CONDITIONS OF
THE PRESENT

CONDITIONS OF THE PRESENT SELECTED ESSAYS

LINDON BARRETT

Edited and with an introduction by Janet Neary

WITH CONTRIBUTIONS BY Elizabeth Alexander, Jennifer DeVere Brody, Daphne A. Brooks, Linh U. Hua, Marlon B. Ross, and Robyn Wiegman

Duke University Press   Durham and London   2018

© 2018 DUKE UNIVERSITY PRESS. All rights reserved.

Text design by Courtney Leigh Baker
Cover design by Matthew Tauch
Typeset in Garamond Premier Pro and Trade Gothic by Westchester Publishing Services

Library of Congress Cataloging-in-Publication Data
Names: Barrett, Lindon, 1961–2008, author. | Neary, Janet, editor, writer of introduction. | Alexander, Elizabeth, [date] writer of supplementary textual content. | Brody, Jennifer DeVere, writer of supplementary textual content. | Brooks, Daphne, writer of supplementary textual content. | Hua, Linh U., writer of supplementary textual content. | Ross, Marlon Bryan, [date] writer of supplementary textual content. | Wiegman, Robyn, writer of supplementary textual content.
Title: Conditions of the present : selected essays / Lindon Barrett ; edited and with an introduction by Janet Neary ; with contributions by Elizabeth Alexander, Jennifer DeVere Brody, Daphne A. Brooks, Linh U. Hua, Marlon B. Ross, and Robyn Wiegman.
Description: Durham : Duke University Press, 2018. | Includes bibliographical references and index.
Identifiers: LCCN 2017036793 (print)
LCCN 2017056119 (ebook)
ISBN 9780822372066 (ebook)
ISBN 9780822370321 (hardcover)
ISBN 9780822370512 (pbk.)
Subjects: LCSH: American literature—African American authors—History and criticism—Theory, etc. | Literature and society—United States—History—20th century. | African Americans—Intellectual life—20th century. | African Americans in literature.
Classification: LCC PS153.N5 (ebook) | LCC PS153.N5 B297 2018 (print) | DDC 810.9/896073—dc23
LC record available at http://lccn.loc.gov/2017036793

Cover art: Hank Willis Thomas, *Hang Time Circa 1923*, 2008. Inkjet on canvas. Courtesy of the artist and Jack Shainman Gallery, New York.

MELISMA, *n.*

A melody or melodic sequence of notes. Usually spec. (in singing and vocal composition): the prolongation of one syllable over a number of notes; an instance of this.

Contents

Preface: Contrary to Appearances xi
JENNIFER DEVERE BRODY

Acknowledgments xv

Introduction: Unruly Knowledges 1
JANET NEARY

I. IN THE CLASSROOM, IN THE ACADEMY
Situating African American Literature, Theory, and Culture

Introduction 25
LINH U. HUA

1. Institutions, Classrooms, Failures: African American Literature and Critical Theory in the Same Small Spaces 31

2. The Experiences of Slave Narratives: Reading against Authenticity 48

3. Redoubling American Studies: John Carlos Rowe and Cultural Criticism 61

II. GESTURES OF INSCRIPTION
African American Slave Narratives

Introduction 87
DAPHNE A. BROOKS

4. African-American Slave Narratives: Literacy, the Body, Authority 92

5. Hand-Writing: Legibility and the White Body in *Running a Thousand Miles for Freedom* 119

6. Self-Knowledge, Law, and African American Autobiography: Lucy A. Delaney's *From the Darkness Cometh the Light* 139

III. IMAGINING COLLECTIVELY
Identity, Individuality, and Other Social Phantasms

Introduction 165
MARLON B. ROSS

7. Identities and Identity Studies: Reading Toni Cade Bambara's "The Hammer Man" 171

8. The Gaze of Langston Hughes: Subjectivity, Homoeroticism, and the Feminine in *The Big Sea* 193

9. Black Men in the Mix: Badboys, Heroes, Sequins, and Dennis Rodman 212

10. Dead Men Printed: Tupac Shakur, Biggie Smalls, and Hip-Hop Eulogy 237

IV. CALCULATIONS OF RACE AND REASON
Theorizing the Psychic and the Social

Introduction   273
ROBYN WIEGMAN

11. Presence of Mind: Detection and Racialization in
"The Murders in the Rue Morgue"   278

12. Family Values / Critical Values: "The Chaos of Our Strongest Feelings"
and African American Women's Writing of the 1890s   299

13. Mercantilism, U.S. Federalism, and the Market within Reason:
The "People" and the Conceptual Impossibility of Racial Blackness   320

Afterword: Remembering Lindon Barrett   353
ELIZABETH ALEXANDER

Contributors   357
Index   361
Credits   375

Preface: Contrary to Appearances
JENNIFER DEVERE BRODY

It is a pleasure to open this volume that collects and collates the singular work of the late Professor Lindon Barrett. The essays provide readers with an opportunity to engage with Barrett's prescient and probing ideas about literature, law, theory, criticism, the West, print culture, the Enlightenment, black feminisms, material violations, slavery, sexuality, capitalism, corporatism, and, preeminently, the conceptual conundrum of racialized blackness that obtains to them all. This collection gives us a better understanding of Professor Barrett's thinking that emerged over the more than two decades that he worked in the profession.

Lindon's brand of anarchical argument arrested all of us who knew him. For example, in the conclusion to his brilliant book, *Blackness and Value: Seeing Double*, he wrote, "Whatever certainty race as an index of value would seem to provide is a false certainty dearly bought. The binary of race and the binary of value (which contrary to appearances are at least tripartite) are such compound falsehoods.... Indeed, one is left to assume—and the irony is profound—that there may be much less than one imagines 'of value' in value."[1] This passage suggests Lindon's quality of mind: his love of language, his complexity, and his commitment to an ethics of everyday existence. Lindon helped us to understand the violence that underwrites signs and figures of value. His theorizations of the forms and figures of racialized violence mark this volume, which can be seen, doubly, as a troubled remainder. Lindon saw how "value remembers itself by dismembering the Other"—and, in the face of such oppositions, Lindon saw double... and listened as he looked. The tripartite structure to which he alludes in the conclusion included sexuality—or rather desire—something he witnessed in the excess of the sounds resonating as material traces emanating, even breaking free, from captive (black) bodies. Such significations make waves across space and time and move me to recall his own body now transfigured as ashes scattered among the waves of the Pacific.

Lindon and I had forged a friendship as "girls together," as Lindon liked to say, in graduate school at the University of Pennsylvania. I recall our first meeting in Philadelphia in the fall of 1987 outside a restaurant named Le Bus. Both of us were doctoral students in the English Department and became part of a community of scholars that included Kim Hall, Elizabeth Alexander, Roland Williams, Nicole King, Laura Tanner, and James Krasner. There, in that time and place, Lindon and I became neighbors, colleagues, collaborators. Then, Lindon was a vegetarian who fasted on Tuesdays in solidarity with folks who were underfed around the globe. We lived in a food-insecure area on the edge of the ghetto and used to drive miles to the suburbs in his brown Pinto in search of fresh vegetables. Lindon was a devotee of the short story (James Joyce's "Araby" in *Dubliners* and Toni Cade Bambara's "Hammer Man" from her collection *Gorilla, My Love* were among his favorites); he wrote a creative master's thesis about the singer Diana Ross and never tired of talking theory. His interest in multiple forms of textuality—exemplified if not epitomized by his work on "singing and signing" in *Blackness and Value*—was apparent in the first conference he organized after we had graduated from Penn. Titled "Contesting Boundaries in African-American Textual Analysis: Period Revisions, Theory, Popular Culture," the 1993 conference was held just after Lindon took a post as assistant professor at University of California, Irvine. It included nine scholars, all of us then junior faculty. The interdisciplinary gathering marks a watershed in my own thinking about African American textual analysis. As Lindon wrote in the proposal for the event, "the conference will present research arising from a highly expansive and re-definitional period [in which] the substitution of the word 'textual' for 'literary' attests to far-reaching changes within the field . . . [such that] poststructuralist theories . . . speak to the conditions of African American cultural expressivity and social reality." I remember the conference included a performance by the troupe Pomo Afro Homo. The current volume honors Lindon's commitment to various modes of textuality and to interdisciplinary scholarship.

It remains a privilege to be among his interlocutors—to bear witness to his diverse intellectual obsessions that centered on the problematics of value in the wake of the abolition of African slavery in the New World. His unfettered (a word I use explicitly) desire for thinking difference gifted him with a sense of openness and a rigorous commitment to theory. He wrote against prescribed notions of normativity and indeed lived his life according to expansive forms of fellowship. For us, dancing served as a way to solidify our friendship: by dancing we performed communitas—and we seemed to be dancing all the time—in Philadelphia, DC, Chicago, LA, and San Bernadino. Even as we found solace on the dance floor, we knew that, contrary to appearances, the Southern California where we felt privileged to live and work as assistant professors was a dangerous place. Once, on a midnight ride in Lindon's drop-top Saab, we were stopped by the police. As we turned around in the driveway of a cheap motel, the squad car, manned by a single officer, pulled us over. The area skirts the city that Mike Davis writes about in his book *City of Quartz*, which was the home of white supremicists, abandoned factories, and the long arm of the then recently militarized LAPD. When the lone officer, who no doubt mistook us for an interracial couple—irony indeed—saw Lindon's UC Irvine ID, he waved us on without an arrest. We danced even harder that night and listened more carefully to the lyrics of Queen Latifah's hit song "U.N.I.T.Y."—one of the three songs that make me think about Lindon every time I hear them. Even now, it is easy to recall Lindon's luminous smile and to hear his effusive laugh.

As several scholars cited in this volume suggest, Lindon's scholarship remains critical in both senses of the term: its interest in blackness and value, in the violent virgule that split them both into multiple forms and falsehoods, has much to teach us. The idea behind what was presumed to be fair, implicit, rational and calculable served as an impetus for the albeit all-too-brief lifetime of inquiry that he pursued so passionately. Lindon's work elides, in the name of ethics, certain certainties in favor of expounding upon the excess value created by the African American singing voice, by inscriptions of marked black presence and other subversive forms. This scholarship allows us to see American failures and futures as well as their interrelation in more nuanced ways. I hope that your encounter with this brilliant work bodies forth meaningful insights and bears some trace of its author's extraordinary presence—of mind, voice, and body. I will close my remarks by repeating the inscription Lindon wrote to me in the copy of his book: "years and counting. Won't say the number. My friendship with you is one of the richest in my life … Love, respect and a couple of giggles. Lindon"

NOTE

1. Lindon Barrett, *Blackness and Value: Seeing Double* (New York: Cambridge University Press, 1999), 242.

Acknowledgments

There are many people to thank for the constitution of this collection.

John Carlos Rowe and Winston James, Lindon's friends and longtime colleagues, were the first to see the need for a Barrett essay collection. They gathered Lindon's body of work, safeguarded his unpublished papers, helped acquire permission to reprint essays, and entrusted me to edit the collection, for which I cannot thank them enough. They have been dedicated, encouraging, patient, and wise advisors every step of the way.

The collection would not exist without the unparalleled research assistance of Max Gottlieb, Nicole McBride, Arielle Irizarry, Maria Elizabeth Rodriguez Beltran, and Maha Haroun, who helped prepare the manuscript. Maha's exquisite labor, insight, and attention deserve particular mention. She is a phenomenal research assistant, and I am lucky to have worked with her.

The most unwieldy part of putting together a collection like this is obtaining permission to reprint essays in this context. Thank you to the many rights and permissions holders that enabled us to reprint Barrett's essays here on behalf of Lindon's estate, which is administered with care by Winston James and Barry Copilow: Marcia Henry with the Modern Language Association, Yi Deng at Columbia University Press, Louise Eyre and Kayla McLaughlin at Oxford University Press, Jeff Moen at the University of Minnesota Press, Ariane de Pree-Kajfez at Stanford University Press, and Shannon McCullough at Johns Hopkins University Press.

Hunter College has provided essential financial support for the book. Thank you, in particular, to Dean Andrew Polsky; Luz Ramirez and Annemarie Rivera, who are both a dream to work with; and the Office of the President. The support of the Presidential Fund for Faculty Advancement and a Schuster Award were essential to completing the project.

My thinking about these essays and the potential of this collection has been enriched by conversations with colleagues at Hunter, including Tanya Agathocleous, Kelvin Black, Nijah Cunningham, Kelly Nims, and Jeremy Glick. The chairs of my department—Cristina Alfar, followed by Sarah Chinn—were steadfastly supportive and encouraging. Thom Taylor quietly makes all of the work emanating from the Hunter English Department possible. Dual thanks and apologies to the many students who came to talk with me while I was in the thick of the editing process. Whatever you came to talk with me about, I connected it to Barrett's work.

A number of people encouraged the project in its earliest stages, such as Larin McLaughlin and Dawn Durante, as well as many of Lindon's former colleagues, interlocutors, and debate partners, including Gabriele Schwab, Fred Moten, Hortense Spillers, Pier Gabrielle Foreman, and Dwight McBride. Their support was instrumental at points when the project felt bigger than me.

I am deeply grateful to the collection's contributors: Jennifer DeVere Brody, Linh U. Hua, Daphne A. Brooks, Marlon B. Ross, Robyn Wiegman, and Elizabeth Alexander. Even though some of them did not know me, they signed on without hesitation, lending their formidable voices and brilliance to the project. These scholars not only provide important intellectual context for the essays and calculate their impact on the academy, but also traverse their own loss in the wake of his death to do so, effacing the bright line between the scholarly and the personal in a way that I admire and draw from.

Amy Parsons, Jennifer Brody, and Brandon Callender have each played multiple roles in bringing this collection to print (and are therefore thanked here in multiple places). They have been invaluable sounding boards and have helped me think through editorial decisions large and small—from the structure of the collection to typographical and stylistic decisions. I gratefully acknowledge their smarts, guidance, and support.

Duke University Press has been an ideal home for this project. Courtney Berger's editorial leadership improved the book at every stage. Her intellectual vision and publishing acumen are matched only by her thoughtfulness and compassion, which meant a lot to me as I navigated this sometimes emotional work. Thanks, also, to Sandra Korn, Karen M. Fisher, and Liz Smith, who were a joy to work with. I am grateful to the anonymous readers of the manuscript for their keen suggestions, which improved my introduction to the book immeasurably.

I first learned how I might think about Lindon's work in a reading group he formed at UC Irvine in which we read other people's work. That group—Jeff Atteberry, Bruce Barnhart, Mrinalini Chakravorty, Naomi Greyser, Ginger Hill,

Linh Hua, Leila Neti, Arnold Pan, Amy Parsons, and Radha Radhakrishnan—remain the well I return to when I am puzzling out one of Lindon's ideas or wondering what he would think about something happening today. I hope we can celebrate the book's publication where we started our academic lives together, throw a copy into the Pacific Ocean, and pour out some rum.

Thank you to The Team, who have supported me in so many ways, including Lorraine Pirro, Susan McCloskey, Beth Neary, Amy Parsons, Tanya Agathocleous, Kyra Grosman, Coral Leather, Rebecca Goldberg, Cara Fitzgerald, Emma Heaney, Kyla Schuller, and Jordan Stein, with whom I talked over the project and who reminded me to celebrate each small success as the book came together. Amy Parsons, Linh Hua, Brandon Callender, Selamawit Terrefe, Susan McCloskey, Cara Fitzgerald, my sister Beth Neary, and my parents, Gwen and Jim Neary, all read drafts of my introduction, encouraged me, and improved it vastly.

My greatest thanks is reserved, as it is in all my academic endeavors, for Lindon himself. Thinking deeply with him has been a gift. Lindon's essays are hard, and engaging with them so closely made me smarter. Inhabiting his mind in the role of editor made me miss him both more and less.

As a facet of his incredibly rich intellectual life, these essays hold Lindon's own debts and acknowledgments. They bear the traces of a deeply engaged scholar whose thinking was enriched, but not bound, by the institutions of which he was a part: the University of Pennsylvania; University of California, Irvine; and University of California, Riverside. His lively—and sometimes epic—debates with colleagues and friends are evidenced in these pages. He was supported by a fiercely loving group of colleagues, friends, and family. I wish he was here to thank you himself.

I am grateful to Lindon's parents, Dorothy and Leslie Barrett Sr., who are generous, gracious, and open. It makes me happy to share this project with them.

Of the many things I have learned and continue to learn from Lindon, perhaps the most important is that academic rigor is not at odds with playfulness and joy. His vibrancy lit up academic space. In that spirit, it is my hope that this collection will continue the work of radically restructuring our understanding of the operations of identity and power, will make us ruthlessly guard pleasure and abundance in the face of institutional austerity, and will also inspire dance parties, which Lindon believed are essential to living a deeply engaged scholarly life.

INTRODUCTION. Unruly Knowledges

JANET NEARY

Our aim, even in the face of the brutally imposed difficulties of black life, is cause for celebration. This is not because celebration is supposed to make us feel good or make us feel better, though there would be nothing wrong with that. It is, rather, because the cause for celebration turns out to be the condition of possibility of black thought, which animates the black operations that will produce the absolute overturning, the absolute turning of this motherfucker out. Celebration is the essence of black thought, the animation of black operations, which are, in the first instance, our undercommon, underground, submarine sociality.—FRED MOTEN, "Blackness and Nothingness (Mysticism in the Flesh)"

A Critique of Criticism Itself

Conditions of the Present begins with a series of negations. In the first essay collected here, "Institutions, Classrooms, Failures," Lindon Barrett diagnoses the institutional aporia between African American literary studies and critical theory by considering the offhanded lament of a student in one of his African American literature classes: "No comment I have encountered from an undergraduate illustrates more acutely the strong sociopolitical, institutional, and intellectual tensions converging on the limited number of classrooms in which African American literature is taught than one offered rather confidently from the front row of a lecture hall filled with sixty or so students. I remember the comment as follows: 'I'm not sure how I'm going to write the paper for this class, because I've never been a slave and can't fully relate to this experience.'"

Observing how unlikely it would be to hear a similar remark in a class on Renaissance or Victorian literature, Barrett deconstructs the student's operating assumptions—that African American literature is reducible to a record of experience and that racial identity and experience are indistinguishable—to identify the peculiar elision between text, historical experience, and identity that accrues to African American literary studies. "Textuality," he reminds us, "is always a locus of authority, the fixed site of an author; African American literature, however, takes its place in the cultural system in which authority—self-authority or any other—has been traditionally denied the texts' authors."[1] By contrast, critical theory is treated as the disembodied domain of abstract thought—defined in opposition to praxis or political expediency. This divide, Barrett argues, amounts to an obfuscation: "It should be made clear to students that the dangers of conflating the experiential and the discursive are the dangers of diminishing the issue of power."[2]

Barrett prompts his readers to consider the role of power in the way "what stands as experience, in fact, comes to stand as experience" ("The Experiences of Slave Narratives"). In pursuit of this question, he draws a direct parallel between the literature under consideration and our formulation and devotion to fixed critical categories, particularly "the assumed stability and independence of rubrics of identity," writing, for example, that "an understanding of slave narratives that esteems them for more than their supposed fidelity to an unrecoverable past allows them to complicate what people in the United States believe and what they think their beliefs are based on."[3] In another essay, he asserts that "it may be misleading to believe that cultural doxa in need of explanation does or would correspond—as a matter of course—to those categories offered by the culture under investigation in the first place" ("Identities and Identity Studies").

However, for Barrett, the diagnosis is also in large measure the cure. To recognize that African American literature has been institutionally positioned in opposition to the abstract work of critical theory is to shift our focus to the cultural system that produces the division and to disrupt the conservative pull of their separation: "If African American literature and critical theory appear to fail each other," he concludes, "then this failure itself is highly instructive in pursuing an understanding of both fields" ("Institutions, Classrooms, Failures"). From this vantage, the rhetorical and intellectual matter of African American literature and the historically grounded, ideologically bounded nature of critical theory can come into focus. By opening with the assumptions governing what African American literature is not, Barrett shows the revelatory potential of recasting that horizon itself as the subject of inquiry, transforming the boundaries, limitations, and ultimately the failures of each field into a productive moment of disorientation and dislocation.

This first essay in the collection reveals the agility that characterizes Barrett's thinking: his ability to stand inside a field—to be "in the position of theory" as he puts it—and see its constructedness, its implications, and its dialectics; to see how it has been constituted by that which it sets aside, renounces, or refutes ("Institutions, Classrooms, Failures"). Rather than adopting the organizational logic of the text or system in question, he examines how that logic came into being, asking, for example, "Do opposed formations—racial blackness and whiteness, for example—share a colluded ground?" ("Identities and Identity Studies"). What is at stake in this shift from text or object to cultural system is a clear-eyed view of power and its operations. Thus this first essay, like all of the essays in this collection, reveals not only "the dangers of conflating the experiential and the discursive," but also that "when these dangers remain unacknowledged, authenticity seems to emerge through the variables of space and time independent of all matters of social power and cultural regimes. Categories of meaning appear given rather than produced" ("The Experiences of Slave Narratives").

Throughout his scholarship, Barrett eschews the assumed, the given, and the expedient in favor of an analysis of texts' material and intellectual conditions of production. With an acute understanding of the historical constitution of African American literature in particular, and a keen sense of the importance of rhetorical analysis in the treatment of these texts, Barrett advances our understanding of the operations of power in both the texts under consideration and the critical categories we use to address them; in short, Barrett offers us a critique of the practice of criticism itself.

The Collection

In the spring of 2012, I received a call from Winston James, Barrett's literary executor, asking if I would be interested in editing a collection of Barrett's essays. James and John Carlos Rowe, longtime friends and colleagues of Barrett's, were in the last stages of assembling the manuscript of his final, epic monograph, *Racial Blackness and the Discontinuity of Western Modernity*, which he had been close to finishing before his life was violently cut short. In the course of collecting and collating material for the book, they uncovered two unpublished, stand-alone essays and reencountered a number of Barrett's published essays that were striking in their prescience and urgency. Rather than include the unpublished works as an appendix to the book (a proposition they considered), they envisioned an essay collection that would showcase the scope and import of Barrett's thinking and writing beyond *Racial Blackness* and his field-defining first book, *Blackness and Value: Seeing Double*. As one of Barrett's final doctoral students at UC Irvine, I had studied nineteenth-century African American literature with him since 2002, when I took my first class with him on slave narratives, which became my field of study. His essays—and the joy of working with him—taught me how to think and provided the foundation for my academic life. Recognizing the importance of a Barrett essay collection, I immediately said yes, eager to share the vision of these essays more broadly, but was also overwhelmed by the significance of the work and the depth of my loss, which are entangled. Editing this book has been another intellectual gift from Barrett, who has given me so much, and it is, for me, a labor of love. I live and work in Lindon Barrett's debt, in the best possible ways, and I hope, here and elsewhere, to do it justice.

Conditions of the Present: Selected Essays collects the full range and scope of Lindon Barrett's work for the first time. In addition to presenting the two previously unpublished essays discovered by James and Rowe, *Conditions of the Present* collects all of Barrett's published essays except those that were reworked into *Blackness and Value*. Traversing autobiography, slave narrative, fiction, pop culture, and journalism, these diverse and compelling essays confront critical blindnesses within both academic and popular discourse. In them, Barrett presents precise readings of cultural and literary texts, speaking across institutional divides as well as the separation between the academy and the street. Characterized by their dense rhetorical precision, the essays "highlight the power and coercion that gives shape to subjective and social structures."[4] The through line is his tireless commitment to interrogating the processes of consolidation and division that grant certain people status while withholding recognition from others. At the center of each essay is a sophisticated analysis of desire, and Barrett puts his analysis of race—as a set of libidinal prohibitions calculated to produce and preserve certain phenotypical traits—to a striking set of conclusions. Whether he is analyzing the autobiographies of Lucy Delaney, Langston Hughes, or Dennis Rodman, articulating the relationship between mercantilism and the formation of U.S. nationalist discourse, or addressing the phenomenon of the hip-hop eulogy, Barrett's goal is to explicate the interrelationship of desire and subjection and to bring to the fore the relations of coercion and violence so often recast as efficiency or progress. Located at the nexus between African American literature, cultural studies, and critical theory, the essays augment and challenge received notions of materiality and individuality through their deployment of Marxism, psychoanalysis, feminism, and queer theory.

The collection organizes Barrett's critical output into four parts, each prefaced with an introduction by an important voice in American studies orienting scholars to the work of the essays collected there. Part I, "In the Classroom, in the Academy: Situating African American Literature, Theory, and Culture," introduced by Linh Hua, focuses on the institutional status of race, literature, and critical theory in the classroom, the text, and the discipline. The first two essays argue—as discussed above—that the institutional situation of African American literary study can be productively brought into conversation with the literary texts themselves. The final essay in the section, a previously unpublished, full-length review essay of John Carlos Rowe's contribution to American studies, turns from the classroom to the broader situation of African American literature within the academy by way of a careful analysis of the trajectory of Rowe's scholarship. Taken together, the essays in this part reveal the centrality of African American aesthetic and critical production to the workings of the academy, which would understand them as marginal or supplementary.

Part II, "Gestures of Inscription: African American Slave Narratives," introduced by Daphne Brooks, brings together Barrett's field-defining essays on the genre. Opening with his foundational essay on literacy, the body, and authority, followed by his influential readings of William Craft's *Running a Thousand Miles for Freedom* and Lucy Delaney's *From the Darkness Cometh the Light*, Barrett identifies "the spurious homology" between literacy/whiteness and illiteracy/blackness, revealing the symbolic function of literacy within the slave narrative through readings of ex-slave narrators' presentations of their bodies in a variety of contexts.[5] According to the cultural logic of race in the United States he outlines, the black body is understood in terms of "obdurate materiality," while the white body signifies beyond its materiality, "attain[ing] its privilege by seeming to replicate the dynamics, the functioning, of the symbolic itself."[6] By appropriating literacy, ex-slave narrators overturn the mind/body split, the primary exclusionary principle that has cast blackness outside of Western notions of humanity. The three essays in this part show how the treatment of "the vexed African American body" is "the central textual dilemma for ex-slave narrators" and its management is a key strategy of authentication ("Hand-Writing"). The essays analyze the inextricability of representations of literacy and the body in order to intervene in the discursive constructions of race that obtain in the narrative, in the courtroom, and in the national imagination.

Part III, "Imagining Collectively: Identity, Individuality, and Other Social Phantasms," introduced by Marlon Ross, collects what are arguably Barrett's most urgent essays on notions of individuality, race, and identity, focusing specifically on the imbrication of black masculinity, sexuality, and violence across a broad range of cultural discourse. In these essays, Barrett brings together a cultural history of the U.S. advertising industry, the commodification of young African American men in the NBA, and narratives of racial and sexual coming of age—including Toni Cade Bambara's short story "The Hammer Man" and Dennis Rodman's autobiography, *Bad as I Wanna Be*—to elucidate figures of racial violence in the most quotidian exchanges, such as the marketing of NBA stars or the perfunctory "Have a nice day" that punctuates consumer exchange. Always keeping in focus race as "a set of libidinal prohibitions," Barrett's readings demonstrate that "public circulation of private desires seems the constitutive project of subjectivity itself."[7] Consequently, "race, gender, and sexuality, as popularly prescribed, are mutually reinforcing terms of ideal and abstract efficiency that, in their co-implications, promote even more attenuated forms of 'efficiency' within the most intimate circuits of human exchange" ("The Gaze of Langston Hughes"). Barrett's critique of the constitution and maintenance of individual subject positions in this part is situated at the productive intersection between queer theory, literary analysis, and black feminism, showing the irreducibility of "the homoerotic, the feminine, and race ... to the discrete terms of queerness, femininity, and blackness" ("The Gaze of Langston Hughes").

Part IV, "Calculations of Race and Reason: Theorizing the Psychic and the Social," introduced by Robyn Wiegman, most fully articulates Barrett's challenge to the foundations of modern subjectivity at the nexus of race, capitalism, and the nation. The essays in this part chart U.S. racial thought through a detective story by Edgar Allan Poe, a previously unpublished analysis of the critical reception of African American women's writing of the 1890s, and an account of the origins of U.S. national discourse in the mercantilist episode of the late eighteenth century. The questions posed in his essay on late nineteenth-century African American women's writing, "Family Values / Critical Values," express the overarching concerns of all the foregoing essays: "If race and family amount to sometimes competing, sometimes conflated sets of prohibitions on the discharge of sexual energy, by what means ... do these prohibitions fuse purposefully with the strict protocols of capitalist consumption? What relations do these sets of prohibitions on the discharge of sexual energy bear to a national culture fully engaged in ... the social and psychic relations of incipient consumer capitalism?" The final essay answers these questions by turning from the literary to the historical. Analyzing the stakes of the interrelationship between federalism and mercantilist capitalism, Barrett grounds a psychoanalytic account of subjectivity in the historical phase of transatlantic modernity while at the same time enriching our understanding of the discursive emergence of the basic unit of the democratic state: "the people." The title of the collection as a whole is drawn from Wiegman's introduction, in which she affirms that these essays, like all of the essays in the collection, "are not only performative instances of Barrett's ability to register and rework the epistemological conditions of the present; but also articles of faith, quite literally, in the possibility of criticism as the venue and vehicle for dismantling the calculating mind as the supreme figure and fiction of white racial essence."

Knowledge Arriving Recklessly

One of the most valuable contributions of *Conditions of the Present* is the sustained, overarching challenge these essays present to the individual subject as an analytic horizon for both academic and popular discourses of identity. Positing what he calls the "subject-effect," Barrett asserts that "the self . . . is always a questionable fiction," remarking that it is "most remarkable for the abiding insistence placed on it rather than its utility or relevance."[8] Moreover, the "subject-effect" is constituted by our attempts to secure and control the "unruly," "unreasonable" force of the libidinal, which is ultimately Barrett's powerful working definition of race:

> Race, conceived as a set of libidinal prohibitions, reveals a peculiar circuit which works to stabilize and ensure the transmission of identifying phenotypical traits from generation to generation through the mechanism of procreative heterosexual practice, because the visibility, recognition, materiality, and certainty of race depend precisely on their tenuously guaranteed stability—the color of skin, the texture of hair, the shape of noses, eyes, buttocks, etc. Race begins to seem a peculiarly libidinal complex, a sexual scheme conscripting desire in apparently absolute ways so as to position gay and lesbian sexuality (whether interracial or intraracial) not simply as a breach of normative gender roles, but, moreover, as a breach of, a challenge and antithesis to, racialization itself in the same manner as miscegenation. ("The Gaze of Langston Hughes")

Drawing on Audre Lorde, Naomi Zack, Elaine Scarry, Gilles Deleuze, and Félix Guattari, among others, Barrett identifies bodily knowledge and desire—and, specifically, the libidinal—as the signal challenge to the individual, writing that "sexual pleasure and orgasm recurringly present themselves as incompatible with the very proposition of the individual. . . . Sexuality in its pleasurable and unruly recklessness, distresses and may *necessarily* abrogate, even if only momentarily, all formalities to which it would be bound."[9] As the point of articulation of the racial subject, African American autobiography is an ideal site "at which a critical reader can witness, in diverse realms, the dynamics animating fictions of the self" ("Self-Knowledge, Law"). For example, in his analysis of a figure taken to be the epitome of individuality, Dennis Rodman, Barrett argues that "what is in evidence [in Rodman's autobiography] are the warring trajectories of a variety of appeals to social meaning, which vie with each other through the figure of the individual, and which do not necessarily find coherent resolution in any singular configuration or body" ("Black Men in the Mix"). To fully recognize the libidinal (and the prohibitions placed on it) is to admit race as central to notions of selfhood—even and especially those privileged locations and iterations of identity that would seem unmarked—and to acknowledge sexuality as fundamentally disruptive to the foundational unit of liberal humanism: the individual subject. Quoting Elaine Scarry, Barrett describes the psychic, social, physical, and affective possibilities represented by the libidinal in terms of nonsubjective, collective knowledge, declaring, "These knowledges arrive recklessly, ... by drawing 'a single, overwhelming discrepancy between an increasingly palpable body and an increasingly substanceless [social/civic] world'" ("Family Values / Critical Values").[10]

The sharpest examples of the ways in which "public circulation of private desires seems the constitutive project of subjectivity itself" are in Barrett's analysis of scholarship, rather than his analysis of primary texts (though they are there, too; see, e.g., "Identities and Identity Studies" and "Black Men in the Mix"). It is, finally, our investment in the individual that leads us to ask the wrong questions when championing those who are marginalized, foreclosing the possibility of understanding the process of marginalization itself. This is most evident in "The Gaze of Langston Hughes: Subjectivity, Homoeroticism, and the Feminine in *The Big Sea*," and his previously unpublished "Family Values / Critical Values: 'The Chaos of Our Strongest Feelings' and African American Women's Writing of the 1890s." In his analysis of Hughes's memoir, *The Big Sea*, Barrett notes that much of the criticism has focused on Hughes's silence around his sexuality. Barrett takes up the question of Hughes's silence, jettisoning what he considers the overly narrow and even misleading interest in Hughes's sexual identity: "A too-strict concern for a sexual resumé, like a too-strict concern for a racial or gender resumé, neglects the coimplications of [the homoerotic, the feminine, and race] that allow masculinist subjectivity to accrue on symbolic, psychological, and material violations of agents who—by either biological markings or erotic preferences—stand as targets."[11] Rather than the question of whether or not Hughes makes himself legible as a gay man, Barrett is interested in "what specific silences allow Hughes to avoid breaching important orthodoxies so as to appear a recognizable rather than an untoward speaking subject." In his assertion of the subject as a product of collective fantasy—"no individual posture is ever entirely about fantasy and, equally, no fantasy is ever simply about an individual posture"—Barrett shifts the critical question from "*whether or not* African Americans (and young black men in particular) are a site of cultural and social crisis" to "precisely what kind of social subject is allowed to take public form in collective recognition and negotiation of the crisis" ("Dead Men Printed"). In so doing, he makes clear that without looking at the conditions and dynamics that make social recognition possible, critics and artists—marginalized or otherwise—risk reproducing the violence and outcomes of those very dynamics.

Similarly, in "Family Values / Critical Values," Barrett indicts a scholarly conversation that has been hamstrung by its critical presumptions. Taking stock of the limitations of the debate about African American women's writing of the 1890s, Barrett elucidates the ways a consideration of gender is always (though often unacknowledged) a consideration of race. Untangling the interrelated but decidedly not interchangeable logics of race and family, he argues that "what has come to stand as the foremost debate in the field, contesting whether or not this body of work measures up as radical racial discourse, . . . mistakes important features of the cultural situation under examination." While one side argues that the sentimental novel, the formal template for women writers of the period including Frances Harper and Pauline Hopkins, "is bad art, white art, bourgeois art—or all three" and therefore "'incompatible with political protest fiction,'" the other side "credit[s] the writers with innovative use of constricting narrative forms," reading their "use of sentimental forms as a means of cultural intervention." Emblematic of his work elsewhere, Barrett explodes the either/or premise of the debate, "subtended foremost by gender," by attending to the ways "unexamined reiterations of normative domestic agendas are never fully in dispute, so that cultural capital steadfastly accrues, even in never fully accounted ways, to the disciplinary construct of the family, which in significant measure secures the abjected cultural position of racial blackness, even as the most routine terms of African American advocacy in the 1890s attempt to resignify the construct." The essay goes on to provide a nuanced account of the intercalated but distinct logics of family and race, taking into account the different historical circumstances under which Harper and Hopkins "champion[ed] racial blackness by idealizing a set of conditions that do not define the circumstances of the majority of African Americans." He concludes that "the family and its structures do not strictly exhaust the possibilities of affective arrangements, racial, gendered, sexual, economic or any set of arrangements one might imagine or pursue; as clearly, race and its structures do not consume the possibilities of affective arrangements, familial arrangements, gendered, sexual, or economic arrangements." Whether beginning in the classroom or dwelling in critical space, Barrett always returns us to the world—or, rather, the ways criticism takes its cues from social and material organizations in the world. Thus, for Barrett, criticism is a place to imagine possibilities, but it has to question its own deployment of categorical thinking, even when those categories are used in the service of radicalizing the canon.

Imagining Collectively

The most powerful implications of Barrett's focus on the libidinal are, perhaps, expressed in Barrett's "Dead Men Printed: Tupac Shakur, Biggie Smalls, and Hip-Hop Eulogy," an essay I find particularly piercing to read in the wake of Barrett's own violent death. In his examination of the murders of Shakur and Smalls, and the ways they have been represented in the press, Barrett brings to bear the full range of critical and social theory to demonstrate the fundamentally irrational force of the libidinal as central to what we might call the perverse pleasures of state violence. As Marlon Ross states in his contribution, Barrett "refuses to normalize or naturalize the death of young black men as a self-violating death-wish, the expected cost of being young, black, and too talented to survive the darkening streets of America's promised land."[12] Locating black men as a primal site within the libidinal economy of racial capitalism, Barrett writes that "capitalism looks to young black bodies as sites of open, unregulated flows of desire but, paradoxically, only in order productively and profitably to inscribe and channel these unregulated flows" ("Dead Men Printed"). He describes the paradoxical situation of young black men—who are uniquely vulnerable and uniquely threatening in what Barrett calls the "visual regime of abolished racial enslavement"—in terms of Hegel's master/slave dialectic. The master's sense of self "arrives at itself through a violent will or force" that must be displaced and disavowed to be maintained. Thus, "in these highly publicized incidents, violence 'returns' to African American male bodies, even though violence does not necessarily emanate from those persons in the first place, and it is this mystified circuit of what [Judith] Butler terms white paranoia that, one might say, positions the several discrete incidents as equivalent for U.S. culture logic (the beating of [Rodney] King, the shootings in Brooklyn, the murders of Shakur and Smalls)." But more than merely offering an explanation of racial violence, as the foregoing suggests, Barrett demonstrates how our collective response to the murders of these young black men recirculates as ways of knowing ourselves that perpetuate this violence: "To imagine such a profound situation of non-sociality *as sociality* requires an enormous feat: the feat seems to be the denial of one's own relative—relating?—difference in an inscription of galvanizing—absolute?—difference elsewhere, the inscription of a horizon making one's own relative position of difference disappear, just as the absolute, visible difference of the physical horizon reaffirms the impossibility of seeing the relative position at which one is at that moment standing. One thing certainly happens: one imagines collectively." For Barrett, these modes of grief expressed in hip-hop eulogy instrumentalize brutality against black people in part by obscuring the relational dialectic within racial capitalism that places young black men in a position of extreme precarity.

One of the benefits of this collection is that these essays bear surprising and dynamic relationships to one another that continue to unfold in the shifting historical coordinates of the present, which rely on the precarity Barrett elucidates. To give just one example, the juxtaposition of Barrett's essays on slave narratives, which argue that "facts prove instruments of will," takes on new meaning in relation to the journalistic treatment of police brutality addressed in "Dead Men Printed" in our own moment of institutional and state-sponsored antiblack violence.[13] One contemporary strain of the national conversation about police violence, specifically, has called for evidence, clarification of the facts of the case, unbiased arguments, and clear camera angles. However, drawing on Ahmed Aijaz's articulation of colonial discourse, Barrett reminds us that "in terms of the cultural logic of the United States, to speak of Reason is already to a very significant degree to make a racially exclusive move" ("Presence of Mind"):

> To "describe" is to specify a locus of meaning, to construct an object of knowledge, and to produce a knowledge that shall be bound by that act of descriptive construction. "Description" has been central, for example, in the colonial discourse. It was by assembling a monstrous machinery of descriptions—of our bodies, our speech acts, our habits, our conflicts and desires, our politics, our socialities and sexualities—in fields as various as ethnology, fiction, photography, linguistics, political science—that the colonial discourse was able to classify and ideologically master the colonial subject, enabling itself to transform the descriptively verifiable multiplicity and difference into the ideologically felt hierarchy of value. To say, in short, what one is presenting is "essentially descriptive" is to assert a level of facticity which conceals its own ideology and to prepare a

ground from which judgments of classification, generalisation, and value can be made. (Aijaz, qtd. in "Institutions, Classrooms, Failures")

Reminiscent of Ida B. Wells's 1893 indictment of lynch law, that "those who commit the murders write the reports," Barrett reminds us that "the knowledge that courts are charged to research, discover, and possess emanates from and returns to the civic and political communities from which the law is constructed" ("Self-Knowledge, Law").[14] There are no facts that are not implicated in the system of power-producing violence, which is to say that we cannot expect that state-sponsored antiblack violence will be ameliorated by the very matrices of "description," logic, and reason that violently constitute blackness as "the impossible point of human conception."[15]

Multiplicity, Plurality, and Difference:
UC Irvine as a Theoretical Epicenter

Barrett's seventeen years at UC Irvine, an epicenter of critical theory, inform the aims and methods of these essays.[16] Barrett's theoretical substrate is decidedly post-structuralist, and his literary criticism might be described as philosophically inflected historical materialism. In his rigorous deconstructions of difference and his pursuit of how we come to know what we know, one can see his engagement with Jacques Derrida, Louis Althusser, and Ferdinand de Saussure, among others. Continuing the project of *Blackness and Value*, in his essays on slave narratives, for example, Barrett reads the representation of bodies—and the prohibitions on slave literacy—in light of structural linguistics as it gets taken up within post-structuralist accounts of subjectivity: "As we have been instructed by Saussurian linguistics and poststructuralist thought, multiplicity, plurality, and difference are the conditions that make possible significance, signification, language, meaning. Saussure, in his pioneering investigations of the synchronic dimensions of linguistics, argues that the 'content [of a linguistic unit] is really fixed only by the concurrence of everything that exists outside it. Being part of a system, it is endowed not only with a signification but also and especially with a value, and this is something quite different' " ("Hand-Writing"). Rather than ontology, Barrett understands race within a cultural system that determines meaning and value through the production of difference. As in the first essay of the collection discussed above, Barrett does not apply critical theory to particular texts but rather demonstrates the parallel and intertwined operations of critical theory and the production of racial meaning that are often masked or obscured; in this case, Barrett argues that race and the racial body are fundamentally linguistic propositions. His methodology is of post-structuralism while also demonstrating the limits of post-structuralism: a tendency toward abstraction. If race is fundamentally linguistic, the reverse is also true: language reflects power and value, influenced by and entailing specific material, political realities.

Barrett's post-structuralist methodology, philosophical inquiry, and uniquely interrogatory interdisciplinarity are nowhere more evident than in his never-before-published review of John Carlos Rowe's scholarship. Explicating Rowe's influence on American studies, Barrett lingers in their shared intellectual domain, the domain of critical theory as seen from a historical materialist perspective:

> John Rowe's imperative, as clear from the beginning of his career, is an engagement with the sign as articulated by deconstructive theorizing, an engagement seeking to return the phenomenological force of the sign to the material historicity of the modern, that is, to outline modernity as the exorbitance of the sign, in which the United States is locatable as a sign (in political as well as aesthetic modes) indicative of the zenith of the linear progression that is the modern.... [His] insistent interest in re-tracing the ground of canonical U.S. literature mobilizes the deconstructive critique of this structuralist critical posture beyond the aporia of textuality, cognition, and experience into specific semantic determinations that enact material, historical, and aesthetic traditions that demonstrate how the endless chain of signification coalesces an extraliterary "reality" always holding political force.[17]

The essay, first delivered at a conference celebrating Rowe's work at UC Irvine, offers a preview of the line of thinking Barrett develops in the last essay of the collection, "Mercantilism, U.S. Federalism, and the Market within Reason." In it, Barrett describes the emergence of the United States within the context of mercantilist capitalism—both of which depended on the exclusion of African-derived people from the concept of "the people" (in the case of the nation) and of human being (in the case of the subject). At issue for both Rowe and Barrett is our understanding of the republican synthesis and the constitution of modern forms of subjectivity and personhood. For both, a post-structuralist account of the processes of signification is central to understanding the operations of power and national consolidation.

Lindon arrived at UC Irvine in the midst of the deconstructive turn. At the end of Barrett's time there, coinciding with Jared Sexton's and Frank Wilderson III's arrival in the African American Studies program, another theoretical paradigm was emerging for which Irvine would become the/an epicenter:

Afro-pessimism.[18] It is in debates over Afro-pessimism that I most acutely feel the loss of Barrett's inimitable voice and nuanced critique. Although Barrett was taken from us before he could fully articulate his response, I had the opportunity to be in reading groups with Barrett and Sexton, among others, where the tenets of Afro-pessimism were being discussed and debated. Drawing on these conversations, and pursuing the most speculative line of inquiry offered here, I want to suggest that these essays are keyed in an alternative modality to Afro-pessimism and that they might be limned for what I believe is Barrett's nascent response to an Afro-pessimist paradigm.

Like Afro-pessimist thinkers, Barrett identifies slavery as the fundamental ground of racial capitalism that structures the organization of the modern state and governs contemporary race relations; however, he resolutely rejected an assessment of black life and death as reducible to a reaction formation to this instantiation of organized, institutionalized racial violence. In this way, Barrett's thinking forecasts Christina Sharpe's work in *In the Wake: On Blackness and Being*, in which she writes that "to be *in* the wake is to occupy and to be occupied by the continuous and changing present of slavery's as yet unresolved unfolding"; but rather than an ontological position, it is a linguistic proposition, a material reality, a dialectal positioning, such that "*to be* 'in' the wake, to occupy that grammar, the infinitive, might provide another way of theorizing, in/for/from what Frank Wilderson refers to as 'stay[ing] in the hold of the ship.' . . . At stake is not recognizing antiblackness as total climate."[19] Similarly, Fred Moten's 2013 response to Afro-pessimism, laid out in his essay "Blackness and Nothingness (Mysticism in the Flesh)," resonates with Barrett's articulations of racial blackness as nonontological.[20] Moten asserts "blackness [as] ontologically prior to the logistic and regulative power that is supposed to have brought it into existence," declaring, "blackness is prior to ontology."[21] Barrett rejected the notion of race "conceived as an ontological condition," arguing that it "always has been and continues to be foremost an intellectual matter" ("The Experiences of Slave Narratives"; "Institutions, Classrooms, Failures"). Consequently, his analysis of the various textual crises in slave narratives, in "The Experiences of Slave Narratives," for example, demonstrates how the supposedly fixed poles of a black-white racial dialectic are, in actuality, continually strained.

Barrett's sharpest divergence from Afro-pessimism, however, is his insistence on the vitality of forms of black sociality and his insistence on race as a future-oriented temporal structure. Barrett's critique of the individual subject as both the fundamental unit of liberal humanism within modernity and a racist formation is crucial. In his essay on mercantilism and federalism, Barrett argues that "the disposition of racial blackness constitutes the impossible point of human conception in the enterprise—foreclosed as the unnamed violence of human visibility.... At stake originally, as the 'modern' is the phantasmatic animation of the conceptual form (the commodity) in the face of the already fully animate individual and collective material forms (in human proportions) of racial blackness" ("Mercantilism, U.S. Federalism"). While this shares an understanding of the libidinal economy of modernity with Afro-pessimism, Barrett refuses the ability of modernity—"the enterprise"—to proscribe the limits of social engagement and arrangement. For Barrett, to accept the premise of social death, whether it be Frantz Fanon's iteration in *Black Skin, White Masks* or Orlando Patterson's in *Slavery and Social Death*, would be to adopt the terms of modernity's dialectic—to reproduce its fundamental conceit—rather than to think about how that dialectic is constructed and maintained and what it forces from view. Furthermore, Barrett's account of the future-oriented temporality of modernity's libidinal economy is at odds with Afro-pessimist temporality which posits, in Wilderson's words, that "the capacity to redeem time and space is foreclosed to the Black because redemption requires a 'heritage' of temporality and spatiality, rather than a past of boundless time and indeterminate space."[22] By contrast, Barrett understands race as a set of historically specific social and libidinal regulations designed to foreclose what Bruce Barnhart has called "the kinds of inventiveness that threaten to redistribute the future."[23] Consequently, blackness is not locked in a historically determined position of ontological death; to reclaim the unruly knowledge of the libidinal is to recognize that "race and its structures do not consume the possibilities of affective arrangements, familial arrangements, gendered, sexual, or economic arrangements" ("Family Values / Critical Values"). Whereas Afro-pessimism stipulates that "*Blackness* refers to an individual who is by definition always already void of relationality," blackness and subjectivity, for Barrett, are constituted by relationality.[24] Consequently, blackness exceeds the prescriptive force of modernity's limits on human experience, encompassing potential futures that modernity cannot predict.[25]

The Beginning and the End

Originally published over a span of thirteen years (between 1993 and 2006), the essays in *Conditions of the Present* chart the evolution of African American literary studies. The language designating this body of literature has shifted over time from "black literature" to "Afro-American written art" to "African-American literature" to "African American literature," the term I use here, each idiom reflecting different perspectival, political, social, ideological, and cultural demands. I have chosen to preserve Barrett's original terminology for his objects of study, rather than making the language consistent across the collection. The scholarly potential in retaining the linguistic variance between, for example, "African-American" and "African American" is exemplified in Barrett's essay "African-American Slave Narratives: Literacy, the Body, Authority" (originally published in 1995), in which Barrett mobilizes the shifting language and disciplinary codes used to address these texts to parse slave narrative scholarship into three distinct phases—historical, literary, and cultural analysis. In the first phase, slave narratives entered the academy under the rubric of history; scholarship in this period (the 1960s and 1970s) treated these texts primarily as historical documents and eyewitness accounts, valued for the window they offered onto historical conditions. In the second phase (the late 1970s and early 1980s), slave narratives began to be read in English departments and treated as literature; during this phase critics prioritized "what is literary (as opposed to sociological, ideological, etc.) in Afro-American written art" (in the words of Robert Stepto).[26] In this phase critics emphasized "interpretations of the language, rhetorical strategies, and predominant tropes of the texts, especially in relation to structuralist and poststructuralist theories" ("African-American Slave Narratives"). Barrett's own essay, "African-American Slave Narratives," inaugurates the third phase—what he calls cultural analysis—in which "rather than separating history and literature, one might see them as equally 'textual' and place them in conversation with one another, reconstituting and revitalizing the confusion of the realms of art and propaganda." To echo a point above, the benefit of this critical turn is that the literary text comes into view as an artifact enmeshed in and reflecting a set of extratextual power relations that are located and negotiated there, rather than simply a record of experience or a "closed linguistic event." This mode of analysis constitutes a self-reflexive turn in that it illustrates the ways African American literary study mandates a consideration of our critical vocabularies and ideological investments: "With acute sensitivity to its own politics, as well as the political dimensions of its objects of study, cultural analysis yields insights into the manner in which a particular worldview authorizes, implements, and structures the commonplace rituals, spaces, and interpretive activities of those interpellated by a particular cultural regime" ("African-American Slave Narratives"). The methodology we inherit from Barrett insists on integrating precise rhetorical analysis with acute attention to a text's historical conditions of production and our own ideological horizons of interpretation. Thus, in keeping with Barrett's dedication to understanding language as an index of power, the collection keeps these linguistic and methodological shifts in view across the essays. The only exception to this is that I translated each of the essays into the same citation style and removed inconsistencies produced by different journals' variant house styles to unify the collection.

It is my hope that the editorial decisions and scaffolding offered here encourage multiple critical paths through the essays. Although the collection is organized thematically rather than chronologically, each essay's original date of publication is included next to its title so one might pursue a set of historical arguments yet to be made. Similarly, the section introductions offer an essential critical history of Barrett's scholarship, naming his scholarly ancestors as well as his legacy, a partial list of which includes work by Alexander Weheliye, Aliyyah I. Abdur-Rahman, Saidiya Hartman, Fred Moten, Farah Griffin, Stephen Best, Jacqueline Goldsby, P. Gabrielle Foreman, Tavia Nyong'o, Jayna Brown, Soyica Colbert, José Esteban Muñoz, Sharon Holland, Christina Sharpe, and Simone Browne, as well as the contributors collected here.

A brief note on the book's arresting cover image: Hank Willis Thomas's 2008 *Hang Time Circa 1923*. Like Barrett, Thomas has long worked at the intersections of race, gender, and commodity culture in series such as *B(r)ANDED* (2006) and *Pitch Blackness* (2008). In *Hang Time*, Thomas reproduces the iconic Air Jordan logo—a graphic representation of Michael Jordan performing a layup—with a noose around Jordan's neck, forcing us to confront the pleasure of black masculine prowess in the context of the violence of racial capitalism. The image intersects with Barrett's essays at multiple points: his analysis of the commodification of young African American men within what he calls "capitalism as culture and culture as capitalism" in his essays on black masculinity in the NBA and in hip-hop eulogy, and in his analysis of a key moment in Toni Cade Bambara's story "The Hammer Man." Barrett discusses one of the main characters' performance of a layup as "a form of black masculine genius and gracefulness at its most thrilling" and, in the mind of the character's adversaries, "at its most repulsive or threatening."[27] Both Barrett and Thomas force us to confront, specifically, the position of black men within racial capitalism as "the most feared and the most revered bodies in the world."[28] The title of Thomas's work also resonates with the historical scope of Barrett's essays. Thomas recalls a specific historical moment in order to simultaneously enact a compression of time that brings together a vision of blackness and black masculinity emerging in slavery and with us now.

Finally, a word about the framing of these scholarly essays with two powerful voices articulating the personal—as well as scholarly and professional—force Lindon Barrett was in the world. The collection begins and ends with a return to the particularly rich foundational moment of Barrett's life in the English doctoral program at the University of Pennsylvania. In their preface and afterword, respectively, Jennifer DeVere Brody and Elizabeth Alexander each give us a snapshot of a young Lindon coming into his own at the moment the vice grip of the canon was giving way to new possibilities in literary study represented by black literature. As this collection shows, this sea change in literary criticism and history was not simply an expansion of our objects of study, but rather a revelation/revolution of the very dynamics and ideological motivations determining social, political, and aesthetic notions of value, a literary referendum on how we come to know what we know. Offering us an intimate portrait of Lindon—animated by his excitement, his focus, his devotion to friends and colleagues and the then new project of black literary study—Brody and Alexander illuminate what was at stake for Barrett in this work: black love.[29] Both emphasize the importance of embodied experience and community to Barrett's thought. It is a portrait that decidedly contradicts what have seemed to me willful misreadings of Barrett's writing and his department building as cynical, isolating, or disaffected. Nothing could be further from the truth. The energy and rigor Barrett brought to his scholarship—and which sometimes fueled his falling out with friends and colleagues—was based on his deeply held belief that knowledge is produced collectively, that the energy between people conditions even what we understand to be the most intimate or private aspects of ourselves.

Although he was embattled at UC Irvine, decamping to UC Riverside in 2007, Barrett never stopped fighting intellectually damaging neoliberal forces, and he never stopped drawing students together in fierce collectives that were both intellectually rigorous and personally sustaining. As antithetical as pleasure and university administration seem, Barrett embodied this paradox in his academic life: he insisted on reclaiming pleasure where it was eyed most suspiciously; he was deeply committed to service and took up the administrative roles necessary to make expansive, revelatory, and challenging institutional and intellectual spaces. Barrett believed, as Moten writes in the epigraph above, that "celebration is the essence of black thought." Though it is perhaps counterintuitive, by centering institutional failures and a racial position designated by violence, negation, and otherness, Barrett reclaims critical space as the space of connection and relationality.

Nearly ten years after his death, the full scope of Barrett's impact in the academy is still being calculated. What is clear is that the need for Barrett's incisive analysis has never been more urgent. The essays are eerily prescient of later crises both inside and outside of the academy, including the 2008 financial collapse, unprecedented levels of black unemployment, the dissolution of many interdisciplinary programs across the country, unrelenting police violence, and the ceaseless assaults on people of color intensified by our new national political administration. However, what is most valuable about these essays is not what they diagnose, but what they propose: taken together they indicate a way forward in the bleakest circumstances. Even while identifying the failure of present epistemes to acknowledge the circuits of social and market desire that coalesce in the "compositely articulated" subject, Barrett offers hope: "If the cause is inertia or blindnesses inherited from institutional (and culturally pervasive) paradigms, then, one can imagine, as already suggested by the work of feminists of color, that the obstacles for self-defined critical and radical thought are far from insurmountable" ("Identities and Identity Studies").

So we end at the beginning, before the sharp impact of his loss and its infinite aftermath, in a moment of "unprecedented possibility" to be harnessed for our present.[30] These essays provide a sophisticated articulation of the way intimate circuits operate, charging us to finish the work they so powerfully inaugurate. As another of Barrett's former students—Leila Neti—has written, "[Barrett]'s theorization of pleasure maps out the ways in which forces of racialization and capital, often in the service of regulatory modes of sexuality, constantly threaten to erode the possibilities of human sociality. Yet, on some level, his work is, most profoundly, about recognizing and rescuing a space for precisely those most vulnerable of pleasures amidst the most powerful social and cultural threats to them."[31] Perhaps the greatest gift of this collection will be the perpetual immediacy of Barrett's call to protect spaces of "open-ended desire" from the regulatory measures and violent appropriations that operate under the name of progress.

NOTES

1. Lindon Barrett, "Institutions, Classrooms, Failures: African American Literature and Critical Theory in the Same Small Spaces," chapter 1, this volume. References to Barrett's essays are given in the text in parentheses after first mention.

2. Lindon Barrett, "The Experiences of Slave Narratives: Reading against Authenticity," chapter 2, this volume.

3. Lindon Barrett, "Identities and Identity Studies: Reading Toni Cade Bambara's 'The Hammer Man,'" chapter 7, this volume; Barrett, "The Experiences of Slave Narratives."

4. Bruce Barnhart, private correspondence.

5. Lindon Barrett, "African-American Slave Narratives: Literacy, the Body, Authority," chapter 4, this volume.

6. Barrett, "African-American Slave Narratives"; Lindon Barrett, "Hand-Writing: Legibility and the White Body in *Running a Thousand Miles for Freedom*," chapter 5, this volume.

7. Lindon Barrett, "The Gaze of Langston Hughes: Subjectivity, Homoeroticism, and the Feminine in *The Big Sea*," chapter 8, this volume.

8. Lindon Barrett, "Dead Men Printed: Tupac Shakur, Biggie Smalls, and Hip-Hop Eulogy," chapter 10, this volume; Lindon Barrett, "Self-Knowledge, Law, and African American Autobiography: Lucy A. Delaney's *From the Darkness Cometh the Light*," chapter 6, this volume; and Lindon Barrett, "Black Men in the Mix: Badboys, Heroes, Sequins, and Dennis Rodman," chapter 9, this volume.

9. Lindon Barrett, "Family Values/Critical Values: 'The Chaos of Our Strongest Feelings' and African American Women's Writing of the 1890s," chapter 12, this volume.

10. Barrett's formulation reminds me of a line from the Last Poets' "When the Revolution Comes," which reasserts the solidity of revolutionary potential in an increasingly substanceless world, prophesying that when the revolution comes, "blood will run through the streets of Harlem drowning anything without substance."

11. Barrett goes on to state that "the attention to sexuality . . . is misconstrued . . . if simply translated into an attempt to settle the question of Hughes's individual sexuality, since the powerful forces assigning valences to race, gender, and sexuality impinge upon Hughes even as he remains shrouded in ambiguities. . . . By ignoring the magnitude of these shared oppressive mechanisms, one fails both to account adequately for longstanding social arrangements, and to recognize that the bedrock of individual identity (or rubrics of identity) is never as determinate as it appears." It ultimately amounts to "the impulse to blind oneself to one's absence from oneself." Barrett makes a similar critical move in his essay "Presence of Mind: Detection and Racialization in 'The Murders in the Rue Morgue,'" chapter 11, this volume, in which he argues that asking if Poe is racist is too limiting a question: "It is not open declarations of racial sentiments on the part of Poe that are so telling but, rather, the continuity between his work and widespread racial and racist constructions."

12. Marlon Ross, introduction to "Imagining Collectively: Identity, Individuality, and Other Social Phantasms," part III, this volume.

13. The full quote, from "Institutions, Classrooms, Failures," is useful here: "Students in African American literature classes discover opposing sets of facts and attendant narratives that no amount of appeals to neutrality might reconcile. . . . Neutrality itself takes up a place within one of the opposing sets of facts, with the result that there no longer clearly exists the certainty (or illusion) of 'getting the facts right'; the *facts* prove instruments of will implicated in, rather than effecting release from, *experience*, interestedness, and the dynamics of cultural, civil, and other forms of power. The facts appear as the discursive gestures of dominant groups 'whose exclusionary behavior may be firmly buttressed by institutionalized structures of domination that do not critique or check [that exclusionary behavior].'"

14. Ida B. Wells, "Lynch Law in All Its Phases," *Our Day*, May 1893.

15. Lindon Barrett, "Mercantilism, U.S. Federalism, and the Market within Reason: The 'People' and the Conceptual Impossibility of Racial Blackness," chapter 13, this volume.

16. Barrett was at UC Irvine between 1990 and 2007, when he took a position at UC Riverside.

17. Lindon Barrett, "Redoubling American Studies: John Carlos Rowe and Cultural Criticism," chapter 3, this volume.

18. As Jared Sexton notes, "Afro-Pessimism is a contemporary phenomenon, some may even scoff that it is trendy, but its political and intellectual evolution is considerably longer and its ethical bearings much broader than one might expect, and there is work yet to be done regarding a genealogy of its orientation and sensibility," "Afro-Pessimism: The Unclear Word," *Rhizomes* 29 (2016), doi:10.20415/rhiz/029.e02.

19. Christina Sharpe, *In the Wake: On Blackness and Being* (Durham, NC: Duke University Press, 2016), 13–14, 21.

20. Fred Moten, "Blackness and Nothingness (Mysticism in the Flesh)," *South Atlantic Quarterly* 112, no. 4 (fall 2013): 737–80. Originally delivered as the UC Irvine miniseminar "Just Friends."

21. Moten, "Blackness and Nothingness," 739.

22. Frank Wilderson, *Red, White, and Black: Cinema and the Structure of U.S. Antagonisms* (Durham, NC: Duke University Press, 2010), 17–18.

23. Bruce Barnhart, American Studies Association session proposal.

24. Wilderson, *Red, White, and Black*, 18.

25. Barrett's understanding of blackness as in relation to but not reducible to white regulatory forces resonates with the temporality of the black radical tradition set forth in Cedric Robinson's *Black Marxism*, which posits black radicalism as a phenomenon and force that "cannot be understood within the particular context of its genesis." Cedric Robinson, *Black Marxism: The Making of the Black Radical Tradition* (Chapel Hill: University of North Carolina Press, 2000), 73. Stephen Best's essay on representations of slavery in contemporary art gets at the heart of these questions, positing what he calls "derealized social relation" as a way of "making those relations apprehensible." Stephen Best, "Come and Gone," *small axe* 48 (November 2015): 186–204, 199.

26. Robert Stepto, introduction to *Afro-American Literature: The Reconstruction of Instruction*, ed. Dexter Fisher and Robert Stepto (New York: Modern Language Association, 1979), 1.

27. Barrett, "Identities and Identity Studies."

28. Hank Willis Thomas in *Juxtapoz*, qtd. on Jack Shainman Gallery website, http://www.jackshainman.com/artists/hankwillis-thomas/.

29. Here there is another connection to Moten's essay, "Blackness and Nothingness." Moten writes "that black life—which is as surely to say life as black thought is to say thought—is irreducibly social; that, moreover, black life is lived in political death or that it is lived, if you will, in the burial ground of the subject by those who, insofar as they are not subjects, are also not, in the interminable (as opposed to the last) analysis, 'death-bound,' as Abdul JanMohaed (2005) would say" (739).

30. Elizabeth Alexander, "Afterword: Remembering Lindon Barrett," this volume.

31. Leila Neti, private correspondence.

I. IN THE CLASSROOM, IN THE ACADEMY
Situating African American Literature, Theory, and Culture

Introduction

LINH U. HUA

To understand classroom pedagogy as transformative practice, one would do well to study three deliberations by Lindon Barrett on the politics of African American literature in the university classroom. The following essays showcase Barrett's signature pedagogy of race and racial blackness in three contexts—the classroom, the text, and the discipline—to demonstrate functional connections between African American slave narratives, notions of experience and authenticity, and the racializing discourse of American studies. Together they illustrate the depth and range of Barrett's teaching, foregrounding the classroom as a crucial arena in which to assess the lived relevance and practical manifestation of theory. Barrett's delincation of African American literature as a site of theory qualitatively changes the nature of the relationship between literature and theory to social justice and liberation writ large. As he teaches it, understanding and undoing the work of race entails capturing all of its contrary dimensions—the many ways that it works as violent metaphor, as static identity, and as material effect. The troubling detail that Barrett identifies across the classroom, the page, and the academy is the ease with which reproduction of the sign of difference gets taken up as a sign of liberation. If liberal theories of diversity and inclusion rehearse experience and identity markers as fixed evidence of race and difference, Barrett models a pedagogy that questions even calls for justice that reify a logic of absolute experiential difference rather than challenge it. The vigilance and rigor of his pedagogy—as demonstrated in the following essays—contribute to dissolving practiced expectations in our reading of texts and of each other to open new possibilities for wonder.

These early essays of Barrett's capture an important moment of crisis in the humanities familiar to those who have read Barbara Christian's seminal essay, "The Race for Theory" (1998), or Ann duCille's "The Occult of True Black Womanhood: Critical Demeanor and Black Feminist Studies" (1994).[1] Although he published the first essay in this collection around the same time that duCille published hers, the seed of his argument was earlier articulated in 1991 in "Speaking of Failure: Undergraduate Education and the Intersection of African-American Literature and Cultural Theory."[2] Amid conversation on the role of theory in relation to literature in general and to African American literature in particular, Barrett's pedagogy responded to a larger question about the relevance of the humanities in a rapidly changing market. In this context, his treatment of texts in the classroom forgoes a defense of literature for literature's sake to address what he saw as the more pertinent question: not how, but *why*, the humanities are integral to contemporary culture. Why African American literature?

Barrett begins with a tenet now fundamental to literary and cultural theory: that the interpretive posture that we inhabit to engage texts reveals an essential grammar of how we imagine our place in the world. He promises that engaging literature—African American literature in particular—in the university classroom will upset the very logic of how we come to understand ourselves as feeling and thinking beings, for race "always has been and continues to be foremost an intellectual matter, either within or without the classroom but most plainly so in the classroom" ("Institutions, Classrooms, Failures"). Dislodging race and racial blackness thus from an overdetermined logic of material embodiment, Barrett names them as neither inconsequential nor incidental and always the material and violent manifestation of systems of libidinal, intellectual, and geopolitical power. Race and racial blackness are violent yet largely fictive concepts with material history and abiding resilience that foremost restrict our imagination in the service of reductive truths and false certainty. Barrett's pedagogy not only identifies these restrictions, it facilitates unlearning that extends past the classroom and beyond the page by honing the pedagogical reach of both sites.

The stakes of Barrett's position on race can be traced in his severing of ethical attachments to questions of difference and identity, all part of his work to eradicate naturalized racial codes. In the first essay, "Institutions, Classrooms, Failures: African American Literature and Cultural Theory in the Same Small Spaces," Barrett argues for the necessary coupling of African American literature and critical theory in the classroom to offset the binary functions that have been relegated to each respectively. Here, Barrett grapples with the implications of a liberal education culture that observes difference but does little to engage its corollary—race—as an analytic that requires intellectual and personal reflection. He provides as example the intellectual impasse experienced by an undergraduate student who has alienated herself completely from the assigned text: an African American slave narrative. The student articulates her impasse as panic and apology for being unable to engage with the text or to write a paper on it because she has never been a slave. While we may presume that the student means to inhabit a progressive posture by giving experiential credit where it is due—for only those who are/were slaves can fully understand the depth of that captivity—the student's disidentification with the assigned text and its African American author rehearses two principal oversights: one, that firsthand experience has seldom been a prerequisite for engaging white-authored texts; and two, that neither has Professor Barrett himself experienced conditions of enslavement. That African American slave narratives were historically authored for a white reading audience at the time of their publication introduces another level of irony to the student's expressed alienation.

As generic literary forms composed of formulaic elements, African American slave narratives are products of cultural, political, and intellectual enterprise that warrant study as exemplars of literary and rhetorical practice. This point is especially important given widespread attempts to withhold education and literacy from African Americans during the antebellum period and after.[3] Rhetorical prowess notwithstanding, the characterization of African American writing as "purely descriptive" itself bears the weight of colonial syntax.[4] On such occasions, Barrett prompts students to do the internal work to "intellectualize [*their*] *position*" by conjoining African American literature and both canonical and contemporary theory ("Institutions, Classrooms, Failures"). As he explains, the discursive negotiations and tensions that present themselves in African American literature require a precise and questioning intellectual labor—namely the labor that has been appointed to theory.

For Barrett, pairing these two seemingly disparate entities—African American literature and critical theory—is not only a fruitful but also an ethical imperative. "The paramount issue," stresses Barrett, "is to place students in the position of theory insofar as this position is both *relevant* and *antagonistic* to African-American literature.... More important than a comprehensive exposure to theory," he clarifies, "is the fixing of a *location* for theory," so as to historicize and properly situate not only these texts but our own positions as readers of these texts ("Institutions, Classrooms, Failures"). Theory enjoys a seemingly disembodied, universal abstraction that, Barrett argues, begs for material historicity—the kind of situated, localized contextualization most often reserved for African American and ethnic literatures.[5] While race and racial blackness have been essential to experiences of whiteness and to white imagination (see Toni Morrison's *Playing in the Dark*), engagement with white-authored texts is not summarily stunted with apologies for experiential deficiency or want of historical authenticity.[6] "It would be unthinkable to raise the same [concerns] in those courses," Barrett reminds us ("Institutions, Classrooms, Failures"). Indeed, students and scholars grapple with theory perhaps precisely because of its inaccessibility. Pairing African American literature and critical theory, then, stages a disruption of theory's high abstraction to hold it accountable to a set of thoughts and circumstances that it has ignored or buried, while nonetheless relying on it.[7] Barrett is clear that "no matter how open or mediated, a disqualification or pathological bracketing of dark-skinned Others remains an invariable premise of both popular and learned traditions of Euro-American thought."[8]

The tenuousness of liberal gestures and apologies are altogether unraveled in the third essay collected here, in which Barrett employs a deconstructive methodology to reveal the faulty premise of liberal philosophy. In his essay-length review of John Carlos Rowe's scholarly contributions, "Redoubling American Studies," Barrett characterizes Rowe's rereading of canonical texts through new extratextual pressures as evidence that fixity of meaning and, therefore, of value closes us off to an ethical encounter, whether that encounter is with a text or with a social other. "In the circumstances of modernity," cautions Barrett, "Meaning is never simply the proposition of the sign but also always already its articulation of violence."[9] From his analysis of Rowe's work in American studies to his attempt to situate African American letters in the classroom and the academy, Barrett's pedagogy requires difficult engagements with the texts of our literary traditions. As with the classroom, the literary text is one site for parsing our attachments to and our understanding of history's impact on our capacity for responsible and ethical literacy.

This last point on reading—reading literature and theory on one hand; reading ourselves and others on the other—brings us to Barrett's enduring contribution to an intersectional hermeneutics. Indeed, notions of race and racial experience as coherent, fixed, and discrete have long signaled a crisis of racial ideology and racial violence for women of color and queer and feminist scholars of color, calling attention to the restrictive nature of race as a fixed framework for understanding violence against communities of color. If intersectionality has become nearly a reflexive intellectual move in this cultural moment, this is in part due to arguments such as Barrett's that racial violence relies on a matrix that produces and reifies racial difference alongside and through sexual and gender ideology that privileges patriarchy and heterosexuality. Barrett's teaching, on this and other interventions, distinguishes itself through sustained conversation with the work of African American and women of color feminist scholars. His formulation of race bears this out: "Only by a circuitous route through matters of gender and sexuality do the dynamics of ethnicity/race lodge themselves in the dissociation by which they are most routinely understood."[10] Evidenced in his pedagogy and citation practices and in his treatment elsewhere of race as a system for managing the "discharge of sexual pleasures," Barrett teaches us that reading well means reading beyond the familiar, in order to recognize and dispel the logic of such distinction in the first place.

Against the everyday consequences of economic despondency, systemic racism, and racially motivated violence, it may on first read seem the height of indifference to underscore the field-changing supposition made by Barrett that places at the center of violence the conceptual nature of race. But it is the conceptual that emboldens our desire for justice; it is the conceptual that names race as the experience of the other, that prevents us from recognizing that in the context of a presumed post(-post)civil rights era, where the unfinished business of justice for the underclass, the dispossessed, and the disappeared is articulated and mobilized en masse, race is most trenchantly produced through an affective economy that is reliant on the simultaneity of embodied alienation and identification, as exemplified by the apologetic student.

When I revisit Barrett's writing, I always sense the liberation that is to come, that his student in the above example could not yet imagine or practice. The movement and dislodging of expectations that he preferred in his everyday life he also enacted in his pedagogy and politics—insisting that students attend to textual crises and eruptions, to acts of rhetorical treason done in the service of resisting the totality of a racial and racist ideology. What legacy will fixed ideologies and expectations of race produce? Do they, as Barrett cautions, bear witness to the fact that the "the limiting nature of blackness has to do with the supposition that those designated *black* remain circumscribed within a very particular set of experiences of, attitudes toward, and perspectives on the world strikingly differentiating them from a broader population that bears a much more open-ended positioning to the world?"[11] Barrett's focus on the intellectual labor and articulation of black sentience in the classroom outstrips social, cultural, and political institutions that are still processing the centrality of black corporality and black death in the making of modern capitalism. Amid the economic, social, and political repercussions of white privilege on communities of color, Barrett's writing underscores the daunting yet critical task for professors and students of African American literature to refuse race and difference as self-evidentiary, to code a challenge to fixed notions of innate difference in order to most authentically acknowledge and disavow the violence pursued and practiced in its name.

NOTES

1. Barbara Christian, "The Race for Theory," *Feminist Studies* 14, no. 1 (1988): 67–79; Ann duCille, "The Occult of True Black Womanhood: Critical Demeanor and Black Feminist Studies," *Signs* 19, no. 3 (1994): 591–629.

2. Lindon Barrett, "Institutions, Classrooms, Failures: African American Literature and Critical Theory in the Same Small Spaces," chapter 1, this volume; Lindon Barrett, "Speaking of Failure: Undergraduate Education and Intersection of African-American Literature and Critical Theory," *Callaloo* 14, no. 3 (summer 1991): 619–30.

3. See Carter G. Woodson, *The Mis-education of the Negro* (Washington, DC: Associated Publishers, 1933), for an early account of the power of miseducation as an instrument of control.

4. Barrett, "Speaking of Failure."

5. Barrett, "Speaking of Failure."

6. Toni Morrison, *Playing in the Dark: Whiteness and the Literary Imagination* (New York: Vintage, 1993); Barrett, "Speaking of Failure."

7. Barrett, "Speaking of Failure."

8. Lindon Barrett, *Blackness and Value: Seeing Double* (New York: Cambridge University Press, 1999), 68.

9. Lindon Barrett, "Redoubling American Studies: John Carlos Rowe and Cultural Criticism," chapter 3, this volume.

10. Lindon Barrett, "Identities and Identity Studies: Reading Toni Cade Bambara's 'The Hammer Man,'" chapter 7, this volume.

11. Lindon Barrett, "The Experiences of Slave Narratives: Reading against Authenticity," chapter 2, this volume.

CH1

Institutions, Classrooms, Failures: African American Literature and Critical Theory in the Same Small Spaces (1994)

No comment I have encountered from an undergraduate illustrates more acutely the strong sociopolitical, institutional, and intellectual tensions converging on the limited number of classrooms in which African American literature is taught than one offered rather confidently from the front row of a lecture hall filled with sixty or so students. I remember the comment as follows: "I'm not sure how I'm going to write the paper for this class, because I've never been a slave and can't fully relate to this experience." This announcement was made in response to my open invitation for questions and comments a few weeks into an upper-division course on African American autobiography. It is remarkable for a variety of reasons. Among other matters, this announcement of an imminent failure to engage meaningfully the terms of African American autobiography codifies what may be the central challenge of courses in African American literature, the task of comprehending—of realizing intellectually—important particulars of African American experiences in the so-called New World. In essence, such intellectual activity stands very clearly in opposition—not apposition—to the traditional materials, monuments, and experiences of American cultural literacy, a term coined by E. D. Hirsch to refer to the general knowledge necessary to reinforce and maintain technical literacy. Students of African American literature—both contrary to and exemplified by my student's appeal to the importance of experience—are placed in a position for which their earlier education has in virtually no way prepared them.

Perhaps this situation ought to be regarded as one not of location but of dislocation. Students of African American literature find themselves—in the materials they are reading and the institutional lives they are leading (even if only for a quarter or a semester)—in a position where the texts they are reading do not resemble literature in terms of its traditional subjects, aims, and consequences and where their classroom does not resemble an institution of higher education in terms of who is allowed to speak and what is allowed to be said. Textuality is always a locus of authority, the fixed site of an author; African American literature, however, takes its place in a cultural system in which authority—self-authority or any other—has been traditionally denied the texts' authors. The situation of students of African American literature, as my student's comment suggests, becomes one in which variant discourses converge and fail to resolve their antagonisms. The situation is one of failure.

One can, with these matters in mind, begin to imagine the relevance and productiveness of pairing African American literature with critical theory in undergraduate education, for the situation of this pairing and the situation of the students who might be introduced to it speak significantly to each other. If African American literature and critical theory appear to fail each other, then this failure itself is highly instructive in pursuing an understanding of both fields. At the very least, the failure provides important definitional information about the contrasted fields, and an instructor conversant with both wants precisely to highlight this peculiar relativity. In fact, it soon becomes clear that their troubled relation reinscribes the governing dualism—the intellectual versus the experiential—of my student's appeal. Theory, on the one hand, is marked by a reluctance to acknowledge itself as a political body of works with *material* determinants and consequences; African American literature, on the other, is characterized by the difficulty of acknowledging itself as anything more than the oversimple redaction of the conditions of a *material* and (by negation) political body. One wants to draw attention to the manner in which their "failed" intercourse raises questions concerning the generally unremarked politics of reading—questions that students of African American literature engage necessarily and directly and at risk to their academic careers. In other words, these texts clearly trouble the tense relation between themselves as texts and the cultural system in which they take their places as texts—so much so that one quickly realizes how unlikely it is that a student would make a similar comment in courses on Renaissance or Victorian literature although the very same circumstances obtain. The materials of these courses necessarily stand outside the student's experience (and I phrased my initial response to my student accordingly). That is, although students have been neither Renaissance courtiers nor besieged gentry swept up in the social and intellectual changes of rapid industrialization, it would be unthinkable to raise the same question in those courses. One must ask why such virtually identical institutional and classroom situations appear dissimilar enough to justify a student's unembarrassed commentary before sixty or so peers.

For what reason does the reading of African American texts elicit appeals to incomprehension based on lack of experience? In exploring the answer to this question and some of the many notable critical errors of the appeal, I restrict myself to two points and, in doing so, attempt to suggest how, by employing theory in the teaching of African American literature, some of those errors might be addressed.

It is first important to note that my student's newly discovered (in)abilities dramatically reverse traditional academic practice. The student abrogates the practice of privileging depersonalized knowledge, which is standard to literary and other academic studies. Whereas one most often repudiates (rather than makes appeals to) personal experience in academic studies, my student conceives it imperative to do exactly the opposite. bell hooks provides cogent insight into the dilemma of this student, as well as into the institutional dilemma it redacts. She writes: "Racism is perpetuated when blackness is associated solely with concrete gut level experience conceived as either opposing or having no connection to abstract thinking and the production of critical theory. The idea that there is no meaningful connection between black experience and critical thinking about aesthetics or culture must be continually interrogated."[1] Traditional American cultural literacy not only distorts or, in large part, dismisses African American cultures and experiences but also fosters an inability to consider or engage those cultures and experiences intellectually, thus promoting what amounts to a "literate resistance" to viewing them in any way other than within the terms of vague and dismissible angst or—to repeat a phrase—the oversimple redaction of the conditions of a material and (by negation) political body. This "literate" impulse is mass-produced and widely circulated, as Hirsch specifies in his theory of predetermined cultural cues, elaborated in his book *Cultural Literacy*.[2] Therefore, in order to "write the paper for [my] class," students must encounter the difficult and novel task of reconsidering and revising this impulse. Theory—to repeat a central point—may prove instrumental in this revision, for the situation of theory, like that of my student in her dilemma and that of the literature she confronts, is one of dislocation. Theory knowingly absents itself from that which it represents. It maintains and reinscribes this absence as the measure of itself; the matter from which theory absents itself can be crudely understood as "practice."[3] Theory attempts to be a signifier removed from signifiers. It thus fails (as sign) to be where it is not and also fails (as nonpractice) not to be where it is. Equally, the situation of African American literature, which determines the dilemma of my student in the front row, is one of pronounced incompatibilities and tensions. To be African American amounts to having those discourses spoken most easily and fluently by the dominant culture fail to imagine you, and, conversely, to locate an African American self within those discourses amounts to failing those discourses. In short, if theory in itself is a site of profound incompatibilities, then theory becomes an immense (re)source for presenting and understanding—as recorded in a literary tradition—African American thought and behavior and the strategies and circumstances of African American thought and behavior, also in themselves sites of profound incompatibilities; the same obtains vice versa.

Yet, more to the point, just as instructive as the similarities of the two are their differences. Critical theory stands as an ostensibly depersonalized form of knowledge; African American literature does not. Bringing the two together clearly engages the dualism of knowledge and experience underlying my student's perplexing appeal to a lack of experience. Insofar as the abstraction (i.e., knowledge) of critical theoretical concerns hardly seems capable of admitting or bearing relation to the resolute materiality (i.e., experience) of African American concerns and cultural productions, the pairing of the two addresses the standard "literate" sensibility underlying, however consciously or unconsciously, my student's appeal. In making the two fields conversant, one aims then at allowing students to see the complication of materiality and abstraction (or second-order discourse) even in the most apparently material of conditions (i.e., African American literature) and vice versa, in the most abstract of pronouncements (i.e., theory). Granted that in the moments immediately following my student's comment, this process begins for her far afield of theory; nonetheless, it is a process to which theory can amply contribute both in the discourse of the classroom and in course reading materials—issues to which I will turn presently.

More immediately, there is an unstated corollary of my student's appeal that must also be considered: Complementing her conception of her own impairing lack of experience seems to be a certainty or presumption of my experience as a slave—indeed, despite a temporal gulf of more than one hundred years making such experience an impossibility, despite my presence at a lectern marking me as the professor (or authority) in the room, not to mention the obligatory accreditation of a PhD underwriting my presence at the front of the room (a certificate not of experience but of, if nothing else, intellectual perseverance). Prompting the student to see her distorting cultural literacy and even racism begins as simply as stating that I have no more experience of being a slave than she does. As a group, we African Americans are imagined to bear little resemblance to the dominant American community while, conversely, each African American is granted an inexorable representativeness in relation to all other African Americans. My student's act of implicitly looking to her professor for experience as a slave, which she acknowledges she lacks, underscores the startling efficacy of mass-produced and widely circulated cultural cues dissuading most inhabitants of the New World from thinking carefully and insightfully about race. Clearly, no one at the present time possesses the experience of antebellum slavery. My student fails to see that race—and here is the unacknowledged crux—always has been and continues to be foremost an intellectual matter, either within or without the classroom but most plainly so in the classroom. While the issue of experience is not irrelevant, neither does it enter the dynamics of the classroom and its impending academic tasks in the manner my student conceives.[4]

Race is not singularly an experience, and experience is not an innocent register of "reality." Both race and experience are implicated in and overdetermined by economic, political, and social struggles. Personal and even collective experience do not define the parameters of race, which is another way of saying that the only interventions in issues of race are not to be made in terms of either personal or collective experience. The belief that this state of affairs holds sway returns one to the odd revision of standard academic practice already noted. Standard academic practice pursues *facts* (which, despite appearances, are also implicated in and overdetermined by economic, political, and social struggles), and if facts are somehow paramount in our institutions and classrooms, the fact of personal African American identity is emphatically not the singular one to be considered in this instance. Indeed, in classrooms of African American literature facts themselves are preemptively questioned and challenged by attention to situations, the situations of those both within and without the classification *African American*. It is, no doubt, at this point that the remarkable difficulties of my student arise.

Undergraduates are tutored to assume "the technique of what might be called methodological neutrality, of 'getting the facts right' before leaping in with our value judgments, [which their institutions of higher education would have them believe] is one of the progressive achievements of [Western] civilization."[5] Nevertheless, students in African American literature classes discover opposing sets of facts and attendant narratives that no amount of appeals to neutrality might reconcile. In ways analogous to my student in the front row, these undergraduates find themselves speaking and writing at odds with those in whose "care" and within whose power of evaluation they are placed. They remain at odds with their professors of African American literature, who must in some measure revise the facts or "certainties" of their earlier education; equally, they remain at odds with their institutions of higher education, which virtually everywhere resist such revision. In African American literature courses, the narratives or "stories" of a previous education are revised in accordance with diverse critiques of a New World civilization founded by and abidingly committed to the vision of a "white-supremacist oligarchy."[6] Neutrality itself takes up a place within one of the opposing sets of facts, with the result that there no longer clearly exists the certainty (or illusion) of "getting the facts right"; the *facts* prove instruments of will implicated in, rather than effecting release from, *experience*, interestedness, and the dynamics of cultural, civil, and other forms of power. The facts appear as the discursive gestures of dominant groups "whose exclusionary behavior may be firmly buttressed by institutionalized structures of domination that do not critique or check [that exclusionary behavior]."[7] (These lessons cannot remain purely "textual" or "academic" when students find themselves in courses that, for all intents and purposes, are brand new to American education—heralded by political and social upheaval in the 1960s and met with bureaucratic and journalistic trepidation three decades later.)[8]

Although my student's response to the "literate" dilemma presented by the course in African American autobiography forms itself as a misrecognition or revision of the binarism traditionally differentiating experience from "methodological neutrality," her inversion of terms is not the key point to be noticed. More significant is her retention of the binarism itself. Indeed, perpetuating the institutional narrative she has long imbibed, the student summarily dismisses both the dynamics of the course and the academic discourse of the classroom in which those dynamics are played out. She construes both as sites at which intellectual configurations no longer obtain. In effect, to resolve her dilemma, she understands her engagement with African American materials as, rather than revising an education already in place, standing curiously *without* that education. In this way, even inverted, the binarism operates to distinguish that which is institutionally (and culturally) valued from that which is not; her articulation of her situation ironically instates within the discourse of the class on African American autobiography the disqualification or bracketing of African Americans, their cultures, and cultural productions long endemic to the dominant communities of the New World. The force of her comment would have African American autobiography virtually inaccessible intellectually; she removes the course in which she is enrolled from the academic tradition she is attempting to master and from the imperatives of the institution in which she is enrolled. She reinstates the textual materials of the course, as well as the ongoing interpretive activities of the classroom, securely within the material realm that, in terms of the popular American mind, almost solely determines African American existence.

Recall that in its central conflict, the conflict of the marginal and the preferred, the study of African American literature exposes and troubles what Hirsch imagines as a supratechnical literacy, the background information or background knowledge—beyond linguistic competence—requisite to reading. Reading African American literature precipitates remarkable encounters with predetermined cultural cues constructing a predetermined reality—to which acknowledged textuality stands in apposition. The acknowledged textuality of African American literature abrogates, in large part, these predetermined cultural cues of official American experience and reality, therefore supplanting expected apposition with disorienting opposition. The appeal of my student can be understood as an attempt to return opposition to apposition. In terms of the pressures of the course, her impulse to disregard, or revise, the tenet that privileges depersonalized knowledge is not misguided; her peculiar revision, however, fails to respond adequately to either the materials or the imperatives of the course. Opposingly, the revision she fails to undertake involves dismissing, rather than keeping intact, the binarism structuring her lament.

More fully considered, her situation and the analogous situations of the sixty or so other students in the class lead to a recognition of the coimplication of *experience* and the *facts* (or more traditional academic concerns). Made otherwise aware of their curious situations, an awareness to which the intersection of critical theory and African American literature can contribute, undergraduates may be prompted to recognize that

> when it comes to knowledge of the world, there is no such thing as a category of the "essentially descriptive"; that "description" is never ideologically or cognitively neutral; that to "describe" is to specify a locus of meaning, to construct an object of knowledge, and to produce a knowledge that shall be bound by that act of descriptive construction. "Description" has been central, for example, in the colonial discourse. It was by assembling a monstrous machinery of descriptions—of our bodies, our speech acts, our habits, our conflicts, and desires, our politics, our socialities and sexualities—in fields as various as ethnology, fiction, photography, linguistics, political science—that the colonial discourse was

able to classify and ideologically master the colonial subject, enabling itself to transform the descriptively verifiable multiplicity and difference into the ideologically felt hierarchy of value. To say, in short, what one is presenting is "essentially descriptive" is to assert a level of facticity which conceals its own ideology and to prepare a ground from which judgments of classification, generalisation and value can be made.[9]

Undergraduates, in their new and difficult situations, discover that facts are replaced by attention to situations and, moreover, that although open regard for situations may seem superfluous or, at best, ancillary to undergraduate (or all) education, this principle does not apply here, for if there is a set of concerns that African American literature privileges, among them are not only African American thought and behavior but just as surely the *situations* of African American thought and behavior and the inevitable politics of reading (and announcing) those situations. With little or no preparation, undergraduates in African American literature courses are confronted directly with the situations of reading and, more particularly, their own situations when reading. My student's apprehension of her (in)abilities and their relation to the limits of her experience demonstrate the manner in which students of African American literature cannot help discovering with greater immediacy the political dynamics of what passes as literature and as the (con)textuality or situations of literature.

My student finds herself in a situation and in a classroom in which she fails to intellectualize the course materials as well as her own position vis-à-vis race. Thereby, she extends the widely circulated "ideologically felt hierarchy of value" that, by definition, cannot hold sway in a class on African American autobiography. As of yet, she fails to comprehend the class and, ironically, announces her fear that she fails to comprehend the class. One might prompt her to begin to intellectualize her position by posing a question as simple as why she might assume I have experience as a slave while she has none. The point is to begin to make her deliberately recognize and estimate a superordinate "literacy" that it is the aim of the course materials and classroom interaction to interrogate and revise. The issue is to make her intellectualize *her position*, a feat that, despite her lament, she has not yet begun to perform. And, as she intuits, this feat should not be undertaken wholly at the expense of experience. She is intuitively correct to question and resist "standards of pyrotechnics" claiming "that intellectual excellence requires depersonalization and abstraction" and the attendant descriptive license of those standards (even though her particular line of reasoning fails to pursue that interrogation or challenge adequately).[10] To her credit, she somewhat aligns herself with the materials and imperatives of the course: How, one might ask, can the mandatory dismissal of "particular personal experience" form part of an education also concerned with traditions of language and literature that attempt to revise long-standing processes of depersonalization, traditions of language and literature that begin with "the process of [random Africans] becoming a single people, Yorubas, Akans, Ibos, Angolans, and others . . . present on slave ships to America and experienc[ing] a common horror [marked by] unearthly moans and piercing shrieks?"[11] African American linguistic and literary traditions necessarily find their beginnings here, preserve and revise those initial sounds, and in large part record heroic, or at least involved, attempts to retreat from, or cast off, the enforced depersonalization those initial moans and shrieks protest. How, one might ask again, can African American literature reconcile itself to conditions of the academy and higher education that call for depersonalization? Indeed, the education of undergraduates in African American literature courses is profitably complicated when we examine the way in which incipient concerns of African American literature and culture are reinscribed within the conditions of its presence—its situation—in the academy, as well as their own situations. This proposition I undertake, in part, by pursuing three categories of theory that can be counterposed with African American texts: canonical theory, institutional theory, and African American (and other subaltern) theory. Canonical theory may be thought of as works such as Aristotle's *Poetics*, Sir Philip Sidney's "An Apology for Poetry," David Hume's "Of the Standard of Taste," Immanuel Kant's *Critique of Judgment*, and Karl Marx's *Capital* that stand as part of a prized tradition of belletristic and philosophical texts. I take institutional theory to refer to the relatively contemporary phenomenon of professional academic writings, such as F. O. Matthiessen's *American Renaissance*, Mary Douglas's *Purity and Danger*, and Michel Foucault's *Language, Counter-memory, and Practice*, that reflexively settle or trouble issues of literature, knowing, and culture.[12] African American (and other subaltern) theory includes texts such as the essays collected by Cheryl A. Wall in *Changing Our Own Words*, Edward Said's *Orientalism*, and Hortense Spillers's "Mama's Baby, Papa's Maybe," which turn the energies of humanistic inquiry predominantly to hierarchies of race, gender, sexuality, and class and their invariable complications of issues pertaining to literature, knowing, and culture.[13] Although these distinctions prove helpful in intellectualizing materials that seem to lie beyond that possibility, it is not necessary that they be introduced to one's students. It is more to the point that they provide ways of structuring discussions. Equally important, the distinctions are neither rigorous nor mutually exclusive; they suggest broad contexts in which to place theory in its fretful relation to African American literature.

Of the three categories, I present or refer to canonical theory first and make most of these references in the introductory meetings of the class. My object is to begin to interrogate (in general as well as personal terms) the immediate problematics of our situatedness in a class devoted to African American literature or other materials and to suggest a tradition of speculation that prohibits or at least diminishes the very activities we are to undertake as a class. I breach most standard notions of critical theory for, to highlight the manner in which a strict—and in no way disappearing—canon of humanist figures and thought takes little (or derisive) account of a tradition of African American thought and behavior and the circumstances of such thought and behavior, I pursue the juxtaposition of broad, historical speculations with African American literature. We may briefly survey works by such European and American intellectuals and leaders as G. W. F. Hegel, Thomas Jefferson, Abraham Lincoln, the noted nineteenth-century scientist Joseph Le Conte (a leading figure of the newly established University of California), and the New Critics (who in standard discussions are generally divorced from their "southern agrarian" incarnation). The notion I want to present, especially in initial meetings, is that, no matter how open or mediated, a disqualification or pathological bracketing of dark-skinned others remains a virtually invariable premise of both the general and learned traditions of Euro-American thought. Indeed, I want to present the notion that examinations of "African American" literature and culture must at some point look necessarily to European males and their New World descendants, since it is precisely these communities and their discourses that have in lasting ways determined the hostile conditions and attitudes in terms of which African American literature and cultural productions must at some point be contextualized.

I prompt my class to consider immediately a history in which respected and prized traditions of Western thought disqualify African Americans a priori from the belletristic and philosophical traditions advertised as universal. The class must begin to think of the educational implications of such histories and predilections and to consider how such implications may or will influence the tasks they have set for themselves by taking up the seats they have chosen for the quarter: Is the institution in which they are enrolled a participant in such histories? Are the educations they have received and will continue to receive implicated? At what point did these histories end, if in fact they did? In what ways, given such histories and widespread predilections, will a course covering African American literature or culture necessarily differ from or challenge the vast majority of the other courses in which the students have been or are enrolled? In short, undergraduates must begin to visualize themselves in a situation of profound contradiction; they must begin to contemplate a second-order, or critical, discourse about their own educational situations as well as about the materials they will encounter.

In the late eighteenth century, Jefferson wrote that "in general, [African American] existence appears to participate more of sensation than reflection."[14] Early in the nineteenth century, Hegel proposed that "we must lay aside all thought of reverence and morality—all that we call feeling—if we would rightly comprehend ['the African']; there is nothing harmonious with humanity to be found in ['the peculiarly African'] character."[15] Lincoln, in the mid-nineteenth century, wrote, "I agree with Judge Douglas [that the African American] is not my equal in many respects—certainly not in color, perhaps not in moral or intellectual endowment."[16] One might draw on a variety of figures and extend the chronology as close to the contemporary moment as one wishes and, in doing so, suggest an enduring theoretical context and problematic for African American literature.

My use of institutional and subaltern theories is not so broadly contextual. I employ these theories, rather, as resources for reading texts chosen for the course. To this end, institutional theory provides general (rather than more culturally specific) speculative concepts, which may be relevant to either individual texts or patterns emerging among a series of texts. Elaine Scarry's *The Body in Pain*, for example, provides a helpful model for considering the "discourse" of pain and physical abuse endemic, particularly, to many early African American texts. Scarry looks foremost to torture and war, suggesting that both are "reality-conferring process[es], in the one [torture] it is the non-believer's body and in the other [war] it is the believer's body that is enlisted in the crisis of substantiation."[17] Her distinction between torture and war is perhaps not crucial in the context of African American literature; I do, however, see as crucial in that context the understanding of pain and physical confrontation as reality-conferring processes. To provide a brief example, the insight is borne out in reading the scene from Frederick Douglass's 1845 autobiography in which Demby is summarily murdered for refusing to take further abuse at the hands of the overseer Mr. Gore. At stake in Demby's rebellion is the "reality" of a system founded on the unaccountable equation of dark skin with subhumanity, a system in which African American bodies stand as sites (and sights) against which whiteness is contradicted and therefore also predicated most forcefully. Nothing fixes the meanings of the signs of blackness and whiteness, in and of themselves in New World landscapes. These matters are fixed instead by such acts of violence as those that reduce Demby to a "mangled body ... [whose] blood and brains marked the water," acts of violence that take on, in the words of Scarry, the significance of "the reality conferring process," "the crisis of substantiation," for a questionable sociopolitical order.[18] In this application of Scarry's formulations, the point of irruptiveness at which established value recovers itself in the American landscape—and most fully asserts itself—is the point at which African American bodies are violated.

Scarry's theoretical speculations seem especially helpful when reading a text such as Mary Prince's "The History of Mary Prince, a West Indian Slave," in which meditations on language, literacy, and culture are clearly subordinate to catalogs of physical abuse and recollections and images of physical pain.[19] Equally, Pierre Macherey's *Theory of Literary Production* seems helpful in considering, say, the opening pages of Toni Morrison's *Song of Solomon*. Macherey is concerned with looking beyond a "false simplicity which derives from... apparent unity of meaning" to "those disparities which point to a conflict of meaning" and reveal "the inscription of an otherness" in certain configurations; he is interested in "that which happens at [the] margins" of certain configurations.[20] In the opening pages of Morrison's novel, the "unity of meaning" that the elected representatives of the white citizens hope to realize and master is relentlessly troubled by the *present absence*, or marginality, of African American communities, whose imaginations are equally at work (re)naming "Mains Avenue" first "Doctor Street" and then, in response to official reprimands, "Not Doctor Street." "The charity hospital at its northern end" is similarly (re)named "Not Mercy Hospital" in the light of its refusal to provide services to African Americans.[21] In a similar manner, the critique of Edmund Husserl in Jacques Derrida's early work *Speech and Phenomena and Other Essays on Husserl's Theory of Signs* may help illuminate the efficacy of the "singing voices" and musical motifs in, say, Ann Petry's *The Street* and *The Narrows* and many other African American texts attentive to the cultural primacy of music.[22] Peter Stallybrass and Allon White's *The Politics and Poetics of Transgression* might be taken up in conjunction with Billie Holiday and William Dufty's *Lady Sings the Blues* to demonstrate how Holiday employs the grotesque as well as the charged values of the body and of urban geography in her critique of the American society that perversely celebrates her talents.[23]

At this point, one begins to see at least one additional issue of failure in proposing such intersections of African American literature and critical theory. One recognizes a failure to acquaint undergraduate students adequately with the histories, factions, and abundance of formulas that compose the relatively heterogeneous field known as critical theory. These intersections yield, in large part, a somewhat random exposure to both concerns—or, at least, to theory. Nonetheless, one should not be daunted by the specter of this failure, for the paramount goal is not to provide undergraduate students with a survey or in-depth acquaintance with the dense expanse of critical theory (a project that I believe is more fully suited to graduate school) but, rather, to place students in the position of theory insofar as this position is both relevant and antagonistic to African American literature. One wants to engage the more pressing failure of an apparent inability of the two to address each other, the apparent failure in classes of African American literature of the traditional academic dualism.

This issue is inherently addressed in the third of the three categories. African American (and other subaltern) theory takes as its focus the coimplication of literary and intellectual activities in social systems of domination and hierarchy—in "the sordid history of colonialist expropriation, material exploitation, and class and race oppression behind European world dominance."[24] William Andrews, for example, in the first chapter of *To Tell a Free Story*, "The First Century of Afro-American Autobiography: Notes toward a Definition of a Genre," draws on speech-act theory to delineate the sociohistorical and, therefore, narrative constraints facing early African American autobiographers; Valerie Smith, in *Self-Discovery and Authority in Afro-American Narrative*, interrogates the tensions and incompatibilities of an unreflective privileging of the notions of literacy and literariness in relation to African American lives and texts.[25] Other texts that come to mind as suitable for undergraduate scrutiny include JoAnne Cornwell-Giles's "Afro-American Criticism and Western Consciousness: The Politics of Knowing," Mae G. Henderson's "Speaking in Tongues: Dialogics, Dialectics, and the Black Woman Writer's Literary Tradition," and Christopher Miller's "Theories of Africans: The Question of Literary Anthropology."[26] These exemplary texts provide an eclectic sample of recent work conjoining the concerns of African American literature and critical theory. Cornwell-Giles examines the problematics of attaining self-knowledge in a philosophical dilemma perpetuated by the hostile point of view of a dominant discourse; Henderson proposes that the manner in which black women write and speak in modulating multiple voices is a central and distinguishing feature of their discourse; Miller explores some of the ways in which mastery proves unattainable for the Western scholar in pursuit of the African other. Spillers's "Mama's Baby, Papa's Maybe" bears mentioning again. This essay, making such distinctions as that between the "body" and the "flesh," is very difficult but worth the time and close attention it requires.[27] Students need not master the essay in its entirety to cull important and original insights from it. Colonial and postcolonial theories also belong in this category: for example, Homi Bhabha's "Sly Civility," outlining pathological contradictions of colonialist discourse; Gauri Viswanathan's *Masks of Conquest*, detailing the formation of

English literary study in British India as a strategy of sociopolitical control; and Jenny Sharpe's "Figures of Colonial Resistance," arguing against the transparency of the intellectual who puts forth narratives of resistance.[28]

It seems clear to me that the incompatibility of the two fields is instructive in aiding undergraduates to "write the paper[s] for [my] class[es]." The inevitable involvement of each field with failure, as well as the apparent failure of the two fields to address each other, does not constitute grounds for their mutual dismissal; it forms the ground on which undergraduate students can begin to read the fields in concert. At the very least, the *opposition* illuminates analogous tensions that students of African American literature must confront in the texts they are considering as well as in the circumscribed spaces of the institutions and classrooms in which they find themselves. The situation of the pairing, like that of students who find themselves in the position of writing papers on African American autobiography despite their different "experiences," is remarkable but not ludicrous. Once undergraduates are made to entertain the difficulty of reading the two fields in concert (not simply, as one would expect, the difficulty of reading theory), these students are placed (although they may not realize it, until someone points it out to them) in the situation of making "analyses of culture within the relations of power which divide [culture] into preferred and marginal categories."[29] Such conflicts constitute preeminent concerns, themes, and references for African American literature, with the result that the study of literature assumes its place, more or less openly, within the dynamics of discursive and cultural conflicts. The remarkable pairing queries both a discrete notion of literary studies and the often unremarked dynamics of reading sustained in institutions that privilege ostensibly depersonalized knowledge and the attendant "descriptive" license such knowledge promotes.

African American literature and critical theory are thought to be ineluctably opposed concerns, resolutely incompatible, and in this apparent dissimilarity lies precisely the benefit of considering them in tandem. I propose that no inherent benefit lies in the fact of theory itself; rather, benefits lie in the troubled convergence of the two fields within the classroom. Clearly, there can be no final word on this matter, for that is precluded by the presence of controversy, in which—by definition—final words appear forever elusive. Still, I offer a tentative final word—insofar as such a paradox is allowed. In classes on African American literature one must remain attentive to the tensions and failures arising before and even around one; one must even create some tensions and failures oneself.

NOTES

Chapter 1, "Institutions, Classrooms, Failures," was previously published in *Teaching Contemporary Theory to Undergraduates*, ed. Dianne F. Sadoff and William E. Cain, 218–32 (New York: Modern Language Association of America, 1994), and is reprinted by permission of the Modern Language Association of America.

1. bell hooks, *Yearning: Race, Gender and Cultural Politics* (Boston: South End, 1990), 23.

2. E. D. Hirsch, *Cultural Literacy: What Every American Needs to Know* (New York: Houghton, 1987).

3. I use the term *critical theory* primarily in agreement with the currency gained by the term as suggested by Gayatri Spivak: "Theory in the United States institution of the profession of English is often shorthand for the general critique of humanism undertaken in France in the wake of the Second World War and then, in a double-take, further radicalized in the mid-sixties in the work of the so-called poststructuralists." Gayatri Chakravorty Spivak, "The Making of Americans, the Teaching of English, and the Future of Culture Studies," *New Literary History* 21, no. 4 (1990): 788. Thus, even further, theory is a site of incompatibilities and tension.

4. Professors of African American literature who are African American are not the only instructors who must confront in the classroom the issues delineated here. On the contrary, insofar as they must be prepared to engage textual materials, any such instructor, regardless of race, must be prepared to negotiate the variety of ways (some more patent and bald than others, as suggested by my student's comment) in which predetermined cultural knowledge enters the classroom. This student's comment raises a particular issue clearly tied to the race of her teacher. Nevertheless, at the same time, it raises a general issue not nearly so restricted. There are, of course, important issues to be considered concerning instructors of African American literature who are not African American; however, this situation is not the primary focus here. In an extended consideration of the more general issue, I hope to delineate the manner in which my student's announcement suggests a paradigm for bringing together the seemingly inimical pair of African American literature and critical theory.

5. Gerald Graff, *Literature against Itself: Literary Ideas in Modern Society* (Chicago: University of Chicago Press, 1979), 86. In the light of the work Graff would go on to produce, this passage, published in 1979, is almost unimaginable.

6. Nell Irvin Painter, "Race Relations, History, and Public Policy: The Alabama Vote Fraud Cases of 1985," in *America in Theory*, ed. Leslie Berlowitz, Denis Donoghue, and Louis Menand (New York: Oxford University Press, 1988), 127.

7. bell hooks, "Essentialism and Experience," *American Literary History* 3, no. 1 (1991): 176.

8. Dinesh D'Souza, *Illiberal Education: The Politics of Race and Sex on Campus* (New York: Free Press, 1991).

9. Ahmad Aijaz, "Jameson's Rhetoric of Otherness and the 'National Allegory,'" *Social Text* 19 (fall 1987): 6.

10. Elizabeth Fox-Genovese, "To Write Myself: The Autobiographies of Afro-American Women," in *Feminist Issues in Literary Scholarship*, ed. Shari Benstock (Bloomington: Indiana University Press, 1987), 163.

11. Sterling Stuckey, *Slave Culture: Nationalist Theory and the Foundations of Black America* (New York: Oxford University Press, 1987), 3.

12. F. O. Matthiessen, *American Renaissance* (New York: Oxford University Press, 1941); Mary Douglas, *Purity and Danger* (New York: Ark, 1984); and Michel Foucault, *Language, Counter-memory, and Practice* (Ithaca, NY: Cornell University Press, 1977).

13. Cheryl A. Wall, ed., *Changing Our Own Words* (New Brunswick, NJ: Rutgers University Press, 1989); Edward Said, *Orientalism* (New York: Vintage, 1979); and Hortense Spillers, "Mama's Baby, Papa's Maybe," *Diacritics* 17, no. 2 (1987): 65–81.

14. Thomas Jefferson, *Notes on the State of Virginia*, ed. William Peden (New York: Norton, 1954), 139.

15. G. W. F. Hegel, *Lectures on the Philosophy of History*, trans. John Sibree (London: Bell, 1914), 97. Hegel continues, "In Negro life the characteristics of point is the fact that consciousness has not yet attained to the realization of any substantial objective existence—as for example, God, or Law—in which the interest of man's volition is involved and in which he realizes his own being."

16. Abraham Lincoln and Stephen Douglas, "First Joint Debate, Ottawa, August 21: Mr. Lincoln's Reply," in *The Lincoln-Douglas Debates of 1858* (New York: Oxford University Press, 1965), 53.

17. Elaine Scarry, *The Body in Pain: The Making and Unmaking of the World* (New York: Oxford University Press, 1985), 150.

18. Frederick Douglass, *Narrative of the Life of Frederick Douglass, an American Slave*, ed. Benjamin Quarles (Cambridge, MA: Harvard University Press, 1960), 47; Scarry, *The Body in Pain*.

19. Mary Prince, "The History of Mary Prince, a West Indian Slave," in *Six Women's Slave Narratives*, introduction by William L. Andrews (New York: Oxford University Press, 1988), 1–44.

20. Pierre Macherey, *A Theory of Literary Production* (London: Routledge, 1978), 79.

21. Toni Morrison, *Song of Solomon* (New York: NAL, 1977), 4.

22. Jacques Derrida, *Speech and Phenomena and Other Essays on Husserl's Theory of Signs* (Evanston, IL: Northwestern University Press, 1978).

23. Peter Stallybrass and Allon White, *The Politics and Poetics of Transgression* (Ithaca, NY: Cornell University Press, 1986).

24. Gauri Viswanathan, "The Beginnings of English Literary Study in British India," *Oxford Literary Review* 9, no. 1 (1987): 22–23.

25. William Andrews, *To Tell a Free Story: The First Century of Afro-American Autobiography* (Urbana: University of Illinois Press, 1986); Valerie Smith, *Self-Discovery and Authority in Afro-American Narrative* (Cambridge, MA: Harvard University Press, 1987).

26. JoAnne Cornwell-Giles, "Afro-American Criticism and Western Consciousness: The Politics of Knowing," *Black American Literature Forum* 24, no. 1 (1990): 85–98; Mae G. Henderson, "Speaking in Tongues: Dialogics, Dialectics, and the Black Woman Writer's Literary Tradition," in *Changing Our Own Words: Essays on Criticism, Theory, and Writing by Black Women*, ed. Cheryl A. Wall (New Brunswick, NJ: Rutgers University Press, 1989), 16–37; Christopher Miller, "Theories of Africans: The Question of Literary

Anthropology," in *"Race," Writing, and Difference*, ed. Henry Louis Gates Jr. (Chicago: University of Chicago Press, 1986), 281–300.

27. Spillers, "Mama's Baby, Papa's Maybe."

28. Homi Bhabha, "Sly Civility," *October* 34 (1985): 71–80; Gauri Viswanathan, *Masks of Conquest* (New York: Columbia University Press, 1989); Jenny Sharpe, "Figures of Colonial Resistance," *Modern Fiction Studies* 35, no. 1 (1989): 137–55.

29. Hazel V. Carby, "The Canon: Civil War and Reconstruction," *Michigan Quarterly Review* 28, no. 1 (1989): 42.

CH2

The Experiences of Slave Narratives:
Reading against Authenticity (1999)

Often students facing the task of having to read and consider African American slave narratives make a notable misstep. They look at slave narratives so intently as experiential records that they virtually neglect them as discursive artifacts. They expect to engage through their experiences of reading the narratives singularly representative or authentic experiences of "blackness" and "enslavement," and these expectations are problematic because they diminish intriguing textual negotiations undertaken by the narrators as well as the powerful sociopolitical imperatives overdetermining racial categorization. Expecting to hit experiential bedrock, students overlook the acts of textual representation with which they are confronted. If the cultural regime underwriting U.S. slavery is one that "cast[s] social practices as biological essences," then its analog in these instances is the casting of social practices as experiential essences.[1] The result is that the textual artifacts before the students are dismissed as transparencies, and the notion of race underpinning enduring U.S. cultural formations is hypostasized. Racialization is reconfirmed and reiterated as obdurate and monolithic. It is imagined as the untroubled and authentic bedrock of social and historical experience, even as the narratives both produce and question the effect of race in their efforts to document and alter a social and cultural landscape. The narratives, that is, propose race foremost as the vexed product of social interactions and delineate and query these interactions. These delineations and queries—not any authentic experience monopolizing blackness or slavery—are the most recuperable performances of the narratives.

Because race is by no means a self-evident principle, the reader of the narratives must consider race on some level as a discursively mediated phenomenon and apparatus. Students must be led to understand that a central lesson to be gleaned from the exercise before them is the way in which race "organizes a range of discursive practices," practices eminently more recuperable than the "authentic."[2]

Arguably the most influential line of thought in contemporary criticism of slave narratives, the now widely articulated African American feminist critique, offers a productive basis for classroom instruction. Raising questions of representativeness and authenticity along lines of gender, the critique of what formerly stood as the archetypal figure and archetypal heroism of slave narratives highlights the idea that "slave experience" and "blackness" are not recoverable as parcels of experience transparently preceding and redacted in the narratives. Dispelling the aim of reading to find a unitary condition of blackness or slavery underwriting the narratives, the critique foregrounds ways in which constructions of blackness (and whiteness) in the texts emerge principally as strategies of cultural dominance or subversion scripting what may come to be understood as totalized "experience." Slave narratives are artifacts in which political, discursive, and textual crises make up the most substantive signifiers of racial blackness (as well as whiteness) and slavery. In reading to recognize these crises, students learn to forgo simple expectations of authenticity and its apparent stability of categories and conditions. They must question self-evident matters like *race* and the ease with which its self-evidence is usually received.

Much of the self-evidence of race as well as the experience of enslavement represented in the narratives is, from the vantage of the African American feminist critique, insistently masculinist, since most slave narratives, in the words of Deborah McDowell, focus "studiously on making the slave a man, according to cultural norms of masculinity."[3] Readers are schooled to be suspicious of what most often passes as authentic slave experience. What passes as the whole story is, in fact, only part of it. In place of a singular, authentic slave or black experience, one discovers attempts to parallel dominant constructions of masculinity. In addition to attempts to authenticate brutal experiences of racial blackness and enslavement, postures central to the narratives complicate or overwhelm gestures at unproblematic authenticity, as demonstrated by the narratives of Frederick Douglass, James W. C. Pennington, and Elizabeth Keckley, for example. These contradictory gestures form points of textual crisis that trouble the specious self-evidence of race and the highly charged and enduring investment of U.S. culture in both the certainty of race and the notion of the limiting nature of blackness.

This is not to say that race should be imagined as a meaningless or insignificant concept. But it must not be conceived as an ontological condition either. Students must be reminded that, even in the circumstances of U.S. slavery, race is not a given but a deployed concept and that the peculiar dynamics of its deployment are especially well illustrated by textual moments that refuse the transparency of authenticity. One well-known example comes early in *Narrative of the Life of Frederick Douglass*. When Douglass recalls that slave songs provide one of the most powerful impressions of the anguish of enslavement, he characterizes them as an authentic measure of African American experience. He also claims that only his subsequent remove from the songs triggered in him recognition of them as such: "I did not, when a slave, understand the deep meaning of those rude and apparently incoherent songs. I was myself within the circle; so that I neither saw nor heard as those without might see and hear."[4] Douglass the ex-slave proclaims a proximity to his white readership that, in effect, alienates him from the condition of racial blackness he is purporting to document. Douglass stakes his authenticity as a cultural informant by marking a gulf between himself and the cultural phenomenon he aims to explicate from the inside. How is it possible, many critics have asked, that attaining the position of "those without" ultimately validates Douglass's ability to represent the experiences and meanings of those "within the circle"? Whatever the answer, the odd address to his readers compromises any apparent immediacy to racial blackness and to the condition of enslavement Douglass advertises. The advertised immediacy to blackness and to the condition of slavery remains finally a strategic appeal, a manner of speaking deployed as a peculiar textual event, a dramatic, emphatic flourish.

There emerges from these statements no self-evidence, no unassailable or strict measure of authentication. If in the context of the narrative and much nineteenth-century thought, racial blackness is powerfully related to the terms of enslavement and if Douglass clearly lines himself up with those distanced from enslavement, then his disclosures trouble or unsettle pervasive codifications of race. Where one is led to expect pure racial blackness, one finds appeals to whiteness, so that the stark racial distinction paramount to the narrative and to the cultural and political intrigue the narrative reports emerges, in these textual moments, as troublingly imprecise and unreliable. If Douglass's address to his readers abandons to some degree "those inarticulate norms and values that determine what can, legitimately be said—or perceived—in any social structure," then routine notions of race are in this instance abandoned.[5]

The enduring U.S. investment in both the certainty of race and the certainty of the limiting *nature* of blackness is placed in crisis. This notion of the limiting nature of blackness has to do with the supposition that those designated *black* remain circumscribed within a very particular set of experiences of, attitudes toward, and perspectives on the world strikingly differentiating them from a broader population that bears a much more open-ended positioning to the world. In the context of slave narratives, this notion has to do with imagining the brutal physicality and anguish of enslavement as the only problem or revelation yielded by the texts; it has to do with belief in a singular, authentic experience monopolizing both the writing and reception of the narratives. The point here is not to minimize or discount the brutal physicality and anguish of either enslavement or racial blackness in U.S. history. Nor is it to espouse a kind of belated liberal humanism: all people ultimately are the same and the human condition transcends incidental social divisions. Certainly not. While the position forwarded here fully acknowledges that the anguish and brutality of U.S. racial regimes provide powerful materials for extended consideration in the classroom as they do in the slave narratives themselves, it also cautions that to conceive the horrors and angst of brutalized lives as the only materials offered for consideration by slave narratives amounts to reiterating notions of the limited nature of blackness contested by the narratives themselves but pervasive in both past and present U.S. culture.

One might ask what it means for students of any racial or ethnic makeup to imagine they might be capable of or charged with recovering the immediacy of the physical or other conditions of enslavement. This type of approach ultimately disengages the narratives from the historical, political, economic, and judicial circumstances that determine the problematic of race and are unaccountable in the terms of oversimple black/white bifurcations. This type of orientation to the academic endeavor may too easily reinforce conceptualizations of racial blackness and African Americans that are comfortable and overly familiar in the cultural imagination of the United States. How might this misstep fail to make students see that race—and here is the unacknowledged crux of the matter—always has been and continues to be foremost an intellectual matter, either within or without the classroom but most plainly so in the classroom? The conditions and anguish of enslavement, as the passage from Douglass implies, are never merely reducible to stark, simple bifurcations nor are they fully recoverable or unmediated. The crux of reading these narratives, then, must also reside elsewhere. In the essay "Stranger in the Village," James Baldwin writes: "The ideas on which American beliefs are based are not, though Americans often seem to think so, ideas which originated in America. They came out of Europe. And the establishment of democracy on the American continent was scarcely a radical break with the past as was the necessity, which Americans faced, of broadening this concept to include black [people]."⁶ However ambiguous United States responses have been to this challenge to expand the concept of democracy, slave narratives stand as ready documents of one episode in this ongoing drama. An understanding of slave narratives that esteems them for more than their supposed fidelity to an unrecoverable past allows them to complicate what people in the United States believe and what they think their beliefs are based on.

Two moments from innumerable possible examples, one from J. W. C. Pennington's *The Fugitive Blacksmith* and one from Elizabeth Keckley's *Behind the Scenes*, underscore this circumstance. These moments offer students textual crises in which race proves highly equivocal. The crises or postures they reveal are not necessarily indicative of any authentic or lived experience but are discursive performances that frustrate readers searching for what might easily pass as the authentic. As readers had in the moment of Douglass's curious consideration of slave songs, they discover not only markers of blackness and slave experience but patent markers of whiteness as well. Pennington and Keckley take up stances that confound uncomplicated expectations placed on race. Pennington's reflections on a decisive moment in his personal quest for freedom and Keckley's reflections on the mind-sets of newly emancipated African Americans reverse routinely assumed premises of racialization.

In the example from Pennington, the peculiar moment of address is precipitated by his witnessing, as a young man, the beating of his father: "Being a tradesman, and just at that time getting my breakfast, I was near enough to hear the insolent words that were spoken to my father, and to hear, see, and even count the savage stripes inflicted upon him."⁷ Witnessing this event causes Pennington to repudiate his condition as a slave and to resolve to escape. "Although it was some time after this event before I took the decisive step, yet in my mind and spirit, I never was a *Slave* after it."⁸ At this heightened moment of his narrative, Pennington makes an unexpected and unusual racial appeal. The incident is recorded in a way that calls attention to more than the pronounced physical violence Pennington witnesses and its disturbing emotional effect on him and the rest of his family. Pennington justifies his determination to no longer be a slave with a rhetorical question: "Let me ask anyone of Anglo-Saxon blood and spirit, how you would expect a *son* to feel at such a sight?"⁹

Pennington's appeal is not to the feelings, judgments, or experiences of African Americans, as one might anticipate, but to the sensibilities and self-assurance of those most emphatically understood as white in the U.S. imagination. Rather than ask his readers to comprehend experiences and matters entirely foreign to them, Pennington asks that they consider what is most familiar in their own attitudes and self-understanding. He asks that, in order to understand his experiences, they draw on their own. He offers them no alien authenticity but a proclamation of shared sensibilities, a shared sense of an appropriate response to witnessing the injury and humiliation of a would-be patriarch. Moreover, Pennington not only poses the question but also implies he knows the answer. Without pausing to offer an explanation, he implies that he understands "Anglo-Saxon blood and spirit" and that he does so with no taxing or unusual effort. Even more, he insinuates that his rejection of slavery and his eventual escape from the U.S. slave regime is a justified, if not obvious, response to his trauma. He presents his readers with a critical reading of his situation forestalling the imagination of stark, impenetrable divisions between racial blackness and racial whiteness and the experiences of both.

Rather than polarized racial positions, masculinist, familial, and sociolegal imperatives that refer to a shared world and discourse are brought to bear on the episode. Much is common across the gulf of race, Pennington assumes, and the apparent effortlessness of the assumption must complicate readers' notions of the experiences documented in slave narratives as well as the experience of reading the texts themselves. A large portion of what Pennington shares with his readers are comprehensions of what they already possess. In documenting U.S. slavery, he offers a vision of an exorbitant "chattel principle" exceeding individual suffering or terror and disturbing widely esteemed institutions such as the family and the sentiments the family fosters.[10] Pennington assumes that, despite barriers of race, he and his readers revile such disturbances.

It is also worthwhile to recognize that Pennington's conception of shared cultural sensibilities underscores the apprehensions and insights of the feminist critique so influential in reforming the reception and teaching of slave narratives. Key to Pennington's trauma is the diminished entitlements of a "son" realized through demonstrations of the belittled circumstances of a "father." Pennington's recollection centers the drama of enslavement, repudiation, and escape in the postures assumed by men and the cultural commerce among men. However, for those not invested in such prerogatives promoted across racial lines such as African American women, this rendition of the travails and triumphs of enslavement is glaringly inadequate. The central figure of the slave presented by Pennington conforms, in this way, to Frances Foster's estimations of the typical figure to appear in slave narratives:

> The Heroic Slave narrates a success story. He has endured the most inhumane environment imaginable and, without stooping to revenge, has escaped with his life and his integrity. He is Every slave, innocent, ignorant,

and abused but a human being who needs only free soil in which to blossom into an industrious, literate, and totally moral citizen. [...] His is decidedly a temporal and essentially parochial theme—liberation in this life of those physically enslaved in the southern United States.

The Heroic Slave struggles not only against physical brutality and oppression but also against the subjugation of his human spirit. [...] He knows only that he lives within an institution that denies his humanity and threatens his very survival and that he is willing to risk his life to save himself.[11]

These conventional portrayals, as Foster points out, marginalize the matters openly pursued by feminist considerations of the genre, the experiences and circumstances of enslaved African American women. Given what is excluded from the purview of this typical figure, one begins to understand the misdirection of reading the narratives to recover, as a matter of course, some unitary condition of blackness or enslavement. Slave narratives become—in intellectually rewarding ways—highly questionable.

Elizabeth Keckley's *Behind the Scenes* similarly illustrates the questionable nature of representative performances undertaken by the narratives. Written several years after the defeat of the South in the Civil War, *Behind the Scenes* recounts Keckley's life as both enslaved and free, including her occupation as a well-respected seamstress, an occupation that allowed her to purchase her freedom before the war. However, the episode of interest here concerns Keckley's commentary on the "extravagant hopes" of African Americans emancipated during the massive military campaign of the midcentury.[12] The initiative and responsibility implicit in her own process of manumission do not obtain. She writes, "Some of the freedmen and freedwomen had exaggerated ideas of liberty [... and] it was but natural that many of them should bitterly feel their disappointment."[13] Having visited many of these disappointed ex-slaves arriving in Washington, Keckley discovers that some of them claim to prefer slavery to their newfound freedom. This is so, she speculates, "because dependence had become a part of their second nature, and independence had brought with it the cares and vexations of poverty."[14] She illustrates the point with her recollection of an old black woman complaining that since she had arrived in Washington, Mrs. Lincoln had not handed down to her any old undergarments in the manner of Southern plantation mistresses. Keckley explains to "Northern readers [who] may not fully understand the pith of the joke" that the old woman does not recognize that this custom is no longer appropriate to her new circumstances.[15]

Keckley, at this moment of her narrative, like Pennington in his, positions herself to underscore her proximity to her readers—their experiences, conditions, and understanding. She advertises that she holds a routine comprehension of U.S. citizenship with its assumptions of economic ingenuity and self-reliance. She shares with her readers the amusement of scoring "the pith of the joke," how alien the old woman's perceptions are. The woeful misunderstandings of the old woman are as unacceptable to Keckley as they are to her readers. The consequence of the remarks lies, then, in Keckley's negotiation of spaces for African Americans both within and without the circle of experience attributed to the dominant U.S. population. If there are a large number of African Americans as misinformed as the old woman, Keckley does not so much privilege or unfold those experiences and sensibilities as repudiate them. Recapitulating postures her readers already hold, her anecdote does not so much pursue what is unknown to her readers in experience or conception, as provide them with familiar matters and the assurance that some African Americans can and do share those familiar matters: "While some of the emancipated blacks pined for the old associations of slavery, and refused to help themselves, others went to work with commendable energy, and planned with remarkable forethought. They built themselves cabins, and each family cultivated for itself a patch of ground."[16] The image drawn of an African American community is a divided one. Some African Americans fully recognize what their new circumstances entail, and some do not, and this twofold vision of Keckley's remarks makes any act of claiming the authentic much more complex than it might first appear. Which of the two positions is more "black"? How is the question resolved? By a mere accounting or tallying? Is Keckley even concerned with this issue? Certainties may be more elusive than available, especially in a text premised on such peculiar dynamics of address as *Behind the Scenes*. It is a text in which an ex-slave glosses in three chapters some thirty years of her life as a slave in order to provide extended and close consideration of four subsequent years spent in service to public figures. It is a text in which an ex-slave is able to provide her white readership with intimate details of the lives of captivating public figures and to take her readers repeatedly and at length into the White House, giving them a kind of access to the national monument and the Lincolns, an access they would never be able to obtain otherwise. In effect, Keckley bears greater proximity to central figures and institutions of the United States than does an audience that intently understands itself as holding much more direct claims and a much more direct relation to these figures and institutions. The address of this text dramatically reverses deeply assumed premises of racialization. The certainties of authentic racial location and experience are powerfully ruptured.

Keckley possesses the freedom, knowledge, and access that place her in a position that by the logic of racialization is as troubling as it is intricate.

These dynamics of address, if the text is attended to appropriately, cannot fail to emerge in the classroom. They cannot fail to arise if one is attentive to the ways racial blackness is produced, or effected, in the very act of its textual representation. The discursive and the experiential are, of course, closely related but are, just as assuredly, not the same. Often the two are mutually constitutive, but students must be reminded that, although the purpose of discourse is frequently to convey or consolidate experience, that goal is never an uncomplicated or wholly attainable one. Considerable humanist thought following Saussure dedicates itself to demonstrating this discrepancy in detail. Taking an act of representation for the represented itself, no matter how seemingly commonsensical or compelling, constitutes a misjudgment albeit a widespread one. One must also point out to students, however, that the issue is not simply one of misperception but ineluctably one of power: There are significant consequences to tally when one considers the relation between discourse and its referents. Who has the means or occasion to govern the relation? To foster and benefit from equating the discursive and the authentic? At what moments and in what circumstances? In other words, the misstep of neglecting the dynamics and subtleties of discursive practices amounts to submitting to those practices too naively, and the literary classroom, one must insist, should never be a site for such submission.

Celebrating and questioning the pioneering work of the critic-activist Barbara Smith, Deborah Chay, in her discussion of the development and fortunes of black feminist criticism, considers how "accounting for differences by reference to experience [. . .] cannot then account for the ideological construction of experience itself."[17] When one considers social difference solely in terms of experience, the purview of what can be explained is limited. What is omitted, Chay argues, are "the conditions which continue to make an appeal to experience as a logical, appealing, and invisible foundation" so enticing.[18] Insofar as experience seems the unimpeachable ground that situates one in the world, one is never prompted to consider how what stands as experience, in fact, comes to stand as experience, how it may be overdetermined by more than authentic lived reality. In accepting experience as the only or fundamental ground of difference, one is not prompted to consider how one comes to "know" an elephant, an African American, a slave, a woman, a gay man, a lesbian, or the destitute before one ever encounters them. One is not prompted to consider how the perceptions detailing experience may be groomed for and channeled to the experience before its occurrence or appearance. Experience, this is to say, may result as much from overdetermining representations as from any singular, undeniable, discrete moment or encounter. Ideological constructions of experience, Chay reminds her readers, define one's situation in the world as much as experiences themselves do, and Chay is concerned ultimately with the irony that "efforts to identify varieties of black feminist critical practice [...] obscure one of black feminism's most persistent commonalities and one which wants theorizing—the use of experience to ground claims about difference and to establish cultural legitimacy."[19]

While the goal here is not simply to reproduce some of the preeminent concerns of African American feminist criticism, the instructiveness of these concerns, as already suggested, cannot be ignored. It is equally important to make clear that the practice Chay identifies is by no means unique to African American feminist criticism but, rather, a pervasive symptom of the conception of social difference in the United States. The near monopoly granted experience in the consideration of social difference more often than not leaves unpursued crucial opportunities for "exploring how difference is established, how it operates, how and in what ways it constitutes subjects who see and act in the world."[20] It leaves unexamined crucial opportunities to uncover very subtle channels of social power. It should be made clear to students that the dangers of conflating the experiential and the discursive are the dangers of diminishing the issue of power. When these dangers remain unacknowledged, authenticity seems to emerge through the variables of space and time independent of all matters of social power and cultural regimes. Categories of meaning appear given rather than produced.

Thus, to gauge race and U.S. slavery primarily in terms of experience would be to see them as given terms of U.S. social reality, rather than as phenomena actively produced and maintained. The exercise or experience of reading slave narratives would seemingly highlight the disparity attributable to difference—rather than to the politics (organized and otherwise) swirling around difference. By transforming their expectations into more useful impulses, students might be prompted to ask what is to be gained by imagining racial blackness and slavery purely in terms of experience and authentication. And by whom?

What is the boon to the students themselves? The comfort of eluding confrontations with "inarticulate norms and values that determine what can legitimately be said—or perceived—in [their own] social structure?"[21] Is there a boon for them in neglecting the question of how difference manages to underwrite political, economic, moral, psychic, and even libidinal formations they take for granted? Which is to ask, Is there a boon in neglect of the crucial question of what is difference itself? There is an intellectual solace in this position that forecloses genuine critical engagement with the narratives and, accordingly, genuine critical inquiry into imperative social constructs like race, gender, sexuality, and class. Kim Hall recognizes as much, and in the appendix to her study *Things of Darkness* urges scholar-teachers to create in their classrooms an atmosphere in which students cannot easily assume comfortable cultural positions that elsewhere are offered to them routinely. Hall proposes a set of alternatives:

> We can create a cultural narrative for the white student based on a family tale of glorious origins and lost (but soon to be regained) power and make the student of color a Caliban, fit only to serve the psychic and social needs of those in power. Or, we can acknowledge the ongoing legacy of "this thing of darkness" (racialization in the New World) and use that knowledge to create new ways of thinking about difference that let students approach the texts of Western culture as equals. If we are successful, we can give students the critical tools for a more meaningful and complex dialogue on race, one that comprehends the intersections of categories without disregarding our differences and that moves beyond racial guilt—but not beyond justice.[22]

If students expected only to engage experience, they would fail to account for the circumstances, addresses, and perceptions of the very narrators to whom they surrender themselves in opening the text, as illustrated by the reflections of Pennington and Keckley. They would gloss rather than meaningfully attend to Pennington's peculiar appeal to fundamentals of racial whiteness and would never be intrigued by Keckley's divided characterization of emancipated African Americans. Such misreadings are to be avoided because they more insistently foreclose intellectual curiosity than foster it. They abrogate the textual authority of Pennington and Keckley in deference to more widespread expectations of what the narrators' experiences must have been—experiences singularly of difference. They replicate widespread gestures of "a cultural system, in which authority—self-authority or any other—has been traditionally denied" African Americans especially in acts of self-declaration.[23] Pennington and Keckley would be refused the authority to characterize their experiences as they chose.

In teaching slave narratives, then, one does not want to make the mistake made by the culture at large, the mistake of reifying U.S. racialization and slavery as historical givens recalcitrant to serious questioning. One wants to excavate the powers of representation that ex-slave narrators struggle to assume not only in the nineteenth century but also in the circumstances of their current reception as writers in a cultural archive. Against common perception, the narrators struggle to represent through records of their experiences the certainty that race only "embodies a pragmatic recognition of how someone's ancestors were socially defined."[24] Race does not so much redact any necessary experience or aggregate of necessary experiences as it does a powerful apparatus of social classification. A paramount vector for social power routinely represented otherwise, race is determined by both experience and the cultivation of experience, not necessarily in equal measure. The influence of each, not to mention the causal relation between them, is not to be taken for granted, ex-slave narrators remind us.

If students can be made to imagine that Pennington and Keckley have the power to accomplish this feat, how much closer are they to imagining the power of others more consistently and unquestionably invested with the power to represent the meaning of race and other signal experiences? An imperative task for teachers of slave narratives is to help students recognize how unlikely it is that those bearing highly uncommon experiences of race would offer the connection between experience and race as the commonplace it is assumed to be in the United States. It is highly unlikely that these narrators would represent race as an experiential given defined solely by the parameters of their particular experiences or, for that matter, any set of experiences. Authentic experience consorts with authentic power. The burden lies in engaging and highlighting these unlikely performances and disclosures on the part of ex-slave narrators. It lies, as do much of the import and interest of the narratives, in crises of representation that include race itself.

NOTES

Chapter 2, "The Experiences of Slave Narratives," was previously published in *Approaches to Teaching* Narrative of the Life of Frederick Douglass, ed. James C. Hall, 31–41 (New York: Modern Language Association of America, 1999), and is reprinted by permission of the Modern Language Association of America.

1. Eva Saks, "Representing Miscegenation Law," *Raritan* 8, no. 2 (1988): 39, 40; reprinted in *Interracialism: Black–White Intermarriage in American History, Literature, and Law*, ed. Werner Sollers (New York: Oxford University Press, 2000), 40.

2. Deborah G. Chay, "Barbara Smith: Black Feminist Criticism and the Category of Experience," *New Literary History* 24, no. 3, "Textual Interrelations" (summer 1993): 639.

3. Deborah McDowell, "In the First Place: Making Frederick Douglass and the Afro-American Narrative Tradition," in *Critical Essays on Douglass*, ed. William Andrews (Boston: G. K. Hall, 1991), 40.

4. Frederick Douglass, *Narrative of the Life of Frederick Douglass, an American Slave*, ed. Benjamin Quarles (Cambridge, MA: Harvard University Press, 1960), 263.

5. Laurie A. Finke, "The Pedagogy of the Depressed: Feminism, Poststructuralism, and Pedagogical Practice," *Teaching Contemporary Theory to Undergraduates*, ed. Dianne F. Sadoff and William E. Cain (New York: Modern Language Association of America, 1994), 164.

6. James Baldwin, "Stranger in the Village," in *Notes of a Native Son* (1955; reprint, Boston: Beacon, 1984), 159–75.

7. James W. C. Pennington, "The Fugitive Blacksmith," in *Great Slave Narratives*, ed. Arna Bontemps (Boston: Beacon, 1969), 198.

8. Pennington, "The Fugitive Blacksmith," 198.

9. Pennington, "The Fugitive Blacksmith," 198.

10. Pennington, "The Fugitive Blacksmith."

11. Frances Smith Foster, "Adding Color and Contour to Early American Self-Portraiture: Autobiographical Writings of Afro-American Women," in *Conjuring: Black Women, Fiction, and Literary Tradition*, ed. Marjorie Pryse and Hortense Spillers (Bloomington: Indiana University Press, 1985), 32.

12. Elizabeth Keckley, *Behind the Scenes; or, Thirty Years a Slave, and Four Years in the White House* (New York: G. W. Carleton, 1868), 139.

13. Keckley, *Behind the Scenes*, 139.

14. Keckley, *Behind the Scenes*, 140.

15. Keckley, *Behind the Scenes*, 140.

16. Keckley, *Behind the Scenes*, 60.

17. Chay, "Barbara Smith," 639.

18. Chay, "Barbara Smith," 649.

19. Chay, "Barbara Smith," 649.

20. Chay, "Barbara Smith," 649.

21. Chay, "Barbara Smith," 164.

22. Kim F. Hall, *Things of Darkness: Economies of Race and Gender in Early Modern England* (Ithaca, NY: Cornell University Press, 1995), 268.

23. Barrett, "Institutions, Classrooms, Failures," chapter 1, this volume.

24. Saks, "Representing Miscegenation Law," 45.

| CH3

Redoubling American Studies: John Carlos Rowe
and Cultural Criticism

As writing formalizes the subject, at once, it formalizes the subject as a historical coordinate in the progressive temporality measuring the distance, as well as the increasing distance, between the premodern and the modern (the conceptual movement that describes the notion of "history" as stated by the postcolonial historian Dipesh Chakrabarty in *Provincializing Europe*). A brief historical, philosophical, and political detour may bear this out. The epistemological and social breach with the premodern out of which the "United States" ultimately arises does not take place exclusively on the Western arc of the Atlantic Ocean. In 1651 Thomas Hobbes deploys in *Leviathan* "America" precisely as the sign of the novel social, administrative, mercantile relations he aims to legitimate:

> It may peradventure be thought, there was never such a time, nor condition of warre as this; and I believe it was never generally so, over all the world: but there are many places where they live so now. For the savage people in many places of America, except the government of small Families, the concord whereof dependeth on naturall lust, have no government at all; and live at this day in that brutish manner, as I said before. Howsoever, it may be perceived what manner of life there would be, where there were no common Power to fear; by the manner of life, which men that have formerly lived under a peacefull government, use to degenerate into, in a civil Warre.[1]

John Locke in his 1698 *Two Treatises of Government* also invokes the sign of America in his effort to restate the terms of social and political authority that would authorize the historical transformations of incipient capitalist relations: "An acre of land that bears here Twenty Bushels of Wheat and other in America, which with the same Husbandry, would do the like, are, without doubt, of the same natural, intrinsick Value. But yet the Benefit Mankind receives from the one, in a Year is worth 5 £. and from the other possibly not worth a Penny, if all the Profit an Indian received from it were to be valued, and sold here; at least, I may truly say, not 1/1000. 'Tis Labour then which puts the greatest part of Value upon Land."[2] The rhetorical gestures of Thomas Hobbes and John Locke toward the Western arc of the incipient Atlantic economies augur revolutionary forms of cognizance. Both texts reveal the signifying efficacy of the new geopolitical realities of the western Atlantic, a signifying efficacy that, at once, invokes new historical possibilities understood as progress, as well as establishing non-European or nonwhite racial identity as categorically deficient human forms constituting inherent threats to the civil order founded on emergent capitalist relations, the determination of private ownership as the virtually exclusive goal of aggregate human relations. Thomas Hobbes proposes the territories of the western arc of the Atlantic as the site of a perpetual state of meaningless war arising from a racially specific social order that the rational historical progression of Europe would supplant. John Locke proposes the territories of the western arc of the Atlantic as mired in economic meaninglessness in comparison to the mercantilist agenda and regulation of labor sponsored by western European powers. Still, the apparently simple referential gestures encode more than the rational correspondence of signifier and signified—America—to material objectivity.

The case is particularly pronounced in the instance of John Locke. For John Locke, the "preeminent theorist of natural liberties, and an influential resource for abolitionist thinkers," is directly involved with and profits substantially from slaveholding interests in both the Bahamas and several mainland British colonies, even to the point of playing an important role in the writing of the constitution of slaveholding South Carolina.[3] In "Three Approaches to Locke and the Slave Trade," the philosopher Wayne Glausser "provides a useful catalogue of the scholarly controversy generated by these inconsistencies"—however, with the shortcoming that he rehearses the controversy so that the issue revolves around the individual figure of John Locke rather than the cultural doxa that affords the inconsistency. Beyond the questions of John Locke's personal motivations, the inconsistency is far reaching for Western investments in the putatively rational order of the sign. John Locke is a central figure in the empiricist turn of Western philosophical thought. The evidentiary gestures John Locke and his contemporaries make toward what is understood as empirical reality, rather than biblical or archival authority, mark a signal transformation in the development of modern thought, the conception of America being a primary gesture in the signal transformation. In this sense, the claim that "'tis Labour then which puts the greatest part of Value upon Land" misrepresents its significance and its putative logical form, insofar as to pose as equivalent systems of labor within European geographies with the systems of labor reified across the western arc of the Atlantic beginning in the sixteenth century misconstrues the cultural violence that yields the legibility of America as an empirical terrain, an empirical sign. The America providing the evidentiary gesture for John Locke proposes the incommensurability of two disparate territories, unequal, however, precisely because of the system of racial subordination providing the logical, significant accessibility of America in the first place—as both empirical information and empirical opportunity. "Every modern scholar who takes him seriously has had to confront an embarrassing fact: John Locke, preeminent theorist of natural liberties, and an influential resource for abolitionist thinkers of the eighteenth and nineteenth centuries, actually participated in the slave trade."[4] The calculus of apparent (un)reason is neither purely textual nor individual but betrays, rather, the foundational cultural information of Atlantic modernity—routinely apparent, but never so much as simply rational as, instead, politically, racially, and economically inflected.

The implication seems to be that, if the question of information is the question of the modern, then it is information always already disclosing the limits of Western civil order, so that the errant condition of the sign—the relations of the signified and the signifier—must be measured not only as an internal, ineluctable structural quandary or contradiction but, at once, as the inexorable press of the violent conventions of modern civil being. This insight John Rowe brings insistently to his considerations of U.S. literature and the humanist enterprise more broadly: two particularly self-reflexive moments in the trajectory from *Through the Custom-House* to *Literary Culture and U.S. Imperialism* openly rehearse these critical interventions as John Rowe articulates them. In the 1985 article "Deconstructing America: Recent Approaches to Nineteenth-Century Literature and Culture," the issue is stated in terms of modernity and modernism: The "various aims in shifting the questions of 'American modernism' into questions of 'literary modernity' share the common goal of overcoming the provincialism of traditional 'American' literary study without lapsing into the trap of the formalists' version of comparativism and internationalism."[5] In this essay, John Rowe documents what he sees as the limitations of his earlier work that his forthcoming scholarship will address: "Indeed, the limitation in Riddel's and my own work may be identified as the nearly exclusive effort to demonstrate affinities between contemporary theory (largely from the Continent) and American literature from transcendentalism to high modernism. This strategic 'crossing,' or 'intertextuality' as I call it in *Through the Custom-House*, has tended to background the other, indispensable aspect of this theory of America as 'modern': the socio-historical particulars of any particular bid for modernity."[6]

In the winter 1985–86 issue of *Cultural Critique*, John Rowe puts the point more generally in the article "'To Live Outside the Law You Must Be Honest': The Authority of the Margin in Contemporary Theory": "Insofar as deconstruction lays claim to its own 'lucidity,' its own 'self-deconstructing' movement, then it will lapse into those sorts of binaries that deny its very methodology. In its own defensive gestures, deconstruction imagines its own antagonists, and it is in that moment that deconstruction loses it power, becomes merely another 'point of view' in a culture that prides itself on its pluralism. Such pluralism is, however, merely the brighter figuration of a darker intention: the culture's preservation of its central governing power as indeterminate, as that metamorphic principle that absorbs differences without losing its 'essence.'"[7] Still the paramount attention is not simply to deconstructive methodology:

> The ways in which such cultural conservation deforms and disfigures its "object" of study should remind us that those attractive estrangements and fictions of literature may carry within them the very methods of a larger cultural imperialism. Indeed, this has been one of our constant themes in this essay: that the "imperialism" of author over reader, of literature over life, is too easily discriminated from geographical imperialism by arguments that valorize the "honesty" of art about its fictional methods. Literature borrows from the culture its most powerful means of appropriating differences and constructing an other; literature cannot be protected from the searching critique of social representation that post-structuralism maps for itself.[8]

John Rowe understands that the complexity of signification rests not only in the oblique contingencies animating signifier, signified, sign, textuality, and referentiality as the play of articulate but always nonetheless suspended or interrupted reason, but a diffuse geopolitical, historical elaboration always posing reason as the final contingency even as it would remain concomitantly the first principle of an exclusive geopolitical property—in short, the elaboration of ownership that defines Western modernity and its justifications for animation.

The sign then always embodies material practice as well as the ideological grounds of material practice even as it invites fascination beyond either. To chart such fascination defines the most subtle executions of deconstructive theorizing, and to pursue such fascination otherwise provides the most difficult and compelling excavations of the human where the fully human routinely would not be imagined. At the conclusion of "'To Live Outside the Law You Must Be Honest,'" John Rowe observes:

> Deconstrutive readings of patriarchal culture and its literacy (as well as other) productions might well serve these feminist aims, insofar as such interpretations might identify the contradictions of a restrictive and repressive ideology. And insofar as those contradictions might be considered to have some coincidence with those identified by ethnic minorities, third-world interests, and other marginalized groups, then the very determinate political aims of feminism might find some common ground with other exiled groups. Thus the insistent "nationalism" of the United States may be viewed both by American feminists and by Latin Americans to be a common subject of deconstructive analysis, insofar as sexual patriarchalism and foreign-policy paternalism are maintained equally by such nationalism in its internal and external conduct.[9]

Stated another way—which is to say, beyond the question of methodological rapprochements—such a pursuit discusses the most powerful signs and signifying processes of the modern codified as the United States. At the conclusion of "Deconstructing America," John Rowe writes:

> Deconstructing "America" is not a task of simply opening American literature to those European influences that Americans have so often strategically repressed. Deconstructing "America" is not a process of "denationalizing" our literature and culture for the sake of some ahistorical literary paradigm. Deconstructing "America" involves a very close and theoretically informed reading of how "America" invented itself by means of those strategic repressions (Europe), exclusions (women and ethnic minorities), and rationalizations (the literary canon and the self-legitimizing "humanities," among others) that constitute (among other hegemonic forces) America as a representational system with a complex and diverse history. Now that our primary national product seems to be what some have called "information" and what I would term "representations," then this project for deconstructing America seems not only relevant but urgently needed.[10]

The observations are trenchant but, nevertheless, the equal imperative in considering the career of John Carlos Rowe is recognizing adequately its scope, its sweep. The impressive compass of his career is notable not only in the number of academic discourses that the scholarship ably traverses—African American and Native American canons, canonical U.S. literature and its criticism, critical theory, deconstruction, Marxist theory, pedagogical theory, postcolonial criticism, postmodern theory—but, moreover, the way in which the body of scholarship expands the central questions emerging from the formation of U.S. literary and cultural studies from its inception. The insistence and innovation with which John Rowe pursues what remains among the most challenging and sometimes unpopular issues of U.S. literary scholarship most distinguishes the value and incisiveness of his scholarship. Needless to say, the origins of the institutionalization of the study of U.S. literature are above all formalist, formalism reckonable in the overwhelming influence of New Criticism during the early portion of the twentieth century but, most particularly, in F. O. Matthiessen's canonical and canonizing 1941 study *American Renaissance: Art and Expression in the Age of Emerson and Whitman*. F. O. Matthiessen, as his subtitle suggests, is intent foremost "to examine an author's resources of language and of genres, in a word to be preoccupied with form," even as he still claims seven literary texts written between 1850 and 1855 as the center of an aesthetic enterprise signifying much more than aesthetic achievement: the specification of the social and political—or extraliterary reality—of the modern nation.[11]

Rather, John Rowe troubles these assumptions to reveal the coimplications of textual meaning and the derivation of the aesthetic. The critical and literary assumptions of John Rowe entail the broadest dynamics of cultural doxa: from the assignation of social identity through the orders of race, gender, class, and sexuality, to protocols of material production, to the historical drive of political machinations. Nonetheless, John Rowe arrives at his insights by retaining attention on the very processes of signification understood to complicate the text and, moreover, define the text by the extremity of the (purposefully purposeless) complication. John Rowe demonstrates that the orders of the imagination, at once, define and exceed the text; orders of the imagination are always already groomed into the formalist attentions from which the study of U.S. literature is derived, the cultural investments on which the originary formalist attentions depend even as they would occlude them. The trajectory from *Henry Adams and Henry James: The Emergence of a Modern Consciousness* (1976), to *Through the Custom-House: Nineteenth-Century American Fiction and Modern Theory* (1982), to *The Theoretical Dimensions of Henry James* (1985), to *At Emerson's Tomb: The Politics of Classic American Literature* (1997), to *The Other Henry*

James (1998), to *Literary Culture and U.S. Imperialism: From the Revolution to World War II* (2000) presses the methodological assumptions invested in the certainty that textual meaning is most faithfully or readily yielded in attention trained exclusively or foremost on the formal principles. This trajectory of the scholarship is compelling and worth pursuing in some detail.

Recall that in 1955 James Baldwin publishes his forthright *Notes of a Native Son* and states, "The American commonwealth chooses to overlook what Negroes are never able to forget: they are not really considered part of it. Like Aziz in *A Passage to India* or Topsy in *Uncle Tom's Cabin*, they know that white people, whatever their love for justice, have no love for them."[12] Although not a practitioner in the emergent field, James Baldwin writes at a formative moment in the florescence of U.S. literary studies as an academic field, the moment of the publication of such classic texts as Richard Chase's *The American Novel and Its Tradition* (1957), Leslie Fiedler's *Love and Death in the American Novel* (1960), Charles Feidelson's *Symbolism and American Literature* (1953), R. W. B. Lewis's *American Adam* (1955), and Leo Marx's *The Machine in the Garden* (1964). If culture can be defined, in brief, as an aggregate point of imagination beyond, but tending both away and toward, material circumstance, then James Baldwin's assertion and his series of essays in *Notes of a Native Son* join these inaugural authors of American studies in the project of mapping that point of aggregate imagination sufficient to signify the United States as a historical and conceptual fixture, even as the coincidence between James Baldwin and these writers remains beyond all points of imagination as the academic discipline elaborates itself at the moment he writes.

Beyond the question of race that Baldwin formulates starkly, there remains also the question of methodology in accounting for the discrepancy. James Baldwin's claims are as complex as they are succinct in this passage. The passage invokes racial whiteness as a culturally visible construct, names this construct in a relation to the adamant exercise of social power, invokes literature beyond formalist analytics, draws comparisons across national literatures, and describes a multicultural paradigm, as well as detailing the issue of affect, all in its effort to consider the question of culture, the aggregate point of imagination beyond material circumstance that nonetheless imbues material circumstance. These points of critical articulation are now commonplace in institutionalized literary studies, the investigation of the construct of racial whiteness as it informs the U.S. literary imagination, the Foucauldian theorization of modern formations of power in the literary imagination, the growth of performance and cultural studies understanding the literary text beyond its formal boundaries, the institutionalization of postcolonial theory to highly consequential effect, the investigation of affect undertaken within structuralist and post-structuralist paradigms, for example. In 1984, twenty-nine years after the publication of *Notes of a Native Son*, as these types of discourses had become commonly established in literary study, James Baldwin reiterates his analysis more broadly and more starkly still in his new introduction:

> The only real change vividly discernible in this present, unspeakably dangerous chaos is a panic-stricken apprehension on the part of those who have maligned and subjugated others for so long that the tables have been turned. Not once have the Civilized been able to honor, recognize, or describe the Savage. He is, practically speaking, the source of their wealth, his continued subjugation the key to their power and glory. This is absolutely and unanswerably true in South Africa—to name but one section of Africa—and, as to how things fare for Black men and women; here, the Black has become, economically, all but expendable and is, therefore, encouraged to join the Army, or, a notion espoused, I believe, by Daniel Moynihan and Nathan Glazer, to become a postman—to make himself useful, for Christ's sake, while White men take on the heavy burden of ruling the world.[13]

More methodologically able to acknowledge James Baldwin's points of imagination, the proposition of culture and its analyses, at the conclusion of the twentieth and opening of the twenty-first centuries, understand literary textuality more diffusely. The impressive career of John Carlos Rowe is an exemplary one in U.S. literary studies, then, impressive precisely for its methodological astuteness in pursuit of these broad questions under the aegis of literary and aesthetic production, the trajectory of the career charting and emphasizing the way in which the possibility of considering the coincident analyses of James Baldwin and those writers who consolidate American studies as a field in the 1950s and 1960s ultimately converge within academic analyses by the close of the twentieth century. The trajectory of the career of John Rowe, as does the institutional field generally, reckons revealingly with the always already implicit discourses fully animating the incipient field of American studies through its marked exclusions.

The Linguistic Turn, Ideology, Pedagogy

Immediately, in John Rowe's book-length projects, from *Henry Adams and Henry James: The Emergence of a Modern Consciousness* (1976), there is the influence of deconstructive theorizing. Deconstructive theorizing is redacted routinely by the querying of textual unities, the querying of the mystifying proposition of the boundaries of texts, the supplementarity on which all sufficiently significant systems depend, the concerted demonstration of the final unreliability of the seeming steadfastness of meaning, the subtle vagaries and belatedness of authorial intentions and processes, the impossibility of the strict rationality of communication and comprehension, the insistently relative ground of epistemological certainty always already exposing the fiction of disciplinary stabilities and—as deconstruction is transformed into a more unruly post-structuralism—the racialized, gendered, and sexualized orders of exclusion and inclusion to which ideational and communicative orders always already return. John Rowe increasingly insinuates historical, material, and political contingencies within these principles derived from the formalist or synchronic analysis of the sign inaugurated by Ferdinand de Saussure, extrapolated as structuralist methodologies that are, in turn, challenged by deconstructive responses—in short, the linguistic turn of the humanities and some social sciences.

In *Henry Adams and Henry James: The Emergence of a Modern Consciousness*, John Rowe poses Henry Adams and Henry James as exemplary of U.S. modernity, because these figures demonstrate the movement from the "earlier transcendent and logocentric vision [of the mid-nineteenth century] to an increasingly speculative and experiential emphasis on methodology." Both "illuminate the unfolding, self-conscious position that has characterized modern literature since the turn of the century."[14] John Rowe's exposition concerns processes of signification that do not so much specify authorial distinctiveness but, rather, the conditions of signification that confuse and conjoin the critical and the literary in and as the works of Henry Adams and Henry James: "The notion of critical activity itself as the subject matter of criticism emerges from Adams's and James's own conceptions of signification and interpretation."[15] John Rowe claims further: "the unfulfilled meaning, the suspended question, and the incomplete sentence are more than mere rhetorical techniques in their works. My attempt to analyze signification as a relational process fundamental to Adams's and James's art must involve a commentary on criticism itself."[16] The final claims of the text arrive in even more straightforward deconstructive terms: "James and Adams's symbolic modes mediate the silence behind man's existence without hiding it. Their symbolism actively sustains the tension between nothingness and interpretation that makes it possible for meaning to come into being. But the interpreter's activity consists of more than simply naming his world, for there is always the problem of the fullness of meaning."[17]

Deconstructive theorizing interrupts or severely defamiliarizes the seemingly naturalized productions of meaning and identity, pursues the arbitrariness of apparently stable meaning in an alternate, wayward production of meaning itself, and these concerns are central also to the study that follows. The critical preoccupation with modernity remains the signal element of the peculiar insight of *Through the Custom-House: Nineteenth-Century American Fiction and Modern Theory* (1982), since the book turns on its curious redeployment of the established critical currency of modernity. Modernity, as it is theorized in this study, becomes the axis along which to conjoin "certain impasses in nineteenth-century thought . . . reflected both in the general cultural climate" and selected works of canonical U.S. writers, as well as the work of modern philosophers and linguists who define the profoundly linguistic turn—particularly as epitomized by Derridean deconstruction.[18] *Through the Custom-House* aligns Henry Thoreau's *A Week on the Concord and Merrimack Rivers*, Nathaniel Hawthorne's *Blithedale Romance*, Edgar Allan Poe's *The Narrative of Arthur Gordon Pym*, Herman Melville's "Bartleby the Scrivener," Mark Twain's *Pudd'nhead Wilson*, and Henry James's *The Sacred Fount* with the "discussions of the metaphoricity of signification, the supplementarity of representation, the divided function of the authorial subject, and the psychic and sociopolitical repressions of metaphysical thinking" that galvanize U.S. scholarship after the reception particularly of Jacques Derrida's *Speech and Phenomena*, *Of Grammatology*, *Writing and Difference*, and *Dissemination*.[19] The enduring question of the study, however, is not the application of deconstructive or post-structuralist strategies of reading and knowing in the generation of novel textual interpretations. Rather, the fundamental question is how this new theoretical charge of mapping the eccentricities of the literary and the tropological within the always already compromised discourses of the rational or the philosophical illuminates the historical drama of Americanness that fractures the nineteenth-century texts chosen for examination. Insofar as this historical drama rendered by the chosen texts in aesthetic terms can never be alethic, to repeat John Rowe's use of the Heideggerian term, the critical platform renders the historical drama—which is to say, the anxiety of the belatedness in relation of the United States to Europe—as the formal problem of history itself, as outlined by Hayden White in *Metahistory*. In White's conception history concerns the always insinuating proposition of the present that is recoded as the linearity or progressiveness assigned to historicity itself, for the present is the always already known point to which the progressive linearity of history proceeds. As a conceptual proposition, then, history approximates an exorbitant rendition of the enclosed relation between the Saussurian signifier and the signified, because the referential gesture of history as a linear narrative would exceed ideally the representational potential of language that is, finally, its premier, adamant proposition. The impasse again is the promise of the signified in the fullness of its referentiality beyond the system of the sign, the dilemma that constitutes the incompleteness shared by the psychological, the philosophical, the historical, the economic, their revelations always already only the traces, structures, and errant courses of the sign that each of these would abandon ideally in order to fix or situate themselves otherwise. In this riddle, John Rowe recognizes the animating anxiety that can be termed modernity, a recognition that ultimately allows the examination of the texts chosen for the study "in relation to those retentions and protentions that may be said to operate in the literary tradition, the author's own oeuvre, and in the linguistic sign itself."[20] The escape from this trap of representation that the texts aim to enact would be spoken in the name of Americanness but, rather, merely specifies the "endless straying or anarchy of meaning" that not only fails the cultural project but, moreover, troubles the chosen texts, in their "generic consistency, narrative progress, and development, organic characterization, and thematic and stylistic coherence."[21]

If, in this way, *Through the Custom-House* rereads the U.S. literary canon through the nineteenth century by means of structuralist and post-structuralist attentions to the linguistic sign that redact finally the anxieties of the philosophical, historical, psychological, and economic conditions of modernity indicated as the United States, then *At Emerson's Tomb: The Politics of Classic American Literature* (1997) more adamantly traces the political and materialist terms of the same formation. The sustained literary readings of Ralph Emerson, Edgar Allan Poe, Herman Melville, Frederick Douglass, Harriet Jacobs, Walt Whitman, Mark Twain, Henry James, Kate Chopin, and William Faulkner seek the diminution of the political in the structures of thought that yield the U.S. literary imagination in its recording and recoding of quotidian practices that are fixed through the most fundamental categories of the political—race, gender, class, and sexuality—even as the meaningfulness of nationality and modernity, as well as their idealizations of subjectivity, would refuse the political as the fundamental point of their origin. In this study, what is more clearly revealed in the impasse of signification is nonetheless the work of the ideological. The dynamic described, then, is a circuit of textuality, materiality, and sociality so adamantly groomed yet so precarious, at once, that the anxieties of the philosophical, historical, psychological, and economic remain the fundamental, not incidental, conditions of signification.

At Emerson's Tomb queries, accordingly, the "romantic idealist assumption that rigorous reflection on the processes of thought and representation constitutes in itself a critique of social reality and effects a transformation of the naïve realism that confuses truth with social convention."²² The limits of this tradition of Emersonian dissent, John Rowe argues, are evident in Ralph Emerson's nineteenth-century context as well as the early twentieth century insofar as "the problems of textual and rhetorical domination are very often the first ones to be addressed by writers, like Douglass and Jacobs and Chopin, who are explicitly committed to the political functionality of literary representation."²³ More broadly stated still, the project is "to reconsider the degree to which the 'classic' American literary text has become the site of dehistoricized, depoliticized 'aesthetic' representation that has been so frequently criticized."²⁴ *At Emerson's Tomb* renders more explicitly the implied ideological concerns of *Through the Custom-House*, ideology in the sense of the historical and social suture premising consciousness, the self-animation coincident with entrance into and negotiation of the established social relations. For example, John Rowe deploys, in this second articulation of a canonical trajectory through the nineteenth century into the twentieth, the familial as an ideological articulation conjoining such disparate literary and historical figures as Herman Melville and Kate Chopin:

> The nineteenth century bourgeois family is one of the primary social forces that constructed subjectivity, especially as Americans confronted the social transformations brought about by industrialization and urbanization. The family is a discursive formation that contributes to the ideological work of interpellating subjects in new social contexts. Because the family appears at once to be based on a natural relation among its members and yet depends crucially upon the production of its members, both in its domestic space and in the larger economy, the family serves a crucial function in naturalizing individuals' relations to ideology. Because the family's means of production seems so self-evidently natural and biological, the family is an especially attractive medium for disguising ideological messages and thus contributing to the naturalization of new social relations.²⁵

As *At Emerson's Tomb* retraces and augments the ground already covered in *Through the Custom-House*, detailing through the exorbitance of the sign, this retracing more readily foregrounds the forms of agency both aligned with and distressing the exorbitance of the sign in the regime of the modern. The exorbitance of the sign demands a scripting of the human that is precisely the terrain of the ideological, the imbrication of signification, subjectivity, and material orders of production both fixed in the canon, as social convention, and as protocols for the production of social value, a fully ideological coimplication, a terrain that reveals the imbrication of the extraliterary and the literary: "As Engels reminds us, sexual production follows the same laws as industrial production under capitalism: the alienation of the mother and children is achieved by the partriarch's transformation of them into his property (surplus value) and their obedience to his domestic law, including public laws against divorce and carefully regulating the transmission of property by inheritance."[26]

In *The Other Henry James* (1998), John Rowe returns to another body of material with which he is profoundly familiar, with the aim of using new theoretical currencies to reassess the literary and cultural profile of Henry James. The insistence of the project—stated immediately—is to trouble the ground between the extraliterary and the literary in order to define the continuing relevance of Henry James as a canonical figure beyond his dexterity with complex ironies, uncertainties of perspective, and labyrinthine prose structures approximating psychological constructions of the social. The return to Henry James would provide more than testimony to notions of an enduring aesthetic standard, rather, testimony to the developments of critical and cultural theory attending to the vital role of the discursive in the constructions, ambiguities, and contestations of social reality never simply circumscribed to the aesthetic posture. The introduction to *The Other Henry James* reports that

> critical theory today is far more concerned with the social consequences of discursive acts than it was in the late 1970s and 1980s, and this turn has been complemented by the rise of cultural studies as a critical movement. Once understood as a term designating various epistemologies, with special attention to the aesthetic and literary roles in knowing, critical theory designates today a much wider range of methods and practices concerned with the construction, maintenance, and transformation of social reality. In this regard, cultural critics have drawn far more directly from the Frankfurt school's modern definitions of critical theory than from the meanings formulated by Anglo-American literary theorists.[27]

In light of these developments, John Rowe's task is to read Henry James's work in order to document Henry James's role as a critical social theorist, to align his fiction with the developing orientations of critical theory. John Rowe acknowledges this task as "quixotic," because there are other figures more clearly suited to be read along these lines, but it is precisely the possibilities of such a reassessment that discloses the heuristic as well as explanatory powers of culturally engaged theoretical currencies.

In *The Other Henry James*, the figure of Henry James is juxtaposed to several points of critical departure: to Marxist paradigms in which he is taken as exemplifying bourgeois mystification "intent on justifying the bourgeoisie's right to rule," to U.S. deconstructive paradigms that underscore "the essential undecidability of language" so emphasized by the complexity of Jamesian prose, to feminist attentions that uncover the subordinate or failed role of the feminine that often enables Jamesian propositions of mastery, to New Historicist paradigms keen "to textualize social reality" as progressive ideological shifts codified in "institutional practices and procedures."[28] These series of juxtapositions mark the project of *The Other Henry James* in relief, for the project finally is to approach "James as a critical theorist in his own right, rather than as constructed by various critical theories."[29] The study, in other words, prompts "the reader to imagine another Henry James, more attentive to questions of class, race, gender, and sexual preference relevant to the changing social order of his time."[30]

The equally innovative turn that concludes the study bears noting also. The final concern is pedagogical: the elaboration of a possible set of classroom practices confronting the problem that the "technique of Henry James . . . appears all too often to be the social utopia of James's characters—the best characters are those able to master the complexities of social rhetoric in ways isomorphic with the task set for the reader of wending his or her way through James's endless sentence."[31] In this way, the question of Henry James is exemplary of a larger issue, which is that "in too many graduate programs, just such an obsession with the rhetorical and stylistic techniques of literature, to the exclusion of other literary functions, remains central to the curriculum and professional training," an issue reconstituted in the inertia that "what is already in place (in terms of the curriculum) is often accepted tacitly as educationally sound and proper, even when it is obvious that humanistic education is closely tied to specific historical circumstances."[32] The point is not to dismiss the language-model approach or formalist approaches to Henry James but to place these types of analyses in the service of intellectual engagements beyond bourgeois subjectification through broader, or more extensive, engagements with the literary. Thus, the boon of rereading Henry James as a social critical theorist, the exercise of *The Other Henry James*, "connect[s] his modernity with our postmodern condition."[33] Figuring these connections does not evade an examination of language and narrative, but expands them:

> Reading Henry James in terms of the ways the dominant ideology operates involves identifying just those topics in the early modern period that are the most ideologically contested. Traditionally, race, class, and gender have been the major issues of social conflict in Euramerican socie-

ties in the period of modernity, and it is just in these respects that newer, ideologically attentive approaches to Henry James have transformed him from an ivory-tower aesthete into an important subject and object of critical theory. More recently, considerations of gender conflict have been broadened to include questions of sexual preference, so that the somewhat restricted consideration of masculine and feminine gender roles must be expanded to include lesbian and homosexual references as important parts of the social construction of identities. In a similar fashion, discussions of race and ethnicity have expanded to include prevailing definitions of nation and empire, whose political functions have significantly determined most forms of social identification in the modern period.[34]

The collectively authored introduction of the volume *Post-nationalist American Studies* outlines again the congress of the extraliterary and the literary, but within the paradigm of U.S. literature as an epistemological system. As the enabling point for this broader project, the concept of nationalism itself is solicited in the Derridean sense of the term through the acknowledgment of the histories of race and colonialism as fundamental to modern national formations, particularly the United States. For example, John Rowe and his colleagues observe, "Within the United States... it is important to distinguish between nationalisms which are aligned with the nation-state and those which challenge 'official' nationalism.... Despite their limitations, black and Chicano nationalism, for instance, are not identical with or reducible to U.S. nationalism. In other words, we need to critique the limit and exclusions of nationalism without forgetting the differences between nationalisms or throwing all nationalisms into the trashcan of history."[35] This point of solicitation remarks immediately the convergence of the extraliterary and literary in the notion of U.S. exceptionalism that codifies the fields of U.S. literature and American studies, insofar as the

> turn away from Europe marks the primary meaning of American exceptionalism—the conviction that the United States marked a break from the history of Europe, specifically the history of feudalism, class stratification, imperialism, and war. Puritan tropes such as the "City on the Hill" and the "Errand into the Wilderness" were later reclaimed to figure American exceptionalism. John Winthrop's words delivered aboard a ship bound for New England in 1630, "We shall be as a city upon a hill, the eyes of all people upon us," came to define the persuasive image of the United

States as literally above other nations, separate and inviolate, righteous and exemplary.[36]

The theme of U.S. exceptionalism provides the refrain of the consensus paradigm of American studies and American literature developed in the mid-twentieth century from the end of World War II to the mid-1960s, as elaborated, for instance, in R. W. B. Lewis's *American Adam* and Leo Marx's *The Machine in the Garden* and as challenged with the force of post-structuralist theorizing in a concerted way by the mid-1980s by such texts as Sacvan Bercovitch and Myra Jehlen's *Ideology and Classic American Literature*. The postnationalist U.S. paradigm augments the challenges of the earlier post-structuralist turn with insights provided from the fields of history, political theory, and, particularly, Marxist scholarship focused on mercantilism and the rise of the world capitalist system as elaborated, for instance, in the work of Ernesto Laclau, Cedric Robinson, and Immanuel Wallerstein. The effects of this intellectual turn are notable not only for the novel insights added to the intellectual archive but also, as dramatically, for the growing interdisciplinarity of humanist inquiry as well as the simultaneously waning fortunes of the humanist academy. That is, the introduction notes how the political effects of this inquiry are marked distinctly within the contemporary university at the newest sites of its bureaucratic apparatus: "Unfortunately, these intellectual developments have occurred at a time in which American universities have been under attack on both political and financial grounds, and interdisciplinary perspectives have often been the main casualties of these attacks. Several Ethnic Studies programs have been significantly downsized or eliminated during the late 1980s and 1990s, and a few once-prestigious American Studies programs, like the American Civilization program at the University of Pennsylvania, have been eliminated entirely."[37] The volume includes, for these reasons, not only analyses of the resituated ground for the study of U.S. cultural production that acknowledges the United States as the outgrowth of an intercontinental economic and colonizing revolution that begins as the cultural florescence known as the Renaissance, but aims to intervene at the most guarded location of university practices, the classroom, by including syllabi that demonstrate the pedagogical dimensions of the arguments forwarded in the individually authored essays.

John Rowe's contribution, "Post-nationalism, Globalism, and the New American Studies," is the first of these essays and surveys the new, more cosmopolitan incarnation of American studies operating under the aegis of globalization. The thesis is that

> a common purpose linking these different versions of American Studies should be the critical study of the circulation of "America" as a commodity of the new cultural imperialism and the ways in which local knowledges and arts have responded to such cultural importations—the study of what some have termed "coca-colonization." What some cultural critics have termed the capacity of local cultures to "write back" against cultural and even political and economic domination should be considered part of American Studies, even as we recognize the practical impossibility of expanding our scope to include all aspects of global experience simply because of the global pretensions of First World nations like the United States.[38]

In short, the international dimensions of U.S. literature and American studies are charted in relation to the ongoing international dimensions of cultural production and sometimes mediated, not only in relation to a rescripted past.

Literary Culture and U.S. Imperialism: From the Revolution to World War II (2000) takes on this task at length and marks John Rowe's most explicit and sustained engagement with cultural studies, which most clearly remarks the convergence of U.S. literary study with the points of imagination set out by James Baldwin in 1955. For the United States is read as an always evolving cultural project, a project instantiated through political action continually reformulated across a progressive linear history as well as providing the imaginative torque by which the hegemonic cultural narrative of the nation is literally and literarily established. The sustained political action has two articulations: an imperialism aimed at the acquisition or control of territories deemed essential to the national self-imagination, as in the impulses of Manifest Destiny or the Monroe Doctrine, and an internal colonization of subordinated Others within the boundaries of the expansive nation-state. The work of internal colonization is as varied and as extensive:

> Including slavery, criminalization, and racism as modes of colonizing African Americans; conventional germ warfare, "removal" and deterritorialization, the various "reservation" systems, and assimilation as means of decolonizing Native Americans; taxation without representation, vigilante violence, "exclusion laws" forbidding or strictly limiting immigration, criminalization, and racism as means of colonizing Chinese, Mexican, Latin-American, and other immigrant populations; gender hierarchies, the fetishism and commodification of the feminine body, and the exploitation of feminine sexual reproduction, as well as the exclusion

of women from a wide range of civil and economic rights as part of the colonial domination of women; and the construction of strict sexual mores for the definition and regulation of "proper" sexual "morality," in order to police lesbians and gays and/or "purge" the nation of their "deviance."[39]

The attention to pedagogy also remains an insistent concern of this further rehearsal of the canonical formation and the most subtle preoccupations of the U.S. literary canon:

> I use this term "curricular standard" to emphasize the importance of our pedagogical purposes in the selection and organization of cultural texts in scholarship. After all, teaching should be one of the primary tests of the validity of our scholarship in many of the humanities and social sciences. How does this scholarly argument help me educate students about the meanings, values, and uses of "American Literature"? Most canonical approaches, including those designed to revise the literary canon, are limited to teaching the "best that has been thought and written" and substituting thereby a history of "genius" (or "history of ideas") for a more nuanced cultural and political history.[40]

The excavation of the U.S. political and textual order and its ramifications in curricular and pedagogical contexts draws this study, more than any of the earlier ones, directly into the purview of documenting the relays of interpretative and declarative formations that hold together the material determinations of social life in varying instantiations of the hierarchical structuring of power and, in an open debt to the work of Michel Foucault, pursues this enactment of power not simply as a repressive, destructive formulation, but as an affirmative, insinuating element of subject formation. John Rowe in this latest return to canonical U.S. literature as well as texts that expand or challenge the canon meticulously discloses—more so than literary influence, generic development, or the autonomy of literature and the aesthetic—the constitution of power as and within the literary artifact.

It is important to recognize that the fundamental imperative of this development of John Rowe's critical work, although aligned with cultural studies, is not the same as the fundamental imperative of cultural studies, with its concentration foremost on the establishment of social relations and the resistances deployed to amending these relations that render static the social articulation of power. John Rowe's imperative, as clear from the beginning of his career, is an engagement with the sign as articulated by deconstructive theorizing, an engagement seeking to return the phenomenological force of the sign to the material historicity of the modern, that is, to outline modernity as the exorbitance of the sign, in which the United States is locatable as a sign (in political as well as aesthetic modes) indicative of the zenith of the linear progression that is the modern. This aim, stated as early as the introduction to *Through the Custom-House*, is to exceed the formalist enclosure of the sign, as John Rowe states in a brief consideration of Roland Barthes's essay "What Is Criticism?" and Hayden White's studies *Metahistory* and *The Tropics of Discourse*:

> It is no coincidence that both Barthes and White argue for a critical discourse that concentrates on "purely formal" relations.... Barthes and White merely shift their attention from the signified—always a "suspended meaning" for them—to the formal order of the signifier. The assumption that such transcoding can be undertaken on a purely formal level that avoids semantic determinations returns us once again to the binary structure of the sign, whose signifier and signified can be distinguished analytically. The structuralists' concentration on the linguistic system of the work inevitably involves the possibility of determining the infrastructure of language and thought that would ground the literary performance or historical event.[41]

Instead, John Rowe's insistent interest in retracing the ground of canonical U.S. literature mobilizes the deconstructive critique of this structuralist critical posture beyond the aporia of textuality, cognition, and experience into specific semantic determinations that enact material, historical, and aesthetic traditions that demonstrate how the endless chain of signification coalesces an extraliterary reality always holding political force. John Rowe, insofar as this dynamic of the sign remains so instrumental to the reality of political force, details the condition of modernity; the modernity that finally both exceeds and allows the entity the United States, which is to say, the historical episode initiated by the rise of the Atlantic economies and which rearticulates intercontinental trade and geopolitical orders and the terms of the profoundly self-conscious anxiety that marks the resultant social organization of aggregate populations, particularly by the turn of the nineteenth century into the twentieth century.

The Sign and the Reason of Modernity

In this way, the movement from *Through the Custom-House* to *Literary Culture and U.S. Imperialism* describes, from within the canon of U.S. literary production, this critical perception: as writing formalizes the subject, at once, it formalizes the subject as a more or less coerced coordinate in the violently stratified "global economy [that] would rely [always] upon social conventions and legal process in countless ways."[42] The insight fosters lines of critical inquiry in cultural and literary studies enabled by the force of deconstructive, feminist, neo-Marxist, post-structuralist, and racialized theorizing from the 1960s onward, reflected increasingly—as the field of American literature retheorizes itself in their wake—in such literary historical studies as Michael Gilmore's influential 1985 *American Romanticism and the Marketplace*. Contextualizing the classic literature of the American Renaissance, Gilmore proposes that "trade also seems to be connected to the appearance of symbolism in the writings of the American romantics," which is to claim that the literary phenomenon remains coimplicated directly with "developments in the economy, specifically [with] the spread of the commodity form," a coimplication in which the "twofold nature of things is a growing economic phenomenon that finds its correlative in the symbolic mode of apprehension."[43]

Insistently clarifying these imbrications, John Rowe's extensive scholarship, his trenchant interventions, particularly the book-length studies, place him in the company and stature of such figures as Richard Chase, Leslie Fiedler, Leo Marx, F. O. Matthiessen, and R. W. B. Lewis who, at one point, defined a field of study that they certainly would not recognize in its present form. Indeed, the title of F. O. Matthiessen's classic study *American Renaissance: Art and Expression in the Age of Emerson and Whitman* suggests the very terms of the presently refigured premises of the study of U.S. literature and culture as they develop through the end of the twentieth century and into the twenty-first. F. O. Matthiessen's title holds the vision of the artist as a discrete principle from which a unique content and form are issued through an act of noninstrumental signification yielding the discretely analyzable aesthetic artifact. However, in an analytic gesture that fully compromises the notion of the artist as the discrete principle original to signification, as well as the noninstrumentalist possibilities of signification, John Rowe observes in the 1987 article "Modern Art and the Invention of Postmodern Capital" that "whereas industrial capitalism struggled to give some natural credibility to its products and the conditions of their manufacture, postmodern economy accepts the utterly fictive origins of human 'information.' Under these conditions, then, everything that belongs to social reality is always already understood to be highly figurative, charged both with its local significance and informed by its more general derivations."[44] In this recognition, the very question of the artist, aesthetic object, and audience is redrawn so that the ground of the critical act itself always already confuses the literary and the extraliterary, contradicting the self-declared formalist principles by which F. O. Matthiessen consolidates the ground of U.S. literary study. As a theorist of the postmodern, John Rowe clearly understands that the divide between the extraliterary and the literary is always already only an effect of signification or, as he emphasizes, representation under determinate historical circumstances. Increasingly, the very grounds of all social production might or must be understood in aesthetic terms, he explains further:

> Capitalism lays special claim to the individual subject as the figure capable of affirming, expressing, and reproducing itself in and through a capitalist economy. This may well be the fundamental irony of capitalism; it is in fact the great artistic achievement of capitalism: to turn into a philosophical original and end up the very individual that capitalist economic practices seem intent upon destroying. By now the "solution" to this apparent paradox is familiar enough. Alienating workers from the coherent processes and products of their own labor-power, capitalism invents a philosophical and idealist "category" of the "subject" that defines itself just insofar as it can distinguish itself from its material circumstances.[45]

The postmodern condition, then, suggests that the representational act can never merely be the measure of itself. Rather, the sign is always already inscribed not merely in but as a social field. This broader dynamic of aesthetic signification remains a given in the study, unconnected to the material terms of production or social identity. The challenge to this unexamined exorbitance of the aesthetic does not require postmodern theorizing as indicated, for example, by even so standard a work as Perry Miller's anthology *The Transcendentalists*, by so important an early feminist work in U.S. literature as Annette Kolodny's *Lay of the Land*, by Paul Lauter's article "Race and Gender in the Shaping of the American Literary Canon: A Case Study from the Twenties" or his full-length study *Canons and Contexts,* or by Gerald Graff and Michael Warner's *The Origins of Literary Studies in America: A Documentary Anthology*. Nonetheless, the answer provided by John Rowe's forthright and steadfast engagement with the riddle of aesthetic signification and the problematic of signification per se in its attenuated relation to material objectivity provides an exemplary engagement with the questions of representation provoked by the foundational work of American studies.

This foundational work refuses—in a way that the scholarship of John Rowe does not—to acknowledge the signifying and material violences that finally are never incidental to the formations of the modern and its most prized geopolitical territories or aesthetic traditions. In the circumstances of modernity, meaning is never simply the proposition of the sign but also always already its articulation of violence. The work of John Rowe suggests that to attend adequately to the sign and its traditions, there is the difficult necessity—to borrow a phrase coined jointly by Akira Lippit and Fred Moten—of "owning the inalienable unaddressable wrong." The act, as difficult and unpopular as it might be, acknowledges not only the promise of the modern but, moreover, the deplorable system of human relations from which the promise must be disentangled. John Rowe is keeping very good company with James Baldwin.

NOTES

1. Thomas Hobbes, *Leviathan* (New York: Norton, 1997), 71.
2. John Locke, *Two Treatises of Government* (New York: Cambridge University Press, 1988), 298.
3. Wayne Glausser, "Three Approaches to Locke and the Slave Trade," *Journal of the History of Ideas* 51, no. 2 (April 1990): 199.
4. Glausser, "Three Approaches to Locke and the Slave Trade," 199.
5. John Carlos Rowe, "Deconstructing America: Recent Approaches to Nineteenth-Century American Literature and Culture," *ESQ* 31, no. 1 (1985): 53.
6. John Carlos Rowe, *Through the Custom-House: Nineteenth-Century American Fiction and Modern Theory* (Baltimore: Johns Hopkins University Press, 1982), 54.
7. John Carlos Rowe, "'To Live outside the Law, You Must Be Honest': The Authority of the Margin in Contemporary Theory," *Cultural Critique* 2 (1985–86): 51.
8. Rowe, "'To Live outside the Law,'" 58.
9. Rowe, "'To Live outside the Law,'" 67.
10. Rowe, "Deconstructing America," 61.
11. F. O. Matthiessen, *American Renaissance: Art and Expression in the Age of Emerson and Whitman* (New York: Oxford University Press, 1941), xi.
12. James Baldwin, *Notes of a Native Son* (Boston: Beacon, 1984), 76.
13. Baldwin, *Notes of a Native Son*, xiii.
14. John Carlos Rowe, *Henry Adams and Henry James: The Emergence of a Modern Consciousness* (Ithaca, NY: Cornell University Press, 1976), 9.
15. Rowe, *Henry Adams and Henry James*, 12.
16. Rowe, *Henry Adams and Henry James*, 12.
17. Rowe, *Henry Adams and Henry James*, 239.
18. Rowe, *Through the Custom-House*, xii.
19. Rowe, *Through the Custom-House*, 4.
20. Rowe, *Through the Custom-House*, 25.
21. Rowe, *Through the Custom-House*, 9, 7.
22. John Carlos Rowe, *At Emerson's Tomb: The Politics of Classic American Literature* (New York: Columbia University Press, 1997), 1.
23. Rowe, *At Emerson's Tomb*, 5.
24. Rowe, *At Emerson's Tomb*, 15.
25. Rowe, *At Emerson's Tomb*, 67.
26. Rowe, *At Emerson's Tomb*, 210.

27. John Carlos Rowe, *The Other Henry James* (Durham, NC: Duke University Press, 1998), 3.

28. Rowe, *The Other Henry James*, 9, 10, 12, 13.

29. Rowe, *The Other Henry James*, 14.

30. Rowe, *The Other Henry James*, 36.

31. Rowe, *The Other Henry James*, 187.

32. Rowe, *The Other Henry James*, 183, 184.

33. Rowe, *The Other Henry James*, 198.

34. Rowe, *The Other Henry James*, 191.

35. John Carlos Rowe, *Post-national American Studies* (Berkeley: University of California Press, 2000), 2.

36. Rowe, *Post-national American Studies*, 3.

37. Rowe, *Post-national American Studies*, 11.

38. John Carlos Rowe, "Post-nationalism, Globalism, and the New American Studies," *Cultural Critique* 40 (1998): 28.

39. John Carlos Rowe, *Literary Culture and U.S. Imperialism from the Revolution to World War II* (Oxford: Oxford University Press, 2000), 5.

40. Rowe, *Literary Culture and U.S. Imperialism*, 23.

41. Rowe, *Through the Custom-House*, 13.

42. Joyce Appleby, *Capitalism and a New Social Order: The Republican Vision of the 1790s* (New York: New York University Press, 1983), 33.

43. Michael T. Gilmore, *American Romanticism and the Marketplace* (Chicago: University of Chicago Press, 1985), 15.

44. John Carlos Rowe, "Modern Art and the Invention of Postmodern Capital," *American Quarterly* 39, no. 1 (1987): 156.

45. Rowe, "Modern Art and the Invention of Postmodern Capital," 160.

II. GESTURES OF INSCRIPTION
African American Slave Narratives

Introduction

DAPHNE A. BROOKS

We might think of critical slave narrative studies and black nineteenth-century studies more broadly as, in some ways, dividing into two categories: before and after the three essays by Lindon Barrett included in this section. For while it is clear that a cluster of field-altering volumes by fellow scholars would emerge in the immediate years following the last of these essays that he published (in *American Literature* in 1997), the critical questions that he maps out here with a deft and trademark combination of rigor, lucidity, and elegance would mark the emergence of a powerful shift in black literary and cultural criticism focusing on the narratives and representational practices of the formerly enslaved. As Barrett himself makes clear in his 1995 *American Literary History* article "African-American Slave Narratives: Literacy, the Body, Authority," the tremendous advances made by black studies scholars in the 1970s and 1980s had, up until that point, galvanized efforts to recuperate, historically authenticate, and contextualize forgotten and marginalized texts in the academy, and their efforts equally sought to illuminate the literary workings of these texts in their own time. The subsequent push in the late 1980s to dissect language and form and to trace the rhetorical strategies of early African American literature was a clear and forceful battle cry at the height of the heady canon wars from that era. But Barrett's essays remind us that the 1990s called for new critical methodologies that might better enable scholars to forsake neither history nor the literary but to instead deploy cultural analysis and critical theory as a means to interrogating and reading the dialectic between both realms. Courtrooms and bodies and the sociocultural politics and poetics of literacy figure prominently in his expansive readings of Frederick Douglass's, Harriet Jacobs's, and William Craft's respective classic texts, as well as lesser-known works by Lucy Delaney, Mary Prince, James L. Smith, and (a then-obscure) Solomon Northup. More still, his bold and imaginative examination of the black body in these three essays would showcase his long-standing investment in revealing the ways that black subjects consistently disturb Enlightenment philosophies that frame body and mind, and blackness and the human as antithetical to one another. His insightful observations would form the blueprint for pathbreaking studies just around the corner that focused, in part, on black corporeality and suffering (Saidiya Hartman, *Scenes of Subjection*), the politics of gesture and insurgent performance in captive cultures (Fred Moten, *In the Break*), the juridical entanglements between slavery and cultural production (Stephen Best, *The Fugitive's Properties*), the intersections of race and modernity in the production of literary culture (Jacqueline Goldsby, *A Spectacular Secret*), and the innovative and alternative modes of black literacy deployed in nineteenth-century black freedom struggles (P. Gabrielle Foreman, *Activist Sentiments*). In short, Barrett's work, which built in particular on the advances made by influential black feminist scholars such as Hortense Spillers, Valerie Smith, and Hazel Carby, opened the door to what we might think of as the new black nineteenth-century studies, which continues to shape scholarly conversations and debates in the field today.

All three essays included here showcase Barrett's formidable talents and resources as a post-structural theorist who clearly reveled in engaging with the critical paradigms of UC Irvine colleagues including Jacques Derrida while also drawing on various theoretical methodologies in order to consistently call attention to the vexed position of blackness in relation to post-Enlightenment Western thought, which held that "the life of the body can be imagined exclusive of the life of the mind only by intricate fiat" and that "the African American body signifies an existence entirely or virtually within the bodily half of the antithesis..., entrap[ped]" in the putative "mindlessness of corporeality."[1] The brilliant intervention that Barrett makes here is nothing short of an epistemic revision of black corporeality as it has been scripted and engineered in dominant cultural imaginaries. What if, he asks, the narratives of ex-slaves offer us the most potent countertheorizations of blackness that demonstrate the ways in which "constructions underlying designations of black and white... exclude bodies within one category from signification altogether," and what if these same narratives can not only expose this fallacy but, in some cases, provide their authors with the means to move black bodies into the realm of "Saussurian linguistics and poststructuralist thought, multiplicity, plurality and difference...

the conditions that make possible significance, signification, language, meaning?" ("Hand-Writing"). In both "African-American Slave Narratives" and "Hand-Writing," Barrett reveals the myriad ways that nineteenth-century black culture workers transformed and reassembled their bodies into vivid templates of the mind while troubling the boundaries between their own absence and presence, literacy and illiteracy, stasis and transfiguration. This work captures Barrett in motion and moving toward some of the most influential arguments that he would go on to make in his monograph *Blackness and Value: Seeing Double*, in which he posits, recuperates, and affirms radical, alternative forms of self-making improvised by captives as a way to counter the hegemony of the signed self. We can see in these essays the roots of the "singing self" theories from that book and Barrett's critical analysis of black embodied, sonic articulations of the human that would ultimately anticipate the work of scholars such as Farah Griffin, Fred Moten, Alexander Weheliye, and others, in effect opening up an entire field of black sound studies made possible by his scholarship.

Self-making lies at the heart of each of these essays, as Barrett returns again and again to the contested terrain on which blackness is controlled and defined, appears and disappears in Western culture—in, for instance, the courtroom, where statutory law "challenges [Lucy] Delaney's sense of herself" and produces "fictions constructed through the determining technologies of legal discourse."[2] As he reveals in "Self-Knowledge, Law, and African American Autobiography: Lucy A. Delaney's *From the Darkness Cometh the Light*," "African Americans and African American autobiographers must revise or recast in the terms of their lives a story already (unacceptably) written—and writ large—by American law and custom. They attempt to write a story already recorded and on which the book, for the most part, has been closed" ("Self-Knowledge, Law"). Discursive autobiographical strategy that "advertises its fictiveness as opposed to its facticity," in the case of Delaney, and counterintuitive corporeal acts that enable the black body "to be recognized as significant in terms other than its physicality," as in the case of cross-dressing, cross-racial fugitive Ellen Craft, are thus some of the tactics that black agents might use to upset Western racial epistemologies ("Self-Knowledge, Law").

Barrett's engagement with black feminist theory marks yet another departure from the 1980s emphasis on form and content analysis in slave narrative studies. In his insistence on taking into account the "racist and sexist system" in which "black women are ... the ur-site of blackness, the site at which the physical and cultural 'pathology' known as blackness is generated," he draws from Spillers, Smith, Carby, and others in order to recuperate the centrality of the black female body as an insurgent and malleable escape tactic in William and

Ellen Craft's 1860 *Running a Thousand Miles for Freedom* ("Hand-Writing"). My own *Bodies in Dissent* as well as the work of black performance studies scholars such as Tavia Nyong'o (*The Amalgamation Waltz*), Jayna Brown (*Babylon Girls*), and Soyica Colbert (*The African American Theatrical Body*) are just some of the works that remain deeply indebted to the strides that Barrett made in this regard.

Above all else, Lindon Barrett's essays on the slave narrative showcase his insistence on tracing the ways in which nineteenth-century black writers perpetually envisioned ways of doing the black body differently and in relation to a field of signification that negated its presence. His work challenges us to consider how these authors manage not only their own bodies but constructions of the white body as well. His attention to a range of undertheorized literary moments in which "the white image in the black mind" (to borrow a formulation from an important anthology of the same name) emerges underscores the ways that Barrett's scholarship was both extending advances in early 1990s whiteness studies to the realm of the African American slave narrative genre and, likewise, forging a new path in reading the ways that fugitive culture producers theorize whiteness. This thread in particular clears a path for the scholarship of performance studies scholars such as Marvin McAllister (*Whiting Up*) and Faedra Carpenter (*Coloring Whiteness*), and it is one that calls for even further study as we continue to generate complex readings of the life of the black mind and body in nineteenth-century culture.

In short, the essays that follow are an incessant reminder of the scholarly and aesthetic moment that Lindon Barrett made possible, and likewise they remind us of the promise and possibility of early African American expressive cultures as the site where sly and incisive critical commentary on race has the power to take hold. As we move deeper into the twenty-first century, we might draw on the tools that Barrett has given us here to read new cinema (*12 Years a Slave*, *Django Unchained*), new theater (Branden Jacobs-Jenkins's *An Octoroon*, Marcus Gardley's *The House That Will Not Stand*), Jennifer Kidwell and Scott R. Sheppard's *Underground Railroad Game*, Suzan-Lori Parks's *Father Comes Home from the Wars, Parts I and II*, and new art installations (Theaster Gates's *To Speculate Darkly: Theaster Gates and Dave the Potter*, Kara Walker's *A Subtlety*). Think of these essays, then, as letters of a sort, sent out into the world, like Jacobs's shrewd and subversive epistolary endeavors—but, in this case, sent with love to the world of black studies. They return to us now with a kind of clarity, conviction, and explanatory force that might guide us into yet another new era of thrilling discovery about the past that remains perpetually present.

NOTES

1. Lindon Barrett, "African-American Slave Narratives: Literacy, the Body, Authority," chapter 4, this volume; Lindon Barrett, "Hand-Writing: Legibility and the White Body in *Running a Thousand Miles for Freedom*," chapter 5, this volume.

2. Lindon Barrett, "Self-Knowledge, Law, and African American Autobiography: Lucy A. Delaney's *From the Darkness Cometh the Light*," chapter 6, this volume.

| CH4

African-American Slave Narratives:
Literacy, the Body, Authority (1995)

Although there exist numerous and illuminating investigations of issues surrounding conceptions of literacy as they inform the analysis of African-American slave narratives, few explore fully the notion that, beyond the immediate relation it bears to issues of power and powerlessness, literacy bears an equally important and immediate relation to "the most contracted of spaces, the small circle of living matter."[1] That is to say, few seem to consider fully the manner in which a paramount element of the project facing ex-slave narrators is an intricate negotiation of the mind/body split that remains so important to post-Enlightenment Western thought and that, with equal insistence, is so often redacted in the terms of the black/white racial dichotomy indispensable to the U.S. cultural imagination. To speak of issues of literacy within the context of the U.S. slave regime and the autobiographical narratives of its ex-slaves is to a very great extent to speak of issues of the body—and of the African-American body in particular. For the social and imaginative imperatives of this regime and its legacies promote a conflation of the distinctions between literacy and illiteracy, on the one hand, and black and white, on the other. These four terms, in effect, form a spurious homology, with the result that, as much as literacy represents a privileged state of mind, it also connotes the material body and, ultimately, the alleged overwhelming corporeality of blackness. This peculiar set of relations, it seems to me, deeply informs the complex relationship between ex-slave narrators and their texts and, by considering this inexorable connection between literacy and African-American corporeality, I offer in this discussion an extension of the theorizing focused on issues of literacy as it informs the relationship between ex-slave narrators and their texts.

To begin it is useful to provide a very brief rehearsal of the scholarly attention slave narratives and their narrators have received in the recent academy: in the past fifteen years or so, African-American slave narratives have enjoyed unprecedented academic lives, especially in departments of literature. These texts have come to bear the intense scrutiny of close readings and of sophisticated theoretical speculations. The aim of this essay is to extend those speculations into the purview of what is now called cultural analysis. With acute sensitivity to its own politics, as well as the political dimensions of its objects of study, cultural analysis yields insights into the manner in which a particular worldview authorizes, implements, and structures the commonplace rituals, spaces, and interpretive activities of those interpellated by a particular cultural regime. These studies understand dimensions of culture as dimensions of power, and, in this way, it is not difficult to see that they find a rewarding cache of materials in texts produced by African Americans who record their experiences as chattel personal.

However, slave narratives entered academic concerns far afield from elaboration of issues of culture and power as construed by cultural analysis. These texts entered the academy within the terms of a debate concerning their legitimacy as historiographical evidence of U.S. slaveholding society. A rehearsal of the central concerns of this debate forms the greater part of John Blassingame's introduction to the anthology *Slave Testimony*. Preoccupied with "the reliability of various sources," this debate illuminates the status of slave narratives as gauges of or monuments to a compelling social reality, a series of past events accessible beyond provisional representation within any text or collection of texts.[2] This positive status was withheld from slave narratives for most of the twentieth century because of reservations about the influences of editors and amanuenses, or conversely the very literacy of the ex-slave, as well as the skewed sample of the slave population that produced the narratives.

As these concerns were overcome, the narratives attained a more widespread currency within the academy. Frances Foster's 1979 *Witnessing Slavery* provides the first published full-length literary study of the narratives. It examines the social and historical conditions of their production and peculiarities of plot construction, as well as their nineteenth-century readership and popularity.[3] Foster's study obliquely reflects what became an overriding consensus among African-American literary critics for the 1980s. The status of the slave narrative as a reliable redaction of matters beyond its text was bracketed in deference to considering the text as an artifact open to investigation itself. Foster, to this end, provides an examination of important forces influencing the production of the artifact. However, those most fully committed at this time to consolidating new approaches to African-American texts were concerned with textuality as a primarily closed linguistic event. Their manifesto was the 1979 volume *Afro-American Literature: The Reconstruction of Instruction*, in which the urgency is to emphasize "what is literary (as opposed to sociological, ideological, etc.) in Afro-American written art."[4] In the collection of essays, Henry Louis Gates's "Preface to Blackness: Text and Pretext" elaborates this concern most explicitly. Eschewing "the confusion of realms, of art and propaganda" and "the tendency toward thematic criticism [that] implies an inferiority complex" in order to advocate "sophisticated verbal analysis," these new attentions yielded detailed interpretations of the language, rhetorical strategies, and predominant tropes of the texts, especially in relation to structuralist and poststructuralist theories.[5] In various guises and with good reason, these attentions remain at the forefront of the criticism of texts of ex-slaves; nonetheless, it seems somewhat misguided to believe, as William Andrews does, that "looking to the 1990s, it is hard to imagine that critics and scholars of black American autobiography will veer sharply away from the interests and concerns that preoccupied criticism of this genre in the 1980s." It seems to me unlikely that examining the African-American autobiographical text "as a site of formal revisionism and the free play of signification" exhausts its possibilities for critical investigation and interpretation.[6]

The point here is not to reject earlier and important studies and approaches that developed as slave narratives gained unprecedented currency in the academy. It is to extend those inquiries by exploring possibilities for the transfer of critical energies from the symbolics of a textual event, that is, a linguistic, literary, or verbal system, to the symbolic dimensions of extratextual systems and links between the two. A text—verbally or otherwise constructed—speaks to rituals of identity formation, to the way a multiplicity of personal and social identities are culturally maintained. Engaging these dynamics is among the aims of cultural analysis insofar as such aims are ever expressly defined.[7] One might consider three stages in this critical history of slave narratives: a historical phase, a literary phase, and, as I am hoping to suggest, a phase of cultural analysis. In the historical phase, the literacy or, conversely, illiteracy of the ex-slave defines contentions and controversies regarding the reliability of the text in question; literacy is pondered as an index of historical veracity. In the second phase, issues of literacy, as well as the narratives themselves, are mostly taken out of "history." Literacy provides the critical-interpretative focus for reading the texts, as well as suggesting methodological-theoretical schemas, and, in doing so, dispels "the confusion of realms, of art and propaganda."[8] However, in a cultural analysis phase, rather than separating history and literature, one might see them as equally "textual" and place them in conversation with one another, reconstituting and revitalizing the confusion of the realms of art and propaganda. The premise here is that cultural discourse, systems of shared symbolic-expressive conventions, form the zero-degree "reality" from which both history and literature emerge.[9] What is more, issues of literacy play a central role in this third approach as well.

For as it does in the primary texts, literacy remains central to the academic criticism of slave narratives; no single issue holds the preeminence granted literacy. Robert Stepto in his influential study *From behind the Veil* posits that "the primary pre-generic myth for Afro-America is the quest for freedom and literacy."[10] James Olney echoes this position in his important essay "'I Was Born': Slave Narratives, Their Status as Autobiography and as Literature." Olney states that "the social theme [of the narratives], the reality of slavery and the necessity of abolishing it, trifurcates on the personal level to become subthemes of literacy, identity, and freedom . . . altogether interdependent and virtually indistinguishable as thematic strands."[11] Henry Louis Gates Jr., in the essay "Literary Theory and the Black Tradition," his most extended consideration of literacy, writes, "sheer literacy was the very commodity that separated animal from human being, slave from citizen, object from subject" in the cultural imagination of the West.[12] Literacy is conceived in terms of empowerment and the transformation of identity it grants those long excluded from it in a society in which letters were indispensable. Nonetheless, this empowerment and transformation are ambiguous, as Valerie Smith recognizes. Smith warns that to privilege heedlessly the notion of literacy is to "pay homage to the structures of discourse that so often contributed to the writer's oppression."[13] In Smith's mind, to reproduce without qualification the priority of literacy is to reproduce ideological frameworks intended to dehumanize slave communities, since this privileging "suggests that, without letters, slaves fail to understand the full meaning of their domination."[14] It suggests that, without letters, slaves somehow fail to understand or participate appreciably in the life of the mind.

These important analyses, despite their differences, conceive of literacy from the perspective of its attainment, as an achievement, though (to a greater or lesser extent) a vexed one. On the other hand, if one draws on the approaches of cultural analysis, it may prove equally rewarding to investigate literacy as an unattained condition, as a prohibited condition, for literacy as a prohibited condition is not simply to be equated with enforced illiteracy but rather, I contend, finds its significance in the body. The body, within the ideologies of the dominant American community, holds the ultimate terms of identity for African Americans. As the dominant community would have it, the identity of African Americans is bound up primarily, if not exclusively, with "the most contracted of spaces, the small circle of living matter." This proves a signal identification, because in European philosophizing the body "can only be an object of thought not its subject."[15] Thus, African Americans who are forced to live illiterate lives, who are forcibly identified with the limited sphere of the body, are in as manifest a fashion as possible seemingly restricted to being the objects of thought and never its subjects. Because literacy provides the most manifest formalization of the life of the mind, it is central in this elaborate intellectual and social construct. Literacy provides manifest testimony of the mind's ability to extend itself beyond the constricted limits and conditions of the body. To restrict African Americans to lives without literacy is seemingly to immure them in bodily existences having little or nothing to do with the life of the mind and its representation. Conversely, to enter into literacy is to gain important skills for extending oneself beyond the condition and geography of the body. In effect, I am arguing that in terms of African-American slave narratives, the body and issues of literacy (and illiteracy) are to some extent indistinguishable.

In consideration of this claim, however, it is important to keep in mind the highly nuanced history of antebellum policies and attitudes—both legal and extralegal—toward African-American literacy. The work of historian Janet Duitsman Cornelius proves valuable on this point. Cornelius documents, in her study *"When I Can Read My Title Clear": Literacy, Slavery, and Religion in the Antebellum South*, the perhaps surprising fact that legal sanctions restricting slave literacy were not as widespread as generally believed (even by slaves themselves).[16] Cornelius complicates the historical issue further in several ways. She rehearses actions taken by Southerners, whether or not in accordance with legal policies, to restrict African-American literacy—"the most common widely known penalty for learning to read and write was amputation"; Cornelius equally rehearses the efforts of considerable segments of Southern society to promote literacy among African Americans (as exemplified most dramatically by the efforts of prominent South Carolina slaveholder Richard Fuller).[17] A further noteworthy dimension of this complex history concerns equivocal policies and actions of American tract societies, such as the American Bible Society, in their concerted efforts to preserve the Union while still placing "repeated emphasis on the value of reading for all people."[18] Nevertheless, beyond these contingencies, it is important to recognize that uniformly underlying the less than straightforward history of social and legal barriers to African-American literacy is the powerful, unequivocal fact that "literacy, especially the ability to write, signified an establishment of the African's human identity to the European world."¹⁹ Spanning the highly scrutinized gulf between illiteracy and literacy amounts to entering the fretfully theorized condition of the most fully human—which is the same as the least "racialized."

Race as a symbolic boundary is conflated with literacy as a symbolic boundary, a conflation both overdetermined by and reifying the antithesis of body and mind. While, needless to say, we all assume that the lives of the body and the mind are not simply coincident or coterminous, still, as Richard Rorty argues in *Philosophy and the Mirror of Nature*, neither does there exist any self-evident or ineradicable distinction to be drawn between the two. The central question Rorty poses in his demonstration of the speciousness of crediting two ontologically distinct realms is "How ... do we know when we have two ways of talking about the same thing ... rather than descriptions of two different things?"²⁰ He aims to demonstrate that what passes for an ontological distinction, "the non-identity of mental and physical states," proves upon close scrutiny merely an epistemological one. He begins by recognizing in the position of neodualists, or those continuing to "distinguish mind from body ... in a more or less Cartesian way," that "not only have [they] a clear intuition of what 'mentality' is, but that it has something to do with non-spatiality."²¹ The physical is spatial, whereas the mental is not. Examined more judiciously, however, this difference only reflects markedly different mediums by which information is received. It reflects also markedly different relations one sustains to this information.²² To Rorty's mind, the issue deals, ultimately, with an appearance/reality split: neodualist reasoning, taken on its principles, posits "a physical property as one which anyone could be mistaken in attributing to something, and a phenomenal [mental] property as one which a certain person cannot be mistaken about."²³ The differentiation is one between competing modes of knowledge and certainty and concerns itself, fundamentally, with one's relation to the information with which one is faced. In this way, what amounts to a matter of epistemology is accepted mistakenly as one of ontology, mistakenly because "there seems no reason for the epistemic difference between reports of how things feel [or seem] and reports of anything else to produce an ontological gap."²⁴

On a less abstract level than that pursued by Rorty, the neodualist distinction proves specious because, as is abundantly clear in the narratives, extending oneself beyond the condition and geography of the body and (through literacy) into a manifest life of the mind is not equivalent to entrance into a nonspatial, nonmaterial realm but, instead, into a realm of intentional, phenomenal, and perceptual power that superintends and assuredly returns to matters of the physical, spatial, and geographic. Literacy determines for whom the physical, the geographic, and the bodily will remain an overwhelming concern and source of identity and for whom it will remain an index of power and valuable apparent remove. Simply put, the life of the body can be imagined exclusive of the life of the mind only by intricate fiat. In the symbolic practices of antebellum America, literacy as prohibition stands as this fiat, and, although a necessarily doomed attempt to exile African Americans from the life of the mind, it bore vast social consequences. That African Americans live within a culture where they are forced to deal first and foremost with the spatiality-materiality of their existences (which finds its hyperbole in attention to their bodies) is recorded in the physical brutalities described again and again in slave narratives.[25] To choose one brief passage from a vast number of possible examples: "Blow after blow was inflicted upon my naked body.... I thought I must die beneath the lashes of the accursed brute. Even now the flesh crawls upon my bones, as I recall the scene."[26] In the American slaveholding regime, the primary and recurring location marking crisis within or reaffirmation of the instituted relations and ideologies of master and slave remains the African-American body.

The urgency and primacy given to spatial-material existence in African-American lives is more subtly recorded by the characteristic opening statements of slave narratives. Henry Bibb (1850) opens his text as follows: "I was born May 1815, of a slave mother in Shelby County, Kentucky"; William Grimes writes (1855): "I was born in the year 1784, in J———————, County of King George, Virginia"; Frederick Douglass writes (1845): "I was born in Tuckahoe, near Hillsborough, and about twelve miles from Easton, in Talbot county, Maryland."[27] Similarly, in an 1863 interview undertaken by the American Freedmen's Inquiry Commission, Mrs. Joseph Wilkinson says: "I had never been but 15 miles before from home in my life."[28] This primary attention given to geography suggests or parallels the primary attention necessarily given to the narrators' bodies in the narratives. The drama of these texts is spatial (both bodily and geographical); geography, a local physical space, even more than the year of birth, becomes, as does the disposition of one's body, the most ineradicable marker of self and identity.

In the texts and contexts of these narratives, issues of literacy underscore the fact that African Americans are removed in large part from presenting as ineradicable markers of self and identity: the mind, the intellect, or any other aspect of their existences less mediated by physical and sensational imperatives attributable to "the most contracted of spaces, the small circle of living matter." Reading and writing, in the Western worldview, rather than anchoring themselves in the relatively immediate concerns of the body, represent avenues of direct access to an abstract "conceptual apparatus we inherit from our culture," an apparatus acting as arbiter of fact and fantasy, the primary and the secondary, the valuable and dross.[29] This apparatus delineates the world as well as interactions most appropriate for taking place in it. Reading and writing and the cultural apparatus they represent make *sense*, which proves, in turn, the principle and end of "government" in the post-Enlightenment West. This inherited cultural apparatus is, therefore, to be carefully guarded or managed. Literacy and its activities symbolize in the American cultural conversation entrance into this conceptual arena in which the facticity of the body and, indeed, of the world are determined (and, at best, controlled). Undertaking a study of predominant metaphors of reading in the latter nineteenth century, Catherine Sheldrick Ross, in consideration of the metaphor "reading is a ladder," states, "We have seen that, on the ladder of up/down the following are all up: nonfiction, utilitarian information, realism, factuality, and rationality."[30] Reading is understood as a ladder with these genres as its rungs, which one ideally ascends. Of the most prevalent and consequential metaphor—"reading is eating"—Ross observes:

> The hierarchy of genres . . . which stretches from romance at the bottom to realism to travel, biography, and history and finally up to nonnarrative prose, is thus brought into alignment with a hierarchy of foods. The counterpart to the work of romance is the sugary confection. . . . Just as one climbs the hierarchy of foods by leaving behind the sugary dishes and the milk puddings in favor of "stronger foods" and pure meat, so one climbs the ladder of genres by successively leaving behind the fictional and narrative elements that give delight rather than instruction.[31]

Literacy and its activities superintend a hierarchy with "instruction," "factuality," and "rationality" at its zenith, an engagement with the world neither fanciful, primarily passive, nor inconsequential. It is this arena of "rationality," rather than the body, that stands as the primary realm of human agency, superintending an engagement with the world that ultimately constructs physical and social realities. These predominant metaphors, although reliant on the physical, suggest a transcending of the physical. They suggest a realm of agency that "precedes . . . determines . . . [and] stands outside the play of the sensible [or physical]."[32] One sees in their hierarchies a desire to attain a full presence of mind—or, put differently, the philosophical idealism central to traditional Western thought.

In the same way that "in Western thought . . . it has seemed 'natural' to think in terms of a series of hierarchies in the individual, in society, and in the world of nature," so too the metaphors of reading investigated by Ross reinforce "the notion of a hierarchical ordering of the verbal universe into distinct levels and the related imperative of leaving behind the lower in favor of the higher."[33] This discourse of reading underscores the fact that to prohibit African Americans from literacy is equivalent, in terms of social organization, to proscribing African Americans from the highest realms of value and the hierarchical constructs leading to them. These metaphors illustrate in one further way that to separate segments of a population according to a legislated division of body and mind amounts, ingeniously but mistakenly, to conflating hierarchies of race with hierarchies of sense and sensibility. African Americans, as the dominant culture would have it, are apparently barred from the full presence of their own minds and, more importantly, the full presence of mind characteristic of traditional Western thought, which never represents itself in terms of geography or spatiality. Hence, the paramount dilemma of ex-slave narrators might be understood as follows. In giving account of slavery and "themselves," their paramount task is to reproduce the experiences and trials of a "body"—their bodies—in a medium necessarily antithetical to that project. Written language is an abstract medium recalcitrant to mimicking or reproducing bodily experience; what literacy affords those who acquire it is precisely the ability to some extent to do away with the body (in deference to the mind and abstraction). Yet to accomplish their project as ex-slave narrators, these writers must assuredly make their bodies appear for their readers, since to be an African American or slave is to be foremost a body and to be fixed in a particular kind of space—a particular geography, but most especially the immediate space of one's own body.

Yet the opposite may initially appear true when one takes into account the cultural and historical context of these narrative projects. I have in mind, particularly, the terms of literature of sensibility and the sentimental novel, which are the dominant literary modes of representation during the era of the classic slave narrative (1836–65). One might wish to claim that exactly what slave narratives manage to do in borrowing techniques from sentimental literature is to appropriate and make political use of the reader's body by means of the bodily reactions sentimental techniques aim to elicit. Rather than working in a medium recalcitrant to the body, ex-slave narrators might be said to disclose, in the estimation of Karen Sánchez-Eppler, for instance, "the bodily nature of the genre itself."[34] Sánchez-Eppler claims that "the ability of sentimental fiction to liberate the bodies of slaves is intimately connected to the bodily nature of the genre itself. Sentiment and feeling refer at once to emotion and to physical sensation."[35] However, despite Sánchez-Eppler's observations, it is paramount to recognize that the body in question in the sentimental literary transaction *never* enters the transaction on its own terms. On the contrary, it enters the transaction, foremost and always, as a measure of a prioritized, immaterial sensibility or character, as an emblem of a state of mind and consciousness. Contextualizing the bodily reactions elicited by sentimental literature, M. H. Abrams underscores this point when noting that "it was a commonplace in popular morality that readiness to shed a sympathetic tear is the sign of both polite breeding and a virtuous heart, and such a view was often accompanied by the observation that sympathy with another's grief, unlike personal grief, is a pleasurable emotion, hence to be sought as a value in itself."[36] Bodily response to sentimental literature stands, then, as a sign or cipher of character. These responses make references to states of mind and decidedly not to the body itself. Only insofar as the body remains a primarily transparent point of reference, only insofar as its materiality stands in for and defers to the immateriality of "polite breeding" and of "emotion[s]" of value, can it be understood as integral to the sentimental literary transaction. The body is not itself the issue; it merely stands as a supplement for the primary and truly integral appearance of "human capacities of sympathy and wishing others well... social consciousness and a sense of communal responsibility in an era of expanding commercialism and of an economics based on self interest."[37] Janet Todd in her historical study of sentimental culture, *Sensibility*, also makes this point: "Sentimental literature... is a kind of *pedagogy*... clarifying when uncontrolled sobs or a single tear should be the rule, or when the inexpressible nature of the feeling should be stressed."[38] In short, bodily responses to sentimental literature remain part of a generic enterprise characterized, above all, by attention to the life of the mind and spirit, not the body.

This highly compromised role of the body in the sentimental literary transaction is illuminated by Elaine Scarry's shrewd analysis in *The Body in Pain* of the process she terms "analogical verification." In processes of analogical verification (Scarry has in mind primarily the instances of torture and war), "the sheer material factualness of the human body is borrowed to lend th[e] cultural construct [in question] the aura of 'realness' and 'certainty.'"[39] Restated, "the incontestable reality of the body... is separated from its source and conferred on an ideology or issue or instance of political authority impatient of, or deserted by, benign sources of substantiation."[40] What Scarry's formulation allows one to recognize is that "the sheer material factualness" or "incontestable reality" of the body is of a kind notably different from that of discursive experience, even as discursive experience may actively pursue or covet that nature or "source." No matter how violent, elegant, or naturalized the effort to make them parallel, mirror, or stand in for one another, the realms of the body and of discursive, narrative, and ideological configurations are separate (although certainly not unrelated). What is more, like torture and war, though to a much less physically violent extent, sentimental culture is greatly concerned with responding to a troublesome "crisis of belief" enacted by this separation between the two.[41] In this way, claims for the "bodily nature" of any genre seem, upon close scrutiny, facile formulations. Despite their use of sentimental techniques that fleetingly announce a bodily presence in the literary transaction, ex-slave narrators still face the task of working in a medium resistant in many ways to the translation of the *bodily* experiences they aim to convey to their readers.

Still, a further, more troublesome consideration for these narrators is the fact that the mark of their inferior status as African Americans in U.S. society is precisely their bodies, bodies symbolizing a mythical distance from the mind and mythical entrapment in corporeality. The bodies they would reproduce in language are paradoxically the very marks of a remove from language and the life of the mind. Their bodies are concomitantly the focus of their new literacy and agency yet emblems of an apparent disqualification from literacy and self- or social agency. Presenting their bodies as primary emblems of their personal identities and histories proves, then, an extremely vexed exercise, and, it is fair to say, their dilemma is resolved only by careful management, not simply of the appearances of African-American bodies in the narratives, but also of the glossing of these bodies from the texts. In the same way that appearances of these bodies are crucial, so too are their disappearances, as illustrated by James L. Smith's 1881 autobiography, for example.

Smith, an effective abolitionist speaker at one point after escaping from Virginia in 1838, ably negotiates the problem of presenting the African-American body as both an indispensable marker of self-identification and the anchor of political and social ideologies of unbearable hostility. The opening chapter of his narrative presents incident after incident of the mishaps, injuries, beatings, and whippings befalling virtually every African American introduced to his readers. Smith, himself, is injured and made lame at a very young age. In defiance of his bedridden mother, he helps two other slaves cart lumber, until a very large piece drops on his knee and crushes the foot of the other boy with him. While the other boy dies as a result of his injury, Smith's knee is so badly damaged it never heals. His peculiarly marked body becomes an enduring marker of identity. In this vein all African Americans introduced in the narrative at this point are sketched primarily in terms of their bodies and impositions threatening or marking their bodies (his father is poisoned; the slave found responsible is beaten until she is unrecognizable; she is sold south, etc.). Smith rehearses an overwhelming set of physical obstacles and conditions that define the world of his slave community. These conditions solicit brutal recognitions of one's own physicality.

What is more, these impositions stand as both the upshot and defining feature of black and white interactions. Without fail white Americans appear in the first chapter simply to comment upon or cause African-American injury. Smith's most memorable beating as a child forms the most detailed account of the appearance of a white American in the chapter. One afternoon he falls asleep instead of "driv[ing] the calves for the milk-woman to milk."[42] When his transgression is discovered, he stands before his mistress "trembling about mid-way of the [kitchen] floor."[43] This is an important detail to note because of what follows. Smith writes that Mrs. Mitchell, "taking the cow-hide, and lifting her large arms as high as she could, applied it to my back."[44] The rest of the scene, which is increasingly cartoonish, almost slapstick, is related as follows:

> Jinny (the cook) told me afterwards, that when Mrs. Mitchell struck me I jumped about four feet, and did not touch the floor again till I was out doors. She followed me to the door and just had time to see me turn the corner of the "great house." I then ran towards the cow-pen. The cook told me the way I was running as I turned the corner, that she did not believe that there was a dog or horse on the plantation that could have caught me. . . . To my astonishment when I went to the kitchen again, behold, there . . . [Mrs. Mitchell] was still waiting for me. She asked me why I ran from her, I told her that it hurt me so bad when she struck me, that I did not know that I was running. She said the next time she whipped me that she would have me tied, then she guessed I would not run. She let me off that night by promising her that I would do better, and never run from her again.[45]

What Smith's readers encounter, at various levels, is the literal removal of the African-American body from its premier crisis of physical and spatial instantiation in antebellum America and, equally, from a narration it apparently dominates. The incident is one of flight, at the simplest level: Smith flees from his position "mid-way of the [kitchen] floor," the site of the pain inflicted by Mitchell. His body disappears, correspondingly, in the textual reconstruction of the incident. The disappearance constitutes a narrative unraveling of the logic that characterizes African-American existence in terms of a mythical distance from the mind and mythical entrapment in corporeality. Smith suggests by telling Mrs. Mitchell he did not know he was running from her that his responses and reactions lie outside cognition—most particularly, at the "embodied" moment in question. Nonetheless, his escape from further punishment rests precisely on his certification of his cognitive abilities, his "promise" never to run again in similar circumstances. The promise is accepted by Mitchell and releases him from further punishment.

In this episode, a body that is voided of language becomes a body filled again with language. Manipulations of the body are, in effect, supplanted by manipulations of language. Smith transforms his interactions with Mrs. Mitchell from those between physical tormentor and physically tormented into the dynamics of verbal, nonphysical transactions. Paramount by the end of the encounter are not the sensational dimensions of his corporeality but a moment of profitable disembodied self-identification—his verbal promise. Manipulating the fiction of African-American noncognition to advantage, Smith both claims and disclaims thoughts he cannot have. This is to say, Mrs. Mitchell accepts a promise from him to do what, by definition and—more importantly—by his own admission, he cannot. For the moment he must justify to her is one at which he decidedly does not "know" what he is doing. Thus, the scene turns, despite his admitted reasonlessness, precisely on his reasonableness. It turns ironically on his word.

Crucially, therefore, the African-American body so central to this first chapter both appears and disappears, and Scarry's study is once again useful for understanding the particulars of this sleight of hand, one shared by Smith with other ex-slave narrators. Scarry outlines the three central premises of *The Body in Pain* as the inexpressibility of pain, the political and perceptual consequences of this inexpressibility, and, accordingly, the interrelated nature of material and verbal expressibility. Physical pain is inexpressible because it "does not simply resist language but actively destroys it."[46] As a result, pain has vast political consequences, for "the relative ease or difficulty with which any given phenomenon can be *verbally represented* also influences the ease or difficulty with which that phenomenon can be *politically represented*."[47] With these observations in mind, Scarry aims at detailing the manner in which physical pain, when intentionally inflicted, is translated into the fiction of power. As above, Scarry's concept of "analogical verification" or "analogical substitution" constitutes a signal moment in her exposition, for, in more than merely obvious ways, she argues, the body is central to the "structures" of torture and war. During these activities, the highly contestable abstractions of a political or cultural regime are substantiated or verified by the "incontestable reality" of selected physical bodies. The certainty of pain experienced by the victim or combatant seems to confer its quality of "incontestable reality" on that power which has brought the pain into being. However, it is precisely because "the reality of that power is so highly contestable, the regime so unstable," that it is necessary to inflict the pain in the first place.[48]

In antebellum America, the legally woundable African-American body serves as this locus of incontestable reality for the violent processes verifying the ideologies of slaveholding and white supremacy. The African-American body anchors, to borrow Scarry's concept, hostile American ideologies, and, for these reasons, it is problematic for the writers of slave narratives to represent, without reserve, African-American bodies in narrative form, bodies too long appropriated to substantiate the reality of antagonistic cultural regimes. In short, when representing African-American bodies, these writers must contradict what is being culturally represented. The *acts* of representation must gainsay *what* is being represented.

The fundamentally discursive nature of this state of affairs cannot be overstated. Indeed, the issue of mulatto bodies makes this circumstance eminently clear since they are, for cultural and legal purposes, read and disposed of as black regardless of their apparent bifurcated or "biracial" constitution. According to the logic of race, mulatto bodies should stand as compromised entities, entities different by nature from unadulterated black bodies. Nonetheless, just as the biological or genetic substantiation for popular notions of race remains ultimately unforthcoming—an argument elegantly summarized, for example, by Kwame Anthony Appiah in his study *In My Father's House: Africa in the Philosophy of Culture*—so too the cultural logic that should apply to mulatto bodies proves inconsistent.[49] If mulatto bodies are products of the union of black and white Americans, then it seems they should constitute a separate biological grouping, and, what is more, in a political regime where biological status is insistently translated into social status, they should be subject to legal and cultural conditions defined differently from those attendant to blackness. This, however, is not the case. For although the possession of a mulatto body carries its own peculiar dynamics (for example, some may be able to "pass" for white), the conditions of racial subordination reserved for mulattos—no matter how well these conditions may be dodged in particular circumstances—are identical to those reserved for unadulterated black bodies. This is to say, bodies, or biology, are never so much the issue as are the meanings assigned to them, the way in which they are read, the discursive universe in which they are placed.

It is fair to conclude, then, that just as does attention to or respect for literacy, attention to the body remains a preeminent point of focus in slave narratives. The body is concomitantly a term of presence and absence—as also are issues of literacy. The African-American body (a category made to subsume the mulatto body) marks a social presence but an absence of mind. Literacy marks the presence of the higher values of Euro-American civilization and an apparent absence of "meaningless" entrapment in the body. While negotiation of issues of literacy remains relatively uniform, the negotiation of representations of the African-American body is not nearly as stable. Literacy, even though it may have its dangers—as it does for Harriet Jacobs's Linda Brent, who must suffer both the oral and written entreaties of her licentious master—is a tool of empowerment to be acquired and skillfully employed. But, as a result of the vexed cultural significance of the African-American body for its possessors, representations of this body are not treated nearly so singularly or unequivocally. Each narrator struggles differently to determine how best to deal with the exigencies of representing her or his "embodiment" and the "embodiment" of other African Americans and, while the attempts are various, patterns do emerge. Four patterns are most perceptible: the body as intensive and extensive, the body in its relation to self-authorization, the body as a form of knowledge, and figurations of the master's body. These modes of representation might be classified, respectively, by the concepts: presence, erasure, transformation, and displacement.

Of the four categories, the first, the body as intensive and extensive—the body in its mode of narrative presence—returns one most clearly to issues concerning the dichotomy between literacy and the body—that is, the legislation and enforcement of a body/mind split. Henry Bibb provides in his narrative an excellent example:

> My clothing was stripped off and I was compelled to lie down on the ground with my face to the earth. Four stakes were driven in the ground, to which my hands and feet were tied. . . . Fifty lashes were laid on before stopping. I was then lectured with reference to my going to prayer meeting without his orders, and running away to escape flogging.
>
> While I suffered under this dreadful torture, I prayed, and wept and implored mercy at the hand of slavery, but found none. After I was marked from my neck to my heels, the Deacon took the gory lash, and said he thought there was a spot on my back yet where he could put in a few more.[50]

In this mode of representation the body is an entity imposed upon and, in its tortured or injured state, tellingly juxtaposed to the voice and language. The African-American body is voided of language, while the adversarial, torturing, or injuring slaveholder or overseer is most fully vocal. The African-American body (and individual) is defined by spectacular physical pain, a circumstance that, as a matter of course, "bring[s] about an immediate reversion to a state anterior to language, to the sounds and cries a human being makes before language is learned."[51] African Americans, at these moments in the narratives, appear most fully confined within the limits of their bodies, bodies transformed into entirely self-referential, unbearably discrete and intensive artifacts, violently denied the possibility of extending into the world the selves, the voices, the language, the minds that they house.[52] Even more than the withholding of adequate education, the spectacularly painful body renders the individual starkly illiterate; the obdurate materiality of "the body in pain" denies all other possibilities for the individual.

Narrative representations of the tortured or injured body are virtually ubiquitous in the texts of ex-slave narratives; however, Mary Prince's 1831 *The History of Mary Prince*, Henry Bibb's 1850 *Narrative of the Life and Adventures of Henry Bibb*, and Solomon Northup's 1853 *Twelve Years a Slave* might be understood as narratives in which this form of representing the body is paramount. It is important to note further that especially in the narratives of male narrators, the ultimate figure in this mode of representation is the adult female slave. The figure of the black woman in bodily distress is employed by male narrators to provide dramatic testimonies concerning the evils of slaveholding. Northup, for example, presents repeatedly to his reader Eliza, whose deterioration after separation from her children is read primarily through the text of her body; more usually, however, reference is made to the sexual persecution of female slaves, as in William Craft's opening pages of *Running a Thousand Miles for Freedom*. In short, in the texts of male narrators, impositions upon or violations of the African-American woman's body stand as the ultimate transgression of the U.S. social order. The body becomes the primary means of identifying the textual presences of African-American women so that, oddly enough, this representational insistence very often reinscribes the valorizations of a body/mind split within constructions of gender. The upshot is that within these texts struggling with the separation of body and mind as read in terms of race, the separation, while nonetheless challenged, is also reread in terms of gender. Underscoring this point, texts authored by African-American female ex-slaves rarely forward these images as the primary means of self-representation. Lucy Delaney, Jacobs, and Elizabeth Keckley provide important cases in point.

Douglass's account of the whipping of his Aunt Hester provides a well-known example of this transposition of the mind/body split that stands as a salient feature of male-authored texts. In an early incident of the autobiography, Aunt Hester is beaten for visiting a suitor she is forbidden by her master from seeing. Because she disobeys, Hester is beaten, a beating Douglass describes as "the blood-stained gate, the entrance to the hell of slavery, through which I was about to pass."[53] Hester is "stripped... from neck to waist, leaving her neck, shoulders, and back, entirely naked," then whipped until "warm, red blood (amid heart-rending shrieks from her, and horrid oaths from him) came dripping to the floor."[54] One might say that in this instance Douglass's literacy emerges as an analogue of the whip implementing Hester's subjugation in the first place, since his rendition of her physical torture reinstates the violence by which Hester is denied the possibility of extending into the world the self, the voice, the language, the mind her body houses. Douglass merely reproduces, for highly dramatic and rhetorical effect, the hostile "embodying" of Hester, rather than discursively challenging it as he does his own or even that of the murdered slave Demby, briefly introduced three chapters later. Prominently informing the narration of Demby's murder by the overseer is the sense of Demby as a martyr protesting the lack of the most meager rights one might extend to even reviled members of U.S. society. Rebelling against the savage treatment he is expected to endure as a matter of course, Demby is rendered by Douglass to symbolize an active, antiphonal, even if counterintuitive, stance to the discourses and physical practices of a white supremacist community. The treatment of Demby in Douglass's text suggests an alliance of body and mind never glimpsed in Hester's scene of torture; Hester's presence in the text is marked only by "her neck, shoulders, and back, entirely naked," "warm, red blood," and "heart-rending shrieks." In short, representations of the bodies of African-American women in the texts of male narrators reinscribe (in terms of gender) the dynamics these narrators would challenge (in terms of race): African-American women remain peculiarly voided of language, and their bodies are circulated in symbolic and textual systems meant precisely to challenge such "corporealization" on behalf of all African Americans. It is this contradictory figuration of African-American women that remains the centerpiece of the most common mode of representing African-American bodies in the narratives.

 The second category, the body in its relation to self-authorization, is perhaps best exemplified in the now classic pair of texts, Douglass's 1845 *Narrative of the Life of Frederick Douglass* and Jacobs's 1861 *Incidents in the Life of a Slave Girl*. In these texts the measure of the narrators' achieved will or self-authority bears a direct relation to the disposition of the body. In Douglass's *Narrative of the Life of Frederick Douglass*, this is evident in his repudiation of the body. For while important figures in his text are often vividly embodied, as is Aunt Hester, Douglass himself is increasingly disembodied. Douglass is careful to interrupt his narrative again and again in order to alert his reader to the emotional and intellectual presence shaping the tale of his formerly brutalized self.

He is careful to overshadow the rendition of himself as brutalized chattel with the rendition of himself as the shaping agent and intellect of the text. One might recall two highly rhetorical passages that disrupt the recollected narrative early in the text. After considering the often misunderstood slave songs, Douglass announces to his reader a tear making its way down his cheek as he writes at his desk, and, after describing the harsh winters he endured in Maryland without adequate clothing, he observes that the pen with which he writes might be laid in the cracks of his feet, cracks attesting to his frostbite and pain. In short, the reader is instructed that the former condition of his body is now self-consciously gauged by marks of sensibility and instruments of intellect. Equally, much later in the narrative, during Douglass's dramatic confrontation with Covey, close attention to the prose and imagery of the text reveals that Douglass's rendition of this crucial "turning-point in ... [his] career as a slave" is one in which his own bodily presence is not primarily or even predominantly at issue.[55] Rather, most fully embodied is Covey's would-be accomplice Hugh, who is "fairly sickened" by a kick dealt by Douglass, as well as Covey himself, who is left "puffing and blowing at a great rate" and from whom Douglass draws blood.[56] Indeed, insofar as it is highlighted in the scene, Douglass's presence is rendered in terms of the rekindling of "the few expiring embers of freedom" and the revival of "a sense of ... [his] own manhood."[57] In short, although Douglass's physical actions certainly do not become less important as the narrative progresses, this climactic episode underscores the manner in which narrative attention to the bodily presence of Douglass becomes less pronounced in deference to the establishment of what might be called an overshadowing presence of mind and spirit. Most importantly, to this end, when he refuses to provide the details of his successful escape to the North, Douglass denies the expected climax of his narrative in order to announce and display his mastery over his readers: whereas the narrative begins with his enumeration of all the information withheld from slaves by slaveholders, it concludes, in a highly dramatic and rhetorical reversal, with Douglass as master and withholder of important information. Douglass's body is at issue at the climax of the narrative only insofar as it is primarily absent, an absence that precisely marks his self-authorizing achievement. As his body is increasingly obscured in or removed from the text, Douglass's self-authorization is rendered more and more manifest.

In Jacobs's narrative the body does not disappear yet still functions as an important gauge of self-authorization. *Incidents in the Life of a Slave Girl* records circumstances very different from those faced by Douglass, and, in contrast, it is at the moments when the body of the narrator is most enduringly menaced and figures most prominently in the narrative that the narrator attains her greatest measure of authority. In order to escape the persecutions of her master, Flint, Brent hides in a garret in the roof of her grandmother's house. For her reader, she recounts the physical distresses of her seven-year tenure in the interstices of the house: "For weeks I was tormented by hundreds of little red insects, fine as a needle's point that pierced through my skin, and produced an intolerable burning.... The heat of my den was intense, for nothing but thin shingles protected me from the scorching summer's sun."[58] She writes further, "I suffered much more during the second winter.... My limbs were benumbed by inaction, and the cold filled them with cramp. I had a very painful sensation of coldness in my head; even my face and tongue stiffened and I lost the power of speech."[59] Nonetheless, just as Brent/Jacobs's "loophole of retreat" proves the site of her most graphically recounted bodily distress, so too it proves the site of her most effective manipulation of her adversaries. From her garret she manufactures false evidence of her presence in the North. She writes letters to Flint and to her grandmother that are carried North and mailed from there by "a trustworthy seafaring person"; she watches with great satisfaction as Flint is entirely duped and believes she has truly escaped to the North: "This was as good as a comedy to me."[60] At this point in the narrative, Jacobs controls her own situation, as she does at no other point in the text, as well as controlling those vying to impose hostile authority on her. These moments of self-authorization even surpass those gained later by an actual escape to the North, where she is forced, for example, to take an ambivalent stand toward a bill of sale that bears her name and where she is never fully in control of the activities of such benefactors as Lydia Maria Child or Harriet Beecher Stowe or of her own situation vis-à-vis these benefactors.[61] Perhaps most remarkably, as attested by numerous passages throughout the narrative, Jacobs can by no means be certain of the reactions of her readers to and from whom she alternately exposes and conceals herself. In *Incidents in the Life of a Slave Girl*, unlike Douglass's *Narrative of the Life of Frederick Douglass*, the greatest moment of self-authorization and the most graphic representations of the body coincide. Indeed, this episode that "was as good as a comedy" concludes on a note of self-assurance for the narrator marked by a new allowance "to leave my cell, sometimes, and exercise my limbs to prevent becoming a cripple."[62] Here the issues of self-authorization and the body seem inextricably linked.

The third pattern of representations, the body as a form of knowledge, strongly informs Lucy Delaney's *From the Darkness Cometh the Light*, written c. 1891, and William Grimes's 1855 *Life of William Grimes, the Runaway Slave*. Delaney's narrative is perhaps the first (and only) narrative in which the U.S.

courtroom figures centrally and is graphically rendered.⁶³ The courtroom scene of the text provides the climax, for Delaney's status as a free or enslaved black woman is determined in the courtroom, where the central legal issue involves establishing the biological relationship between Delaney and her mother (who was legally free but wrongly enslaved at the time of Delaney's birth). Insofar as bodies are paramount in this narrative, they are so as bearers of meaning and, in particular, legally ascertainable meaning. The African-American body is presented, above all, as *significant*, and the drama and dynamics of determining this significance are foregrounded: How does one go about reading, and what can be read as the significance of, an African-American body (or an African-American life)? Indeed, Delaney's suit for her freedom is precipitated by her unapologetic renunciation of the usual meanings assigned to African-American bodies—in this instance, that the particulars of menial labor are somehow innate to dark-skinned bodies. Without any instruction, she is placed in charge of her mistress's laundry, and, accordingly, placed in the waters of the Mississippi, the clothes grow "darker and darker, until they nearly approximated ... [her] own color."⁶⁴ Delaney resists her mistress's attempts to physically punish her, and these events lead to the climactic courtroom deliberations concerning her status as free or enslaved. Most often, in Delaney's narration of enslavement and emancipation, the body is not voided of language but becomes a central premise for or focus of language. Simply put, more than it is brutalized, the body is meaningful in this mode of representation; there are attempts, whether positive or negative, undertaken by many to make *sense* of the African-American body rather than to apparently remove it from *sense* (as in scenes of brutalization).

The final image of Grimes's text presents this notion with intense bitterness and rancor. After he declares his hope that he is prepared for death, Grimes writes: "If it were not for the stripes on my back which were made while I was a slave, I would leave my skin as a legacy to the government, desiring that it might be taken off and made into parchment, and then bind the constitution of glorious, happy, and free America. Let the skin of an American slave bind the charter of American liberty."⁶⁵ This series of images, even on the purely semantic level, is extremely complex. The two declarations given here confound one another to a significant extent. The first suggests that the scars of U.S. ideology lacerating his back render his skin inadequate to serve as parchment fastening or holding together the most prized rhetoric of the American republic; just as his abused skin belies American self-definition, its lacerated surface disqualifies his skin as an appropriate surface to touch and hold the physical printed word. Nevertheless, the second declaration calls abruptly for that incongruity or impossibility. There is no better parchment, Grimes seems to say, than the lacerated skin of an American slave to gird the nation's prized but hyperbolically false self-declaration and self-knowledge. The "binding" pact of the United States is rendered necessarily and profoundly unreadable when placed in proximity to the openly legible marks on his abused skin.

Indeed, the multiple valences of the verb *bind* register keenly the confusion of these sets of images, ranging provocatively between several possible meanings from "hold[ing] together or . . . form[ing] . . . into a single mass" to "bandag[ing]," "cover[ing] a wound with dressings and bandages," or "mak[ing] fast (any one) with bonds or fetters; depriv[ing] of personal liberty, mak[ing] a captive or prisoner," et cetera (*Oxford English Dictionary*). Concomitantly, it connotes the social wounds and disunion in fact characterizing the nation, social wounds that are literally legible on his skin, as well as a social cohesion represented ideally by the "constitution" that is its grammatical object. The distinction between parchment (a vessel or apparatus of literacy) and the African-American body is both upheld and collapsed by Grimes's declarations. The peroration turns on confusing the distinctions between literacy, technologies of literacy, and a hyperbolic corporeal opposite—African-American bodies. Grimes's African-American body is placed within the highest processes of literacy in the United States, and the mind/body distinction superintending U.S. race relations falters here, as the verb *to bind* vacillates under the pressures applied to it. According to this passage the African-American body bears important, even nationally devastating, knowledge. For there is inscribed in Grimes's text and skin alike the knowledge that the impact of literacy, or "*sets of techniques for communications and for decoding and reproducing written or printed materials*[,] . . . is determined by the manner in which human agency exploits it in a specific setting."[66] In the specific setting of antebellum America, literacy is exploited in the service of racial domination and mythologizing.

Figuration of the master's body, as might be expected, is the least prevalent of the four modes of representing the body in slave narratives. However, Mary Prince's *The History of Mary Prince, a West Indian Slave* and William and Ellen Craft's *Running a Thousand Miles for Freedom* exemplify this mode of representation. In Prince's narrative the peculiar crisis that seemingly overwhelms the many horrible and vivid images of injured African-American bodies is marked by her master's "ugly fashion of stripping himself quite naked, and ordering . . . [her] then to wash him in a tub of water. This was worse to me than all the licks."[67] The master's body enters the narrative not as an emblem of physical danger or distress but, it seems, as the embodiment of a mental state not to be endured. Besides the sexual persecution implicit in the episode, the act of washing this body rehearses with patent symbolism the extremes of subjugation and degradation implicit to New World slavery.

In the narrative detailing the escape of the Crafts, the master's body is crucial but also purely fictional. Ellen is disguised as an ailing Southern gentleman accompanied by her body servant who rides the railroad north. Ironically, here the master's body represents the increasing self-authority gained by the Crafts, as well as masking or erasing the dominant cultural meanings assigned to their own bodies. Their masquerade challenges the stability of bodies, identities, and emblems of mind by constructing the body that holds the most stable and revered of meanings in American culture and imagination. Whereas the black body is understood in the redundant terms of its own materiality, the white body is understood as referential, in other words as significant and meaningful. Since meaning implies both a syntax and an associational schema—a conjunctive arrangement of units or elements as well as a nonlinear integrity—the white body is eminently divisible in its situation beyond the redundant terms of its own materiality, and the final encounter of the Crafts' escape bears out this opposition between divisible white and indivisible black bodies.

When William is detained in Baltimore, the final major station before Pennsylvania, by "a full-blooded Yankee of the lower order," the Yankee instructs William that before he and Ellen can pass into free territory the disguised Ellen must be able to account for him as a rightfully owned slave.[68] The two of them, of course, know no one in Baltimore who can vouch for their master-slave relationship, and very quickly their seemingly insurmountable dilemma begins to "attract... the attention of the large number of bustling passengers" around them.[69] Their fellow passengers watch the unfolding dilemma and mutter their disapproval but, as William informs us, "not because they thought... [the Crafts] were slaves endeavoring to escape, but merely because they thought... [his] master was a slaveholder and invalid gentleman, and therefore [that] it was wrong to detain him."[70] That is, Ellen's disguised and bandaged "white" body provides an urgent narrative. Covering Ellen's seemingly weak eyes are "a pair of green spectacles."[71] Her face is "muffled in... poultices, &tc. [that] furnished a plausible excuse for avoiding general conversation."[72] Her hand is similarly bound. These body parts form a legible script much more comprehensible than verbal attestations concerning the relationship between Ellen and William. For in the same manner that all parts invoke or prompt expectations of a whole, the white body and its parts prompt similar expectations. The highlighted parts of Ellen's "white" body imply, then, an integrity of the white body, just as the white body itself implies the wholeness of transcendent logos, self-sufficient spirit. The white body, as understood in the set of social relations that grew out of the Enlightenment, possesses a motive power that leads elsewhere (as does a syntax), possesses an associational integrity that leads elsewhere (as does synchrony or system).

Thus, it is all too fitting that the white body literally inscribes the most unsettled and expectant moment of the narrative: "Just then the bell rang for the train to leave, and had it been the sudden shock of an earthquake it could not have given us a greater thrill. The sound of the bell caused every eye to flash and with apparent interest, and to be more steadily fixed upon us than before."[73] The escape turns, quite literally, on the turning of eyes on the white body. The white body, both metaphorically and literally in this instance, is never a space of entrapment. The railroad official, his own white body spectacularized in its proximity to Ellen's, takes this assumption for granted and resolves the tension. He "all at once thrust his fingers through his hair, and in a state of great agitation said, 'I really don't know what to do; I calculate it is all right.'"[74] In short, what the white body makes legible is in fact so legible that sometimes paper need not be wasted.

On the other hand, reference to one's own African-American body in "a culture that fiercely debate[s] the intellectual capacities of black people and, by implication, their basic humanity" proves a complex and equivocal undertaking.[75] These four categories—the body as intensive and extensive, the body in its relation to self-authorization, the body as a form of knowledge, and figurations of the master's body—account for the primary ways in which ex-slave narrators struggle with the exigencies of long-standing U.S. beliefs and customs positing that African-American bodies betoken a social presence curiously marked by a *visible* absence of mind. The body and mind, within this view, are taken to be radically separate in activity and, most especially, radically separate in value. Thus, as many scholars have fruitfully documented and considered, the curiosity of the black body writing itself remains a cultural event startling enough in itself. Yet perhaps even more noteworthy is the black subject knowingly scripting—by means of patterns of presence, erasure, transformation, and displacement—this startling cultural event. Both the event of the black body writing itself and its narrative configurations, as evinced in slave narratives, lead one to reconsider the compelling ways in which issues of literacy (as achievement and, even more, as prohibition) inevitably remain issues of the body.

NOTES

Chapter 4, "African-American Slave Narratives," was originally published in "Imagining a National Culture," special issue, *American Literary History* 7, no. 3 (autumn 1995): 415–42. Reprinted by permission of Oxford University Press.

1. Elaine Scarry, *The Body in Pain: The Making and Unmaking of the World* (New York: Oxford University Press, 1985), 22.

2. John Blassingame, introduction to *Slave Testimony: Two Centuries of Letters, Speeches, Interviews, and Autobiographies*, ed. John Blassingame (Baton Rouge: Louisiana State University Press, 1977), xvii.

3. Marion Wilson Starling's pioneering 1946 dissertation was not published until 1981 as *The Slave Narrative: Its Place in American History*. Other studies of African-American autobiography also preceded Foster's work; however, these texts do not deal exclusively with the slave narrative. For a rendition of the history of this criticism, see William Andrews, "African American Autobiography Criticism: Retrospect and Prospect," in *American Autobiography*, ed. Paul John Eakin (Madison: University of Wisconsin Press, 1991).

4. Dexter Fisher and Robert B. Stepto, eds., *Afro-American Literature: The Reconstruction of Instruction* (New York: MLA, 1979), 1.

5. Henry Louis Gates Jr., "Preface to Blackness: Text and Pretext," in Fisher and Stepto, *Afro-American Literature*, 54, 67.

6. Andrews, "African American Autobiography Criticism," 208.

7. Of the intricacies of defining cultural studies, Peter Brantlinger writes, " 'Cultural studies' has emerged from the current crises and contradictions of the humanities and social science disciplines not as a tightly coherent, unified movement with a fixed agenda, but as a loosely coherent group of tendencies, issues, and questions. The outcome partly of the theory and canon wars of the 1960s and 1970s, cultural studies does not reflect a single 'field,' theory, or methodology, but makes use of several—Marxism, feminism, deconstruction, psychoanalysis, ethnography." Peter Brantlinger, *Crusoe's Footsteps: Cultural Studies in Britain and America* (New York: Routledge, 1990), ix. See also Cary Nelson, Paula A. Treichler, and Lawrence Grossberg, "Cultural Studies: An Introduction," in *Cultural Studies*, ed. Lawrence Grossberg, Cary Nelson, and Paula A. Treichler (New York: Routledge, 1992), 1.

8. Gates, "Preface to Blackness," 54.

9. In the analysis to follow, the historical component of the convergence I see effected by the example of cultural studies is not as fully explored as the textual component. This historical component is more fully elaborated in the longer version of this study in which the racialized discourses of the slave narratives are contextualized in terms of the competing narratives of race offered by published statements of Southern slaveholders, advice codified for newly emancipated freedmen, and discourses of scientific racism dominant in the late nineteenth century. The emphasis of the particular remarks to follow is on strategies of power that confirm themselves most potently as strategies of seeing and, consequently, as strategies of knowing. In particular, the historical and textual object of sight is the African American body.

10. Robert B. Stepto, *From behind the Veil: A Study of Afro-American Narrative* (Urbana: University of Illinois Press, 1991), xv.

11. James Olney, "'I Was Born': Slave Narratives, Their Status as Autobiography and as Literature," *Callaloo* 20, no. 4 (1984): 53–54.

12. Henry Louis Gates Jr., *Figures in Black: Words, Signs, and the Racial Self* (New York: Oxford University Press, 1987), 24–25.

13. Valerie Smith, *Self-Discovery and Authority in Afro-American Narrative* (Cambridge, MA: Harvard University Press, 1987), 6.

14. Smith, *Self-Discovery and Authority*, 3.

15. Alexander Koyre, introduction to *Descartes: Philosophical Writings*, ed. Elizabeth Anscombe and Peter Thomas Geach (New York: Macmillan, 1971), xliii.

16. Cornelius writes, "The sweeping extent of these laws [restrictive literacy laws] has been exaggerated.... Laws banning the teaching of slaves were only in effect in four states for the entire period from the 1830s to 1865." Janet Duitsman Cornelius, *"When I Can Read My Title Clear": Literacy, Slavery, and Religion in the Antebellum South* (Columbia: University of South Carolina Press, 1991), 33.

17. Cornelius, *"When I Can Read My Title Clear,"* 66.

18. Cornelius, *"When I Can Read My Title Clear,"* 127.

19. Cornelius, *"When I Can Read My Title Clear,"* 16.

20. Richard Rorty, *Philosophy and the Mirror of Nature* (Princeton, NJ: Princeton University Press, 1979), 29.

21. Rorty, *Philosophy and the Mirror of Nature*, 22, 17.

22. Rorty, *Philosophy and the Mirror of Nature*, 28–29.

23. Rorty, *Philosophy and the Mirror of Nature*, 29.

24. Rorty, *Philosophy and the Mirror of Nature*, 30.

25. The fact that this condition persists today is easily and overwhelmingly confirmed by even cursory consideration of the urban "centers" of major American metropolises.

26. Solomon Northup, *Twelve Years a Slave*, ed. Sue Eakin and Joseph Logsdon (1968; reprint, Baton Rouge: Louisiana State University Press, 1990), 25.

27. Henry Bibb, *Narrative of the Life and Adventures of Henry Bibb, an American Slave* (Salem, NH: Ayer, 1990), 13; William Grimes, *Life of William Grimes, the Runaway Slave: Brought Down to the Present Time*, in *Five Black Lives: The Autobiographies of Venture Smith, James Mars, William Grimes, the Rev. G. W. Offley, and James L. Smith*, ed. Arna Bontemps (Middletown, CT: Wesleyan University Press, 1971), 62; Frederick Douglass, *Narrative of the Life of Frederick Douglass, an American Slave*, ed. Benjamin Quarles (Cambridge, MA: Harvard-Belknap, 1960), 23.

28. Quoted in John Blassingame, ed., *Slave Testimony: Two Centuries of Letters, Speeches, Interviews, and Autobiographies* (Baton Rouge: Louisiana State University Press, 1977), 409.

29. Michael Ryan, *Marxism and Deconstruction: A Critical Articulation* (Baltimore: Johns Hopkins University Press, 1982), 2.

30. Catherine Sheldrick Ross, "Metaphors of Reading," *Journal of Library History, Philosophy and Comparative Librarianship* 22 (1987): 150–54, 155.

31. Ross, "Metaphors of Reading," 156.

32. Michael Ryan, *Marxism and Deconstruction: A Critical Articulation* (Baltimore: Johns Hopkins University Press, 1982), 22.

33. Ross, "Metaphors of Reading," 150, 160.

34. Karen Sánchez-Eppler, "Bodily Bonds: The Intersecting Rhetorics of Feminism and Abolition," in *The Culture of Sentiment: Race, Gender, and Sentimentality in Nineteenth-Century America*, ed. Shirley Samuels (New York: Oxford University Press, 1992), 100.

35. Sánchez-Eppler, "Bodily Bonds," 99–100.

36. M. H. Abrams, *A Glossary of Literary Terms*, 6th ed. (Fort Worth, TX: Harcourt Brace Jovanovich College, 1993), 190.

37. Abrams, *A Glossary of Literary Terms*, 190.

38. Janet Todd, *Sensibility: An Introduction* (New York: Methuen, 1986), 4, emphasis added.

39. Elaine Scarry, *The Body in Pain: The Making and Unmaking of the World* (New York: Oxford University Press, 1985), 14.

40. Scarry, *The Body in Pain*, 62.

41. Scarry, *The Body in Pain*, 14; Karen Halttunen, *Confidence Men and Painted Women: A Study of Middle-Class Culture in America, 1830–1870* (New Haven, CT: Yale University Press, 1982).

42. James L. Smith, *Autobiography of James L. Smith*, in Bontemps, *Five Black Lives*, 152.

43. Smith, *Autobiography of James L. Smith*, 153.

44. Smith, *Autobiography of James L. Smith*, 153.

45. Smith, *Autobiography of James L. Smith*, 153.

46. Scarry, *The Body in Pain*, 4.

47. Scarry, *The Body in Pain*, 12.

48. Scarry, *The Body in Pain*, 27.

49. Kwame Anthony Appiah, *In My Father's House: Africa in the Philosophy of Culture* (New York: Oxford University Press, 1992), 35–37.

50. Bibb, *Narrative of the Life and Adventures of Henry Bibb*, 132.

51. Scarry, *The Body in Pain*, 4.

52. A similar claim can be made concerning the inevitable silence following such anguished cries: "Only in silence do the edges of the self become coterminous with the edges of the body it will die with" (Scarry, *The Body in Pain*, 33).

53. Douglass, *Narrative of the Life of Frederick Douglass*, 28.

54. Douglass, *Narrative of the Life of Frederick Douglass*, 29, 30.

55. Douglass, *Narrative of the Life of Frederick Douglass*, 104.

56. Douglass, *Narrative of the Life of Frederick Douglass*, 103, 104.

57. Douglass, *Narrative of the Life of Frederick Douglass*, 104.

58. Harriet A. Jacobs, *Incidents in the Life of a Slave Girl: Written by Herself*, ed. Jean Fagan Yellin (Cambridge, MA: Harvard University Press, 1987), 115–16.

59. Jacobs, *Incidents in the Life of a Slave Girl*, 122.

60. Jacobs, *Incidents in the Life of a Slave Girl*, 128, 130.

61. Jean Fagan Yellin, introduction to Jacobs, *Incidents in the Life of a Slave Girl*, xiii–xxxiv; Jean Fagan Yellin, "Texts and Contexts of Harriet Jacobs' *Incidents in the Life of a Slave Girl: Written by Herself*," in *The Slave Narratives*, ed. Charles T. Davis and Henry Louis Gates Jr. (New York: Oxford University Press, 1985), 262–82.

62. Jacobs, *Incidents in the Life of a Slave Girl*, 132.

63. For an extended reading of Delaney's courtroom scene, see Lindon Barrett, "Self-Knowledge, Law, and African-American Autobiography: Lucy Delaney's *From the Darkness Cometh the Light*," chapter 6, this volume.

64. Lucy A. Delaney, *From the Darkness Cometh the Light: Or, Struggles for Freedom*, in *Six Women's Slave Narratives*, ed. Henry Louis Gates Jr., Schomburg Library of Nineteenth-Century Black Women Writers 2 (New York: Oxford University Press, 1988), 25.

65. Grimes, *Life of William Grimes*, 120.

66. Harvey J. Graff, *The Legacies of Literacy: Continuities and Contradictions in Western Culture and Society* (Bloomington: Indiana University Press, 1986), 4.

67. Mary Prince, *The History of Mary Prince, a West Indian Slave*, in Gates, *Six Women's Slave Narratives*, 13.

68. William Craft and Ellen Craft, *Running a Thousand Miles for Freedom*, in *Great Slave Narratives*, ed. Arna Bontemps (Boston: Beacon, 1969), 308.

69. Craft and Craft, *Running a Thousand Miles for Freedom*, 309.

70. Craft and Craft, *Running a Thousand Miles for Freedom*, 310.

71. Craft and Craft, *Running a Thousand Miles for Freedom*, 289.

72. Craft and Craft, *Running a Thousand Miles for Freedom*, 290.

73. Craft and Craft, *Running a Thousand Miles for Freedom*, 31.

74. Craft and Craft, *Running a Thousand Miles for Freedom*, 310.

75. Frances Smith Foster, *Written by Herself: Literary Production by African American Women, 1746–1892* (Bloomington: Indiana University Press, 1993), 32.

| CH5

Hand-Writing: Legibility and the White Body
in *Running a Thousand Miles for Freedom* (1997)

The African American body is a vexed artifact, and my purpose here is to pursue the implications of this vexation as it bears on the genre of slave narratives, in particular, on William Craft's 1860 *Running a Thousand Miles for Freedom; or, The Escape of William and Ellen Craft from Slavery*. Since the vexed African American body proves to be the crucial element underwriting the social reality of both free and enslaved African Americans in the United States, it seems to me unsurprising that it also underwrites a central textual dilemma for ex-slave narrators. This dilemma derives from the overwhelming singularity of what the African American body is understood to mean, even, as I will argue, as it is placed in a position outside of signification. Given that African American bodies are understood in terms of a "fleshliness" that overdetermines all other possible aspects of their identity, the dynamics of composing slave narratives might be formulated as follows: In giving an account of slavery and "themselves," the paramount task of ex-slave narrators is to reproduce the experiences and trials of a "body"—their own. In order to authenticate themselves as African Americans, these narrators must highlight the primary terms by which African American identity is construed—the body and the life of the body. Nevertheless, because the claims these narrators are making on the government and culture of the United States are based on denunciations of an enforced and spurious confinement to a life merely of the body, to an existence as obdurate materiality, these narrators must not only recover their bodies within their narratives but also, more importantly, remove their bodies from these narratives. This task is accomplished in *Running a Thousand Miles for Freedom* by supplanting the attention usually given to the black body with a focus on the white body. This move constitutes an exceptional turn in slave narratives and accounts for a radical revision of the "scene of writing" so often central to slave narratives. The coincident prioritizing of the white body and revision of the "scene of writing" is not merely arbitrary, however, for what the Crafts underscore in their unusual escape from slavery is the manner in which the white body attains its privilege by seeming to replicate the dynamics, the functioning, of the symbolic itself.

The "scene of writing" is a phrase borrowed from Jacques Derrida's famous deconstructive reproof of Jacques Lacan's reading of Poe's *The Purloined Letter*, in which Derrida claims that Lacan fails to consider the peculiar condition of inscription or discourse itself.[1] What I am calling the "scene of writing" in slave narratives is the scene to which many critics of the narratives are again and again drawn, the scene in which narrators either recount the difficulties faced in becoming literate, identify literacy as a necessary instrument of social power, or demonstrate newly acquired powers directly attributable to the achievement of literacy. Important criticism on slave narratives theorizes both the liberating and confining aspects of the literacy highlighted in these scenes. One insight widely circulated in this criticism is the notion that the realm of textuality often proves as hostile and difficult for ex-slave narrators as the realm of their social and physical confinement. Robert Stepto, in *From behind the Veil*, schematizes a generic struggle of ex-slave narrators to wrest authorial control of the text from the competing voices of authenticating documents, intrusive prefaces, editors, amanuenses, and the like.[2] Frances Foster claims that "though ostensibly individual life stories, these narratives created a protagonist who was not an individual but a type."[3] James Olney counterposes notions of autobiography as a "unique tale, uniquely told, of a unique life" with the overwhelmingly formulaic nature of the narratives, a formula overseen by and most useful to an abolitionist movement interested primarily in documenting "slavery as it is." He observes that these narrators, although provided access to the power of the written word, are "denied access, by the very nature of [their] venture, from the configurational dimension of narrative."[4] Laura Tanner, pointing out discursive and rhetorical ruptures in Harriet Jacobs's *Incidents in the Life of a Slave Girl*, argues that ex-slave narrators create texts divided between being "historical evidence worthy of use in a political argument" and individual "effort(s) to remain true to . . . [a] unique history and consciousness."[5] Importantly, Valerie Smith, in the introduction to *Self-Discovery and Authority in Afro-American Narrative*, constructs the issue in terms of a suspicion of literacy without which one risks "paying homage to the structures of discourse that so often contributed to the [black] writer's oppression."[6] The following analysis of *Running a Thousand Miles for Freedom* aims to contribute to this criticism by illuminating the relation of literacy and its problematics to what might be seen as their vexed opposite, the black body, a body purportedly "outside rightful participation in *logos*, whether understood as reason and its expression in speech or as divine spirit."[7]

The reflections of Thomas Jefferson on the meaning of African American bodies in *Notes on the State of Virginia*, written in the inaugural period of the U.S. republic, provide an always useful gloss. Jefferson proposes that "in general, their [African Americans'] existence appears to participate more of sensation than reflection. To this must be ascribed their disposition to sleep when abstracted from their diversions, and unemployed in labour. An animal whose body is at rest, and who does not reflect, must be disposed to sleep of course." These are not merely casual musings on the part of Jefferson but part of his central argument against "incorporating the blacks into the state." These conclusions, along with his beliefs concerning "the foundation of a greater or lesser share of beauty between the two races," form his justification for continued African enslavement.[8] "The Negro," an 1858 article by Georgia physician John S. Wilson, both underscores and elaborates Jefferson's conclusions. Wilson's description of "the [negro's] *anatomical peculiarity* . . . the wooly head, the black skin, the shorter thicker muscles, and longer sinews, with the absence of that softness of outline, and that symmetry which are generally found in the physical structure of the other races" attests to the nineteenth-century vision of the lower and overwhelmingly corporeal status of African American life.[9] Wilson continues: "Everybody knows that negroes are deficient in reason, judgment and forecast—that they are improvident, and thoughtless of the future, and contented and happy in the enjoyment of the mere animal pleasures of the present moment. If negroes can have plenty to eat and to wear, if they can freely indulge their amourous animal propensities, and then if to these are added a liberal allowance of whiskey and tobacco, they are indeed supremely blessed, and they sigh for no higher or brighter state of existence."[10] In sum, the "ontological" situation of African Americans in these accounts is a bodily one. African American bodies signify an obdurate materiality that is singular, unrelenting, and, above all, abundantly recognizable.

To put the issue in terms of the mind/body split so central to post-Enlightenment Western thought, the African American body signifies an existence entirely or virtually within the bodily half of the antithesis. It signifies a supposed remove from privileged mindfulness and an entrapment in the mindlessness of corporeality. Paradoxically, the bodies ex-slave narrators are required to reproduce *through* language are the very marks of their remove *from* language and the life of the mind. The African American body (the darknesses of our skins, the textures of our hair, the shapes of our noses, cheekbones, and buttocks) becomes the emblem through which notions of race are conflated with notions of sense and sensibility. Our bodies become marks of our exclusion from a privileged presence of mind, a presence of mind diacritically opposed to "the most contracted of spaces, the small circle of living matter."[11] For the "enlightened" Western mind, no better justification for slavery or obfuscation of its economic motives can be found than one *visibly* grounded in nature and the "natural" order. Given the *visible* "certainty" of this particular accounting, Western "reason," "rationalism," and "enlightenment" sanction an oppressive disposition of African Americans in the "New World." Reason, rationalism, and enlightenment sanction a hostility toward African Americans endemic to the U.S. social, political, and economic order. The black body stands as the point of "certainty" underwriting New World hostility; as a result, ex-slave narrators are faced with the task of revising the meaning given African American bodies. They must reject the hostile terms of absolute corporeality and also refigure and represent white bodies.

There are, it seems to me, four principal ways in which ex-slave narrators undertake this task, four principal patterns by which bodies are represented in slave narratives: the body as intensive and extensive object, the body in its relation to self-authorization, the body as a form of knowledge, and, finally, figurations of the master's body. These patterns might be glossed, respectively, by the concepts presence, erasure, transformation, and displacement.[12] The least common and perhaps most intriguing of these is the final pattern, which mediates representations of the black body with representations of the white body. In addition to *Running a Thousand Miles for Freedom*, *The History of Mary Prince* (1831), and Elizabeth Keckley's *Behind the Scenes; or, Thirty Years a Slave, and Four Years in the White House* (1868) provide notable examples of this type of representation. Although *The History of Mary Prince* is in large part a litany of the bodily injuries and abuses endured by Prince and others with whom she is enslaved (and, hence, fulfills the imperative to reproduce in the slave narrative the black body and its trials), its catalogue of injuries is pointedly interrupted by Prince's description of her master's "ugly fashion of stripping himself quite naked, and ordering [her] then to wash him in a tub of water." Prince remarks that "this was worse to me than all the licks," and she recounts her resistance to his demands and its consequences.[13] This appearance of the white body marks perhaps her greatest trauma and certainly her greatest moment of resistance to this point. Her rebellion includes both physical resistance and the temporary removal of herself from her master's home.

In the early moments of *Behind the Scenes*, Elizabeth Keckley also shifts attention from the black body to sustained representations of the white body. Only briefly, in the first three of fifteen chapters, does Keckley recount her own physical abuse. In her later occupation as a dressmaker in Washington, in particular as dressmaker to Mrs. Lincoln, she is able to present images of white bodies at length; these images, broached through the synecdoche of dress and fashion, define her text much more fully than images of black bodies. Far more sustained than the images in *The History of Mary Prince*, Keckley's representations of the white body are also much more subtle.

But William Craft's *Running a Thousand Miles for Freedom* provides the most extensive narrative treatment and most blatant narrative privileging of the white body. For, while Craft's title evokes the image of a laboring black body, and hence greatly emphasizes its physicality, this image turns out to be misleading. Rather than immediately presenting the reader with descriptions of the conditions and trials of bodies designated as African American, the narrative begins and resolves itself by rehearsing the sometimes insurmountable difficulties of distinguishing white from black bodies. By the second page of the narrative, William Craft announces, "I have myself conversed with several slaves who told me their parents were white and free; but that they were stolen away from them and sold when quite young."[14] The opening ploy of the narrative is to point out that under racial rubrics bodies are indeterminate texts; this indeterminacy is particularized in the body of Salomé Muller, a German child who is kidnapped and enslaved for some twenty-five years. Craft writes that "there was no trace of African descent in any feature of Salomé Muller. She had long, straight, black hair, hazel eyes, thin lips, and a Roman nose."[15] The body of Salomé Muller, like those of African Americans of mixed heritage, is read in terms of the unambiguous legal binarism of black and white—unambiguous, that is, until in a court of law the midwife who assisted at Salomé's birth interprets her body and its peculiar marks in terms of a personal and family history that dismisses the reading that would make her a slave.

This opening treatise on the ambiguities of bodies, in particular of the body of Salomé Muller, underscores not simply the arbitrariness of constructions underlying designations of black and white but also, much more importantly, the manner in which these constructions attempt to exclude bodies within one category from signification altogether. This move frees bodies within the other category to be read in terms of multiplicity, plurality, and difference, which is to say, in the realm of signification. As we have been instructed by Saussurian linguistics and post-structuralist thought, multiplicity, plurality, and difference are the conditions that make possible significance, signification, language, meaning. Saussure, in his pioneering investigations of the synchronic dimensions of linguistics, argues that the "content [of a linguistic unit] is really fixed only by the concurrence of everything that exists outside it. Being part of a system, it is endowed not only with a signification but also and especially with a value, and this is something quite different."[16] What this means, he tells us, is that

> in language there are only differences. Even more important: a difference generally implies positive terms between which the difference is set up; but in language there are only differences *without positive terms*. Whether we take the signified or the signifier, language has neither ideas nor sounds that existed before the linguistic system. The ideal or phonic substance that a sign contains is of less importance than the other signs that surround it. Proof of this is that the value of a term may be modified without either its meaning or its sound being affected, solely because a neighboring term has been modified.[17]

This insight is recapitulated in Jacques Derrida's deconstructive philosophy. Derrida, in a 1968 interview with Julia Kristeva, stated that "the play of differences supposes, in effect, syntheses and referrals which forbid at any moment, or in any sense, that a simple element be *present* in and of itself, referring only to itself. Whether in the order of spoken or written discourse, no element can function as a sign without referring to another element which itself is not simply present."[18] Signs, as we have come to understand them, are defined necessarily and only by their meaningful referral to something other than themselves. In the words of theorist Michael Ryan in *Marxism and Deconstruction*, the "being" of signs always "lies elsewhere (because a sign is always a sign of something else; it cannot not refer to something other). Its 'being' is predicated upon reference."[19] Whiteness as defined by U.S. cultural logic is, within these terms, coterminous with nonidentity, displacement, and self-differentiation, the markers of signification.

It is crucial to see that Craft's narration of Salomé Muller's predicament and peculiar emancipation outlines the manner in which her body is transformed from a mere location of meaning (a hostile meaning, at that) to a *sign* of meaning—a condition, as it turns out, synonymous with whiteness. To put the point more bluntly, this anecdote (and the Crafts' subsequent escape from slavery) speaks not only to the "special" circumstances of mulattos or bodies ambiguously marked in terms of race but also to the circumstances of bodies that are unmistakably African American and those believed to be unmistakably white. Beyond the possibility of "passing" available to light-skinned African American slaves, *Running a Thousand Miles for Freedom* illuminates the field or grid of cultural logic by means of which the binary opposition of black and white bodies is instantiated. Above all, the dynamics of passing concerns the testing, interrogating, and subverting of what Amy Robinson provocatively calls "the manifest truth of melanin," and although *Running a Thousand Miles for Freedom* certainly lends itself to such a discussion, that is not what this analysis pursues.[20] The goal here is not to provide an explication of how passing works, or to pursue questions such as how the happenstance of Ellen Craft's light skin and its centrality to the escape might speak to the way dark-skinned black bodies may or may not elude the "corporeality" of blackness; I aim instead to outline the systematic cultural topography that provides highly valenced locations for blackness and whiteness, locations open to being undermined in a number of ways, as the narrative and Ellen's racially ambiguous appearance suggest.

One begins to recognize, beyond the dynamics and mechanism of passing, that the condition of nonsignification from which the body of Salomé Muller is released is the meaninglessness of complete, entirely closed self-referentiality, understood to be the usual condition of African American bodies. The story of Salomé Muller illustrates the manner in which African American bodies are taken as signs of nothing beyond themselves—signs of the very failure of meaning—for these bodies are able to signify, in their obdurate physicality, only a state of obdurate physicality. Conversely, the anecdote also illustrates the manner in which white bodies are taken, as a matter of course, to be signs of matters beyond "the most contracted of spaces, the small circle of living matter." Only when Muller's body is grafted to alternative narratives—that is to say, when it is read in multiple ways that include family histories—is her membership in the realm of whiteness confirmed and made available to her. Whiteness, one comes to understand, amounts to a state in which more than mere self-reference is possible. Only when "the existence of certain marks upon [Muller's] body" are read in relation to a narrative other than mere physical embodiment is her release secured.[21] The freedom she gains with her physical emancipation is the license for her body to be recognized as significant in terms other than its physicality.

This turn of events foreshadows and instructs the reader about the nature of the Crafts' later escape, for the lightness of Ellen's complexion makes their escape possible. With Ellen disguised as a white slaveholder and William masquerading as her body servant, the two take public transportation, "a combination of boat, trains, and coaches," from Georgia to freedom in Philadelphia and eventually Boston.[22] They escape by constructing Ellen's racially ambiguous body as white, a body to be read within the terms of relationality and differentiality, a body—to borrow a phrase from Derrida—"foreign to the self-presence of the living present."[23] For signs and bodies that would be otherwise understood as fully "self-present" in "the living present" repeat, by definition, nothing but themselves, so that, in effect, they are meaningless. The central act of the Crafts' escape is the removal of what is designated as an African American body from this position of meaninglessness to the condition of meaning and signification—one in which there exists no "absolute proximity of the signifier to the signified."[24] In *Bodies That Matter*, Judith Butler writes that the abject designates "precisely those 'unlivable' and 'uninhabitable' zones of social life which are nevertheless densely populated by those who do not enjoy the status of the subject, but whose living under the sign of the 'uninhabitable' is required to circumscribe the domain of the subject."[25] Given this definition of the abject, the narrative of the Crafts' escape demonstrates the way in which the form of abjection reserved for African Americans is tied to the conditions of significance and meaninglessness.

Scenes of writing and the signifying power of texts are basic even to the conceptualization of the escape. With forethought, the Crafts choose the Christmas holidays for their escape because slaveholders often presented favorite slaves with passes allowing them to be absent for several days. These passes, the Crafts know, grant them several days' head start over potential pursuers. When they secure passes, the Crafts share an early but fleeting moment of triumph. "On reaching my wife's cottage she handed me her pass," William Craft writes, "and I showed mine, but at that time neither of us were able to read them."[26] One might say, accordingly, that this exchange, in which instruments of literacy are passed vacantly back and forth, is largely meaningless; it represents in a single, compelling image the Crafts' seeming exile to a mindlessness where only the mechanics of physicality obtain, to an existence of mere bodily gesture.

The pantomime derives (as the narrative immediately points out) from the legally enforced conflation of race and literacy: "It is not only unlawful for slaves to be taught to read, but in some of the States there are heavy penalties attached, such as fines and imprisonment, which will be vigorously enforced upon anyone who is humane enough to violate the so-called law."[27] This conflation undisguisedly attempts to legislate the obdurate materiality of African American bodies. For, if literacy is the most manifest formalization of the life of the mind, if it provides testimony of the mind's ability to extend itself beyond the constricted limits and conditions of the body, then to restrict African Americans to lives without literacy is to immure them in bodily existences having little or nothing to do with the life of the mind. It is to attempt to create a social reality in which the physicality of African American bodies is taken as the entire measure of their significance. Attaining literacy thus becomes equivalent to extending oneself beyond the condition and geography of the body. Hence, the importance of scenes of writing in many slave narratives and the priority given these scenes in the work of many critical commentators. Dramatizing the "barriers raised against slave literacy and the overwhelming difficulties encountered in learning to read and write," the scene of writing presents either an initial move toward or the attainment of literacy.[28]

An odd scene in *Running a Thousand Miles for Freedom*, however, provides what seems the inverse of the usual scene of writing. Rather than acknowledging the Crafts' potential entry into literacy, it strictly recapitulates their disbarment. At best, it continues the pantomime of literacy with which it begins. Rather than provide the circumstances for them to begin manipulating literacy, the scene recounts the moment at which they most profoundly recognize and deftly manipulate their illiteracy. Whereas formerly their plan had covered only the contingencies of complexion and wardrobe, the Crafts are here prompted to a new recognition of the dynamics of materially representing the white body. Yet, even as this episode complicates their understanding of their dilemma, they realize that their only certain resources for resolving their predicament are their bodies: "At first, we were highly delighted at the idea of having gained permission to be absent for a few days; but when the thought flashed across my wife's mind that it was customary for travellers to register their names in the visitors' book at hotels, as well as in the clearance or Custom House book at Charleston, South Carolina—it made our spirits droop within us."[29] They realize that they must overcome both the fact and—more importantly—the *meaning* of Ellen's illiteracy. Put differently, they discover that in order to construct or materially represent a white body, they must somehow represent the power to sign understood to be inherent in the white body. Light or racially ambiguous skin is ultimately insufficient as an "ontological" marker of whiteness. The Crafts must display or illustrate, despite their own illiteracy, the fact that Ellen's "white" body does not lack the condition of the sign and literacy. William writes: "So, while sitting in our little room upon the verge of despair, all at once my wife raised her head, and with a smile upon her face, which was a moment before bathed in tears, said, 'I think I can make a poultice and bind up my right hand in a sling, and with propriety ask the officers to register my name for me.' "[30] Their solution is to underscore what would amount to the betraying illegibility of Ellen's handwriting were she to attempt to write. They highlight, in sum, the very incapacity that would render them suspect. Yet concomitantly, and more importantly, their solution invokes the capacity of the white body to be read multiply, to be read in relation to other terms and narratives. Simply put, Ellen's "illegible" hand will be read not as a sign of illiteracy but as a sign of illness that will earn her credibility and sympathy. By calling attention to "the small circle of living matter" of her fraudulent white body, the Crafts also knowingly call upon the capacity of this white body to be understood within the play of "differential structures from which [meaning, representation, and, indeed, writing] spring."[31] The Crafts recognize that the inherent meaningfulness of white bodies calls for and depends upon their disappearance, their disappearance in deference to their legibility, their ability stand in for terms and narratives that do not inhere in their physical presence. The Crafts act upon the knowledge that the condition of the white body is synonymous with the condition of signification, a condition in which "language as such is already constituted by the very distances and differences it seeks to overcome. To mean, in other words, is automatically *not* to be."[32] The white body, in effect, refers to narratives whose very distance and difference provide the primary marks of its whiteness. The self-difference of the white body thus proves its ultimate self-evidence. Understanding that the meaning and privilege of white bodies resides in their ability to disappear meaningfully, the Crafts deploy the fact that white bodies never signify foremost their own materiality, even in a state that prioritizes attention to that materiality.

Joy S. Kasson's "Narrative of the Female Body: *The Greek Slave*," an essay on the nineteenth-century American sculptor Hiram Powers, a contemporary of the Crafts, underscores this point. Powers was the creator of a famous statue of "a nude [white] woman in chains" that was "the first American sculpture to receive national and international acclaim." Kasson points out that in order to ensure the success of the sculpture in the United States, Powers "carefully established a narrative context that allowed audiences to subdue the discomfort that the subject might have otherwise provided." She documents that "when Powers sent *The Greek Slave* on tour of American cities in 1847, he made sure the sculpture was accompanied by texts that would instruct and direct the viewers' gaze." This peculiar episode in American cultural history suggests that Powers engineered his success by playing upon the ease and inevitability with which the white body routinely disappears in deference to narratives it either generates or represents. In an enterprise that can be seen as both analogous and opposed to that of the Crafts, Powers is able to negotiate "the symbolic significance of the [white] female body." Powers profits, like the Crafts, by training attention on the white body; his sculpture of the nude white female body masks that nudity with what is understood here as the racialized ability of the white body to "direct [its] viewers' gaze" to a narrative with which it is taken as synonymous. Certainly gender is not the only element responsible for the phenomenally successful textualization of the nude; as Kasson insightfully acknowledges, "much of [the statue's] audience was apparently oblivious to the ironies of driving past American slave marts to shed tears over the fate of the white marble statue"—slave marts in which the narratives employed to contextualize the statue were repeatedly played out in reality but unrecognized by most white Americans. That is, in this American cultural context, fictionalized white female bodies more readily bear a relation to narrative and the condition of signification than actual black female bodies, and this irony was not completely lost on shrewd political commentators of the time, as Kasson points out: "When *The Greek Slave* was displayed at the Crystal Palace exhibition in 1851, the British magazine *Punch* published an engraving showing a black woman chained to a pedestal, with the caption: 'The Virginian Slave.' Intended as a companion to Powers's 'Greek Slave.'"[33] What this political parody underscores is the vast discrepancy that existed between (white) representational and (black) actual human bodies within the cultural context of the sculpture.

Thus, the bandaging of Ellen's hand is anything but an arbitrary element of the Crafts' escape. Rather, as a substitute for literacy, it is the indispensable correlate to Ellen's racially ambiguous skin. In this context it is the ultimate sign of whiteness. It articulates or supplements a literacy that is only for the moment glaringly absent. Instead of being read within the terms of African American meaninglessness and "animality," the apparently injured hand betokens only a temporary "symbolic incapacity." In its meaningfulness and privilege, the white body—in addition to always standing in for, articulating, representing, or supplementing that which is not present—marks the realm of culture that is valued over nature. In his extended reading of Rousseau's essay on the origin of languages, Derrida explicates the distinction between nature and culture, the animal and the human, as it bears on the condition and process of signification:

> Animal language—and animality in general—represents [in Rousseau] the still living myth of fixity, of symbolic incapacity, of nonsupplementarity. If we consider the *concept* of animality not in its content of understanding or misunderstanding but in its specific *function*, we shall see that it must locate a moment of *life* which knows nothing of symbol, substitution, lack and supplementary addition, etc.—everything, in fact whose appearance and play I wish to describe here. A life that has not yet

broached the play of supplementarity and which at the same time has not yet let itself be violated by it: a life without differance and without articulation.[34]

The Crafts correctly assume that the act of calling attention to Ellen's hand—and, thereby, her inability to write—will not signal the fixity of animal language supposedly underwriting the enforced illiteracy of African American bodies; it will signal instead "the progressiveness of human languages [which] is not dependent on any one organ, any one sense, [not] to be found in either the visible or the audible order."[35] The Crafts' ruse creates the illusion that Ellen's inability to write does not reflect a location purely within nature—the "animality" of dark-skinned bodies—but rather a location within the truly human and the truly symbolic, a location within *logos*.

Needless to say, there are several socially explosive ironies in the Crafts' refiguring of African American bodies within the symbolic, within the condition of language. The first involves the inevitability of linguistic or symbolic free play, the impossibility of completely controlling the chain of supplementarity characterizing language and, hence, the impossibility of foreclosing completely certain possibilities of representation. Just as Ellen's bandaged hand stands in for an absent literacy, so too it stands in for a legally absent whiteness and a legally absent emancipation. If one accepts the notion that language, representation, and experience inhere in the attempt to provide a presentation of the nonpresent, then the Crafts display keen insight into the conditions, dynamics, and ambiguities of language. They manipulate for their own ends the image of Ellen's hand as "the mark of the absence of a presence, an always already absent present, of the lack at the origin that is the condition of thought and experience."[36] They manipulate for their own ends, one might say, the Derridean or deconstructive "trace" which, by definition, "call[s] attention to the absence of univocal meaning, truth, or origin" attributable to the incommensurability or tension between presence and absence.[37]

Moreover, one begins to understand the extent to which the Crafts' scheme amounts to a powerful expression of mind through the materiality of the body. One recognizes the extent to which literacy is a strikingly inadequate measure of the life and acuity of the mind. The mind/body split proves specious, as does its overdetermining role in the estimation of peoples designated black and white. The Crafts employ the resources at their disposal (representations of bodily materiality) to effect expressions of mind, which, as African Americans, they supposedly do not possess. Illiteracy, which might be taken for mental impairment, is cleverly transformed into feigned physical impairment and thus—ironically—

becomes the singular mark of their noteworthy and ingenious participation in the life of the mind.

The ingenuity is equally notable in the revisionary scene of writing it produces, for this scene foregoes the attainment and circumvents the power of literacy. As already suggested, the scene never fully recovers or departs from the opening pantomime of literacy. The apparent injury to Ellen's hand would render any writing produced by it ineffectual as a means of putatively but definitively distinguishing who is black and white, enslaved and free, in the U.S. republic. The issue of "hand-writing" is dismissed; what is usually privileged, the ability of the hand to produce legible, cursive script as it gives expression to the mind, is replaced by what is only very rarely focused on in slave narratives, the body of the white American. The Crafts illuminate, in effect, what is often illegible: the peculiarly readable (and, as their narrative suggests, peculiarly writeable) dynamics of the white body.

It is important to note that these dynamics, insofar as they are rehearsed by the Crafts, might equally well be rehearsed by those already legally designated white. Needless to say, although literacy may stand as a legislated sign of whiteness, it is not coincident with light-colored skin. One can easily imagine circumstances in which the pantomime of the Crafts as they exchange their passes might be played out at any number of meetings of black and white bodies. William Craft reminds his readers that in the antebellum South a white American could demand at will that an African American produce legible, cursive signs of his or her emancipated status or "whiteness":

> There are a large number of free Negroes residing in the Southern States; but in Georgia (and I believe in all the slave States) every colored person's complexion is *prima-facie* evidence of his being a slave; and the lowest villain in the country, should he be a white man, has the legal power to arrest, and question, in the most inquisitorial and insulting manner, any colored person, male or female, that he may find at large, particularly at night and on Sundays, without a written pass, signed by the master or someone in authority; stamped free papers, certifying that the person is the rightful owner of himself.[38]

These circumstances by no means guarantee the literacy of all whites; they merely assume literacy as a sign of white privilege. As this passage suggests, the black body, in its position outside language, may be taken as providing, as a matter of course, a legally sanctioned location for "hand-writing," a location at which one might demand at any time an indisputable sign of the privileged condition of the white body, its privileged situation within the order of logos "not dependent on any one organ, any one sense, [nor] . . . to be found in either the visible or the audible."³⁹ Necessarily embedded within the terms of this transaction is the assumption that the signs extracted from the black body are not self-penned or self-authored, since, although the black body is proximate to meaning, it holds no meaning itself beyond its own materiality. Although never a sign of meaning, the black body functions as a widely accepted location of meaning, the end point of a chain of signification but never its point of initiation.

The Crafts' scene of writing, then, does not focus on the ability to produce cursive script but rather yields insight into the fictions highlighted by the ability to produce cursive script, fictions connecting as much as separating black and white bodies. The black body holds meaning, while the white body is synonymous with meaning. The black body is taken as a "designated" site of writing, while the white body remains the "essential" site of writing. To write the white body—to inscribe oneself as white regardless of whether one is in fact black or white—is equivalent to writing itself, for the white body is, above all, the site of "a movement of differential referring" without which meaning is not possible.⁴⁰

The crux of the scene is Ellen's elaborate disguise, a disguise allowing her not only to approximate whiteness but also to mask her gender. The particular white body that will provide her greatest license is, of course, the white male body. Karen Sánchez-Eppler, in her treatment of the intersecting tropes of feminism and abolition, writes aptly that "for both women and blacks it is their physical difference from the cultural norms of white masculinity that obstructs their claim to personhood."⁴¹ In other words, the white male body is the preeminently meaningful trace. Given that "every referent, all reality has the structure of a differential trace, and that one cannot refer to this 'real' except in an interpretive experience," the white male body is the most highly valued point of interpretation or writing in this system.⁴² It is not the case, as Sánchez-Eppler also writes in her essay, that "the body [i]s the privileged structure for the communicating of meaning."⁴³ Rather, only the white male body fully enjoys this privileged structure.

The clerks at the hotels, the officials at the Custom House, and the officials of the public conveyances with whom the Crafts must deal all possess the privileged body that grounds U.S. social, legal, psychological, and economic reality. In her male disguise, Ellen mirrors for them their own meaningfulness. "I cut off my wife's hair square at the back of the head," William writes, "and got her to dress in the disguise and stand out on the floor. I found that she made a most respectable looking gentleman."⁴⁴ The cropping of Ellen's hair initiates a movement into whiteness that begins with her *re*gendering. To regender Ellen and thereby remove her from her reproductive capacity is, of course, one way of apparently removing her from her body; but, more importantly, the transformation removes her from an invariable, incontestable, insurmountable connection to blackness. If U.S. slavery can be defined as "an economic and political system by which a group of whites extracted as much labor as possible from blacks (defined as the offspring of black or mulatto mothers)," then the black woman constitutes the only generative space of blackness.[45] She is hyperbolically black. Within this system her identity inheres in her reproductive system, in her capacity to perpetuate a black and degraded labor force. "The female, in this order of things," writes Hortense Spillers, "breaks in upon the imagination with a forcefulness that marks both a denial and an 'illegitimacy.'"[46] Within this racist and sexist system, black women are what one might call the ur-site of blackness, the site at which the physical and cultural "pathology" known as blackness is generated. On the other hand, while the black female figure is seen to perpetuate the line of blackness, the white male figure perpetuates the line of whiteness. The two stand in distinct matrilineal and patrilineal orders. They order largely separate worlds, and to exchange one figure for the other is to exchange one world for the other. The cropping of Ellen's hair effects a chiasmus that profoundly redacts the racial ambiguity inscribed in her light complexion. Whereas in her disguise Ellen is figured as a white father, she is usually comprehended as a black mother to whom the invisible white father shifts all responsibility for her condition.

Like the bandaged hand, the inscription of the white male figure on the black female body of Ellen is an essential element of the Crafts' escape. For the conflation of black matrilineal and white patrilineal figures in Ellen's disguised form, a conflation also visible in her complexion, further refigures the indeterminacy of signification. The same body, Ellen Craft's black female body, is at one moment the most illegible of material ciphers, the generative space of the abjectness known as blackness, and at the next the most meaningful of signs, one that stands for the very condition of meaning itself. Like the bandaging of her hand, Ellen's regendering refigures advantageously "the absence of a presence, an always already absent present" on which signification depends. One sees by means of this transfiguration, more clearly than at any other point in the narrative, that entrance into the "body" of writing amounts to an entrance into a "body" of power.

What is more, the transfiguring of Ellen's body, like the bandaging of her hand, divides her body. The new status of this body within the condition of meaning necessitates that it be divisible. The bandaging of her hand and cropping of her hair redirect and redistribute the interpretive gaze aimed at her. Black bodies are not various. Black bodies generally—like each individual black body—betoken a meaninglessness from which they cannot be recovered. The materiality to which black bodies redundantly refer is an undifferentiated one, one that remains unqualified by the variety of its parts. Put differently, the black body does not necessarily possess a distinguishable anatomy, and some of the most dramatic and ubiquitous images in slave narratives illustrate this point: images of the tortured or injured black body. Recall Frederick Douglass's rehearsal of the stripping and beating of Aunt Hester or Solomon Northup's account of the stripping and beating of Patsey: "By this time her back was covered with long welts intersecting each other like net work. Epps was yet furious and savage as ever.... The painful cries and shrieks of the tortured Patsey, mingling with the loud and angry curses of Epps, loaded the air."[47] James Pennington, recalling how his childhood play and imagination lead to his first whipping, writes that the overseer Blackstone "came along from the field, and ... fell upon me with the [hickory stick] he then had in his hand, and flogged me most cruelly."[48] Harriet Jacobs briefly recounts the tale of the runaway slave James, who after being recaptured "receives hundreds of lashes ... [and is] placed between the screws of the cottin gin ... to stay as long as he had been in the woods." James's body, when finally unscrewed from the gin, is "found partly eaten by rats and vermin."[49] These images and innumerable similar ones present the black body as opened up or pierced in order to foreground its materiality, its physicality. Attention is directed not to specific parts of the body but to the general spectacle of its fleshliness and its subjection to white power.

Conversely, since meaning implies both a syntax and an associational schema—a conjunctive arrangement of elements as well as a nonlinear integrity—the white body is eminently divisible in its ability to transcend its materiality. Parts of the white body may be emphasized or inflected in the generation of meaning, and the final encounter of the Crafts' escape bears out this opposition between divisible white and indivisible black bodies. When William is stopped by "a full-blooded Yankee of the lower order" in Baltimore, the final major station before Pennsylvania, the Yankee informs William that before he and Ellen can pass into free territory Ellen must be able to account for him as a rightfully owned slave.[50] The Crafts, of course, know no one in Baltimore who can vouch for their master-slave relationship, and very quickly their seemingly insurmountable difficulty attracts "the attention of the large number of bustling passengers" around them.[51] Yet as their predicament becomes a public spectacle, it is precisely the manner in which the divisible white body is able to manage spectacularization that solves their problem.

The Crafts' fellow passengers watch the unfolding drama and mutter their disapproval, but, as William informs us, "not because they thought we were slaves endeavoring to escape, but merely because they thought my master was a slaveholder and invalid gentleman, and therefore [that] it was wrong to detain him."[52] Overwhelming the crisis presented by William's vexed dark body, Ellen's disguised and bandaged body provides a more urgent narrative. Covering Ellen's seemingly weak eyes are "a pair of green spectacles."[53] Her face is "muffled in . . . poultices, &tc., [which] furnished a plausible excuse for avoiding general conversation."[54] Her hand, of course, is similarly bound. These body parts call attention to themselves by their absence from view. Hidden under bandages and screens, their ironically heightened presence provides an authenticity that Ellen cannot provide legally. These parts form a legible *script* more readily comprehensible than any oral attestations concerning the relationship between Ellen and William. Just as parts invoke or prompt expectations of the whole, the white body prompts expectations of legitimate signification. That is, the relation of part to whole seems to mirror the relation of the white body to what might be imagined as an "increasingly *substanceless* world" of knowledge, mind, and spirit.[55] The highlighted parts of Ellen's "white" body imply the integrity of a white body, just as the white body itself—despite its endless differentiality—implies the wholeness of transcendent *logos*, self-sufficient spirit. The divisibility of the white body attests to its status as an only provisionally indicative space; the white body has an associational power that leads elsewhere.

Since the white body necessarily inscribes expectation, it is fitting that it literally inscribes *the* most unsettled and expectant moment of the narrative: "Just then the bell rang for the train to leave, and had it been the sudden shock of an earthquake it could not have given us a greater thrill. The sound of the bell caused every eye to flash and with apparent interest, and to be more steadily fixed upon us than before."[56] The escape turns, quite literally, on the turning of eyes on the white body. Both metaphorically and literally, the white body is never a space of entrapment. The railroad official, his own white body spectacularized in its proximity to Ellen's, takes this status for granted and resolves the tension in this situation. He "all at once thrust his fingers through his hair, and in a state of great agitation said, 'I really don't know what to do; I calculate it is all right.'"[57] What the white body makes legible is in fact so legible that sometimes paper need not be wasted. The official takes for granted the coincidence of the white body and the power to sign(ify).

Tellingly, however, this coincidence or coimplication of the white body and the condition of language revolves around the preeminence of absence. Accordingly, the Crafts manage their escape by means of the preeminently legible "hand-writing" of a hand that never writes. They reproduce a hostile symbolic order and take advantage of a logocentric notion of writing in which African Americans are, if not functionally, always ontologically illiterate. The Crafts thus translate their illiteracy into a supraliteracy and establish, contrary to an untenable cultural logic of race, that there is no abject outside of writing to which African Americans are confined, if writing is understood as standing exclusively for the life of the mind. *Running a Thousand Miles for Freedom* curiously and successfully constructs a "scene of writing" in which no writing occurs.

NOTES

Chapter 5, "Hand-Writing: Legibility and the White Body in *Running a Thousand Miles for Freedom*," was originally published in *American Literature* 69, no. 2 (June 1997): 315–36. © 1997.

1. Jacques Derrida, "The Purveyor of Truth," in *The Purloined Poe: Lacan, Derrida, and Psychoanalytic Reading*, ed. John P. Muller and William Richardson, trans. Alan Bass (Baltimore: Johns Hopkins University Press, 1988), 198.

2. Robert Stepto, *From behind the Veil: A Study of Afro-American Narrative* (Urbana: University of Illinois Press, 1979).

3. Frances Smith Foster, "Adding Color and Contour to Early American Self-Portraiture: Autobiographical Writings of Afro-American Women," in *Conjuring: Black Women, Fiction, and Literary Tradition*, ed. Marjorie Pryse and Hortense Spillers (Bloomington: Indiana University Press, 1985), 31.

4. James Olney, "'I Was Born': Slave Narratives, Their Status as Autobiography and as Literature," *Callaloo* 20 (winter 1984): 48.

5. Laura E. Tanner, "Self-Conscious Representation in the Slave Narrative," *Black American Literature Forum* 21 (winter 1987): 424.

6. Valerie Smith, *Self-Discovery and Authority in Afro-American Narrative* (Cambridge, MA: Harvard University Press, 1987), 6.

7. William L. Andrews, *To Tell a Free Story: The First Century of Afro-American Autobiography, 1760–1865* (Urbana: University of Illinois Press, 1986), 7.

8. Thomas Jefferson, *Notes on the State of Virginia*, ed. William Peden (New York: Norton, 1954), 139, 138.

9. John S. Wilson, MD, "The Negro," in James O. Breeden, *Advice among Masters: The Ideal of Slave Management in the Old South* (Westport, CT: Greenwood, 1980), 212, italics in original; reprinted from *American Cotton Planter and Soil of the South*, November 1858.

10. Wilson, "The Negro," 212.

11. Elaine Scarry, *The Body in Pain: The Making and Unmaking of the World* (New York: Oxford University Press, 1985), 22.

12. For a more extended discussion of African Americans in relation to the fundamental Western notion of the mind/body split, as well as an elaboration of these four patterns of

representative black bodies in slave narratives, see my article "African-American Slave Narratives: Literacy, the Body, Authority" (chapter 4, this volume).

13. Mary Prince, *The History of Mary Prince, a West Indian Slave*, in *Six Women's Slave Narratives*, ed. William L. Andrews (New York: Oxford University Press, 1988), 13.

14. William Craft, *Running a Thousand Miles for Freedom*, in *Great Slave Narratives*, ed. Arna Bontemps (Boston: Beacon, 1969), 272.

15. Craft and Craft, *Running a Thousand Miles for Freedom*, 273.

16. Ferdinand de Saussure, *Course in General Linguistics*, ed. Charles Bally and Albert Sechehaye, trans. Wade Baskin (New York: McGraw-Hill, 1959), 115.

17. Saussure, *Course in General Linguistics*, 120, italics in original.

18. Jacques Derrida, *Positions*, trans. Alan Bass (Chicago: University of Chicago Press, 1981), 26.

19. Michael Ryan, *Marxism and Deconstruction: A Critical Articulation* (Baltimore: Johns Hopkins University Press, 1982), 22.

20. Amy Robinson, "It Takes One to Know One: Passing and Communities of Common Interest," *Critical Inquiry* 20 (summer 1994): 717.

21. Craft and Craft, *Running a Thousand Miles for Freedom*, 273.

22. R. J. M. Blackett, *Beating against the Barriers: The Lives of Six Nineteenth-Century Afro-Americans* (Ithaca, NY: Cornell University Press, 1986), 89.

23. Jacques Derrida, *Speech and Phenomena and Other Essays on Husserl's Theory of Signs*, trans. David B. Allison (Evanston, IL: Northwestern University Press, 1973), 58.

24. Derrida, *Speech and Phenomena*, 80.

25. Judith Butler, *Bodies That Matter: On the Discursive Limits of "Sex"* (New York: Routledge, 1993), 3.

26. Craft and Craft, *Running a Thousand Miles for Freedom*, 288.

27. Craft and Craft, *Running a Thousand Miles for Freedom*, 288.

28. Olney, "'I Was Born,'" 50.

29. Craft and Craft, *Running a Thousand Miles for Freedom*, 289.

30. Craft and Craft, *Running a Thousand Miles for Freedom*, 289.

31. Barbara Johnson, "Translator's Introduction," in Jacques Derrida, *Dissemination* (Chicago: University of Chicago Press, 1981), ix.

32. Johnson, "Translator's Introduction," ix, italics in original.

33. Joy S. Kasson, "Narrative of the Female Body: *The Greek Slave*," in *The Culture of Sentiment: Race, Gender, and Sentimentality in 19th Century America*, ed. Shirley Samuels (New York: Oxford University Press, 1992), 172, 174, 172, 179, 172, 185, 186.

34. Jacques Derrida, *Of Grammatology*, trans. Gayatri Spivak (Baltimore: Johns Hopkins University Press, 1974), 242, italics in original.

35. Derrida, *Of Grammatology*, 241.

36. Spivak, "Translator's Preface," in Derrida, *Of Grammatology*, xvii.

37. *Columbia Dictionary of Modern Literary and Cultural Criticism*, s.v. "trace."

38. Craft and Craft, *Running a Thousand Miles for Freedom*, 290.

39. Derrida, *Of Grammatology*, 241.

40. Jacques Derrida, *Limited Inc* (Evanston, IL: Northwestern University Press, 1988), 148.

41. Karen Sánchez-Eppler, "Bodily Bonds: The Intersecting Rhetorics of Feminism and Abolition," in *The New American Studies*, ed. Philip Fisher (Berkeley: University of California Press, 1991), 229.

42. Derrida, *Limited Inc*, 148.

43. Sánchez-Eppler, "Bodily Bonds," 240.

44. Craft and Craft, *Running a Thousand Miles for Freedom*, 290.

45. Jacqueline Jones, *Labor of Love, Labor of Sorrow: Black Women, Work, and the Family from Slavery to the Present* (New York: Vintage, 1985), 13.

46. Hortense Spillers, "Mama's Baby, Papa's Maybe: An American Grammar Book," *diacritics* 17 (summer 1987): 80.

47. Solomon Northup, *Twelve Years a Slave*, ed. Sue Eakin and Joseph Logsdon (Baton Rouge: Louisiana State University Press, 1968).

48. James W. C. Pennington, *The Fugitive Blacksmith*, in Bontemps, *Great Slave Narratives*, 208.

49. Harriet Jacobs, *Incidents in the Life of a Slave Girl*, ed. Jean Fagan Yellin (Cambridge, MA: Harvard University Press, 1987), 48, 49.

50. Craft and Craft, *Running a Thousand Miles for Freedom*, 308.

51. Craft and Craft, *Running a Thousand Miles for Freedom*, 309.

52. Craft and Craft, *Running a Thousand Miles for Freedom*, 310.

53. Craft and Craft, *Running a Thousand Miles for Freedom*, 289.

54. Craft and Craft, *Running a Thousand Miles for Freedom*, 290.

55. Scarry, *The Body in Pain*, 30, italics added.

56. Craft and Craft, *Running a Thousand Miles for Freedom*, 310.

57. Craft and Craft, *Running a Thousand Miles for Freedom*, 310.

CH6

Self-Knowledge, Law, and African American Autobiography:
Lucy A. Delaney's *From the Darkness Cometh the Light* (1993)

The autobiographical text this discussion considers is a recollection of antebellum slave life and of release from chattel slavery. Published some twenty-five years after the Civil War, Lucy A. Delaney's *From the Darkness Cometh the Light*, subtitled *Struggles for Freedom*, recalls as its climax events from 1844, the year in which Delaney's mother, Polly Berry, sued successfully for Delaney's freedom in a Missouri courtroom.¹ The legal case and judgment for Delaney's freedom turned upon the status of Delaney's mother, who was born free in Illinois, kidnapped as a child, and taken to slaveholding territory. Legally a free woman, Berry could not bear enslaved children in the eyes of the law. Thus, successfully establishing the biological mother-daughter relationship between Berry and Delaney amounted to a demonstration of Delaney's legally free status. Despite the singularity of this movement from slavery to freedom in terms of classic slave narratives, Delaney's recollections bear central characteristics of the classic antebellum text in which, during the years from 1836 to the end of the Civil War, "the stigma traditionally associated with slavery [was transferred] from the slave to the slaveholder."² What is significant about Delaney's text is that the working out of these traditional concerns and themes occurs at a very novel site: the American courtroom.

The climax of Delaney's narrative in the setting of an American courtroom tellingly resituates the "scene of writing" so peculiar to African American autobiography. The "scene of writing" in these narratives is the scene in which the autobiographer learns to read, write, or respect fully the power of literacy and discursive conventions. The scene provides a sometimes veiled but always undeniable commentary on the construction of the autobiographical self presented by the narrative. The revision suggested by Delaney's narrative tellingly documents the manner in which each African American autobiographer must in some measure recast the hostile construction of African American identity already undertaken by dominant American society. The courtroom setting in Delaney's narrative dramatizes the convergence of the scriptive and the prescriptive, the private and the public, the individual and the social. Put another way, it dramatizes "a complex political technology" by which the self is represented.[3] This "complex political technology," as *From the Darkness Cometh the Light* reveals, is ultimately implicated in the terms of American law. The critical reader sees in the courtroom scene of writing the African American self as a manifest fiction—a provisional composite of self-declaration and judicial arbitration.

In addition to prompting the critical reader to consider the American courtroom as a primary site for "political and conceptual" determinations (as well as disclosures) of African American identity, Delaney's text prompts recognition of the technological and epistemological fiction of the genre of autobiography.[4] This essay examines these intersecting exposures. It begins by analyzing Delaney's portrayal of the nuclear family and her presentation of her own representativeness vis-à-vis all other African Americans; these subordinate elements of the narrative underscore the exposures of the climactic scenes in the courtroom. The essay concludes by claiming a central place for the American courtroom as a site for the writing of African American identity and autobiography.

The convergence at this site is important for investigations of the situation of the self of African American autobiography, because the foremost concern of African American autobiographies has been the relation between the individual and the communal. Accordingly, the academic study of African American autobiography is perennially concerned with this relation. In 1974, in the introduction to his *Black Autobiography in America*, Stephen Butterfield writes: "The 'self' of black autobiography is not an individual with a private career.... The self is conceived as a member of an oppressed social group with ties and responsibilities to the other members."[5] Almost twenty years later it is now routinely acknowledged that there are important distinctions to be made along these lines between autobiographies written by African American women and African American men. These distinctions concern the relation that the narrated subjects of the autobiographies bear to the community of African Americans with whom they share their oppression, or in other words the extent to which the narratives are or are not individualistic, celebrating individual struggles and individual triumphs. The now-classic pairing of Frederick Douglass's *Narrative of the Life of Frederick Douglass* and Harriet Jacobs's *Incidents in the Life of a Slave Girl* is taken to exemplify such distinction. Douglass more fully fashions a mythic tale of individual perseverance and ingenuity, while Jacobs more fully records her indebtedness to and enduring concerns for the familial community in relation to which she defines herself. The pairing brings together strikingly different models of the way in which African American autobiographies present the dramatic actualization or realization of the self, given a set of intellectual, civic, and legal circumstances operating to prevent precisely that.

Needless to say, one recognizes equally important similarities. One critic describes the shared complexities of African American autobiographical projects as follows: "Autobiography as a genre should be the history of individual craziness, but in black autobiography the outer reality in which heroes move is so massive and absolute in its craziness that any one person's individual idiosyncrasies seem almost dull in their normality."[6] African American autobiographies present readers with narratives that are, in terms of the dominant society, unimaginable. In these texts, what is normally taken for granted becomes, as a matter of course, eccentric. These eccentricities involve defying socially assigned identities and undertaking their revision in light of personally proclaimed identities. The autobiographies of Douglass and Jacobs share, in addition to these traits, more widespread characteristics of autobiography. Both suggest, for instance, that the genre offers "not a simple recapitulation of the past; it is also the attempt and the drama of [persons] struggling to reassemble [themselves] in [their] own likeness at a certain moment of [their] history."[7]

Differences and similarities notwithstanding, these estimations of African American autobiography depend upon notions that Candace Lang, in her reprimand of traditional scholars of autobiography, terms a relatively "unskeptical acceptance of the unified, autonomous self." Writing of Georges Gusdorf and James Olney, among others, Lang invites one to see that "few of the critics in question here manifest an entirely unskeptical acceptance of the unified, autonomous self, but virtually none goes so far as to ponder the consequences of a total rejection of that notion of the subject. To do so would constitute ... a serious and sustained critique of the 'genre' and its ideological foundations."[8] My contention is that the circumstances of African American autobiography prompt such a sustained critique. That critique operates at the level of the ideological foundations of the genre, but it also operates beyond them, putting into question the ideological foundations of American social custom and law. It thus identifies discursive practices from which African American autobiography must extract itself, practices that it must revise. This critique is suggested, but only suggested, by the pairing of Douglass and Jacobs. The issues setting the two narratives in opposition imply the problematics troubling any definitive declaration of the limits and boundaries of the self. The self, as it turns out, is always a questionable fiction, whether that fiction is exposed in terms of relations to a community, or in terms of narrative complexities that betray a self performing the narration over and against a self being narrated.

African American autobiography stands as a peculiar site at which a critical reader can witness, in diverse realms, the dynamics animating fictions of the self. In addition to observing narrative disturbances fretting a discourse generically premised on the viability of a discrete identity, the reader is privy to disturbances of the enduring national fictions in the United States that propose it is impossible and undesirable, in the words of Abraham Lincoln, to "introduce political and social equality between the white and black races . . . [as a result of] a physical difference between the two, which . . . will probably forever forbid their living together upon the footing of perfect equality."[9] Lucy Delaney's *From the Darkness Cometh the Light* articulates this coincidence of generic and social fictions, providing a fiction of personal identity that also rehearses a systemic fiction of national identity, a coincidence that one might attribute to the terms of all African American autobiography. One is openly prompted by Delaney's narrative to see the autobiographical heroine as multiple and as defined in deeply conflicting ways. Additionally, the climax of the narrative—the courtroom scene that eventually secures Delaney her freedom—graphically conjoins the fictitious self-evidence of autobiography with the imperatives of social and legal systems in the United States that remain hostile to African Americans. The "ideological foundations" of the generic, unitary self and of a racial, gendered, and classed national configuration appear there in powerful complementarity. The equivocal fiction of the self is set in relief against the assumed univocality of an overwhelming system. Accordingly, the official site of the courtroom takes its place as the paramount scene for multiple fictive selves, or what amounts to the same, multiple fictions of the self. The tenuous fiction of the self is inevitable, but is taken as less tenuous at some sites than at others.

Not so oddly, then, the autobiographical self-knowledge to be accrued from reading Delaney's narrative—and by extension all African American autobiography—proves to be the ironic knowledge of another/an Other. For Delaney this odd self-knowledge is a foreign and contrary knowledge imposed by a hostile and dominant other party and is, furthermore, knowledge of an estranged and, at best, marginalized Other that/who must be understood as one's self. African American autobiographical acts recapitulate the hostile "knowledge" that discounts them in the first place, as well as the marginalized personal and community "knowledge" that, opposingly, promotes them in the first place. For an African American "simply to write the story of his or her own life represent[s] an assault" on the line of reasoning that assumes and perpetuates the construct that African Americans do not live—at the very least—as fully imaginative, significant, intellectual, and complex lives as the dominant American community, "since to make oneself the subject of a narrative presumes both the worth of that self and its interest for a reader."[10] Given this set of circumstances, *From the Darkness Cometh the Light* underscores correspondences between the generic dimensions of a social configuration and the social dimensions of a generic configuration; *From the Darkness Cometh the Light* challenges "ideological foundations" that obscure these conjunctions.

There are two principal ways in which the text imputes the fictive status to the self. The first returns us to the exemplary concerns of *Incidents in the Life of a Slave Girl*, since the construct of the family holds priority in both narratives. Delaney's narrative begins with the abduction of her mother at the age of five from the state of Illinois "across the Mississippi River to the city of St. Louis" and shortly "up the Missouri River [where she is] sold into slavery."[11] Sold and resold as a slave, Polly meets "a mulatto servant, who was as handsome as Apollo" and eventually the two are married and begin to raise two daughters.[12] With foreshadowing irony, Delaney characterizes her early childhood: "With mother, father, and sister, a pleasant home and surroundings, what happier child than I!"[13] A state of domestic unity and happiness is recuperated from the opening misdeeds of the narrative; however, as one suspects, the archetypal unity and happiness prove ephemeral. The ensuing episodes of Delaney's narrative seem to chronicle a quest to reconvene the blissful family unit.

Delaney recalls that "though in direct opposition to the will of Major Berry, my father's quondam master and friend Judge Wash tore my father from his wife and children and sold him 'way down South'!"[14] This disbanding of the family marks the beginning of the misfortunes from which Delaney must continually extricate herself. Although the evil of slavery underlies the whole narrative, the disbanding of the family also marks the first of only two occasions when the text calls the evil by its name. Delaney decries "Slavery! cursed slavery . . . [which means] bondage as parts husband from wife, the mother from her children, aye, even the babe from her breast."[15] The terms of this initial and most enduring distress are those of the separation of family member from family member. Conversely, the terms of greatest consolation are implied to be the return of family members into each other's presence. The narrative is structured so that its penultimate moment appears to effect such success, but the equivocal nature of this success suggests the fictiveness that the notion of family bears in Delaney's autobiography—despite the fact that it determines both the autobiographical narrator's dilemma and her delivery from that dilemma. Years after the initial catastrophe, and years after her own emancipation as well as the emancipation and death of her mother, years after the abolition of "slavery [and] involuntary servitude, except as a punishment for crime whereof the party shall have been duly convicted," Delaney is haunted by the impulse to redress the long-standing disintegration of her family.[16] She locates her father, and calls her sister Nancy down from Canada, then she writes of her triumph of sorts:

> Forty-five years of separation, hard work, rough times and heart longings, had perseveringly performed its work, and instead of a man bearing his years with upright vigor, he was made prematurely old by the accumulation of troubles. My sister Nancy came from Canada, and we had a most joyful reunion, and only the absence of our mother left a vacuum, which we deeply and sorrowfully felt. Father could not be persuaded to stay with us, when he found his wife dead; he longed to get back to his old associations of forty-five years standing, he felt like a stranger in a strange land, and taking pity on him, I urged him no more, but let him go though with great reluctance.[17]

Delaney's triumph in effect recapitulates the initial loss. The passage begins with "separation" and ends with references to leavetaking, "a strange land," and "reluctance"—the very markers of the distress wrought forty-five years earlier. Indeed, the brief mention of "a most joyful reunion" is encircled by references to "the accumulation of troubles" and "a vacuum . . . deeply and sorrowfully felt." It would appear that the configuration of "family," so heavily privileged in depictions of the African American experience by nineteenth-century white writers like Harriet Beecher Stowe, is one that is strangely never sustained or realized at this or any other point in the narrative. The configuration of "family" is an absent term that nonetheless maintains a brooding, fantastic, and highly rhetorical presence. One must remember that the reunion inevitably falls short of the original union it seeks, since the death of Delaney's mother starkly precludes the possibility. Polly never again faces her husband "who was as handsome as Apollo"; the benevolent romance that introduces and privileges the term "family" within the text survives only as a lost, unattainable fiction.

The teasing impossibility of this presiding fiction is underscored by the scenes immediately preceding the narrative's penultimate episode: after the accidental death of her first husband, Frederick Turner, Delaney is importuned by her mother to remember that death proves a better fate than enslavement.

The unexpected separation Delaney must endure is not ordained by American law and privilege, as is the arbitrary legal separation of her father from her mother. In her grief Delaney submits to the judgment that the burden of slavery outweighs the burden of death: "I had been taught that there was hope beyond the grave, but hope was left behind when sold 'down souf.'"[18] Even in light of further misfortunes, the fiction of the original family unit and the trauma of its fracture presides. Equally, when the four children she bears in her second marriage (to Zachariah Delaney) all die either in childhood or by the age of twenty-four, Delaney reflects that "one consolation was always mine! Our children were born free and died free! Their childhood and my maternity were never shadowed with a thought of separation."[19] No doubt this claim is an odd one to be made by a mother who endures the deaths of two of her children in childhood and two in young adulthood, for the reader is asked to understand that, as she witnessed the death of each child, she is never troubled with "thought[s] of separation," even though that separation might be effected by physical death as opposed to enslavement. The ultimate outrage of American chattel slavery is portrayed in the narrative in terms of the customary priority accorded to the family in nineteenth-century American life. The principal evil of slavery is the arbitrary severing of African American families. So too the narrative represents this arbitrary severing of families as the preeminent despair of Delaney's life. The fiction of the family represents or pursues the fact of Delaney's despair.

The third in the series of deaths enumerated immediately prior to the scene of the curious family reunion is the death of Delaney's mother, her most cherished and long-standing companion. The focus and tone of this passage is substantially different from that registering her distress at her mother's forced removal. Delaney remarks that she is pleased her mother "had lived to see the joyful time when her race was made free, their chains struck off, and their right to their own flesh and blood lawfully acknowledged."[20] The death of her mother represents in the narrative not a traumatic separation but an occasion for satisfying and almost calming reflection. As in describing the death of her children, Delaney moves, if not to hyperbole, to measured lyricism: "Her life, so full of sorrow was ended, full of years and surrounded by many friends, both black and white, who recognized and appreciated her sufferings and sacrifices and rejoiced that her old age was spent in freedom and plenty. The azure vault of heaven bends over us all, and the gleaming moonlight brightens the marble tablet which marks her last resting place, 'to fame and fortune unknown,' but in the eyes of Him who judgeth us, hers was a heroism which outvied the most famous."[21] Once again, the reader is asked to overlook the trauma of this separation, while the narrative itself is structured so as never to overlook the imposed separation outlined early in the events of Delaney's life. Strikingly, the episode that immediately follows, Delaney's attempt at a family reunion, returns to the consequences of that early separation.

It is clear that the privileged form of self-definition in Delaney's narrative is the family, yet it is equally clear that within the circumstances of her life and narrative this privileged form operates foremost as a tantalizing fiction. In her life and narrative, Delaney's family disintegrates even as it is invoked. The term enters the narrative to recapitulate its rupture and absence. As Frances Smith Foster comments, "the problem of distinguishing between the individual self and the community self and the desire to present the symbolic nature of one's personal experiences while maintaining one's own inimitability is traditional for autobiographical writers"; nonetheless, for the African American autobiographer "the question is complicated by his [or her] status... in the United States." That status is an alien and inferior one that in large part abrogates the prerogatives of self-definition. "The slave narrator" and subsequent writers are aliens "whose assertions of common humanity and civil rights conflict with some basic beliefs" of the society they address.[22] African American autobiographers define themselves in relation to at least two communities, a dominating American community that brooks no identification with African Americans and a community of African Americans with whom they share an imposed singularity. Delaney's narrative outlines ways in which defining oneself beyond these options amounts to pursuing a tantalizing and forever absent fiction. Thus, the privileged term of her narrative, the primary register of her self-evidence, proves unprocurable. The central family in her narrative, which the prerogatives of American chattel slavery violate, remains above all in the text what the *OED* calls "a supposition known to be at variance with fact." Delaney recounts her life and defines her self in terms of a fiction, unfortunately a hostile fiction authored by American law and custom. What is more, the fictive status of her family in both the autobiographical narrative and the "reality" of American life implies an equal fictiveness for the self that reference to this family records. Defining the self in terms of what is ultimately fantastic calls into question its "unified and autonomous" nature, because this fantastic self remains, by definition, "at variance with fact." Presented without fact, the unity and autonomy of the self are not those of a first-order reality faithfully recorded by the autobiographical act, but of a fiction manifestly invented by others. The principal sign of Delaney's autobiographical self-presence rests outside her self in what is "known to be at variance with fact," so that the text gives the lie to "the assumption that the... [autobiographical] work is the expression (however inadequate) of an anterior idea originating in the writing subject and for which that subject was the sole authority."[23] One must remember that in large part Delaney's persevering fictions represent a struggle with American law and custom for authorship of and authority over the terms of her life. Given the plainness of these circumstances and their attendant fictions, *From the Darkness Cometh the Light* advertises its fictiveness as opposed to its facticity. The autobiography restates the conditions of invention determining autobiographical representation as much as it appears to redact a fixed presence, a unified and autonomous self.

The even larger irony to be noted here is that every African American autobiographer wishes to pursue options of self-definition beyond the two imperatives that allow her or him either no room for resemblance or no room for difference. In the negative relation African Americans are assumed to bear to the dominating American community we are granted conversely an inexorable representativeness in relation to all other African Americans, and the second of the two principal ways in which Delaney's text imputes the fictive status of the self concerns this assumption of representativeness. Following her rehearsal of the partial, belated reunion of her family, Delaney concludes her text with an enumeration of her personal accomplishments, an enumeration immediately recuperated as racial exemplar. Both the brief listing that includes such items as her election as "President of the first colored society, called the 'Female Union,' which was the first ever organized exclusively for women," as well as the narrative in its entirety, are offered in the hopes that either "may settle the problem in your mind, if not in others, 'Can the negro race succeed, proportionately, as well as the whites, if given the same and an equal start?' "[24] Delaney briefly fashions herself as representative of all African Americans and of their potential. Nevertheless, only three paragraphs earlier, she writes: "There are abounding in public and private libraries of all sorts, lives of people which fill our minds with amazement, admiration, sympathy, and indeed with as many feelings as there are people, so I can scarcely expect that the reader of these episodes of my life will meet with more than a passing interest, but as such I will commend it to your thought for a brief hour."[25]

Delaney acknowledges a vast multiplicity of individuals who are not easily reducible to one another, and acknowledges as well a multiplicity of feelings that may animate any of those individuals. She characterizes herself as acutely aware that for one to read her text is to make a single choice among many and, accordingly, she asks only "for a brief hour" devoted to her own. In effect, at the moment in the text when she sets her own life as a standard or gauge for millions of other lives she also considers her life in terms of the infinite differences that implicitly make such a substitution impossible. Furthermore, she suggests that not only is it troublesome to imagine one life standing in the place of another or many others, it is equally troublesome to imagine any of the many "feelings" that play their part in any one life somehow standing as indicative of that individual life. Oddly, then, at the same time the impossibilities of representation are briefly considered, the narrative nonetheless claims a representative posture for Delaney. One sees that this representative understanding is openly provisional at best and, therefore, in one further and pronounced way, Delaney's reader witnesses (and witnesses Delaney witnessing) her self as "a supposition known to be at variance with fact."

As with the persistent attention to family, the form of the self being invoked responds to the invocation with rupture and withdrawal. The presented self-evidence underscores its own contrivance. The notion that African Americans are invariably more similar than different, and that one African American may always stand in the place of another, is sometimes a profitable fiction and sometimes is not. The notion remains, in any case, always a fiction, as made clear emphatically and irrevocably by the urbanization of large populations of African Americans early in the twentieth century: "After the war, black intellectuals had to confront the black masses on the streets of their cities. . . . After World War I, the large-scale movement of black people into the cities of the North meant that intellectual leadership and its constituencies fragmented. No longer was it possible to mobilize an undifferentiated address to 'the black people' once an urban black working class was established."[26] The closing paragraphs of Delaney's autobiography comprehend and imply deep conflicts that disturb assumptions of a unitary identity attributed by law or custom to African Americans. Indeed, this is an outcome her narrative shares generally with African American autobiographies. (Of course, this description is necessarily ironic, insofar as it advances a unitary identity.) The conflicts of racial representation are registered in Delaney's text in the terms of her autobiographical self, inasmuch as Delaney equivocally proposes a role for her self in that representative fiction.

In effect, as does the genre in general, Delaney's autobiography leads the critical reader to a meditation on fiction. Importantly, however, suggesting perennial concerns of African American autobiography, the fictions to be imagined and reimagined in this instance are not simply personal or generic, but also and necessarily social and legal. As much as the scene of writing here is generic, it also is "constitutional" in the social and legal senses of that word—a scene of writing from which one necessarily infers the civic and judicial. Hence, if African American autobiography, this overdetermined scene of writing, always undertakes "a total rejection of the notion of the subject," then it troubles, by definition—even beyond the ideological foundations of autobiography—the foundations of powerful social and legal practices.[27]

The climactic scenes of Delaney's text powerfully illuminate this imperative and intricate cathexis. Her text lays bare the deeply composite nature and unquestioned priority of these scenes. Although the importance of scenes of writing is well acknowledged within African American autobiographies and the commentaries on them, Delaney's text manifestly draws out and elaborates the nonsubjective and systemic nature of this peculiar scene of writing in which she, as African American "subject," discovers her self. The novelty of Delaney's rendition becomes clear if one considers briefly well-known scenes of writing in *Narrative of the Life of Frederick Douglass* and *Incidents in the Life of a Slave Girl*.

In Douglass's text, in keeping with the more individualistic focus attributed to his narrative, the scene is in large part self-centered. Douglass's lessons in literacy provided by Mrs. Auld are stopped by Mr. Auld, since attaining literacy invariably spoils slaves by making them "unmanageable." At this juncture Douglass understands the white man's power to enslave as well as "the pathway from slavery to freedom."[28] He undertakes learning to read and write by tricking and bribing white boys in his neighborhood and by using for practice such communal markers as fences and such markers of his alienation from that community as the discarded schoolbooks of his master's son. The scene of writing outlined here underscores individual acumen, ingenuity, and the remove imposed by hostile, dominating agents. In Jacobs's text, by contrast, the more miscible, promiscuous, or indiscreet nature of the scene of writing is suggested. Initially, Linda Brent's literacy seems a liability, since it means she must endure an additional form of entreaty from Dr. Flint. However, much later in the narrative, Brent writes letters to Flint (from within the garret to which she "escapes") that are mailed and postmarked from New York. She convinces Flint of her successful "escape" to the North, ensuring "he had no suspicion of [her] being anywhere in the vicinity."[29] The scene of writing sketched here is more mediated; literacy and the construction of texts are taken up by diverse and conflicting hands and acquire their truth or potency by means of circulation and marks of that circulation. Here, one sees how language, literacy, and the construction and interpretation of texts operate "constitutionally"—that is, in a formative but always incomplete manner—to "confer explanatory power with regard to a wide range of evidence."[30] Scenes of writing are scenes in which occur struggles for and determinations of "explanatory power," as well as the disposition "of evidence." Certainly, the texts of both Douglass and Jacobs suggest this state of affairs; nevertheless, they have been traditionally understood to do so in a manner that privileges the more private interstitial and marginal aspects of their inscriptional scenes.

Conversely, the climactic scenes of Delaney's text place the dynamics of language, literacy, and interpretation as they bear on African American "subjectivity" at the most literal and open site of interpretive activity, the American courtroom. The courtroom is a site at which one is not prompted to understand the scene of writing in terms of inscriptions made between the lines or in intramural spaces. The courtroom neither resembles a garret nor confines its proceedings to the margins of used, discarded sheets of paper. Rather than an interstitial space, it is apparently one in which matters are brought into the open and settled. Moreover, the courtroom is a space in which presentations of "evidence" and conferring of "explanatory power" concerning African American identity have sweeping and enduring repercussions. At the site of the courtroom, statutory law is interpreted and upheld and, all too plainly, the particulars of the presence of African Americans in the United States have been meaningfully determined by statutory law. Scenes of writing in African American autobiographies, in this sense, are the site of struggles for the right of individuals to control this "explanatory power" and to determine the disposition of the "evidence" of their own existence. The setting of Delaney's climactic scene of writing in a courtroom brilliantly allows her text to represent the problematic nature of this struggle. It allows her to stage, via the representation of an autobiographical self, the multiple fictions of selfhood that are the only resort of those for whom the "constitutional" issue of their identity already has been settled without their participation or consent. Just as the "fact" of her family is an elusive fiction, so is the ostensible subject of Delaney's narrative. In the end, what the courtroom scene allows her to represent is the enforced fictionality of any subject defined by the impersonality of the law's "constitutional" power, even when that power is employed on behalf of the freedom of the subject.

It is useful to consider briefly the nature of statutory law.

> Statutory law is a distillation of some of the society's most cherished values, or at least of the class that wields the hegemonic power that produces laws. Statutes are one way, and a solemn and formal one, for the elite that imposes its values on a society to state what those values are and how behavior should conform to them. No other social act performs this function so conspicuously and directly. Statutory law is thus a valuable window on the hopes and fears of a society, of its images of itself, and of the ways it hoped to shape the time to come.[31]

Statutory law represents the convergence and "distillation" of a plurality of discourses, a formalizing of values, practices, and customs. The courtroom is the site at which this synthesis is understood and rehearsed. Historically, this site has provided the most far-reaching determinations of African American identity, an identity that cannot be understood as a "unified and autonomous" subjectivity in light of its determination at a site so open to the influences of diverse pressures, agencies, and convergences. Although "the idea of racial inferiority certainly did not appear in colonial law with the introduction of Negroes," and although "the legal determination of who might be slaves developed slowly," as American colonial law was refined, according to William E. Moore, it allowed African Americans identity only as a collective, "not as individuals." Colonial law, in its attempt to confine slavery "to those who quite obviously were different in appearance," and in its attempt to justify itself "on the basis of [African Americans'] inferior background as a people, not as individuals ... [took] the position that slavery is justified as a status properly attaching to a different and inferior people."[32] Thus, one finds in the colonial courtroom the binding interpretation (promoted by mechanisms of "explanatory power") that African Americans bear little estimable resemblance to any community other than that of African Americans and that African Americans bear little estimable difference from one another. The dilemma of the African American autobiographer—and of African Americans—is part of the story American law has written.

The construction of the African American self in this way has been contested as a fiction by African American rebellions, by expressive cultures (dance, song, oral performance) and, within the concerns of this discussion, by autobiographical texts. To grant that, in the words of Paul Finkelman, a leading scholar of early African American legal history, "slavery must be understood not only as a social, economic, or political institution but also as a legal institution" is not simply to acknowledge the brutalizing determinations of African American identity in the legislature and then in the courtroom; it is to recognize, in addition, the persistent challenges to those determinations, as well as their troublesome ramifications.[33] The fictiveness of the established legal "facts" concerning African Americans requires that interpretations separating fiction from fact be made again and again in the American courtroom. The courtroom remains a site of powerful interventions into these perpetual deliberations.

> The establishment of the legal principle that slavery was a status properly belonging to the Negro, as inherently inferior, went far toward the legal determination of who might be slaves. But because slavery was not

uniformly the status of Negroes from their first introduction, because not all Negroes were slaves even after slavery was established as being proper to them, and finally, because anti-miscegenation laws were not in force from the first and not uniformly obeyed thereafter, so that physiological criteria were variable and fallible, for all these reasons the legal criteria of the status of slavery required further elaboration.[34]

This is to say, the identity of African Americans "required further elaboration." Ultimately, however, this conflict between fiction and fact concerning African American identity proved unmanageable even for the "explanatory power" of the antebellum courtroom. Historian Eugene Genovese observes in his review of Paul Finkelman's *An Imperfect Union: Slavery, Federalism, and Comity* that "the 'judicial secession' that Finkelman describes paralleled a moral and ideological secession that struck the deepest sensibilities, and together they prepared the way for the political secession that formally declared the existence of contrasting views of civilization."[35] Equally, one might say the political secession dramatically declared the existence of contrasting views of African Americans in that civilization.

The courtroom, in its interpretation of statutory law, thus stands as a preeminent site for the construction of African American identity. It allows Delaney to dramatize the fictional nature of the forms that identity has been forced to take. Her courtroom scenes heighten the ideological drama of perceiving the fictive nature of the self; they heighten the ideological drama of "a total rejection of that notion of the subject." In the text, Delaney's appearance in court in a suit for her freedom is precipitated by an altercation with her mistress, Mrs. Mitchell. Several times Delaney is entrusted "to do the weekly washing and ironing... [even though she] had no more idea how it was to be done than Mrs. Mitchell herself."[36] Delaney is treated as if the particulars of menial servitude are innate, and her failures and protestations to the contrary prompt Mrs. Mitchell to sell her. Delaney flees and hides in the home of her legally free mother, who subsequently "on the morning of the 8th of September 1842... sued Mr. D. D. Mitchell for the possession of her child."[37] The issue brought before the court is who rightfully possesses the child Lucy Ann Berry, and it is precipitated by Delaney's headstrong self-determination—self-determination out of place in a situation in which that determination is a foregone conclusion.

In the courtroom the tale of the illegal abduction of Delaney's mother is rehearsed, and witnesses attest to the fact that Delaney "to the best of [their] knowledge and belief" is her biological child, and hence illegally enslaved.[38] It is important to note that Delaney's defense is not premised on Delaney's personal identity, but on the very law that defines the status of African American slaves—taken as a collective entity—as perpetually the property of their masters. Delaney's defense depends on the condition of her mother, since "a master who owned a female slave owned also her increase."[39] It is the courtroom scene that occurs after the testimonies, however, that is most memorable to Delaney:

> After the evidence from both sides was all in, Mr. Mitchell's lawyer, Thomas Hutchinson, commenced to plead. For one hour, he talked so bitterly against me and against my being in possession of my liberty that I was trembling, as if with ague, for I certainly thought everybody must believe him; indeed I almost believed the dreadful things he said, myself, and as I listened I closed my eyes with sickening dread, for I could just see myself floating down the river, and my heart-throbs seemed to be the throbs of the mighty engine which propelled me from my mother and freedom forever![40]

The power of the law here resides in the power of Thomas Hutchinson's rhetoric and his construction and interpretation of the "facts" before the court. This power is not negligible, for it challenges Delaney's sense of herself. The words "I could just see myself" introduce a vision of herself that strongly contradicts the identity she is struggling to maintain and to validate by means of legal sanction. Moreover, this vision may well be the one that will receive that sanction. Delaney recalls that "on the day the suit for [her] freedom began ... the jailer's sister-in-law, Mrs. Lacy, spoke to [her] of submission and patience; but [she] could not feel anything but rebellion against [her] lot."[41] This rebellion matches her earlier one against the "government" of Mrs. Mitchell for, in the dispute over the laundry, Delaney "would not permit [Mrs. Mitchell] to strike her; [Mrs. Mitchell] used shovel, tongs and broomstick in vain, as [Delaney] disarmed her as fast as she picked up each weapon."[42] Nevertheless, that rebellious character dissipates as Hutchinson pleads, and the character in which Mrs. Mitchell would cast her seems confirmed—even in Delaney's own mind. In the arena of the courtroom, Delaney represents herself as having no say concerning who she is to be.

Only when Hutchinson concludes his pleading does Delaney find respite from the "constitutional" power of the law over her identity. "Oh! what a relief it was to me when he finally finished his harangue and resumed his seat! As I never heard anyone plead before, I was very much alarmed, although I knew in my heart that every word he uttered was a lie! Yet, how was I to make people believe? It seemed a puzzling question."[43] Yet that respite is brief. Delaney, in her apprehension, stumbles upon the disconcerting issue that "explanatory power alone does not guarantee the truth of interpretation. Nothing does and nothing could."[44] It is apparent that fictions may assert themselves in any circumstances, in any place, in any construct, even those that may appear most legitimate and convincing. It is also apparent that, as Delaney represents herself, her "self" is essentially a fiction constructed by others. It becomes clear that in the courtroom what are determined as facts are for Delaney fictions constructed through the determining technologies of legal discourse.

Confronting Delaney is the overwhelming trouble that "problems of multiple authorship," the competing textual activities of various agents, "have ... separated the text from its original authors and given it a life of its own."[45] The terms "life" and "text" become interchangeable in this scene and at this point of the narrative. They achieve a strange equivalence, as they do in all autobiographical acts, but with recognizably greater force in African American autobiography. Delaney's autobiographical self-representation exposes the way in which the always preexisting construction of her life in the impersonal text of the law relies on "structures of discourse that so often contribute to the [African American] writers' oppression."[46] The life that is written in this scene is literally not her own. Even though the scene ostensibly produces her freedom, it dramatizes an enduring state of subjugation. Of course, such a predicament or analogous predicaments in the courtroom are not exclusive to African Americans. Nevertheless, it is imperative to see that for African Americans the issue does not involve any precipitating activity on their part. At issue in the case of African Americans are not the complications of precedent actions but an a priori state of being, the determination of an identity on which social existence and relations depend. One immediately understands, then, that African Americans and African American autobiographers must revise or recast in the terms of their lives a story that is already (unacceptably) written—and writ large—by American law and custom. They attempt to write a story already recorded and on which the book, for the most part, has been closed.

Among the issues in the balance is the issue of "authorship," and most particularly self-authorship. Hence, it proves more than incidental that the power to resist and abrogate Hutchinson's interpretations of the "facts"—or, equally, to elaborate an alternative fiction—rests not with Delaney, but with Edward Bates, who acts as her attorney. In this representation of her life, he "represents" her, not just as her advocate, but also as one more practitioner of the law who wields its power to construct and construe her life in accord with its letter. "Judge Bates arose, and his soulful eloquence and earnest pleading made such an impression on my sore heart, I listened with renewed hope. I felt the black storm clouds of doubt and despair were fading away, and that I was drifting into the safe harbor of the realms of truth. I felt as if everybody *must* believe *him*, for he clang [*sic*] to the truth, and I wondered how Mr. Hutchinson could so lie about a poor defenseless girl like me."[47]

The eloquence and "explanatory power" of Judge Bates are beyond question, as is his role in securing the relief and victory of Delaney. The emphasis falls on his actions and influence, while Delaney appears as merely acted upon. The turning point in the crisis of her self-determination depends upon the force and efficacy of a self constructed by another. In her own rendition of the climax of her quest for and attainment of self-determination, Delaney has no authority, self-authority or any other kind. Indeed, in Delaney's self-representation in this scene she ironically dramatizes her inability to represent herself in any terms but those supplied by those whose law and customs have enslaved her and will also set her "free." The conventional bathos of "a poor defenseless girl like me" underlines her self-representation as a tactic undertaken within a world of always polite fictions that systematically determine the discourse of self-representation and identity for African Americans. Drawn in the courtroom and in anxiety as "a poor defenseless girl," she possesses less proximity to her "self" than Bates, or, for that matter, Hutchinson. Delaney, in deference to the commanding power of the competing renditions of her self, is a negligible player at this point, and the irony is underscored rhetorically; "defenseless" is an interesting term to employ in reference to a life that turns precisely on a legal "defense" successfully upheld.

As with the narrative's privileging of the term "family" and its equivocal representation of Delaney's representativeness, the courtroom drama belies the notion of a "unified and autonomous" subject. Delaney represents her identity as decisively and variously constituted by the representations of others. The proceedings of the court as well as the autobiographical act that both renders them and is rendered possible by them expose the fictiveness of such a belief. This autobiographical act and its central terms—the privileging of the family, the claim of representativeness, and the climactic legal drama—also challenge the "ideological foundations" of that belief, the principles determining which fictions do and do not count. Because it alludes to the manifest fiction operating at the site of the courtroom itself, the peroration of Judge Bates forms a further element of this exposition, Bates commends the court as a site at which laws attain their most imposing, and thus inviolate, status, and Delaney transcribes his statement as follows: "'Gentlemen of the jury, I am a slave-holder myself, but, thanks to the Almighty God, I am above the base principle of holding anybody a slave that has as good right to her freedom as this girl has been proven to have; she was free before she was born; her mother was free, but kidnapped in her youth, and sacrificed to the greed of negro traders, and no free woman can give birth to a slave child, as it is in direct violation of the laws of God and man.' "[48] This ultimately successful argument turns on a larger set of ironies. What ultimately secures the court's determination of Delaney's identity is an act of self-definition by her legal representative ("I am a slave-holder myself") enabling a local, limited condemnation of slavery that remains clearly subordinate to an approbation of slavery in general. In his argument the laws of God and man rest surely on Delaney's side, yet the laws of God and man stand as surely behind slavery in general.[49] And to assert thus confidently the unequivocal meaning of divine and human law in this setting is to advance one further fiction. As Bates's activity as an advocate and Delaney's anxiety over whose definition of her identity will prevail attest, the courtroom is a site of equivocation. It is a site at which multiple determinations converge, conflict, and are deliberated. Delaney, furthermore, sets out explicitly a critique of the notion of unquestioned determinacy, a notion that assigns her an identity by a process that her narrative puts into question.

The courtroom would be transformed by Bates's appeal to the uncontestable will of God and to the mandates of man, not of men (not of individuals but of a species), into a site where there is no room for interpretation, since all determination has already been made. Because the courtroom is the site and mechanism of statutory interpretation—of the choosing of a particular meaning because a variety of possibilities presupposes and demands the deliberation—Bates's rhetorical gesture can only be understood as another fiction, "a supposition at variance with the facts." Rather than accepting appeals to unquestioned determinacy, courts make determinations "in the way that all knowledge is secure[d], by virtue of its acceptance within a community of interpretation whose existence is prerequisite to the production of knowledge itself."[50] In other words, the courtroom gathers representatives of a community in order to determine what the community knows because conflicting interests have put into question what it knows. The knowledge that courts are charged to research, discover, and possess emanates from and returns to the civic and political communities from which the law is constructed.

This point is underscored by the lack of clear legislative origins for the law of American slavery. "Slavery was not established by law in any American colony, but its development by custom was later recognized by legislation."[51] Law and custom interact to the point at which their distinctions blur; upon scrutiny law is premised on custom, while custom manages to manifest itself as law. The two equally enlist one another, as colonial laws of American slavery continually remind us.

> When Rhode Island legislators began the gradual statutory abolition of slavery in their state in 1784, they declared in a preamble that slavery "has gradually obtained in [Rhode Island] by unrestrained custom and the permission of the laws." This pithily restated the accepted explanations of the legal origins of slavery in the American states. To create slavery by law it was not necessary, as United States Supreme Court Justice John McLean later observed, to pass legislation providing that "slavery shall exist"; and no such statute was ever adopted in any American jurisdiction. However, as an anonymous Garrisonian abolitionist maintained in a retrospective survey of the statutory law of slavery in the British American mainland colonies, the legal origins of slavery are found in "the provincial legislative acts, which establish and sanction the custom [of slaveholding] and stamp it with the character of law."[52]

The situation Delaney narrated in her courtroom scene was related to the collective wills, conflicts, machinations, and imaginations of those segments of civic and political communities best able to command "the legal process . . . as an expression of social control."[53] The determined intermingling of custom and law composing the legal process demands that both be understood in relation to one another.

What law, custom, and the court, as it superintends them, struggle to define in Delaney's autobiography is her identity, her self as that self is complicated by being African American in communities in which African Americans are at worst enslaved and at best marginalized. If one understands the climactic courtroom scene of *From the Darkness Cometh the Light* as the autobiography's preeminent scene of writing, one understands—in addition to the manifest fictiveness of self-determining inscriptions—the manner in which some fictions are enforced and thus acquire greater sanction and power than others. Fictions transcend their provisional status always to someone's or some group's interest. In doing so, they acquire a further provisional status that is less discernible. Scenes of writing turn on issues of power, as is made clear by the conclusion Delaney assigns to the courtroom drama. The conclusion of the scene directly represents her continued confinement by a process of "constitutional" definition that always will determine her identity, even after it has defined her as "free." After Bates's peroration, "the case was then submitted to the jury, about 8 o'clock in the evening, and I was returned to the jail and locked in the cell which I had occupied for seventeen months, filled with the most intense anguish."[54] The courtroom is a site at which fictions are fabricated and acquire legal and social sanction, one at which the peculiar situation of African American identity is made clear. The determination of freedom and of the various forms of her continued subjugation rests with a community that takes it upon itself to measure, imagine, and (re)cast who she must be. Indeed, once American slavery was a fully formed legal institution, "statutory provisions directly or indirectly securing the rights of slaves were scanty. The only positively accorded right [in the mid-eighteenth century] appears in South Carolina's code of 1740 and Georgia's derivative code of 1755, where blacks could bring suit to test the legality of their enslavement."[55] Equally illustrative of the distinct association courts bear to African American subjectivity is the observation that "these suits, the only type of civil action a slave could take, did not begin until the nineteenth century."[56] Besides criminal prosecution, American courtrooms admitted African Americans primarily to determine their identity.

Hence, the individual scene of writing of the African American autobiographer is always matched by socially and legally prescriptive scenes of writing best imagined in terms of the courtroom, and for these reasons Delaney's autobiography effects an exposition of the concerns of the genre. Delaney seizes and begins to fill for African American autobiography "a prime fictive space" that holds great priority for African Americans in determining the terms of their lives.[57] It would seem that to write African American autobiography is not only to write "from behind the veil" but so to write in the public yet confining "constitutional" space of American custom and law.

It is fair to say that Delaney's "story undercuts the authority of both points of view presented in the story: the personal and the legal."[58] In Delaney's text "the personal and the legal" converge at the peculiar nexus that is the courtroom, enabling the critical reader to see in the interrelated fictions of the personal and the legal how African American autobiography necessarily challenges the ideological foundations of the genre and the ideological foundations of American life. In undercutting both, Delaney exposes the dual fictions of unity and autonomy in the autobiographical subject and its claim to self-identity. Fictions may assert themselves in any circumstances, in any place, in any construct, even those that may appear most legitimate and convincing. The self is one such fiction, legality another, and the convergence of the two in terms of African American identity another still.

NOTES

Chapter 6, "Self-Knowledge, Law, and African American Autobiography," was originally published in *The Culture of Autobiography, Constructions of Self-Representation*, ed. Robert Folkenflik, copyright 1993 by the Board of Trustees of the Leland Stanford Jr. University, all rights reserved. It is reprinted by permission of the publisher, Stanford University Press, sup.org.

1. Lucy A. Delaney, *From the Darkness Cometh the Light, or Struggles for Freedom* (c. 1891), in *Six Women's Slave Narratives*, ed. William L. Andrews (New York: Oxford University Press, 1988).

2. Marion Wilson Starling, *The Slave Narrative* (Washington, DC: Howard University Press, 1988), 106.

3. Michel Foucault, *The History of Sexuality: An Introduction* (New York: Vintage, 1978), 127. I am prompted to use this phrase by Teresa de Laurentis's understanding and explaining of it in her essay "The Technology of Gender." De Laurentis suggests that cultural formations and identities such as gender, race, and class are produced by cultural technologies "in the sense in which industrial machinery produces goods or commodities, and in so doing also produces social relations. Teresa de Laurentis, *The Technologies of Gender: Essays on Theory, Film, and Fiction* (Bloomington: Indiana University Press, 1987), 12.

4. Mark Tushnet, *The American Law of Slavery, 1810–1860: Considerations of Humanity and Interest* (Princeton, NJ: Princeton University Press, 1981), 229.

5. Stephen Butterfield, *Black Autobiography in America* (Amherst: University of Massachusetts Press, 1974), 2–3.

6. Roger Rosenblatt, "Black Autobiography: Life as the Death Weapon," in *Autobiography: Essays Theoretical and Critical*, ed. James Olney (Princeton, NJ: Princeton University Press, 1980), 174. Rosenblatt also makes the observation that "no black American author has ever felt the need to invent a nightmare to make his [or her] point" (172).

7. Georges Gusdorf, "Conditions and Limits of Autobiography," in Olney, *Autobiography*, 43. The terms supplied in brackets, however awkward they may seem, open the possibilities of the genre in ways that the original's gendered nouns and pronouns prohibit.

8. Candace Lang, "Autobiography in the Aftermath of Romanticism," *Diacritics* 12 (winter 1982): 5.

9. Abraham Lincoln, "First Joint Debate, Ottawa, August 21: Mr. Lincoln's Reply," in *The Lincoln-Douglas Debates of 1858*, ed. Robert W. Johannsen (New York: Oxford University Press, 1965), 52.

10. Valerie Smith, *Self-Discovery and Authority in Afro-American Narrative* (Cambridge, MA: Harvard University Press, 1987), 21.

11. Delaney, *From the Darkness*, 10.

12. Delaney, *From the Darkness*, 11.

13. Delaney, *From the Darkness*, 13.

14. Delaney, *From the Darkness*, 14.

15. Delaney, *From the Darkness*, 14–15.

16. Constitution of the United States, Thirteenth Amendment (1865).

17. Delaney, *From the Darkness*, 61.

18. Delaney, *From the Darkness*, 57.

19. Delaney, *From the Darkness*, 58.
20. Delaney, *From the Darkness*, 59.
21. Delaney, *From the Darkness*.
22. Frances Smith Foster, *Witnessing Slavery* (Westport, CT: Greenwood, 1979), 5–6.
23. Lang, "Autobiography in the Aftermath of Romanticism," 5, 10.
24. Delaney, *From the Darkness*, 62, 63–64.
25. Delaney, *From the Darkness*, 61–62.
26. Hazel Carby, *Reconstructing Womanhood: The Emergence of the Afro-American Woman Novelist* (New York: Oxford University Press, 1987), 164. At this point in her argument, Carby is considering the vexed dynamics of representation both "in relation to art and creative practices, and as it applies to intellectuals who understand themselves to be responsible for the representation of 'the race,' defining and constructing in their art its representative members and situating themselves as representative members of an oppressed social group" (164).
27. Lang, "Autobiography in the Aftermath of Romanticism," 5.
28. Frederick Douglass, *Narrative of the Life of Frederick Douglass, an American Slave, Written by Himself*, ed. Benjamin Quarles (Cambridge, MA: Harvard University Press, 1960), 58, 59.
29. Harriet A. Jacobs, *Incidents in the Life of a Slave Girl, Written by Herself*, ed. Jean Fagan Yellin (Cambridge, MA: Harvard University Press, 1987), 132.
30. Walter Benn Michaels, "The Fate of the Constitution," in *Interpreting Law and Literature*, ed. Sanford Levinson and Steven Mailloux (Evanston, IL: Northwestern University Press, 1988), 391.
31. William W. Wiecek, "The Statutory Law of Slavery and Race in the Thirteen Mainland Colonies of British North America," in *The Law of American Slavery*, ed. Kermit L. Hall (New York: Garland, 1987), 683.
32. William E. Moore, "Slave Law and the Social Structure," in Hall, *The Law of American Slavery*, 332.
33. Paul Finkelman, *Slavery in the Courtroom* (Washington, DC: Library of Congress, 1985), 14.
34. Moore, "Slave Law and the Social Structure," 338–39.
35. Eugene D. Genovese, "Slavery in the Legal History of the South and the Nation," in *Law, the Constitution, and Slavery*, ed. Paul Finkelman (New York: Garland, 1989), 162.
36. Delaney, *From the Darkness*, 24.
37. Delaney, *From the Darkness*, 33.
38. Delaney, *From the Darkness*, 40.
39. Moore, "Slave Law and the Social Structure," 340.
40. Delaney, *From the Darkness*, 40.
41. Delaney, *From the Darkness*, 39.
42. Delaney, *From the Darkness*, 27.
43. Delaney, *From the Darkness*, 40–41.
44. Michaels, "The Fate of the Constitution," 391.
45. Michaels, "The Fate of the Constitution," 390. It is important to note that in this and all my uses of quotations from Michaels's "The Fate of the Constitution," I am using the

author's prose in the service of a position that he particularly argues against. In its entirety the sentence I am now quoting reads: "Instead, they [theorists who think that texts can be separated from intention] imagine that the passage of time and the problems of multiple authorship have eventually separated the text from its original authors and given it a life of its own." Michaels states that at present "it may seem perverse not only to defend intention but to claim that every interpreter is always and only looking for authorial intention" (390); he writes further that, despite this climate, it is precisely his intention to do so. I repudiate Michaels's stance in regard to autobiography generally and African American autobiography in particular. Indeed, the issue, or problem, is exactly who the author is. The problem is especially exasperating for the African American autobiographer for whom the terms of life to be written appear (unacceptably) already written.

46. Smith, *Self-Discovery and Authority*, 6.

47. Delaney, *From the Darkness*, 41, emphasis in original.

48. Delaney, *From the Darkness*, 42.

49. Perhaps one might even go so far as to say that in this discourse Delaney emerges as an ironic figure in a proslavery argument. Certainly, these passages strike a very different chord from, say, the somewhat analogous concluding moment in Harriet Jacobs's *Incidents in the Life of a Slave Girl*, when Jacobs's freedom is purchased.

50. Kenneth S. Abraham, "Statutory Interpretation and Literary Theory: Some Common Concerns of an Unlikely Pair," in Levinson and Mailloux, *Interpreting Law and Literature*, 129.

51. Moore, "Slave Law and the Social Structure," 325.

52. Wiecek, "The Statutory Law of Slavery," 661.

53. A. Leon Higginbotham Jr., *In the Matter of Color: Race and the American Legal Process—The Colonial Period* (New York: Oxford University Press, 1978), 13.

54. Delaney, *From the Darkness*, 43.

55. Wiecek, "The Statutory Law of Slavery," 668.

56. Moore, "Slave Law and the Social Structure," 342.

57. Robert B. Stepto, telephone conversations, June 22 and 23, 1991. One might imagine the courtroom as "a prime fictive space" because, in the words of Stepto, "barred from a certain context, especially as it involves voice and telling one's own story," it is inevitable that you finally arrive there.

58. Brook Thomas, *Cross-Examinations of Law and Literature: Cooper, Hawthorne, Stowe, and Melville* (New York: Cambridge University Press, 1987), 110.

III. IMAGINING COLLECTIVELY
Identity, Individuality, and Other Social Phantasms

Introduction

MARLON B. ROSS

Race, gender, and sexuality, as popularly prescribed, are mutually reinforcing terms of ideal and abstract efficiency that, in their co-implications, promote even more attenuated forms of "efficiency" within the most intimate circuits of human exchange.
—LINDON BARRETT, "The Gaze of Langston Hughes"

Reading Lindon Barrett on cultural identity makes for a special kind of intellectual odyssey that hails in/tangible pleasures of surprise nestled within the rigors of scholarly thought that is nonetheless fully socially engaged. Barrett does not intend to be a facile read, exactly because the everyday experience of identity formation is itself so falsely solicitous. Unlike the un/canny sociopsychic-discursive process of identification—which elides, evacuates, redacts, adapts, and dissembles—his theorizing of identity demands an alertness to its innumerable intricacies, intractabilities, eruptions, and disruptions. As the above quotation indicates, Barrett grasps, certainly as instructively as any contemporary critic, the paradox by which cultural identity is deployed through highly abstract, impersonal, efficient repetitions of social reproduction, appearing to come out of nowhere and to proliferate everywhere—reproduction that nonetheless also cocoons us in deeply intimate human interactions, as distant as macroeconomy, as personally binding as a mother's hug, rooted in the blood, or a lover's caress, routed through individual choice and destiny. Rather than aiming at a theory (stable, uniform, rationally systematic, deeply structured, liberally progressive), he instead cultivates the theorizing of identity as an ongoing radical act that calls out and struggles against identity's persistent demand to be simply enacted as ready-made acculturation. Barrett's theorizing helps us to see how a large part of the problem of identity concerns its patent insistence on the naturally familiar, as it waffles between, from one side of its mouth, a comforting rhetoric of universal humanity (pivoting in a friendly capitalist kiss on the cheek) and, from the other side of the same mouth, a cozy invitation to intimate kinship within a known body (self, race, religion, nationality, class, gender, sexuality). While recognizing the joys attendant both on belonging to a community and on the constant replay of others' differentiation, Barrett does not shy away from the brutalities of identity subjection, a violence that bleeds from many wounds, from the social and psychic effects of stigma to the lethal lynchings of post–civil rights racial profiling.

The four essays included here were written in the late 1990s. Two of them were published in *Callaloo*, indicating Barrett's unrelieved commitment to, and troubling of, the field of African diaspora studies; the other two in *Yale Journal of Criticism* and *Cultural Critique*, respectively, manifesting his commitment to, and demands on, the advance of cultural theory. Very much at home in Barrett's corpus, these essays talk to each other and also dialogue with his landmark book *Blackness and Value: Seeing Double*, where he asks, "Still, what exactly does it mean to pursue an understanding of race (as a value) in these terms—as both fluid and hypostasized, as concomitantly a series of transactions and the representation of a formal essence, as agonistically systemic?"[1] Taken together, the essays provide one of the most unsettling accounts of identity that can be found in contemporary cultural criticism. Each essay contains a variation of a definition that understands identification as a cycle of codependent clauses in a contract that masks itself as merely what we need to desire to achieve everyday reality. In "Black Men in the Mix," the redefinition reads like this: "Race, since it is not a genetic reality, might be more assuredly characterized as a series of prohibitions on social desire and sexual practice, prohibitions stabilizing and ensuring the transmission of identifying phenotypical traits from generation to generation."[2] Barrett tracks how identity is transmitted across generations and geographies through four interdependent economies: bodily (the corporate self as a relation of individual to social body), libidinal (the disciplining of subjects through the collective ordering of desire), discursive (the sensory, technical, and social vectors of representation), and economic (the marketing of desire through commodified social interactions and objectified social groupings). If desire is the fuel that runs cultural identification, the laissez-faire market is the engine that keeps identity on track through time and space. As we see in a different way for each essay, however, even as desire fuels visible (that is, identifiable) subjects conducive to the market's ingenuity (engine-unity), it also powers other, less recognizable flows of energy inimical both to monetary exchange and to familiar fixities of sociality.

The essay "Identities and Identity Studies" can be taken as a manifesto or blueprint.[3] Posing a challenge to the way cultural studies so quickly calcifies according to academic discipline, Barrett objects to any formulation of culture that too easily aligns disciplinary subjects with proper cultural objects (women's studies for gender, African American studies for race, queer studies for sexuality, etc.). Insisting that cultural studies, if it is to realize its iconoclastic impulse, must find grounding in theories fleshed out by feminists of color, Barrett proffers intersectionality, as theorized by Kimberlé Crenshaw and others, as a way to observe the power of fixed "categories of identity" while resisting the tendency to assume the "stability and independence of rubrics of identity."[4] Barrett's choice of a little-known short story by black feminist Toni Cade Bambara, "The Hammer Man," performs what he urges. At a moment of crisis for her black community, the female protagonist of the story, a rambunctious tomboy, retreats to a heteronormative gender identity, abandoning her antagonistic relation to the community's standards of feminine decorum as she adopts the conventional role of supportive "sister" to a young black boy faced with police brutality. Brilliantly, Barrett highlights the theoretical import of the short story, which plots intersectionality as seamlessly as social experience itself circuits racial cognition through gender dis/affiliation, and gender cognition through racial dis/affiliation. The dis/associative power of an identity (binding the character to one group by cutting her from another) hinges on a concomitant dis/associative vulnerability of another identity (opening her to blood affection with one group by shielding her from another's harm). Like José Esteban Muñoz's theory of disidentification, Barrett's disassociation draws attention to identity's trickster double-edginess, his concept of "seeing double" from *Blackness and Value*, always pulling us from one box to push us into another.[5]

In two essays that should be read intertextually, Barrett shows how two black male queer memoirists exploit, and trip on, the shady line demarcating an individual's free flow of erotic desire from identity's (and the publishing market's) concupiscent prohibitions. In "The Gaze of Langston Hughes" and "Black Men in the Mix," he explores how narrative self-masking and self-exposure, rather than being contraries, operate under the same rules governing the sexual expression of racialized subjectivity—in this case young black queer autobiographical narrators.[6] We can hear echoes of Michel Foucault's theories of subjection here, but tweaked, twisted, and fully bent in an intersectional direction not imaginable to Foucault himself. While Langston Hughes in *The Big Sea* presents a narrator who falls into silence and passivity when confronted with scenes of sexual aggression and violation, Dennis Rodman in *Bad as I Wanna Be* presents a narrator who exposes the self (quite literally) as an ostensibly unique vector of scandalous desire ironically only to reverberate into an autobiographical persona that "splinters into irreducible, but functional, points of identification." Hughes's technique of self-absenting dissemblance seems especially appropriate for a Jim Crow epoch in which heteronormative violence against women can seem to disassociate the narrator from the lynching violence that reduces all black men to the status of queers. Just as white queers lurked in black sex districts to hide their stigmatized sexuality from dominant society, a black queer writer like Hughes could hide behind the Jim Crow curtain that emphasized the homoracial battle (my own phrase, not Barrett's) between black and white men over the violated bodies of women.[7] In Rodman's post–civil rights epoch, when same-sexuality has exploded into public view as part of a multicultural front demanding visibility, postmodern exposure displaces Jim Crow masking. As Rodman refuses the dutiful role of the erect black athlete, however, he cannot help but perform "the seemingly impossible incorporation of African-American 'young guys' within structures to which they are characteristically considered alien." In the violent concatenation of the big black athlete who exposes himself as a cross-dressing suicidal punk, we can easily miss blatant contradictions chaining Rodman's free flow of desire to an engine of marketable racial and sexual clichés. In both essays, Barrett reads the readers of these texts (eminent critics and salacious reviewers) with stunningly brilliant critiques of how "the notion of the individual remains, more than a vested principle, a fetish through which other fetishes are refracted" ("Black Men in the Mix"). And yet, Barrett's reading of Rodman reminds us that "cultural orders [are] never fully able to contain all the energies they invoke."

In the essay that is perhaps Barrett's sine qua non, "Dead Men Printed," we learn how nothing theoretical is alien to him.[8] The essay ranges across every conceivable discipline, from Deleuze and Guattari's post-psychoanalysis to Susan Strange's post-Keynesian economic theory, from Bill Maurer's social anthropology to Gerald Horne's sociological numbers. It is an essay deserving of as much influence as Hortense Spiller's groundbreaking "Mama's Baby, Papa's Maybe," and certainly one deserving a more attentive, extended exegesis than can be mounted in a brief introduction of this sort.[9] Be on guard. Anyone having known Lindon personally or having been acquainted with Barrett solely through his written texts, through his intellectual achievement and promise, will find hard going this essay on eulogies for young black men—in this case the rappers Tupac Shakur and Biggie Smalls—violently felled. Reminiscent of

Sharon Holland's bracing anti-eulogy, "'I'm in the Zone': Bill T. Jones, Tupac Shakur, and the (Queer) Art of Death," Barrett refuses to normalize or naturalize the death of young black men as a self-violating death wish, the expected cost of being young, black, and too talented to survive the darkening streets of America's promised land.[10] Instead, Barrett unsparingly theorizes the transfiguration of young black men into deadening print, reproducing the economic logic of a U.S. moral imagination that needs to cast young black men as dangerous weapons whose performed alienation (think gangsta rap) nonetheless stokes untold profits when parlayed to the most intimately harmless habitats (think young white men's suburban bedrooms). This is why at the heart of this essay is a barrage of lethal statistics, an unusual strategy in Barrett's work, but one fully in keeping with the attempt to goad the culture's accommodation of such black facts into a thoughtful enragement. The persons of young black men, even in death or especially in death, are turned into profiteering weapons against which persistent social violence is justified. Rather than coyly liminal like Hughes and Rodman, these hip-hop boys Tupac and Biggie, Trayvon, Oscar Grant and Jonathan Ferrell, and all those countless, nameless young black men so un/like them, create radically unnerving possibility at the very limits of identity's unceasing subjection. "Young African Americans and their postures," Barrett writes poignantly but unsentimentally, "in more ways than merely marked by hip-hop, revile and reject the collective phantasm of human relations by which the cash nexus is falsely and officially advertised." It is exactly their creative assault on the project of identity domination "that is met with exorbitant and untenable violence" ("Dead Men Printed").

Guiding us through this unstinting, difficult knowledge of the ongoing brutality perpetrated by identity as a project of property and discipline, Barrett wants us to know ourselves beyond this zigzag of us-them, either-other, up-down, wants us to know the delights of connecting in untested places across and within difference. And thus Lindon's voice resonates sonorously and resolutely—inviting us to hear ourselves, our own intellectual challenges, in the difference that is forever him.

NOTES

1. Lindon Barrett, *Blackness and Value: Seeing Double* (New York: Cambridge University Press, 1999), 55.

2. Lindon Barrett, "Black Men in the Mix: Badboys, Heroes, Sequins, and Dennis Rodman," chapter 9, this volume.

3. Lindon Barrett, "Identities and Identity Studies: Reading Toni Cade Bambara's 'The Hammer Man,'" chapter 7, this volume.

4. See especially Kimberlé Crenshaw, Neil Gotanda, Gary Peller, and Kendall Thomas, "Introduction," in *Critical Race Theory: The Key Writings That Formed the Movement*, ed. Kimberlé Crenshaw, Neil Gotanda, Gary Peller, and Kendall Thomas (New York: New Press, 1995), xiii–xxxii.

5. José Esteban Muñoz, *Disidentifications: Queers of Color and the Performance of Politics* (Minneapolis: University of Minnesota Press, 1999).

6. Lindon Barrett, "The Gaze of Langston Hughes: Subjectivity, Homoeroticism, and the Feminine in *The Big Sea*," chapter 8, this volume.

7. On homoraciality, see Marlon Ross, *Manning the Race: Reforming Black Men in the Jim Crow Era* (New York: New York University Press, 2004), 11–12.

8. Lindon Barrett, "Dead Men Printed: Tupak Shakur, Biggie Smalls, and Hip-Hop Eulogy," chapter 10, this volume.

9. Hortense Spillers, "Mama's Baby, Papa's Maybe: An American Grammar Book," in *Black, White, and in Color: Essays on American Literature and Culture* (Chicago: University of Chicago Press, 2003), 203–29.

10. See Sharon Holland, "Epilogue," in *Raising the Dead: Readings of Death and (Black) Subjectivity* (Durham, NC: Duke University Press, 2000), 175–81.

| CH7

Identities and Identity Studies:
Reading Toni Cade Bambara's "The Hammer Man" (1998)

In many ways, this article reiterates critical perspectives championed by feminists of color. As documented, for instance, in the collection *This Bridge Called My Back*, feminists of color have long led the way in recognizing and theorizing the manner in which categories of identity, made most salient by dominant cultural codes, ineluctably intersect, transfigure, and remain coimplicated in one another. Beverly Smith, in an interview in *This Bridge Called My Back*, states the matter forthrightly: "In reality, the way women live their lives those separations just don't work. Women don't live their lives like, Well this part is race, and this is class, and this part has to do with women's identities, so it's confusing."[1] Gloria Anzaldúa similarly laments that she lives in a world in which "they chop me up into little fragments and tag each piece with a label."[2] It is well known that feminists of color have for many years attempted to critique and transform the very category of woman as well as undertake critiques and transformations of the social categories of sexuality and race.

Nonetheless, widely understood conceptions of ethnicity and race remain largely untransformed by critical visions sponsored by feminists of color, as evidenced, for instance, by the codifications of Werner Sollers in "Ethnicity." "Ethnic, racial, or national identifications," writes Sollers, "rest on antitheses, on negativity, or on what the ethnopsychoanalyst Georges Devereux has termed their 'dissociative' character."[3] While it is certainly true that acknowledging this "dissociative" character is indispensable to assessing the psychological, social, and political potency of ethnicity/race, it is still as incomplete a gesture as it is an enabling one.⁴ For, as much as ethnic/racial formations prove dissociative or diacritical, they are also profoundly syncretic. An often unconsidered dimension of ethnic/racial specifications is the masking of the more subtle information ethnicity/race, gender, and sexuality hold for one another.

Forwarding the notion that the integrity and intersectionality of these categories often remain underestimated, the following discussion suggests that, as generally configured, the new academic concerns codified as cultural studies often miss opportunities to interrogate important imbrications of what are routinely considered separate categories of identity. This investigation considers the way predominant epistemes of cultural studies, in the very gesture of attempting to foster counterknowledges, display widespread respect for the assumed stability and independence of rubrics of identity, a state of affairs ironically reflecting— at least on one level—institutional and disciplinary inertia. The alternative perspective offered in this analysis is pursued through a reading of Toni Cade Bambara's short story "The Hammer Man" in which the coimplications of fixed categories of identity are evident in the figure of the central ethnic/racial subject, the narrator. Reading "The Hammer Man" with the predominant configurations of cultural studies in mind, one begins to imagine that, in the same way other options and recalcitrant knowledges are foreclosed for the narrator by the conclusion of the narrative, they are foreclosed for cultural critiques, overlooking the fact that it may be misleading to believe that cultural doxa in need of explanation does or would correspond—as a matter of course—to those categories offered by the culture under investigation in the first place. In other words, the question of cultural studies and disciplinary alliances to rubrics of cultural identity forms the critical limit against which this analysis presses. The literary reading and ensuing discussion aim to explicate not only the imbrication of cultural identities but also the formation of institutional knowledges in terms of putatively separate identities. The aim is to extend the analysis of cultural identities begun by feminists of color into a consideration of ongoing academic configurations of knowledge.

The claim is that, at present, the extent to which these kinds of cultural coimplications remain generally undocumented in the epistemes of cultural studies seems inversely related to their articulation in the crises of Bambara's "The Hammer Man." That is to say, if one were to read this story within standard epistemological configurations, one would be completely at a loss to account for the narrator's assumption of imposed gendered and sexual identities through what is *foremost* a crisis of racialization. By the conclusion of "The Hammer Man," the protagonist comes to "know" and respect the forceful, dissociative nature of ethnicity/race but, in addition, by means of the same trauma, she comes to "desire" and inhabit normative gender roles and their implied heterosexuality. Normative gender and sexual roles transcend what should be the definitive, racialized cleavage of the text. On both sides of what emerges as a stark narrative (and ethnic/racial) divide, the protagonist is pressed toward identical gendered and sexual postures. This syncretism is exposed in terms of the dynamics of the black/white racial dichotomy in the United States.

Indeed, once one foregoes the notion that dissociation is the single or preeminent issue defining ethnicity/race, what becomes evident is a more complex, asymmetrical configuration determining ethnic/racial membership. For ethnicity/race depends ultimately on a "heteronormative vision"—to borrow Kendall Thomas's apt phrase.[5] Its ultimate logic fixes individuals foremost in a procreative relation to social organization. This relation is intent on cultural transmission and/or the transmission of visible physical characteristics speciously and belatedly guaranteeing what seem self-evident divisions and dissociations. The crisis of ethnicity/race, on close examination, proves libidinal, invested ultimately in a set of fundamental prohibitions on the discharge of sexual energies. Ethnicity/race might be thought of as a series of prohibitions on social desire and sexual practice, prohibitions intent on stabilizing and ensuring the transmission of identifying phenotypical (or cultural) traits from generation to generation. Only by a circuitous route through matters of gender and sexuality do the dynamics of ethnicity/race lodge themselves in the dissociation by which they are most routinely understood. By not attending fully to the circuitousness of these dynamics, cultural studies may unintentionally reiterate ideological systems it often sets out to critique or expose. This is an ironic critical position that historian Joan Scott, in "The Evidence of Experience," instructively details in the context of social history.[6]

One notable site where imbrications of categories of identification are intuitively comprehended and intuitively play themselves out is that of the family. In consideration of the existential (rather than biological) "reality" of race in the United States, philosopher Naomi Zack outlines, for example, the "asymmetrical kinship systems" constituting the family as a paramount site of these imbrications. Asymmetrical kinship systems, Zack informs us, comprise the most crucial ground and index of ethnicity/race in the United States because, whereas phenotypical or other evidence may in some cases be so unreliable as to allow particular individuals to "pass," family membership negotiates more assiduously the tensions between the contingencies of individual circumstance and communal dissociative belonging. Zack, concerned with the particular animus between "blackness" and "whiteness" in the United States, spells out the manner in which family, understood as the primary site of ethnic/racial formation, exposes the cathected ground of ethnicity/race, gender, and sexuality:

> Designated black physical racial characteristics are genetic. The mechanism of human genetics is heterosexual sexual intercourse. That fact alone is enough to account for much of the obscenity, fear, fascination, lust, scorn, degradation, and both real and pseudo-revulsion with which white people have considered the sexuality of black people. Individuals who are designated black have the ability, through the mechanism of their heterosexuality, to destroy the white identity of families, and because race of kin determines race of individuals, to destroy the white identity of the relatives of their descendants. Thus the asymmetrical kinship system of racial inheritance in the United States not only is intrinsically racist in favor of white people, but it defines black people as intrinsically threatening and dangerous to white families.[7]

What is evident, then, in the one-drop rule of U.S. "black" and "white" racial specifications is the fact that, as much as ethnicity/race is a civic, legal, and psychological discourse of dissociation, it also operates as a civic, legal, and psychological discourse of sexual practice and gender specification.[8] The logic of ethnicity/race demands a heterosexual paradigm with its attendant instantiations of gender imbalance, and this set of mutual information finds its principal point of cathexis in the figure of the family.[9] The consequence of making these recognitions is to obviate to some degree the exhaustiveness of critical attentions that principally imagine "processes of generating feelings of dissociative belonging."[10] Moreover, it obviates epistemological and institutional agendas based on "increasingly territorialized interpretations of social and subjective being."[11]

It may be somewhat counterproductive to consider the rubrics of ethnicity/race, gender, and sexuality as primarily independent sites of psychic and political subjection, even though it is along these lines that cultural studies for the most part manages the production of academic "knowledges" of identity. The enabling gesture of cultural analysis is most often, as in the larger culture, one marking these sites as generally discrete (though sometimes overlapping) categories of identification, instead of pursuing the manner in which they are articulated through and in one another. In this way, more than speaking to the broader conditions of modern subjection and subjectivity, this move may speak to a recent history of transforming challenges to the unacceptable "isolation of [academic] ideological analysis from concrete cultural struggles."[12]

This is not to say that significant work is not being produced beyond dominant epistemological and institutional frameworks. The work of Judith Butler, Kimberlé Crenshaw, Lee Edelman, Phillip Brian Harper, Hortense Spillers, Kendall Thomas, Robyn Wiegman, and Jean Walton comes to mind, to name only a few leading scholars in this regard; the work of each in the context of black/white relations in the United States investigates the circumstance that ethnicity/race, heterosexuality, and gender norms rely on—are actually constituted through—each other in their reproduction. As already noted, it is imperative to acknowledge that in the context of the post-1960s academy, the cultural and literary criticism of feminists of color form one strand of scholarship that has been insistently aware of these matters and has pursued a more syncretic investigative tack than generally taken in the academy.

African American feminist criticism provides a significant antecedent for the type of ongoing critical work now gaining increasing currency. Important exchanges initiated by African American feminist critics with a largely masculinist African American critical institution and a largely white feminist critical institution have produced widespread effects on the post-1960s academy, although these effects are rarely as openly acknowledged as they are by Cheryl Wall, who states: "Not only has the criticism of black women's writing been transformed over the past two decades; this criticism has transformed other critical discourses as well.... The extent to which feminist and African Americanist writing and, yes, even the criticism that claims the center are more inclusive than they were twenty years ago owes much to black women's writing and its critics changing as many words as they pleased."[13] Wall rehearses the fact that research initiatives underwritten by African American feminism have had, in addition to an extraordinary breadth of influence, a powerful transformative effect on the very rudiments of the academic conversation itself, of which one sign is the advent of earnest examinations of the undertheorized intersections of cultural and social identity. By no means can African American feminist criticism singularly claim responsibility for the productive critical syncretism of the recent academy, but it does constitute one of the earliest and most visible scholarly fields insistent on demonstrating the intellectual gains of refusing to conceive of the main categories of modern identity as merely separate and independent. In this way, African American feminist interventions played a crucial role in charting present possibilities for reconceiving what are usually understood as fundamental but "separate" markers of identity in the modern West or ascendant New World. Such interventions exposed and, with others, continue to expose some of the most subtle machinations of the potent and oppressive cultural logic of the modern West. In the epilogue to *Things of Darkness*, her study of race and gender in early modern England, Kim Hall traces such a debt as well as its radical consequences for what matters have become "visible" at some institutional sites of inquiry.[14]

It bears emphasizing that the issue is not choosing between competing propositions about ethnicity/race—dissociation or syncretism—but imagining, instead, how these propositions are mutually supplementary. Toni Cade Bambara's short story "The Hammer Man" (from her 1972 collection *Gorilla, My Love*) is a brief, exemplary text in this regard. The play of both dissociation and syncretism is paramount in determining the conflicts and crises of Bambara's unnamed pubescent protagonist, a virtually fearless tomboy who finds herself at odds at the opening of the narrative with a variety of people in her African American community. These tensions internal to the community form the preoccupation of the narrative until, in a climactic showdown, the narrator and Manny (her greatest enemy) are paired off one evening in "Douglas Street park" against two white policemen.[15] This heightened confrontation—bringing the greatest tensions of the story to bear through the prism of racial division—profoundly reshapes the protagonist's relation to both her community and larger environment. Not only in terms of racialization but in terms of gender and sexuality as well, this reorientation holds dramatic consequences for her sense of self.

The narrator's account of these events begins with her characteristic humor and insouciance. She proclaims, "I was glad to hear Manny had fallen off the roof," then proceeds, in her rambling, energetic way, to explain how Manny's fall simplifies her life.[16] Indeed, the first two pages or so of the seven-page story comprise her high-spirited explanation of why Manny lay in murderous wait for her on the stoop of her parents' apartment building, "all day and all night, hardly speaking to the people going in and out . . . with his sister bringing him peanut butter sandwiches and cream sodas."[17] Manny seeks revenge for a verbal attack on him (and his mother) made by the narrator—an arbitrary verbal attack motivated only by her mischievous disregard for Manny's reputation as crazy and therefore not to be messed with. After several days and nights of his vigil, Manny is somehow enticed to the roof of the building, perhaps by "Frankie [who might have] got some nasty girls to go up on the roof with him," and Manny's fall releases the narrator from a supposed bout of yellow fever and, therefore, self-confinement in her parents' apartment.[18]

The end of Manny's vigil allays tensions that have spread throughout the neighborhood. The narrator's father, in response to Manny's self-declared intent to kill his daughter, jams the head of Manny's older brother, Bernard—"who was more his size"—into a mailbox which, in turn, elicits angry taunts from an uncle of Manny and Bernard.[19] Similarly, Miss Rose, a friend of the family, confronts Manny's mother several times on the narrator's behalf; Manny's mother chases Miss Rose into the street several times, and everyone in the neighborhood "would congregate at the window sills or on the fire escape" to watch the two of them "[commence] to get with it, snatching bottles out of the garbage cans and breaking them on the johnny pumps and stuff like that."[20] Even as they eagerly watch, everyone agrees "that it was still much too cold for this kind of nonsense," and the narrator herself marvels at the sight that one could use "the garbage cans as arsenals . . . [yielding] sticks and table legs and things . . . and scissor blades and bicycle chains."[21]

This world of seemingly bizarre interactions seems natural and normal to the narrator, but she ultimately encounters institutional agents who do not share her view and who, much more harshly, denigrate and violently handle people from this world. Ironically, then, her escape from Manny's wrath brings her into confrontation with greater and more daunting forces than the tenacious Manny. What she begins abruptly and inadvertently to face is the dissociative significance of ethnicity/race—and precisely at one of the many institutional sites both manufacturing and maintaining that dissociation. She is bribed by her mother into going to the neighborhood community center, where her mother hopes that contact with activities organized and prescribed for girls will reform her tomboyish ways. Instead, as unreformed and irreverent as ever, the narrator sneaks into the office of the community center and discovers in "one of those not-quite-white folders . . . that I was from a deviant family in a deviant neighborhood."[22] As she chafes at her cultural positioning as "deviant," the consequences of which she does not yet fully understand, she imagines herself more than equal to the encounter. She claims the word "deviant" for her own, running "it into the ground till one day my father got the strap just to show me how deviant he could get."[23] Decidedly, then, both she and her narrative world remain largely unchanged by this encounter. Dramatic and climactic changes in narrative style, her perceptions, and her behavior are yet to come.

A subsequent and more intense moment of racialization holds very different consequences; the long final episode of the narrative draws the lines of enmity and violence most extremely. One night after she is "thrown out of the center for playing pool when [she] should've been sewing," the narrator and Manny are antagonized by two white policemen, and this second, more intense, more immediate encounter with the dissociative dynamic of ethnicity/race profoundly alters her sense of self, as well as radically divides the narrative itself into two dissociated halves.[24] The apparently ubiquitous violence (or threats of violence) marking the initial environment of the story pales in comparison to the possibilities of much more drastic and arbitrary violence brooding over the latter half of the story. The rambling circuitry that characterizes the initial rehearsal of events is superseded by a rehearsal of events that is, by contrast, starkly linear and tightly paced. The humor, levity, and high spiritedness of the initial portion of the story dissipate. In deference to the dynamics of the "contrastive identification" endemic to ethnicity/race, the tone and trajectory of the narrative become starkly polarized.[25] So much so, in fact, that in the latter half of the narrative, the protagonist finds herself declaring solidarity with the very person who is patently perceived as her enemy at the beginning of the narrative: "Now, when somebody says [black boy] like that, I gets warm," she states, as tensions mount in the park, "And crazy or no crazy, Manny was my brother at that moment and the cop was the enemy."[26]

Even as her anger and sense of solidarity with Manny grow, the narrator never entirely imagines the full force of the antagonisms playing themselves out. As the police question the two of them for being in the park so late, Manny mindlessly continues to play basketball until one cop "finally grabbed the ball to get Manny's attention. But that didn't work. Manny just stood there with his arms out waiting for the pass so he could save the [imaginary] game. He wasn't paying no mind to the cop. So, quite naturally, when the cop slapped him upside his head it was a surprise."[27] The stark change in the narrative invites the reader to see that the violent confrontations of the latter half of the story are driven by an institutionally sanctioned animus much more menacing than the "deviant" circle of interactions joining together such community figures as Manny and the narrator, Miss Rose and Manny's mother, the narrator's father and Manny's brother Bernard. By comparison, these earlier interactions seem benign, if vitiated, forms of community converse. For example, in the narration of these earlier events there is the suggestion that Miss Rose and Manny's mother find in their very public battles an odd measure of relief from their usual circumstances. For, when Manny's fall from the roof for the most part settles their disagreement, "Miss Rose went back to her dream books and Manny's mother went back to her tumbled-down kitchen of dirty clothes and bundles and bundles of rags and children."[28] The boisterousness and turbulence of frustrated individuals coming together in the first section of the narrative draw out lines and circuits of community, whereas the violence of the latter section reflects the much more damaging and unhealthy effects of institutionalized processes of polarization and abjection. Of the abject, Judith Butler writes that it designates "precisely those 'unlivable' and 'uninhabitable' zones of social life which are nevertheless densely populated by those who do not enjoy the status of the subject, but whose living under the sign of the 'unlivable' is required to circumscribe the domain of the subject."[29]

The apparently definitive issue of the text—the issue underwriting its climactic confrontation as well as shaping the very presentation of the narrative itself—seems, then, the dissociative intervention of ethnicity/race into the world of the narrator. The upshot of this intervention is to draw together the pairs "abject and subject," "black and white," into a definitive homology. The paramount concerns of the narrative are not so deceptively simple, however. Its collective events suggest, quite differently, that to think, speak, and act in deference to ethnicity/race amounts necessarily and already to thinking, speaking, and acting in terms of gender and sexuality. As patently as the events of the narrative are differentiated into two opposed sections by the polarizing dynamic of ethnicity/race, they are united across that divide by powerful citations of gendered and sexual norms. The interplay of all three sites of identification is most evident in the escalating exchanges between the narrator and the increasingly menacing police. After the police assault Manny and take his basketball away, the narrator exhorts them in her characteristically flippant manner to give it back to him, so he can continue practicing to be "Mr. Basketball." She is warned in return by one of her adversaries, who calls her "sister," that if she is not careful she will be "run in" too. To this comment she replies with even greater defiance: "I damn sure can't be your sister seeing how I'm a black girl. Boy, I sure will be glad when you run me in so I can tell everyone about that. You must think you're in the South, mister."[30]

Like Naomi Zack's codification of the fundamental intersection of race and kinship systems, the narrator's retort exposes the interest of race in the heterosexual relations on which family structures depend. Inadvertently hitting on the full scope of the cultural significance of ethnicity/race, the narrator reads her adversary's use of "sister" in an impossibly literal and consequently deflating manner. If, in fact, she is his sister, then they must share one or both parents, a circumstance that would efface his racial designation as white, produce him as black, and, what is more, place him in a resoundingly ironic (and no doubt dangerous) position, especially at the imaginary moment at which he would be forced to face his former peers. At best, the as yet undisclosed moment of heterosexual intimacy that would render them immediate blood relations—and, therefore, racially identical (i.e., black)—would constitute on the part of one or both of "their" parents a reckless disregard of the racial divide the policemen now strictly reiterate through their hostile actions. At worst, that undisclosed moment of heterosexual intimacy would render her adversary's life as a highly effective act of "passing" that, on the one hand, betrays family and ethnic/racial solidarity and, on the other, dupes another race. Redacted and acknowledged in the exchange is an implicit heterosexual paradigm, its gendered roles and responsibilities, as well as its ability to structure and guarantee the ethnic/racial divide and belligerent interaction central to the episode.

This cathexis is also evident in the exchange that follows. Exasperated, and calling her "little girl," the officer exhorts the narrator to take Manny, her "boyfriend," home, and she bristles at the comment, as though it stands as the point beyond all forbearance. "That really got me," she states. "The 'little girl' was bad enough but that 'boyfriend' was too much."[31] Highlighted once again is the fact that gendered and sexual identifications are coincident with her racial identification. The taunt places her directly within the heterosexual and gendered configurations that she has rejected throughout the narrative and that she, only moments before, deployed in her own verbal assault. Further, it reiterates the normative roles already and uniformly foisted on her by virtually every adult she has encountered in the narrative—regardless of the side of the fractured narrative (and ethnic/racial divide) on which they stand. In negotiating the world of her own racial community, as well as the belligerence of another more institutionally powerful one, she insistently is confronted by the fact that "norms of realness by which the subject is produced are racially informed conceptions of 'sex.'"[32] She encounters norms that fix gendered and heterosexual bodies within the culturally and socially (re)productive categories of ethnicity/race.

From the opening moments of the text, the reader finds the narrator's mother admonishing her to be more ladylike and to stop consorting with boys in a manner that supposes she can assume the same roles they do. The community center attempts to discipline her along the same lines, and even the unconventional Miss Rose most often calls her by her "brother's name by mistake."[33] Indeed, as though in culmination of the constant chiding of all the other adults around her, her proper role and her ideal relation to boys is prosaically redacted by her racialized foe in the park. His comment reiterates widespread expectations that situate her squarely within economies of race in which women are understood foremost as "mothers [who] reproduce bodies not in a social vacuum but for either a dominant or a subordinate group."[34] These repeated citations force her to recognize—if not reconcile herself to—understood cultural and social assignments.

Summarily put, these exchanges in the park reflect the widely accounted dissociative dynamic of ethnic/racial membership, yet they do so in ways that, rather than being merely dissociative, are ineluctably insinuated in a "heteronormative vision of racial identity," a vision that largely forecloses gender insubordination and thus implicitly also "expression of sexual difference."[35] What becomes evident is a highly complex and asymmetrical (re)production of ethnicity/race that contemporary epistemologies of cultural studies largely fall short of clarifying or interrogating. The observations of Robyn Wiegman on this point bear repeating. In *American Anatomies: Theorizing Race and Gender*, Wiegman provokes one to consider that if already consequentially circulating categories of identity—race, gender, sexuality—"are finally the only constitutive ground on which [cultural studies] can base its production of counter-knowledges," then cultural studies mounts only a feeble challenge to hegemonic ways of knowing; these counterknowledges would represent negligible challenges to the powerfully oppressive mechanisms, to the "logic of modernity... [and] the disciplinarity that has accompanied the human's emergence as both subject and object of knowledge, an emergence through which bodies have been increasingly anatomized.... [It] does not dismantle the epistemic force of modernity that we engage in, that engages us."[36] Wiegman is concerned in particular with contemporary feminisms, but one might claim more generally that current epistemologies merely reiterate rubrics of cultural identification endemic to the modern cultural imagination. Standard estimations of ethnicity/race, gender, and sexuality are merely reconstituted in academic settings by translating them into the corresponding fields of "African American (or any variety of ethnic and racial designations) Studies," "Feminism(s)," and "Queer Theory."

In the post-1960s academy, the emergence of analytical/disciplinary categories along the lines of deeply entrenched cultural battles makes visible constituencies never before treated as worthy of such institutional expenditures. It "produce[s] a wealth of new evidence previously ignored about these others and ... draw[s] attention to dimensions of human life and activity usually deemed unworthy of mention in conventional" intellectual settings and paradigms.[37] Decidedly, this is extraordinarily important work, and the point here—as decidedly!—is not to characterize it as wrongheaded, frivolous, inept, or in any way in need of coming to a close. Rather, the point is to consider what might be phrased as the institutional exorbitance by means of which that work seems routinely carried out. The issue is the extent to which conversions of new academic concerns into fields of knowledge reiterates "rather than contests given ideological systems," as well as the extent to which they preclude "critical examinations of the workings of the ideological system itself, its categories of representation ... [and] its premises about what these categories mean, and how they operate, and of its notions of subjects, origin, and cause."[38] By construing the rubrics of ethnicity/

race, gender, and sexuality for the most part as discrete and self-evident, this institutional exorbitance creates a situation in which the very protocols for situating newly reckoned lives in academic paradigms and archives may ironically constitute an unconsidered dimension of the larger cultural politics effacing and making these lives abject in the first place. The categories themselves are never called into question.

This criticism is one historian Joan W. Scott mounts against the orthodox historiographical points of departure taken up by even the most radical fields of social and cultural history. Scott critiques the manner in which historians who excavate "human life and activity usually deemed unworthy of mention" leave undisturbed the enabling assumptions of the discipline (and culture) they are challenging, in that they pursue only "an enlargement of the picture, a correction to oversights resulting from inaccurate or incomplete vision."[39] These historians, Scott argues, accept uninterrogated assumptions of the *difference* of their subjects and, therefore, foreclose crucial opportunities for "exploring how difference is established, how it operates, how and in what ways it constitutes subjects who see and act in the world."[40] Scott's objection is that these historians leave in place reified terms and indices never taken to task; her countervailing position arises from the observation that "it is not individuals who have experience, but subjects who are constituted by experience."[41] Her corrective is to see that what is unproblematically taken as a *source* (of reckoning a group) may be no more than the already circulating *effect* (of reckoning a group). She proposes an antifoundational moment and critique in the place of foundational ones.

The foundational moves Scott critiques assume a fixity of difference and the notion that members of different groups share an incontrovertible index of collective experience by means of which they may then be known or considered. Insofar as cultural studies shares with radical social history the impulse to excavate generally unconsidered lives and communities, to make salient areas of cultural life usually never considered in those terms, it seems that an analogy between the missteps of radical social historians and the epistemological routines of cultural analysts holds. In cultural studies, as with social history, terms of difference which might bear closer examination are reified, so that foundational gestures are made when and where it may not be rewarding to make them.

However, this analogy is only a partial one, since the concern with regard to cultural studies is not truly whether one sees its putatively self-evident categories as a source or effect of cultural representations—cultural critics, it seems, are generally aware of this issue. The concern is the degree to which cultural critics may or may not recognize that the designs and effects of cultural representations extend as far as positing the self-evident independence or discretion of identifying categories. The query is to what extent the epistemologies of cultural studies successfully engage the mutually constitutive characters of ethnicity/race, gender, and sexuality. If routine critical protocols elicit a greater fidelity to the ideological systems of institutional sites and archives inherently hostile to the constituencies of cultural studies, then in curious ways these protocols fail to negotiate as adeptly as they might the cultural inequities and disturbances they seek to expose. They repeat in some measure the representational violences they aim to dispute—an observation not made to suggest naïvely the possibility of a pure gesture from within institutional sites that would completely elude or resolve this issue, but only to suggest one way in which a keener sense of the dilemma might inform a more judicious practice. Critical protocols might be reckoned more closely—if not with an incontrovertible presocial essence—at least with the challenges of making visible the multiple and syncretic nature of actual cultural experience. These protocols, to borrow again from Joan Scott, would not allow routinely stable categories to stand as "the origin of our explanation, but [as] that which we want to explain," always with a mind to their pluralities and complicities.[42]

To return to Bambara's "The Hammer Man," it is important to recognize that the brash, unrestrained descriptive style, which opens the narrative, returns briefly at the end of the narrative to present the narrator's dire concluding fantasy of the racially motivated murders of herself and Manny. This peculiar moment that, by recalling the opening style and tone of the story, in this way marks both opposition and resemblance across the narrative divide is one of the many facets of the narrative prompting the reader to apprehend the uncommon mechanisms of power at work in the protagonist's crisis. The initial brash set of descriptions in the narrative records her view, rejection, and deft negotiation of a circumscribed external world and community, whereas the second records her unexpected internalization of both her original community and a wider community's view, grasp, and negotiation of her:

> And I thought to myself, Oh God here I am trying to change my ways, and not talk back in school, and do like my mother wants, but just have this last fling, and now this—getting shot in the stomach and bleeding to death in Douglas Street park and poor Manny getting pistol whipped by those bastards and whatnot. I could see it all, practically crying too. And it just wasn't no kind of thing to happen to a small child like me with my confirmation picture in the paper next to my weeping parents and

schoolmates. I could feel the blood sticking to my shirt and my eyeballs slipping away, and then that confirmation picture again; and Miss Rose heading for the precinct with a shotgun; and my father getting old and feeble with no one to doctor him and all.[43]

It is crucial to recognize that this latter description presents completely fabricated events which, nevertheless, powerfully supersede and overdetermine the "reality" of the first set of descriptions in the narrative, as well as the narrator's original unmindfulness of a variety of categories of cultural identification. The passage is as breathless and unrestrained as the narrative's opening one but, even though its events are entirely imaginary, its significance is more dire and more consequential. Its imaginary violence marks, for the narrator, capitulation on several counts. Her virtual tears witness the singular rupture of the cool bravado that most characterizes her throughout the narrative. Her self-declared alliance with Manny is equally retracted: "And I wished Manny had fallen off the damn roof and died then and there and saved me all the aggravation of being killed with him by these cops."[44] This phantasm of her brutal death signals acquiescent acknowledgment of the remarkable dissociative force of ethnic/racial identifications as well as her recognition of the daunting power of the overwhelming institutional forces zealously enlisted in the endeavor.

The even more peculiar upshot of the fantasy is her very deliberate acquiescence to gender citations she has long resisted, as well as their implicit heterosexual imperatives at which she had just bristled. Given the narrator's attitudes and actions throughout the story, it is remarkable that the narrative concludes with her eager notation that "me and Violet was in this very boss fashion show at the center. And Miss Rose brought me my first corsage—yellow roses to match my shoes."[45] The national academic conversation speaks for the most part past the cathected circumstances of the newly corsaged narrator. In the same way the narrator of "The Hammer Man" is reconciled to a disciplinarity that powerfully forges her vision and actions, independent categories of cultural identity are reconstituted within analytical paradigms claiming revelatory critical distance from cultural doxa. In this particular instance, these paradigms would be unequal to accounting for the appearance of a discourse of homosexuality at the climax of a narrative most seemingly about ethnic/racial division.

In order to admire Manny (even at a crucial moment of ethnic/racial solidarity), the narrator must police and constrain his identity as insistently as it is policed by his adversaries—and, even more ironically, just as insistently as the cultural paradigms she originally flaunts finally police and conscript her:

"What makes power hold good, what makes it accepted, is simply the fact that it doesn't only weigh on us as a force that says no, but that it traverses and produces things, it induces pleasure, forms of knowledge, produces discourse. It needs to be considered as a productive network which runs through the whole social body."[46] Michel Foucault's conception of power as "produc[ing] effects at the level of desire—and also at the level of knowledge" is evident, at the peak of the contest in the park, in the reactions of the narrator to Manny's climactic picture-perfect layup, which precipitates the final tussle between him and the police and, in turn, the narrator's transfiguring fantasy of her death.[47] As she first watches, however, she is not yet terrified: "Manny . . . went right into his gliding thing clear up to the backboard, damn near like he was some kind of very beautiful bird. And then he swooshed that ball in, even if there was no net, and you couldn't really hear the swoosh. Something happened to the bones in my chest. It was something. . . . Obviously he had just done about the most beautiful thing a man can do and not be a fag. No cop could swoosh without a net."[48]

To the narrator's mind, Manny's achievement is a form of black masculine genius and gracefulness at its most thrilling, and, as it turns out, both literally and figuratively, also at its most policed. In the minds of her adversaries, the layup represents a form of black masculinity at its most repulsive or threatening, since in the big "guy [who] watched Manny for a while . . . something must've snapped." He grows immediately "hot for taking Manny to jail or to court or somewhere."[49] His response to Manny's layup is to read it as the sign of Manny's intolerable "deviance" and, hence, the catalyst for his incarceration. This response is diametrically opposed to the narrator's dumbfounded admiration. Nonetheless, the layup remains as policed by her hyperbolic pleasure; although Manny is decidedly not included in their numbers, all "fags" are dismissable. Indeed, it is her assurance that Manny is not a fag that allows her to appreciate his ability to do something beautiful. Her deliberate characterization of Manny as anything but a "fag" provides her the means to recuperate the beauty and gracefulness of his actions within traditional and recognizable citations of the masculine. In her mind, the beauty and the gracefulness showcased here do not mount an effeminate challenge to normative masculinity and gender roles. This is to say, despite herself, the narrator already fully understands and internalizes the gender and sexual prescriptions and proscriptions of both communities—black and white—against which she chafes for most of the narrative.

Whereas present epistemologies generally do not, this climactic self-betrayal suggests that subjection and subjectivity operate across—more so than respect—analytical partitions separating understood codes of identification in the culture and the academy. There is, however, at least one qualification of this commentary still to be made: a more judicious practice of scholarship does not necessarily presume drastic institutional restructuring *of*—but rather *at*— the current locations of cultural studies. It implies the rethinking of the type of work undertaken at institutional sites of scholarship much more so than administrative reconfigurations of departments and programs (undertakings more strongly wedded to the committeed and hierarchical administrative work of institutions). It is not the existence of departments and fields such as "English," "African American Studies," "Women's Studies," and "Queer Theory" that is so much at issue as the type of scholarly practice predominating under these rubrics. A more judicious practice would reform epistemological paradigms, rather than more incidental administrative ones, highlight the fact that identities and identity studies do not exclusively concern fixed and particular social groups, and reveal a more elusive cultural logic that is deeply invested in making various groups visible and divisible in the first place. What set of routine principles underwrites such intuitive partitionings? Given this line of reasoning, it would make little sense, for example, that the agenda of "Women's Studies" would entail only investigations of those gendered female, or that "African American Studies" would attend only to the "experiences" of those understood as black. These fields must also explore those cultural imperatives defining these designations, as well as ascribing and maintaining their peculiar social valences. This is not to say that exactly this type of work is not already being done by a great number of critics beyond those illustrative few mentioned here, but it is to say that this type of work is not yet understood as definitive to the intellectual fields in question. It is not yet commonly understood as work essential to the knowledges these disciplines hope to groom and disseminate.

The set of issues broached by "The Hammer Man" reveals that the compelling issue for radical critical thought is not at all the familiar rubrics by which it can be most easily defined. The issue, rather, is the particular type of work undertaken—work that at some level must be suspicious of the limiting categories of widespread doxa or even acute disciplinarity. Of course, these kinds of substantive conversations are always ongoing; new trajectories in critical thought routinely compromise or overwhelm established intellectual boundaries. The commerce, for instance, between "Women's Studies" and "Queer Theory" is highly productive, even as both fields remain to some extent less responsive to considerations of ethnicity/race. Of the engagement of mainstream feminist literary criticism with African American feminism, for example, Elizabeth Abel deftly observes:

> There has been little in white feminism comparable to the detailed reconstructions of black women's literary traditions produced by Barbara Christian, Mary Helen Washington, Deborah E. McDowell, Gloria T. Hull, Nellie Y. McKay or Margaret B. Wilkerson; or to the mapping of this literature's social and discursive contexts produced by Hazel Carby, Barbara Smith, Valerie Smith, bell hooks, Michele Wallace, Audre Lorde, or June Jordan. Instead, we have tended to focus our readings on the "celebrity" texts—preeminently those by Hurston, Walker, and Morrison—rather than on "thick" descriptions of discursive contexts and have typically written articles or chapters (rather than books) representing black women's texts as literary and social paradigms for white readers and writers. In these texts we have found alternative family structures, narrative strategies, and constructions of subjectivity: alternative that is, to the cultural practices of white patriarchy, with which literature by white women has come to seem uncomfortably complicit. The implied audience for this critical venture has been white.[50]

What Abel describes, needless to say, does not constitute an earnest conflation of analytic categories.

Yet, oddly enough, the disregard of intellectual boundaries remains one of the chief characteristics of the new field of cultural studies, as it has come to greatly influence the type of work Abel characterizes as well as other work; cultural studies is the "newly emergent academic discipline that redefines the boundaries delineating traditional disciplinarities. Cultural studies not only *reframes* the objects of inquiry, but constructs a broader *framework* within which to pursue alternative modes of inquiry. Cultural studies has shifted, redrawn, and sometimes even dissolved the lines demarcating conventional disciplinary boundaries."[51] It may be useful, however, for such inquiries not only to look beyond the boundaries of traditional disciplines but also to look beyond the traditional sites and boundaries of counterknowledges (and identity studies). The emergent questions might be as overwhelming to cultural studies as those now often posed to more conventional disciplines, and while all these questions may not arise directly from "The Hammer Man," Bambara's short story is highly suggestive of what might be the purview of such inquiries. One might ask, for instance, to what extent has gender been grasped as an always fundamentally racial and heterosexist specification? In what ways has sexuality been investigated in terms of its equal reliance on indispensable racial and gendered citations? The same might be asked about the responsiveness of the governing paradigms of ethnic/racial studies to "Women's Studies" and "Queer

Theory." To what extent have these paradigms accounted for ethnicity/race as a gendered and heterosexist concept?

What new questions and answers would emerge from paying earnest attention to the undertheorized nexus of the most salient rubrics "of social and subjective being"? They might look as unfamiliar as they would be energizing. If, for instance, "the sexual emerges as the *jouissance* of exploded limits, as the ecstatic suffering into which the human organism is momentarily plunged when it is 'pressed' beyond a certain threshold of endurance," then to what degree is ethnicity/race implicitly committed or antagonistic to this self-dispersion or *jouissance*?[52] Might ethnicity/race be defined in terms of sexual congress from which all *jouissance* has been strictly economized and overly rationalized, even to a point of nullification? If sexuality (in any of its forms) necessarily troubles "the self [a]s a practical convenience ... promoted to the status of an ethical ideal," do gender specifications in their rationalized (though naturalized) relations to sexuality necessarily exacerbate this trouble?[53] In what ways might race be conceived as a symptom of such trouble? In what specific ways and by what means are these varying productions of and relations to the body (implicit in race, gender, and sexuality) represented as cultural difference and produced as social inequalities?

What would it mean to investigate gay and lesbian sexuality not simply as a breach of normative gender citations but as a breach of, a challenge and antithesis to, racialization itself? What, in other words, would one discover if one investigated whether, or to what extent, the logic of homosexuality defies the premises of racialization? Judith Butler poses one question salient to such an inquiry: "how might we understand homosexuality and miscegenation to converge at and as the constitutive outside of a normative heterosexuality that is at once the regulation of a racially pure reproduction?"[54] Is lesbian sexuality more threatening to racialization than gay male sexuality (or vice versa)? In what ways do the performances of homosexuality as well as ethnicity/race historically explode "the rites and rights of gender function?"[55]

What are the uninterrogated commonalities of groups opposed to each other across the divide(s) of ethnicity/race, gender, or sexuality? Do opposed formations—racial blackness and whiteness, for example—share a colluded ground? In what ways, if any, do points of collusion overwhelm opposition? Phillip Brian Harper, in his probing article on media representations of the death of broadcaster Max Robinson, takes up some of these questions when he characterizes Robinson's cultural position as follows: "The white bourgeois cultural context in which Robinson derived his status as an authoritative figure in the mainstream news media must always keep a vigilant check on black male sexuality, which is perceived to be threatening generally (and is assisted in this task by a moralistic black middle class that seeks to explode notions of black hypermasculinity). At the same time, the African-American cultural context to which Robinson appealed for his status as a paragon of black pride and self-determination embodies an ethic which precludes sympathetic discussion of black male homosexuality."[56] One might ask to what extent do the claims of bourgeois subjectivity necessarily insinuate themselves into the formative grounds of ethnicity/race, gender, and sexuality—and the dissociative stances taken up along these lines? Is it productive to imagine their permutations through the figure of proliferating bourgeois self-disciplinarity? And one might certainly ask, as does "The Hammer Man," in what ways do psychic and social economies dictated by ethnicity/race, gender, and sexuality fracture the individual subjects formed through them?

This critical trajectory clearly concerns measures of interdisciplinarity but, much more so, measures of intersectionality: attentiveness to the inexorable overlapping of the central cultural codes of identification. Even as "The Hammer Man" and its narrative structures reflect the dissociative nature of ethnicity/race, its reader is invited in extraordinary ways to see that there also emerges in the text at least a tripartite complex of subject formation. The positions assumed by the protagonist in resolving her crisis certainly correspond to the rubrics of ethnicity/race, sexuality, and gender, as well as the institutional fields into which they are neatly translated by current epistemologies. She declares ethnic/racial solidarity with Manny: "Manny was my brother at that moment and the cop was the enemy"; she upholds hegemonic sexual proscriptions and allegiances: "[Manny] had just done about the most beautiful thing a man can do and not be a fag"; she surrenders to gender citations she long repudiated: "And me and Violet was in this very boss fashion show at the center."[57] Still, these three positions considered in their coimplications do not correspond to any easily recognized cultural or analytical rubric. Not so neatly, all three remain integral elements of the social subject (re)produced at sites of both pleasure and terror in "The Hammer Man." By means of all these positions, the narrator is compositely articulated as a subject. Present epistemes do not yet routinely aspire to confront or explicate the nature and meaning of this congruence. Even so, if the cause is inertia or blindnesses inherited from institutional (and culturally pervasive) paradigms, then, one can imagine, as already suggested by the work of feminists of color, that the obstacles for self-defined critical and radical thought are far from insurmountable.

NOTES

Chapter 7, "Identities and Identity Studies," was originally published in *Cultural Critique* 39 (spring 1998): 5–29, and is reprinted with permission of the University of Minnesota Press.

Acknowledgments: I dedicate this article to the memory of Toni Cade Bambara. I thank Thelma Foote, Steve Mailloux, John Carlos Rowe, and especially Robyn Wiegman for insightful and generous conversations concerning this article.

1. Barbara Smith and Beverly Smith, "Across the Kitchen Table: A Sister to Sister Dialogue," in *This Bridge Called My Back: Writings by Radical Women of Color*, ed. Cherríe Moraga and Gloria Anzaldúa (New York: Kitchen Table, 1983), 116.

2. Gloria Anzaldúa, "La Prieta," in Moraga and Anzaldúa, *This Bridge Called My Back*, 205.

3. Werner Sollers, "Ethnicity," in *Critical Terms of Literary Study* (Chicago: University of Chicago Press, 1995), 288.

4. In a move that may seem somewhat problematic, the distinction between the concepts "race" and "ethnicity" is for the most part collapsed in this analysis, in fact, much in accordance with the insights of Sollers, who writes: "What is often called 'race' in the modern United States is perhaps the country's most virulent ethnic factor" ("Ethnicity," 289). The hope is that whatever subtleties are neglected and whatever liabilities are incurred by this move will be compensated by the reconceptualization of these terms offered here.

5. Kendall Thomas, "'Ain't Nothing Like the Real Thing': Black Masculinity, Gay Sexuality, and the Jargon of Authenticity," in *Representing Black Men*, ed. Marcellus Blount and George P. Cunningham (New York: Routledge, 1996), 66.

6. Joan W. Scott, "The Evidence of Experience," in *The Lesbian and Gay Studies Reader*, ed. Henry Abelove, Michele Aina Barale, and David M. Halperin (New York: Routledge, 1993).

7. Naomi Zack, *Race and Mixed Race* (Philadelphia: Temple University Press, 1993), 27.

8. Zack defines the one-drop rule as "the logic of an infinite regress" entailing that "[a] person is black if she has a black forebear, and that forebear was black if she had a black forebear, and so on" (*Race and Mixed Race*, 19).

9. For an extended consideration of the highly consequential coimplications of racial, gendered, sexual, commercial, and moral economies in a cultural context, rather than literary and institutional context, see my "Black Men in the Mix: Badboys, Heroes, Sequins, and Dennis Rodman" (chapter 9, this volume).

10. Sollers, "Ethnicity," 303.

11. Robyn Wiegman, *American Anatomies: Theorizing Race and Gender* (Durham, NC: Duke University Press, 1995), 190.

12. Evan Watkins, *Work Time: English Departments and the Circulation of Cultural Value* (Stanford, CA: Stanford University Press, 1989), 24.

13. Cheryl A. Wall, "Introduction: Taking Position and Changing Words," in *Changing Our Own Words: Essays on Criticism, Theory, and Writing by Black Women*, ed. Cheryl A. Wall (New Brunswick, NJ: Rutgers University Press, 1989), 15.

14. Kim E. Hall, *Things of Darkness: Economies of Race and Gender in Early Modern England* (Ithaca, NY: Cornell University Press, 1995).

15. Toni Cade Bambara, "The Hammer Man," in *Gorilla, My Love* (1972; reprint, New York: Vintage, 1992), 39.

16. Bambara, "The Hammer Man," 35.

17. Bambara, "The Hammer Man," 35.
18. Bambara, "The Hammer Man," 36.
19. Bambara, "The Hammer Man," 37.
20. Bambara, "The Hammer Man," 36–37, 36.
21. Bambara, "The Hammer Man," 37, 36.
22. Bambara, "The Hammer Man," 38.
23. Bambara, "The Hammer Man," 38.
24. Bambara, "The Hammer Man," 38.
25. Sollers, "Ethnicity," 288.
26. Bambara, "The Hammer Man," 40.
27. Bambara, "The Hammer Man," 40.
28. Bambara, "The Hammer Man," 37.
29. Judith Butler, *Bodies That Matter: On the Discursive Limits of Sex* (New York: Routledge, 1993), 3.
30. Bambara, "The Hammer Man," 41.
31. Bambara, "The Hammer Man," 41.
32. Butler, *Bodies That Matter*, 3.
33. Bambara, "The Hammer Man," 39.
34. Laura Doyle, *Bordering on the Body: The Racial Matrix of Modern Fiction and Culture* (New York: Oxford University Press, 1994), 5.
35. Thomas, "'Ain't Nothing Like the Real Thing,'" 66.
36. Wiegman, *American Anatomies*, 190.
37. Scott, "The Evidence of Experience," 398–99.
38. Scott, "The Evidence of Experience," 400.
39. Scott, "The Evidence of Experience," 399.
40. Scott, "The Evidence of Experience," 399–400.
41. Scott, "The Evidence of Experience," 401.
42. Scott, "The Evidence of Experience," 412.
43. Bambara, "The Hammer Man," 42.
44. Bambara, "The Hammer Man," 42.
45. Bambara, "The Hammer Man," 42–43.
46. Michel Foucault, "Truth and Power," in *Power/Knowledge: Selected Interviews and Other Writings, 1972–1977*, ed. Colin Gordon (New York: Pantheon, 1980), 119.
47. Michel Foucault, "Body/Power," in *Power/Knowledge*, 59.
48. Bambara, "The Hammer Man," 41.
49. Bambara, "The Hammer Man," 41.
50. Elizabeth Abel, "Black Writing, White Reading: Race and the Politics of Feminist Interpretation," in *Female Subjects in Black and White: Race, Psychoanalysis, Feminism*, ed. Elizabeth Abel, Barbara Christian, and Helene Moglen (Berkeley: University of California Press, 1997), 119.
51. Mae G. Henderson, "Introduction: Borders, Boundaries, and Frame(work)s," in *Borders, Boundaries, and Frames: Cultural Criticism and Cultural Studies*, ed. Mae Henderson (New York: Routledge, 1995), 23, emphasis in original.
52. Leo Bersani, "Is the Rectum a Grave?," *October* 43 (winter 1987): 217.

53. Bersani, "Is the Rectum a Grave?," 222.

54. Butler, *Bodies That Matter*, 167.

55. Hortense Spillers, "'The Permanent Obliquity of an In(pha)llibly Straight': In the Time of the Daughter and the Fathers," in *Changing Our Own Words: Essays on Criticism, Theory, and Writing by Black Women*, ed. Cheryl A. Wall (New Brunswick, NJ: Rutgers University Press, 1989), 129.

56. Phillip Brian Harper, "Eloquence and Epitaph: Black Nationalism and the Homophobic Impulse in Responses to the Death of Max Robinson," in *The Lesbian and Gay Studies Reader*, ed. Henry Abelove, Michele Aina Barale, and David M. Halperin (New York: Routledge, 1993), 165.

57. Bambara, "The Hammer Man," 40, 42, 43.

| CH8

The Gaze of Langston Hughes: Subjectivity,
Homoeroticism, and the Feminine in *The Big Sea* (1999)

What measures might be used to gauge the public voices of those belonging to marginalized and oppressed cultural groups? This question is raised with some urgency by Langston Hughes's first autobiography, *The Big Sea*, for (in the words of Hughes's premier biographer, Arnold Rampersad) "in a genre defined by confession, Hughes appears to give nothing away of a personal nature."[1] Silences, subterfuge, dissemblance, and ambiguity remain enduring elements of self-presentation in African-American cultural practice, as Rampersad himself proposes: "The smiling poise of *The Big Sea* is, in fact, the poise of the blues, where laughter, art and the will to survive triumph at last over personal suffering."[2] But this solution, on close examination, offers only a partial explanation. One must also engage the broader terms of subjection Hughes faces and with which he negotiates in order to speak. In addition to culturally specific expressive traditions, one must examine other factors: biographical imperatives, historical contingencies, and the orthodoxies of a dominant cultural order which insistently "materialize" (in Judith Butler's sense of the word) the speaking subject.[3] Reformulated, the question might run as follows: what specific silences allow Hughes to avoid breaching important orthodoxies so as to appear a recognizable rather than an untoward speaking subject?

The very famous opening image of *The Big Sea* is of Hughes on the deck of the SS *Malone* discarding his books into the Atlantic Ocean as the New York skyline recedes in the night. Having impulsively taken on the job of mess boy on board the freighter that morning, Hughes is bound for the West African coast and likens the discarding of his books to "throwing a million bricks out of [his] heart."[4] Although the act suggests the tossing aside of masks and fetters in order to discover and reveal his *genuine* and as yet obscured "self," the episode that follows is intensely ambiguous, rather than marked by the certainty of revelation.

Below deck, Hughes is faced with a gregarious cabinmate, "George[, who] lay stark naked in a lower bunk, talking and laughing and gaily waving his various appendages around."[5] As he inevitably speaks of women, the naked George boasts that once he returns to the United States he might pay the overdue rent he owes his landlady with "what he had in his hand."[6] The discourse of heterosexual braggadocio is invoked in circumstances that unmistakably belie heterosexual possibilities. The curious inaugural move of *The Big Sea* is from an expectation of certainty to an unresolvable moment of ambiguity realized in homoerotic terms, but couched in heterosexual boasting. At sea, in a cabin with only three laughing men, that any woman might receive "what [George] had in his hand" remains a dramatic impossibility. Starkly inadequate to an episode introducing sexual energy into a clearly all-male social space, George's heterosexist discourse ironically highlights the contradictions governing gender/sexual prescriptives. Are there unnarrated reasons why George's nudity and libidinal imaginings constitute one of the first recollections of the text? Does George, in fact, find someone in this all-male space to receive "what he had in his hand"? Readers are prompted to speculate about the sexuality of an autobiographer doggedly close-mouthed about his sexual encounters but who, on the second page of his narrative, gratuitously directs the gaze of his reader, through his own gaze, to the animated penis of another man and, furthermore, in this spectatorial act, to the discursive subordination of a female agent.

It is crucial to recognize that only female presence, not female subordination, is denied by the peculiar circumstances of Hughes's arrival below deck; the disposition of the female agent in the boast remains as compelling an element of the episode as any questions raised about the sexual identity of Hughes or the two other men in the cabin. The discursive subordination of the female agent who holds legal and financial obligations over George's "head" is a signal upshot of the boast. George attempts, by an appeal to the gendered dynamics of "normative" sexuality, to recast the power relations between himself and his economic adversary. The episode registers the way in which heterosexist discourse and practice, as has long been acknowledged and theorized, strikingly attempts to put women in their place, a place in which "the heterosexual relationship for a man often emerges not as the end but as means to a [self-affirming or empowering] relationship to another man or men."[7] Heterosexist discourse, as much as it is a language of sexual contact, is a marker of prerogative—most readily, of male prerogative. Even so, although the opening moves of the narrative recount male prerogative in pronounced heterosexist terms, the marking of race also occurs in the most attenuated, or inefficient, of ways.

The syncretic features of the scene are easily summarized. One is alerted in a narrative of race to the sexualized imperatives of a dominant "material" order by the curious situation of the feminine in a homosocial scene. This dominant "material" order is implicit, however, because, although the scene certainly does turn on what the political philosopher Carole Pateman terms "the law of male sex-right," it nonetheless skirts or queries the very efficient gender/sexual symmetries that "the law of male sex-right" would be made to underwrite.[8] Altogether, four early episodes of *The Big Sea* draw dramatic attention to these complexities: this scene with Hughes below deck with his cabinmates, the "festival-like" gang rape of a young African prostitute by thirty of the crewmen also below deck on the SS *Malone*, a bizarre shooting in Mexico at the home of Hughes's father, and a brawl in a Paris nightclub where Hughes works for a time as a dishwasher. All from the first half of the book, these scenes expose ways in which the "conditions" of race, gender, and sexuality together define the seemingly incontrovertible limits of self-production for the efficient modern subject, the subject who successfully negotiates the complex of desire and discipline situating her or him in relation to home, family, eroticism, labor, hygiene, consumption, reverie—the various fundamental terms of self-production, the fundamental terms of a dominant "material" order. Like any racialized figure only incompletely or marginally imagined within the terms of idealized subjectivity, Hughes, both consciously and unconsciously, uncovers these limits of self-production (especially in their most intimate forms).[9]

In what follows, I read these scenes of self-production in relation to historian T. J. Jackson Lears's notion of "personal efficiency." Personal efficiency and its protocols produce and are subsequently masked behind "an ideal of unified, controlled, sincere, selfhood—a bourgeois self—[operating] as a counterweight to the centrifugal tendencies unleashed by market exchange."[10] "Personal efficiency" entails managing the vicissitudes of desire and expenditure in the service of an "equipoise" producing the strictly managed, though uneasy, modern subject. These protocols render the modern subject well disciplined even as she or he is incorporated into a society of apparent leisure, desire, and abundance. While Lears's work explores self-production in a commodity culture, "personal efficiency" might also be seen to stand in a troubling relation to libidinal economies in the scenes of sexual subjection that punctuate Hughes's autobiography. Extending well beyond optimal manipulation or exertions of the body in the workplace or systematic husbandry within the household (the theoretical terrain of Martha Banta, Walter Benn Michaels, Mark Seltzer), prized forms of subjection and efficiency, I argue, extend to erotic dispositions of the body (the theoretical terrain of Leo Bersani and Carole Pateman). These matters entail both the "public" and the "private" of desire.

Personal Efficiency and the Primal Scene

Providing a cultural history of the U.S. advertising industry in his study *Fables of Abundance*, Lears outlines some of the ideals of (private) informal management as well as (public) social management conscripting the modern subject by the early twentieth century:

> Advertisements and advice literature alike revealed that the emergent managerial culture offered not a critique but a continuation of Protestant patterns of thought. Religious longings for purification and regeneration were reincarnated in an ethos of personal efficiency. The "soft" side of that ethos was represented by Annie Payson Call and the mind-curists—the temporary withdrawal of affect from frenzied finance, the ingestion of leisure in momentary doses. The "hard" side was epitomized in Frederick Winslow Taylor's scientific management. Taylor and his many followers helped make "the elimination of waste in industry" the chief preoccupation of employers, providing them with a new legitimating language for labor discipline. Advertising played a major role in accelerating this pursuit of efficiency, extending it into the most intimate areas of life.[11]

Lears, in the context of an industry reinventing itself under new social conditions, underscores the disciplined nature of modern subjection, as have a series of other scholars in different contexts. Certainly, this is the project Michel Foucault undertakes in very broad terms and most explicitly in the latter half of his career. A short but notable list of recent literary critical studies focusing on the United States with similar interests includes Martha Banta, whose *Taylored Lives* proposes "it is *especially* family living that the ethos of good management wishes to commandeer"; Walter Benn Michaels, whose *The Gold Standard and the Logic of Naturalism* examines a social system "produc[ing] objects of desire only insofar as it produces subjects, since what makes the objects desirable is only the constitutive trace of subjectivity those objects bear"; and Mark Seltzer, whose *Bodies and Machines* anatomizes crises of agency arising when "the logic of market and of market culture projects a fantasy of perfect reciprocity—the equation of interior states and economic conditions, of desire and goods, that make up, for instance, the subject of 'possessive individualism.'"[12]

The subject of modern consumer culture is "liberated" into an environment not defined by unbounded "chaotic energies" but, contrary to initial appearances, by "a dynamic new form of labor discipline: an incessant cycle of production and consumption."[13] Yet race must be read as a syncretic feature of this complex recuperation of desire, since it remains a glaringly articulated signifier of the social and symbolic field in and through which the forms of desire realize themselves. The prerequisite of this reconceptualization is that race be read within the terms of desire itself rather than the hypostasized terms of the social and symbolic. Ratios of race must be read through ratios of desire and, accordingly, race begins to appear much more attenuated than it otherwise seems. For example, race might appear to be, fundamentally, a series of prohibitions on social desire (especially rendered) as sexual practice, or, differently put, as a fundamental set of prohibitions within the discharge of sexual energy, the ultimate figure of desire itself. Race, conceived as a set of libidinal prohibitions, reveals a peculiar circuit which works to stabilize and ensure the transmission of identifying phenotypical traits from generation to generation through the mechanism of procreative heterosexual practice, because the visibility, recognition, materiality, and certainty of race depend precisely on their tenuously guaranteed stability—the color of skin, the texture of hair, the shape of noses, eyes, buttocks, etc. Race begins to seem a peculiarly libidinal complex, a sexual scheme conscripting desire in apparently absolute ways so as to position gay and lesbian sexuality (whether interracial or intraracial) not simply as a breach of normative gender roles but, moreover, as a breach of, a challenge and antithesis to, racialization itself in the same manner as miscegenation. Neither miscegenation nor homosexuality ensures the transmission and stability of a set of dangerously unstable physical traits. Both must be imagined as aberrant and repugnant because they are so *plainly* about desire (about what one desires at all social costs)—and, in the case of gay and lesbian sexuality, what one might desire to the point of displacing procreation altogether. Like the conscripted energies of labor and consumption, sexual energies conscripted in the name of race would be ideally systematized, in the words of Lears, in the service of "a tighter fit between the supposedly private realm of physical or emotional health and the public world of organized competition."[14] Raising acute anxieties, miscegenation and homosexuality take matters of desire to the point of placing them dangerously out of control; desire is visibly unrecuperated by the articulated terms of order.

If efficiency suggests a strict utilitarianism, the most orderly and least wasteful use of energies and resources, then the ideals of personal efficiency are necessarily frustrated by "the non-utilitarian dimensions of sexuality which are often summarized under the sign of pleasure."[15] Open-ended desire in any form is always a prime target of subjection. Within the most ideal terms of the recuperation of desire, libidinal energies, as well as energies of labor and consumption, would be ruled strictly by a managerial ethos, so that each would mimic the other in its sparing rationalizations. Both would consort with pleasure, distraction, and self-fashioning only to secure them for extremely circumscribed ends.

Race, gender, and sexuality, as popularly prescribed, are mutually reinforcing terms of ideal and abstract efficiency that, in their coimplications, promote even more attenuated forms of "efficiency" within the most intimate circuits of human exchange. The ostensibly independent conditions of race, gender, and sexuality are, in fact, cathected as a virtually unassailable conceptual ground of the dominant cultural order, because the nodes of the cathexis are routinely misperceived as "singular" (rather than confluent). One begins to sense that the opening developments of *The Big Sea* capture this confluence, and one senses in turn the usefulness of juxtaposing critical attentions paid to U.S. commodity culture and to the most intimate features of self-formation. If Martha Banta, Walter Benn Michaels, and Mark Seltzer enumerate cunning subtleties of the seduction and maintenance of the modern subject in public terms, their perspectives do not substantively account for libidinal energies pressed into the mix of such negotiations.

The profound imbrications of public and private desire become evident once Hughes and the ss *Malone* reach the West African coast and the reader becomes privy to scenes of explicit sexual activity. The chief interaction between the crewmen and the citizens of the "some thirty-two ports" at which the ship docks is traffic in "African girls [who] were usually very young, small, with bushy hair, and often henna'd nails," and these scenes diverge dramatically from the ideal sexual arrangements of the eugenically minded nuclear family.[16] Hughes begins to recount one especially noteworthy sexual episode as follows: "No women were permitted on the boat, and often we anchored two or three miles offshore, when the surf was high and the harbor shallow. In such cases, the Captain would issue no money. And even if he had issued money, there was no safe way of getting ashore, unless one paid a boatman extra to carry you on his shoulders through the rolling surf, which was deep and dangerous and often overturned the rowboats."[17] The crew is isolated until one night two African girls steal aboard the ship in order to exchange the use of their bodies for money. Quickly, the interactions become sinister. One of the young girls is taken to private quarters, while the other is thrown "down on the floor on a blanket in the middle of the sailors' quarters and stripped of her flowered dress."[18] If the initial sexual scene takes place in the absence of women, this scene (in which female presence is highlighted) is no less curious. To begin with, it outrageously conflates two "normatively" disparate economies—one pecuniary (public), one libidinal (private)—foiling the independence of their two discrete, though related, circuits of efficiency. The erotic enthusiasms of the crew prove the means by which sexuality is routinely and perversely commodified in monetary terms and money routinely (and with equal perversion) accounted in sexual terms.

Further, the homoeroticism of the first scene still obtains. Once again, men jovially view each other in openly sexual postures: the crew rapes the defenseless girl, each member watching and taking his turn in the exhibitionist display. The scene represents, no doubt, a hyperbolic moment of male homosocial bonding: "Thirty men crowded around, mostly in their underwear, sat up on bunks to watch, smoked, yelled, and joked, and waited for their turn. Each time a man would rise, the little African girl on the floor would say: 'Mon-nee! Mon-nee!' But nobody had a cent, yet they wouldn't let her get up. Finally, I couldn't bear to hear her crying: 'Mon-nee!' any more, so I went to bed. But the festival went on all night."[19] The open violation and explicit sexual activity of this scene as well as the cries of "Mon-nee!" form a dramatic extrapolation of the earlier one below deck with George, and the introduction of a female body provides—it is crucial to note—the means of the extrapolation. Whether or not sexual engagement also took place in the earlier scene, it is only through the signifying presence of a female body that in both scenes the narrative openly acknowledges sexual engagement. The female body does not necessarily mitigate the evident homoeroticism but, in a lateral move, reconfirms masculinity. Not necessarily canceling any homoeroticism, the female body in the group of the thirty men marks a point of mastery over against which masculine identity might be materially or symbolically secured (as it was in the earlier scene by the discursive presence of George's landlady).

The mastery (or masculinization) of the scene is evident in the punctuating cry of the scene: "Mon-nee! Mon-nee!" Money, insofar as it represents a mechanism of orderly exchange, entails a mutual obligation that is altogether abandoned by the crew. The girl steadily protests this abandonment by repeatedly naming the broken obligation. Thus, because money functions as the implicit sign of an agreement fractured so violently along gender lines, the girl's chant "Mon-nee!"—as unheeded protest—comprises the principal sign of violation and masculinization in the scene. Moreover, it is crucial to note that because the effected masculinization depends on the crucial element of the sexual encounter being an act of domination—not the satisfaction of sexual appetites—the heterosexual mechanics of the rape do not diminish or cancel the homoeroticism of the scene. All too clearly, the specular dimensions of the gang rape remain homoerotic. The peculiar homoerotic gaze opening the text is substantially multiplied and redistributed in this later scene. Film scholar Linda Williams describes the analogous dynamics of heterosexual pornography produced for male consumption. Because the money shot, or the image of "external penile ejaculation," forms the most self-consciously spectacular moment of mainstream pornography, its scopophilic enterprise is in the end concerned contradictorily with male self-regard, even though most apparently driven by heteroerotic display.[20]

Indeed, the ruthlessness of the sexual exuberance of the crew is not accounted for by their long isolation prior to the happenstance of the girl getting aboard the ship, and on these points the work of Pateman is particularly instructive. In *The Sexual Contract*, Pateman reviews the terms of the Western "social contract" for its cloaked and invidious assumptions that "sexual mastery is the major means through which men affirm their manhood."[21] Pateman proposes that "political right originates in sex-right or conjugal right. Paternal power is only one, and not the original, dimension of patriarchal power."[22] Hence, Pateman posits rape as the "primal scene" of male power—a "primal scene" certainly congruent with the festival aboard the SS *Malone*. Hughes depicts such a primal scene, yet he withdraws from it. This detail, like his line of sight at the opening of the narrative, seems to question his interpellation of a social and sexual order in which manhood entails "the *enactment* of a masculinity whose distinguishing characteristic is its power."[23] This masculine enactment of power takes gendered *cum* sexual contradistinction as its preeminent measure because "if [masculinized subjects] contracted for use of their bodies among themselves, the competition could shake the foundation of the original [social] contract," the sharing of power among those who fall into the category of "men."[24] If he were already, potentially or in fact, the signifier of another "man's" power, how could a "man" signify his own power within the simple logic of cultural authority? All too clearly, the dynamics of power would become potentially unreadable or, at least, infinitely more complex.

Herein, then, lies so much of the intrigue and much of the danger of the initial scene and line of vision. Not only in these moments are Hughes's desires potentially unreadable but so too are the very particular definitions of masculinity his desires should strictly mirror. The irregular man who refuses or evades "a normalizing sexual taxonomy" represents a threat to those managing to garner whatever cultural authority is available. The irregular man, accordingly, may be threatened himself. Not to speak with a "normalized" voice is to risk having no voice at all. The risk for Hughes, the autobiographer, is great. In the words of Lee Edelman, he risks standing outside "a normalizing sexual taxonomy, generating, for those positioned to exploit it, a surplus of cultural authority through the political recognition and identification of the gay man whose sexuality must be represented as legible precisely because it 'threatens' to pass unremarked."[25] Yet one must not equate the threat posed to the irregular man with that facing women since, of course, "gay men are an oppressed group not only sexually drawn to the power-holding sex but also belonging to it themselves."[26] Neither is the point to imagine that Hughes's response to the gang rape, his refusal to participate, might not be shared by some other men. His withdrawal is not unthinkable but, on the contrary, what is all too plainly *thinkable* is a dominant cultural logic in which the primal scene outlined by Pateman is so normative as to escalate into a sexual festival openly inscribed into a public record.

Further, signal aspects of the risk Hughes broaches in his narration of the scene are the risks of homoerotics and homosexuality, risks which "[come] into focus only as the conflictual undoing of one man's authority by another; [homosexuality] signifies, that is, only a failed, debased, or inadequate masculinity—a masculinity severed from the ground of its meaning in a phallic 'possession' betokening one's legitimate status as a subject. . . . Male-male sexual activity 'means' . . . enforced passivity and *therefore* emasculation for a social order that identifies passivity or penetrability with the emptying-out or abjection of independent will and autonomous selfhood, 'means,' in other words, the humiliation of one man by another."[27] Masculine subjectivity rests on signifying domination, even if, oddly enough, domination of another masculine subject is figured in the name of the feminine. This logic, of course, is unstable, for if the "sacrificial" figure of the feminine can, in fact, prove to be "a masculinity severed from the ground of its meaning in a phallic 'possession,'" how might one explain these self-cleavages of both the masculine and the feminine in the first place? What is at risk in Hughes is the symbolic, interpellative, diffuse *power* to extrapolate these violations far beyond solipsism, to press them into a service that the libidinal characteristically refuses.

The principle of violation defining sexuality no longer plays itself out within a single self-absorbed masochistic figure, but is displaced outward, made specular and spectacular—and so too its violence. The intrinsic masochism of sexuality is translated into and compounded onto the social plane, even though its self-shattering principle invariably remains recalcitrant to the integrity of any subject. The curious homoerotics of male-to-male heterosexual braggadocio, as well as male-for-male heterosexual performance, if not homosexual contact, provide one register of the instabilities of this arrangement. Another is the figure of the feminine.

The moment of disorder theorized by Pateman and the related disorder recounted by Hughes turn out, as it were, to be formative points for the articulation of order. If matters are generally disordered in these scenes, matters of gender positions *cum* sexual roles are not, but, on the contrary, are fully affirmed. These scenes of disorder—nonetheless reflecting order—conscript the inherent masochism of sexuality as Bersani proposes it, which is to say the obvious: sexuality disrupts, rather than simply facilitates, civil order and efficient subjects. The aporia of the opening scene below deck concerns the unreadability of Hughes and George (and Ramon) as efficient sexual subjects. That of the scene of rape exposes the violence constitutive of heteronormative arrangements. In both scenes, the trouble results from the enlistment of the libidinal for the efficient services of subjection.

The Public and the Private

What Hughes makes clear by so carefully documenting his withdrawal is a curious coalescence of the public and the private. He exchanges the scene of public violation and chaos for a less chaotic and public space marked not only by another physical location—his cabin—but marked also as "himself." If the crew takes to violence, Hughes exhibits unmistakable self-containment. His withdrawal serves as one of several signs of disapproval reserved for a number of systems of exploitation he recounts in the autobiography. Disapproval, for instance, is also implicit in his conflicted viewing of a "dozen black Kru boys" hired for work deemed too dangerous for Western crews: "If a boy was caught between the floating black logs, or between a log and the ship, death would often result. Or if the sharks came, death would come, too."[28]

Retreat into privacy as a solution to his uneasiness leaves undisturbed the violent festival disturbing Hughes in the first place. The state of privacy into which Hughes retreats is not so much opposed to as a corollary of the public. His retreat underscores the way in which privacy remains "a threshold between the public and the private rather than a fortified private sphere."[29] It extends an infirm logic in which "sexuality has already been constructed as that which is or belongs to the realm of the private, i.e. opposed to the social" and in which, "if desire is paradigmatically sexual, and the sexual is paradigmatically private, then individuals are far more likely to project expectations for their own fulfillment (and resentment over lack of it) onto the private sphere than to articulate those expectations as an organized social demand, a demand for an organized social response, such as the redistribution and reorganization of basic institutions."[30] In a subsequent episode in which Hughes's fortuitous absence from another scene of sexual violence saves his life, this crucial relation between the public and the private (which is anything but an opposition) is unabashedly exposed.

Sexual prerogative in *The Big Sea* runs even to the extreme of attempted murder. Recalling the brief time he lives in Mexico with his father, Hughes recounts the shooting of Gerta Kraus, a young German woman employed as the housekeeper for the local brewmaster. Gerta comes regularly to visit Frau Schultz, the housekeeper at the Hughes home, and during one visit, the brewmaster—who is also German—enters, draws a pistol from his pocket, and "first ... fire[s] on Gerta point-blank, sending a bullet through her head, another through her jaw, another through her shoulder, before she slump[s] unconscious to the floor beneath the table."[31] The brewmaster shoots and wounds Frau Schultz as well, before searching the premises for Langston whom he also intends to shoot, but who arrives home half an hour after the carnage. "Had I arrived at home that afternoon a half-hour earlier," Hughes states, "I probably would not be here today."[32] Believing himself in love with Gerta, although never once having articulated his feelings to anyone, the brewmaster misconstrues Gerta's visits to Frau Schultz for romantic trysts she is holding with the younger Hughes.

Surviving the ordeal, Gerta bears scars, then, that signify masculine, heterosexual prerogative and its coimplication with ethnicity/race, because the brewmaster's jealous rage is accounted for to a significant degree by the ethnic designation he shares with Gerta, an ethnic designation amounting in their expatriate circumstances to a racialized status. Gerta's appeal to the brewmaster is not simply that she is nubile but, furthermore, that she elicits the opposite of a xenophobic response. Beyond securing normative masculinity, possession of Gerta would allow the brewmaster to construct not merely a domestic space but the most efficient of domestic spaces, since the procreative upshot of the phantasmatic union would realize the transmission of identifying phenotypical and cultural traits from generation to generation. The union would not only secure in expatriate circumstances the trappings of prized masculinity but would in addition reiterate ethnic/racial identity. The extreme irony of the episode, however, lies in the fact that Gerta in her regular visits to the Hughes home seems to recognize the very imperatives of ethnicity/race so important to the brewmaster. In the absence of an alternative explanation, it seems the shared language, nationality, and culture of the two housekeepers draw them repeatedly together in the home—strangely enough—of an expatriate African American and his son.

The ethnic/racial liaison the two women enjoy is ironically misread because the brewmaster privileges such liaisons, above all, through paradigms of heterosexist, domestic arrangements. With catastrophic results for Gerta, the episode lines up domestic spaces and imaginations with sentiments of ethnicity/race. What the brewmaster misinterprets as the thwarting of his desires prompts a rampage in which Gerta is severely injured, and the casting of Hughes as a would-be rival is twofold: he is not merely a masculine but also an ethnic/racial interloper. If the lost prize for the brewmaster is a legal configuration of masculinity traversing gender symmetry and ethnicity/race, he pursues an extralegal remedy.

Once again, Hughes's absence from the scene, like his self-conscious withdrawal from the earlier gang rape, in no way mitigates or affects the violations played out on and through the figure of the feminine. Characteristically, Hughes takes the stance of a nonpartisan reporter. His commentary draws attention to Gerta's enduring scars from the attack, and to the legal sanctions meted out to the brewmaster: "But strangely enough Gerta did not die! She was unconscious for six weeks, and remained in the hospital almost a year—but she didn't die. She finally got well again with the marks of three bullets on her face and body. The court gave the old man twenty years in prison."[33] There is no indication of whether Hughes is attracted to Gerta or could be. Because the specifics of his privacy remain undeclared and unexaminable, he presents his position, implicitly, as contrary to the distracting, impinging disorder, though he might give way guardedly to shock, dismay, or sympathy. Still, it must be noted that his perpetual retreat to the stance of shocked or sympathetic nonpartisan reporter is only available by means of his own (individual) masculinity, the dynamic of subjection inaugurating the disorder in the first place. Notions of discrete individualism available foremost to men (and to some men more than others) subtend the unsettling violence being recorded and the privatized notion of selfhood confirmed through the violence—both in the moment of its occurrence as well as in its subsequent retelling.

Hughes's recourse to the "private" must remain suspect, for the gesture effaces his privileged position: "the illusive security and comfort of the private require[s] that we forget the kinds of violence that women are subjected to within the home. Classically, the private sphere designates men's liberty from the state and the encroachments of others, and ensures their custody of women and children rather than women's safety. This [observation] . . . highlight[s] the masculinist constitution of the private and the forms of encumbrance [attendant to it]."[34] Lacking contravening evidence, Hughes's normative masculinity can or might be assumed so that, in the *absence* of sufficient provocation, "the conflictual undoing of one man's authority by another" remains an "undoing" that is reserved for women.[35] The privacy to which Hughes repeatedly turns—extreme, notorious privacy, for an autobiography—proves in the end a vestibule of the public encounters he rehearses. The repeated turns to the private *articulate no excess* to the disturbing public routines.

The heteronormative dismissal of George's landlady, the carnivalesque gang rape of the African girl, and the shooting of Gerta turn on dynamics of gender subordination undisturbed by the juxtaposition of private and public, and they warrant enumeration of the further principles that, almost to a point, animate the scenes. All are invested in male homosociality. The homosociality of the first two verges on homoeroticism, while that of the last involves "the law of male sex-right," the phantasmatic competition for absolute possession of Gerta.[36] In the first two scenes, naked or half-naked men perform sexually and spectatorially for each other so that this arrangement and its mathematics openly belie the violent heteronormative protocols realized through dialogue in the one and the rape in the other. The near-fatal rampage of the brewmaster equally confirms heteronormative prerogatives. Masculine prerogative installs itself in each scene through one of its most potent symptoms—heterosexual discourse and practice that is undisguisedly brutal. The economic dimensions of each scene also bear comparison: the financial claims of George's landlady are dismissed; the African girl is never compensated for the use of her body; Gerta and Frau Schultz's independent employment contributes centrally to the attack on them.

And these economic dimensions of the three scenes offer the most compelling vantage from which to note some of the connections between the work of Banta, Michaels, and Seltzer and that of Bersani and Pateman. The usual account of the dynamic in which women are immolated is one in which women serve, as it were, as a type of money or specie circulated among men—to follow the work of Lévi-Strauss as well as Gayle Rubin's influential and insightful feminist rereading of Lévi-Strauss.[37] Still, it is equally necessary to understand women as serving concurrently as a type of what might be called "antimoney." As much as they would be made to serve as exchangeable property, women equally would be made to hold a value far exceeding the terms of exchange. Women function—insofar as they would be ideally conflated with the domestic—as markers of selfhood beyond the social and beyond exchange. Gillian Brown, in *Domestic Individualism: Imagining Self in Nineteenth-Century America*, observes to this end "that nineteenth-century American individualism takes on its peculiarly 'individualistic' properties as domesticity inflects it with values of interiority, privacy, and psychology," even as, all the while, "far from an account of the female subject, domesticity signifies a feminization of selfhood in service to an individualism most available to (white) men."[38] Individualism becomes an anterior point from which men might most assuredly enter into the social arena and its circuits of exchange, material or symbolic.

Women, this is to say, operate as a type of "antimoney" because, finally, they are placed at a site more often than not imagined functionally outside the exchangeability, currency, and instability of money, a site understood as inimical to the insistently alienable nature of money. The circulation of women is not an end in itself but, rather, has as its end the situation of the circulated woman in a privatized domestic sphere, her situation in a union between "an 'individual' [her husband] and a natural subordinate [herself]."[39] The circulation of women also supposes an ostensible contrariety of public and private while, in point of fact, describing "a threshold between the public and the private rather than a fortified private sphere" beyond any contingency to a public one.[40]

When Hughes recounts his tenure as helper to Bruce, the formidable cook at the Paris nightclub the Grand Duc, he dramatically presents these arrangements. An enormous fight erupts, Hughes recalls, when one night one of the young danseuses is fired then thrown out of the nightclub. Florence Embry, the sophisticated African-American star attraction at the club, leaves her position beside the stage and her microphone in order to prevent the waiter from ejecting Annette, the danseuse. Although the club's orchestra tries to drown out the noise of the brawl, very soon everyone in the club is fighting man against woman, for Florence's battle cry is "Can't nobody hit a woman in any place where I work!"[41] Hughes describes the battle as monumental, and the club is so badly damaged it must be closed for repairs. According to Hughes, the entire fate of womanhood seems to hang in the balance and the very constructs of gender seem abandoned: "No music now, only good, hard, steady fighting. The women did not even scream as they fought."[42] Women apparently battle against the hegemonic, interpellated, diffuse arrangements and dispensations that mark them as women, and the men fight just as hard, apparently to maintain usually uncontroverted privileges. Hughes maintains his characteristically detached posture. His one reported intervention is to grab "two huge kitchen knives from their racks and [drop] them behind the [ice]box, not wishing to view a murder before [his] eyes."[43] The critical intervention made in the episode is made by Florence, rather than Hughes, and is addressed directly at forceful signs of male prerogative broached though heterosexist protocol. Florence in her brief appearance in the autobiography possesses a kind of passion and intensity Hughes himself at no time displays.

What is more, the predicament of Annette, "the little French danseuse" who sparks the fray, resembles very closely those of the women already discussed.[44] Although she is pregnant, "to make a living, she had to come to work every night, dance with the patrons and drink as much champagne as she could, in order to get her commission. But she was not well and she shouldn't have been there. Of course, if she had had any other way of making a living, she wouldn't have been there."[45] The acute problem arises when, "feeling badly, no doubt, Annette beg[ins] to be very spiteful to those clients who [don't] think that they [can] afford another bottle of champagne, so one night the owner of the place ask[s] her not to come back any more . . . [and] Annette sa[ys] some very unpleasant things to the owner."[46] She is fixed in circumstances that, even though patently invested in heterosexual discourse and engagement, establish male homosociality to be the paramount matter. A crucial component of the male revelry on which the profitability of the Grand Duc depends is the straitened circumstances trapping Annette, endangering her health as well as the health of her unborn child. Masculine prerogative authors the nightly ritual Annette is forced to follow, as well as the dilemma making her current job one of the very few available to her in the first place.

Inasmuch as it conflates public and private, her viselike dilemma confounds what should be separate registers of calculated female subordination—disposition either within exchange or as antimoney, but not both at the same time. Annette already occupies the condition that would mark ideally the "end" of her circulation; her presence in the scene marks another aporia, another structurally crucial moment of undecidability, for in her pregnancy, Annette does not take up a domestic posture, as protocol would dictate, but a public one in which women merely underwrite, above all, "the law of male sex-right."[47]

Fixed in a more glamorous configuration of Annette's job, Florence abruptly determines that transactions of male pleasure might go only so far, even as she negotiates them with substantially greater success than Annette. Florence takes the kind of stand no one else in the autobiography ever does, initiating "a battle royal . . . between the women (and those who sided with the women) and the management (and those who sided with the men)," and at the conclusion of the battle, "Florence . . . still occupied the center of the floor in the midst of the wreckage, hair awry, orchids gone, tears of triumph in her eyes and a run of golden sequins dripping from her dress."[48] Her altered physical appearance—and her cries of "'Nobody'll mistreat a woman in front of me'"—measure her disruption of sedimented masculine transactions triggering the circulation of women and money in the Grand Duc, transactions from which she materially benefits.[49] Once again, Hughes in his presence (or arguably "absence") serves primarily as the means to fortuitous reportage. Florence's intervention, on the other hand, is strong, and the consequences for her are severe.

Rather than counterbalancing controls, centrifugal tendencies define the episode. Personal efficiency, one should remember, refers to "an ideal of unified, controlled, sincere, selfhood—a bourgeois self—[operating] as a counterweight to the centrifugal tendencies unleashed by market exchange," and fomenting and sustaining the brawl, Florence vanquishes any public imagination of personal efficiency.[50] Personal efficiency would ideally reconstitute the private and the public as misaligned in no perpetually excessive way. Public and private would sustain the converse ideally through the parallelism of independent circuits. The marvelous effect is no appearance of disorder, and this is the posture Florence abandons altogether in her cameo role in the autobiography and that Hughes most characteristically assumes, even as he may occasionally register some level of incredulity or dismay at what he witnesses.

Hughes maintains a mysterious transparency by means of which readers see, most clearly and only, the brawl before him. Hughes, in stark contrast to Florence, positions himself as if there were no *excess* to the designs both of them are subjected to witness and on some level scorn (at least no excess marked out in terms of himself as an individual subject or his individual subjection). If there is a position in excess of the ones Hughes encounters, he does not openly or emphatically articulate that excess through his own person. Florence's "excessive" response, on the other hand, disrupts lucrative trafficking in the public circulation of private desires, which is the curious project of the Grand Duc, just as it is for sexual protocols and, less openly, protocols of race and gender. Indeed, public circulation of private desires seems the constitutive project of subjectivity itself. The traffic, in any case, is unmistakably disturbed: "It took the waiters and me," Hughes recalls, "until almost noon to clean up the place after Florence left."[51]

The divergent postures of Hughes and Florence in the episode feature the intrigues and consequences of sexuality's economic and psychological circuits, and reiterate a gender binary, as well as the binarism of public and private. Further, these postures diverge through risks following from exceeding normative male prerogatives, prerogatives aimed at the mastery of women (as well as at men failing to pursue these aims through their primary acknowledged channels, the complementary protocols of violence and sexual engagement). In this arrangement, a universal heteronormative gesture always (re)scripts the terrain of desire, whether material or phantasmatic, whether gendered male or female, whether racially enfranchising or brutalizing, whether publicly acknowledged or privately hoarded. The attention to sexuality demanded by this cultural sedimentation is misconstrued, however, if simply translated into an attempt to settle the question of Hughes's individual sexuality, since the powerful forces assigning valences to race, gender, and sexuality impinge upon Hughes even as he remains shrouded in ambiguities. If there are gay men or gay sexualities to be identified even from the very first scenes, the identification must be accomplished through, despite, and because of heterosexist discourse, since the disposition of the feminine constitutes a prime register of sexual negotiations. If there is a profusion of details in *The Big Sea* that raise questions about Hughes's sexual identity, such profusion is secured through the excessive figure of the feminine. If Hughes seems to dodge participation in the heteronormative agenda in evidence all around him, he manages at the same time to avoid being a target of its violence by never portraying himself in any excessive position. As certainly as there is no explicit gay encounter in the text, his occasional dissenting stances never exceed the limits of efficient reportage. By ignoring the magnitude of these shared oppressive mechanisms, one fails both to account adequately for long-standing social arrangements, and to recognize that the bedrock of individual identity (or rubrics of identity) is never as determinate as it appears.

More important than Hughes's idiosyncratic sexual résumé is the fact that the homoerotic, the feminine, and race within and without the autobiography share a set of social imperatives irreducible to the discrete terms of queerness, femininity, or blackness. A too-strict concern for a sexual résumé, like a too-strict concern for a racial or gender résumé, neglects the coimplications of the three that allow masculinist subjectivity to accrue on symbolic, psychological, and material violations of agents who—by either biological markings or erotic preferences—stand as targets. The fact that this irreducible ground remains unacknowledged in Hughes criticism recapitulates the dynamic of subjectivity, the constitution of self-awareness in the impulse to blind oneself to one's absence from oneself. In other words, if the belated coherence and certainty of consciousness are meant to foreclose the emergency calling for the transfiguring consolidation in the first place, the extent to which this irreducible ground remains so effaced marks precisely its subjectivizing force. Foreclosure of the emergency is purchased for Hughes by a correspondingly uncanny invisibility.

NOTES

Chapter 8, "The Gaze of Langston Hughes," was originally published in *Yale Journal of Criticism* 12, no. 2 (1999): 383–97. Copyright 2000 Yale University and The Johns Hopkins University Press, and reprinted with permission of Johns Hopkins University Press.

1. Arnold Rampersad, *The Life of Langston Hughes, Vol. 1: 1902–1941* (New York: Oxford University Press, 1986), 377.
2. Rampersad, *The Life of Langston Hughes*, 379.
3. Judith Butler, *Bodies That Matter* (New York: Routledge, 1993), 95.
4. Langston Hughes, *The Big Sea* (1940; reprint, New York: Hill and Wang, 1993), 3.
5. Hughes, *The Big Sea*, 4.
6. Hughes, *The Big Sea*, 4.
7. Laura Doyle, *Bordering on the Body: The Racial Matrix of Modern Fiction and Culture* (New York: Oxford University Press, 1994), 82.
8. Carole Pateman, *The Sexual Contract* (Palo Alto, CA: Stanford University Press, 1988), 3.
9. See along these lines, for example, Hortense Spillers's "Mama's Baby, Papa's Maybe: An American Grammar Book," *Diacritics* 17, no. 2 (summer 1987): 65–81; and Hortense Spillers, "'The Permanent Obliquity of an In(pha)lliby Straight': In the Time of the Daughters and the Fathers," in *Changing Our Own Words*, ed. Cheryl A. Wall (New Brunswick, NJ: Rutgers University Press, 1989).
10. T. J. Jackson Lears, *Fables of Abundance: A Cultural History of Advertising in America* (New York: Basic Books, 1994), 75.
11. Lears, *Fables of Abundance*, 183.
12. Martha Banta, *Taylored Lives: Narrative Productions in the Age of Taylor, Veblen, and Ford* (Chicago: University of Chicago Press, 1993), 10, emphasis in original; Walter Benn Michaels, *The Gold Standard and the Logic of Naturalism* (Berkeley: University of California Press, 1987), 20; Mark Seltzer, *Bodies and Machines* (New York: Routledge, 1992), 57.
13. Lears, *Fables of Abundance*, 116.
14. Lears, *Fables of Abundance*, 129.
15. Linda Singer, *Erotic Welfare: Sexual Theory and Politics in the Age of Epidemic* (New York: Routledge, 1993), 36.
16. Hughes, *The Big Sea*, 106–7.
17. Hughes, *The Big Sea*, 107.
18. Hughes, *The Big Sea*, 108.
19. Hughes, *The Big Sea*, 108.
20. Linda Williams, *Hard Core: Power, Pleasure and the "Frenzy of the Visible"* (Berkeley: University of California Press, 1989), 73.
21. Pateman, *The Sexual Contract*, 207.
22. Pateman, *The Sexual Contract*, 3.
23. Lee Edelman, *Homographesis: Essays in Gay Literary and Cultural Theory* (New York: Routledge, 1994), 50, emphasis in original.
24. Pateman, *The Sexual Contract*, 193.
25. Edelman, *Homographesis*, 45.
26. Leo Bersani, *Homos* (Cambridge, MA: Harvard University Press, 1995), 66.

27. Edelman, *Homographesis*, 54.
28. Hughes, *The Big Sea*, 112.
29. Saidiya V. Hartman, *Scenes of Subjection: Terror, Slavery, and Self-Making in Nineteenth-Century America* (New York: Oxford University Press, 1997), 160.
30. Singer, *Erotic Welfare*, 59.
31. Hughes, *The Big Sea*, 76.
32. Hughes, *The Big Sea*, 77.
33. Hughes, *The Big Sea*, 77.
34. Hartman, *Scenes of Subjection*, 157.
35. Edelman, *Homographesis*, 54.
36. Pateman, *The Sexual Contract*, 103.
37. See Gayle Rubin, "The Traffic in Women: Notes toward an Anthropology of Sex," in *Toward an Anthropology of Women*, ed. Rayna R. Reiter (New York: Monthly Review Press, 1975).
38. Gillian Brown, *Domestic Individualism: Imagining Self in Nineteenth-Century America* (Berkeley: University of California Press, 1990), 1, 7.
39. Pateman, *The Sexual Contract*, 55.
40. Hartman, *Scenes of Subjection*, 160.
41. Hughes, *The Big Sea*, 172.
42. Hughes, *The Big Sea*, 174.
43. Hughes, *The Big Sea*, 174.
44. Hughes, *The Big Sea*, 171.
45. Hughes, *The Big Sea*, 171.
46. Hughes, *The Big Sea*, 171.
47. Pateman, *The Sexual Contract*, 103.
48. Hughes, *The Big Sea*, 172, 174.
49. Hughes, *The Big Sea*, 175.
50. Lears, *Fables of Abundance*, 75.
51. Hughes, *The Big Sea*, 175.

CH9

Black Men in the Mix: Badboys, Heroes, Sequins, and Dennis Rodman (1997)

It is an understatement to claim that the anomaly in sports and popular culture that is Dennis Rodman has grown into an equally peculiar national phenomenon, and Rodman's perhaps most notable form of sedition—his brands of cross-dressing both on and off the NBA basketball court—places him in a controversial spotlight he shares with no other sports celebrity and, arguably, no other African-American man in twentieth-century post–civil rights culture. RuPaul may come to mind, but RuPaul does not occupy a national spotlight as a "man" as that designation is commonly taken. Rodman, on the contrary, by virtue of being a highly competitive and successful professional athlete, does present himself and is perceived as a "man." Thus, one of the most startling aspects of the phenomenon of Dennis Rodman is the attention he draws to himself unashamedly wearing sequined halter tops, women's leggings, or leather shorts, or marking his body by conspicuously tattooing himself, dying his hair, as well as painting his fingernails even as he pursues and collects NBA championship rings. He remains in the popular mind neither a drag queen nor one of the innumerable and easily assimilated comedians or actors who make their living by drawing on long and various traditions of male drag in the West. Dennis Rodman—to employ a cliché—is "something else."

The primary sense of this cliché connotes, of course, that Rodman is clearly and highly individual. But, on closer examination, an argument can be made that one of the upshots of his unusual public position is a demonstration of ways in which the notion of the individual proves inadequate to fully understanding the peculiarities of post–civil rights U.S. culture. This analysis proposes the obsolescence of the notion of the individual for assessing Rodman's phenomenal position, and for assessing the potent conjunction of racial, commercial, gendered, and moral economies in the peculiar figure of Rodman. The proposal is that important facets of post–civil rights U.S. culture suggest a fracturing of the "individual" not entirely calculable by recourse to that concept. And this fracturing, as one must suspect of market cultures, occurs through mechanisms aimed at channeling desire and pleasure. In Rodman's self-reflections such fracturing is evident in key rhetorical ploys as well as inconsistencies between his sexual imaginary and exploits. The claim here is that these "individual" instabilities reflect always incomplete attempts on the part of hegemonic cultural orders to contain desire and pleasure. What amounts to the characteristically and strictly rationalized libidinal dynamics of post–civil rights U.S. culture do not always remain so strict or so rational. The resulting eccentricity, however, is not unique to Rodman but endemic to post–civil rights U.S. culture itself. Rodman's state of publicity, in other words, seems to underscore Kobena Mercer's sense that "black struggles over access to the means of representation in the public sphere, in cultural and political institutions alike, require an analysis that is not exclusively centered on individualizing or psychologizing theories of subjectivity, but which acknowledges the contingent social and historical conditions in which new forms of collectivity and community are also brought into being as agents or subjects in the public sphere."[1] The concept of the individual is sometimes most remarkable for the abiding insistence placed on it rather than its utility or relevance, and Rodman's most extended statement on Rodman, his Delacorte autobiography *Bad as I Wanna Be*, foregrounds this circumstance. It becomes clear that—despite the awkward configuration of *Bad as I Wanna Be* as an extended monologue to a reader/confidante, its almost unthinkable repetitiveness, and its structural flirting with incoherence—many of the perplexities of Rodman's rehearsal of his thirty-some years of blackness, maleness, athleticism, travails, and insecurities are not only the result of what must have been the impatience of a publisher and hasty work with his cowriter Tim Keown. These perplexities also arise from Rodman's sometimes shrewd critical remove concerning the incidental circumstances as well as the not so incidental corporate, market, and media forces having careened him to a moment in his life when an eager audience is prepared to seek his autograph, await the latest gossip concerning his comings and goings, embrace his self-proclaimed revisionary style of NBA basketball, and make *Bad as I Wanna Be* a national best seller. As a result of this critical stance and cynical remove and its disclosures, the autobiographical persona and the seemingly singular trajectory Rodman aims to construct for himself splinters into irreducible, but functional, points of identification.

Any proposal of a splintered or decentered autobiographical subject is not a startling one. In the contemporary intellectual climate, assaults on "the metaphysics of subjectivity" are a commonplace of autobiographical criticism, humanist discourses, and cultural criticism generally.[2] For instance, Candace Lang in 1982—to mention only one of numerous possible examples in autobiographical criticism—marshals Roland Barthes and deconstructive analyses to dismiss "entirely unskeptical acceptance of the unified, autonomous subject . . . [as well as reluctance] to ponder the consequences of a total rejection of that notion of the subject."[3] She aims her reprove at less theoretically intent critics James Olney, Georges Gusdorf, etc., even as they already work with various concepts of a somewhat split autobiographical subject. One might construe it as remiss, then, not to discover an analogous autobiographical subject in *Bad as I Wanna Be*. But what remains most intriguing is the particular way Rodman's critique of the circumstances in which he finds himself produces irreducible points of self-identification never quite readable as a composite or refracted "individual." The routine exorbitance of the individual is overwhelmed in the text—even as Rodman dramatically appeals to the symmetry of the individual: "Everybody wants to stop Dennis Rodman"—and thus has everything to do with the convergence of blackness, masculinity, and the market with a moral imaginary for which each of the three, to greater or lesser degrees, may form a crisis.[4]

The convergence of these four concerns, as little as it is noted, proves indispensable to the political economy of the NBA, which is maintained, Rodman states, by "taking these young guys who come into the league and marketing the hell out of them until they become stars . . . [who] show the NBA in the most positive light so everybody buys jerseys with their names on them and votes them into the All-Star game."[5] In the same way Rodman's flamboyant and unorthodox appearance troubles a libidinal circuit undergirding but virtually unexamined within U.S. mass culture, so does this characterization of the NBA. What Rodman exposes as indispensable to the NBA is its "struggle over the relations of representation" and systems of representation and desire, as Judith Butler adeptly demonstrates, mirror one another in a "strangely necessary" relation.[6] Both are premised not only on "displacement, but also [on] an endless chain of substitutions."[7] Displacements and an endless chain of substitutions are easily apparent in Rodman's characterizations. Still, what is of particular interest, for the purposes of this analysis, is the fact that Rodman details how these principles are actualized in the NBA by transforming (primarily African-

American) "young guys" into heroic figures, who are fixed implacably "in the most positive light," then introduced for profit in a variety of forms into the *residences and imaginations* of a mass of enthusiasts. How is it that post–civil rights U.S. culture arrives at a situation in which it nimbly negotiates the allowance to take routine, unbridled pleasure in African-American "young guys"?

The significance of the phrase "in the most positive light" must be scrutinized to recognize fully the libidinal configuration in which both Rodman's arresting physical appearance and the political economy of the NBA as he characterizes it share parallel but unreconcilable interests. While Rodman does so only reluctantly or intermittently, and on very different terms, the NBA traffics indefatigably in heroism made to conform to the most proprietary standards. Heroism, as it is carefully and lucratively managed by the NBA, as well as U.S. moral and commercial culture, entails a proprietary appeal that, above all, enforces market-driven colonizations of desire (and representation). These colonizations—given their way—would reduce desire in all its material, imaginary, and symbolic manifestations to a narrow set of calculable, idealized civilities and affabilities ultimately resolving themselves in "the heterosexual domestic space . . . as an inviolate sanctum."[8] When all is proprietary—that is, when idealized moments and sites of the social imaginary are fully appreciated—culturally and economically circulating displacements and substitutions find their origins and terminations in the equation of certainty with heterosexual domestication. The reflex translation of heterosexual couplings into aseptic domestic wards is privileged as the singular calculus laying claims—impossible to construe as controversial or untoward—on what stands in and as "the most positive light."

Heroism is an idealized form of subjectivity, and the subjectivity Dennis Rodman would claim, both discursively and in terms of the palpability of his body, is decidedly not colonized by "the heterosexual domestic space . . . as an inviolate sanctum"—in Elizabeth Alexander's apt phrase. The subjectivity he would claim is one in which the prerogatives of heterosexual desire are in no way averse to considering or displaying "the feminine side of Dennis Rodman" nor to fittingly resolving themselves, for instance, in the improvisational zest of Madonna "stroking [his] shaft and getting into it . . . [so that] before long [he] was inside her and [they] were fucking."[9] The cultural logic willfully proposing national order (and all human order) as an aggregate of domestic sanctums refuses such prerogatives. And, as best it can, it refuses to imagine or—better yet—to imagine even the imagining of such prerogatives. This logic is given the shorthand of "family values" and is deeply implicated in the economic fortunes of the NBA, corporate culture, and the powerful representations they underwrite. An enormous financial return for the NBA depends on the winsome introduction of (primarily African-American) "young guys" into what U.S. culture insists on regulating as demure domestic wards. Rodman's unusual appearance and cynicism, on the other hand, interrogate these presumptions. They query the NBA's economic/entertainment monopoly, the equally suspect monopoly of moral/ethical discourse in the United States, and the imperatives of those "people in this league who allow themselves to be controlled by the image the league wants to project . . . the ones who are scared they might say the wrong thing and get punished."[10] Reward and punishment, of course, have to do with lucrative player contracts as well as potentially much more lucrative commercial and corporate sponsorships, as "the market extends daily into hitherto neglected areas and niches of opportunity."[11]

Rodman is antagonistic toward the political economy of the NBA and its direct ties to a moral/ethical economy in which "Charles Barkley got crucified for saying he isn't a role model."[12] Embracing the tumultuous position he is placed in vis-à-vis these aggressively promoted interests, Rodman states, "I'm not either. I'm not trying to be a role model."[13] He continues:

> Is it fair for me to pretend I can give you the leadership[,] the guidance, and the direction just because I can play this game? How did you function before I got here? How did you make it to work or school or where you go before I came along? Did you have a great life or a bad life and now—just because you found somebody you really love, idolize, and emulate—you want to trademark yourself as that person? Do you really want to wear that person's jersey and pretend you're him just because he can play a game?[14]

Rodman's queries expose how his league as well as a pervasive moral/ethical refrain are not responsive, in fact, to those they claim to service, but are, instead, disingenuous and even abusive. Fans of the NBA are led to believe that the on-court antics and projected off-court affability and urbanity of "young guys" known for their sportsmanship can and should have directive force on their self-conception and conduct. What is most often unappreciated, Rodman implies, is the fact that such a belief merely ranks among a vast number of "products being created to fill any and every 'need.'"[15]

Rodman's style of making these disclosures is inflected by antinomian acknowledgments of race, class, and sexual enthusiasm not sanctioned by the prevailing structures of desire. His style and the disclosures contravene interpellated market agendas creating and disavowing, through national and international campaigns, communities where, in Rodman's words, "drugs are running wild, like a fucking river down the street. Girls are getting pregnant younger and younger, and AIDS doesn't give a shit how old you are."[16] In one of the initial and only sustained images of *Bad as I Wanna Be*, Rodman symbolizes these communities through his recollection of generations of black kids in Dallas who would "walk five miles through a sewage tunnel to get [in]to the state fair" free.[17] Given this striking redaction of U.S. social reality, it is almost unspeakably peculiar that select African-American men are directly introduced into the material and libidinal economy of a national "sanitary normativity," for "sanitary normativity" in the United States relies on the representation of African-American men and women as paramount threats to its dispensation.[18] This recollection and Rodman's cynicism trouble, then, an extraordinary set of historical circumstances, in which post–civil rights U.S. culture performs the seemingly impossible incorporation of African-American "young guys" within structures of desire to which they are characteristically considered alien. Whereas these structures of desire are defined by the notion that the "sanitary normativity of all the sexual roles within the ... family is a necessary precondition for [the family's] function as the emotional and moral rehabilitative center" of social life, African Americans as a collective are most fully understood as agents antithetical to any "emotional and moral rehabilitative center."[19]

In other words, within the structures of desire detailing "sanitary normativity," the very concept of racial blackness articulates a crisis that would seem to preclude—even if market-driven—the nimble negotiations on which the NBA depends. Moreover, the crisis, on close examination, proves libidinal. Race, since it is not a genetic reality, might be more assuredly characterized as a series of prohibitions on social desire and sexual practice, prohibitions stabilizing and ensuring the transmission of identifying phenotypical traits from generation to generation.[20] Race amounts foremost to a set of fundamental prohibitions on the discharge of sexual energies. The family, of course, is the most routine and acceptable instrument for the management of sexual energies, with the result that from the vantage of hegemonic racial whiteness those "individuals who are designated black have the ability, through the mechanisms of their heterosexuality, to destroy the white identity of white families and ... individuals."[21] If race proves, at bottom, a set of practices worrying over the coding and dissemination of visible but unstable physical traits, then it is ineluctably insinuated into the notion of heterosexual domestication itself, the matrix of wards and libidos Rodman's league seeks deftly to manipulate. Insofar as the "sanitary normativity of all the sexual roles within the ... family" remains an implicit element of the NBA's commercial interests and an explicit element of the aggressive monopoly on moral discourse in the United States, it is imperiled, according to its own logic, by the massive introduction of African-American "young guys" into the residences and imaginations of the populace of U.S. consumers.

The antinomian rendition in *Bad as I Wanna Be* of being in the rough-and-tumble mix of professional play in the nation's arenas as well as the coercive mix of the cultural politics poised around those games highlights the heady mix of African-American men within unprecedented arrangements of desire in the United States. In this mix, the figure of the "individual" is more a cipher for processes of acquisition and accumulation than anything else—processes both capital (financial) and corporeal (racial). In this mix, collectives of select young black men are gingerly transformed into "loci of visual pleasure and spurs to consumption."[22] Perilously, whatever market reflex enacts this unprecedented cultural allowance for African-American men in the post–civil rights United States is a reflex both mutating and mirroring the libidinally charged "process" that is race itself. That is, race as a prohibition on the discharge of sexual energies exceeds the individual, not in the sense of simply connoting an aggregate of individuals but in the sense of a process that, ad infinitum, superintends structures of desire which support the idealized and highly exploitable domestic sanctum. The connection, then, between this dynamic eccentric to (rather than concentric with) the individual and the way Rodman's narrative also belies the dynamics of the individual becomes highly instructive for understanding the meaning of what amounts to the irrationalism of Rodman's national appeal.

Nonetheless, the mix in which Rodman is caught is very seductive and, despite all his cynicism, even Rodman is seduced; he is seduced by his very reliance on the symmetry of the individual. For, as taken as he is with dismissing the cultural order proposed by the NBA, he is equally taken by a fascinated disbelief in the great fortunes of his "whole crazy life."[23] An important motif of *Bad as I Wanna Be* is a rags-to-riches, boy-makes-good narrative, with the result that a significant strand of the text remains invested in at least one brand of heroism, or idealized subjectivity, agreeing in many ways with the cultural order closely supervised in the NBA. Rodman often muses, "I was beaten up and given up for dead, but I made it back to shock the whole world," and "the greatest achievement of my life was turning my life around."[24] The logic of this strand of *Bad as I Wanna Be* seems to propose that individual perseverance, fortitude, and luck affords a binding resolution to the social straits redacted in the image of a "tunnel that got real narrow [and put] sewage right in our noses."[25] Rodman writes with no cynicism whatever:

> There are thousands of kids out there in the projects and the cities, thinking they're going to work hard and get a basketball scholarship. They're going to use the game to get out. I say great. I say go for it. A lot of people will tell you it's a lie, that you can't get out that way. They say nobody does. They have statistics and all that, but I say why not go for it? I got out that way, and as long as there is a living example of the dream, kids are going to chase it.[26]

Rodman's assessment and encouragement are acutely short-sighted, because they leave intact "projects and the cities" teeming with straitened circumstances. Rodman merely imagines the return of select "young guys" with enough perseverance, fortitude, and luck to U.S. urban life with greatly enlarged bank accounts and some measure of local or national celebrity. His pronouncement in no way challenges a social and cultural order, in the same way as does a six-foot-six, 220-pound professional athlete (regularly projected into U.S. homes) matter-of-factly stating "cross-dressing is just like everything else in my life: I don't think about it, I just do it."[27] The persona of a six-foot-six, 220-pound professional athlete unashamedly proclaiming the pleasures of cross-dressing dismisses the relevance of "sanitary normativity" in a way in which the implied heroism of a rags-to-riches notion of individual rehabilitation does not. This is not to say Dennis Rodman should not rejoice in his unique and unlikely accomplishments, but it is to say that the Dennis Rodman who would do so in this manner and the Dennis Rodman wielding an iconoclastic critical remove are not strictly reconcilable in *Bad as I Wanna Be*.

One might go so far as to say that Rodman's repeated fascination with a rags-to-riches characterization of his rise to the national spotlight aligns him with one of the essential and most aggressively championed myths of U.S. exceptionalism, the fable of the United States as a vast site of opportunity. This is a fable that the very league Rodman critiques shares, insofar as it seems to substantiate it. Not only does the NBA furnish exciting athleticism for rapt national spectatorship, it furnishes equally spectacular opportunities for any individual (i.e., young guy) with the wherewithal to seize them. This myth, like the fast-paced professional action itself, is highly suitable for consumption within the matrix of domestic wards and libidos sponsored by the cultural order.

Indeed, Rodman's simple fascination with his own version of a rags-to-riches fable at times renders his autobiographical persona similar enough to that of as disparate an African-American cultural figure as, say, Diana Ross, who in 1993 also published an autobiographical narrative, *Secrets of a Sparrow*.[28] Diana Ross powerfully upholds in her long career conventions of gender, sexuality, race, and deportment that Rodman plainly revels in obliterating. All the more unreconcilable, then, is the fact that Rodman shares as sharp a fascination with the rags-to-riches mythology endemic to U.S. lore as does Ross. To move momentarily to hyperbole, and as astounding as the thought might seem, one might for a moment lose sight in *Bad as I Wanna Be* and *Secrets of a Sparrow* of which D. R. is which.

In any case, since Rodman shares this significant site of pleasure with the order against which he positions himself, one begins to see in the contradiction that his text accommodates no individual Dennis Rodman but—to employ the cliché again—"something else." This peculiarity is apparent in various additional ways. It is difficult not to come to the same conclusion concerning Rodman's rehearsal of his very public relationship with Madonna, for instance. The chapter recounting this relationship follows what might be considered the most controversial chapter of the book, "Man on Man," in which Rodman discusses his cross-dressing, his affinity for gay clubs and communities, his sexual curiosities concerning other men, and the homoerotic dimensions of the male camaraderie displayed in the mix of fervor and athleticism on and around NBA basketball courts. "Man on Man" disregards the usual decorum and purview of the discourse of professional sports. It has unapologetic regard, instead, for provocative and fulfilling sexual license. This regard anthropologist Gayle Rubin codifies as a "concept of benign sexual variation."[29] Desire and the pleasures accruing from desire are matter-of-factly unfixed from their customary moorings in "Man on Man."

However, as one might anticipate, matters are not so easily settled. Even having made his striking series of provocative statements in "Man on Man," Rodman as matter-of-factly seems to forget them when he writes in the next chapter: "Everybody thinks she would have the greatest, wildest sex in the world, and *every guy wants* to sleep with Madonna."[30] There is no trace in this statement of the multiple avenues and permutations of sexual desires and identities contemplated at length in the previous chapter. Rather, there is implied a singularity of sexual desire and identity—according to the logic of which Rodman must be mercilessly ostracized for having made his previous statements. The cultural order in which he lives and which he chafes against is one that claims to be certain about what every guy wants and as a result does, in fact, prescribe what every man and woman wants. In this offhanded description Rodman aligns himself perfectly with this cultural imaginary. How might one account for the dissonance between what Rodman might be trying to say and what he actually states? What, in fact, is he trying to say about the public perception of Madonna and why is it recorded in such a doubtful fashion?

Given the daring stance of "Man on Man" and much of the rest of the book, the reasons Rodman provides for his reluctance to ultimately follow through with his relationship with Madonna raises similar questions:

> In the end it didn't work because I didn't want to be known as Madonna's playboy, her boy toy. I didn't want people to think of me as Madonna's quack-quack duck in the bathtub. . . . I know she didn't think of me that way, but a lot of people looked at it like I was. That bothered me. I admit it. Normally, I don't give a shit what other people think about me. . . . Maybe I gave in to appearances on that, but I think being Mr. Madonna would have been a tough thing to overcome. I didn't want what I had created on my own to be mixed up with what being with her would have created.[31]

The emotional calculations of this point of crisis in his life revolve around gauging public perceptions, a pointedly ironic turn of events in a text and for a figure repeatedly scorning public perceptions and elaborate machinations undertaken to groom them. These concessions to public perceptions are made by an autobiographical figure who, in the previous chapter, devoted an entire page to one sentence set out in enormous bold type: "Don't let what other people think decide who you are."[32] The irreducibility of these postures could be no more glaring, and an important answer to the puzzle lies, as before, in the understated logic of Rodman's statements. Normative prescriptions of the cultural imaginary loom large. Notwithstanding his usual philosophy abrogating conventional standards of sexuality and gender, Rodman's assurance that he would not be able to brook the idea of "being Mr. Madonna" arises, one supposes, because that arrangement explicitly skews gender relations. For, if the prevailing "social construction of masculinity . . . [entails] the stereotype of the ideal man [as] forceful, militaristic, hyper-competitive, risk-taking, not particularly interested in the culture and the arts, protective of his woman, heedless of nature, and so on," then the "man" cannot be subordinate to a female partner so that he is publicly situated as having to take "her" name: "Mr. Madonna."[33] The thought of this arrangement seems insurmountable, notwithstanding Rodman's usual in-your-face iconoclasm: "I can't change anybody's mind, so they can think what they want."[34]

The profundity of Rodman's self-contradiction requires detailed elaboration: Presiding notions of gender, with their direct ties to monopolized notions of sexuality and propriety in general, are routinely dispelled by Rodman. For instance, when writing of the virtual circus of sexual possibilities attendant to life in the NBA, he muses: "Don't get me wrong. I've bought my share of magazines. I've bought my share of movies. I've had my share of lonely nights with Judy (my right hand) and Monique (my left hand). I'm not going to deny that. I'm guilty of that as much as the next guy."[35] In these comments, gender is exposed as a system of merely arbitrary and convenient placeholders. Gender identifications function in the description only to reiterate the reflexively presumed dominance, inexorability, and certainty of heterosexual desire, pleasure, domestication. "Judy" and "Monique" do not exist, except as part of a seemingly requisite imaginary. A flippant naming of left and right hands at one level camouflages the knowledge that both bodily and fantasized pleasures need not conform to standardized notions of heterosexual couplings. Moreover, it camouflages the knowledge that individual desires and pleasures *with notable frequency do not*. The humor of the statements resides in teasingly rending away that camouflage: Orgasm need not arise from heterosexual symmetry; it might as satisfactorily result from solitary performances or sexual couplings far exceeding two. Isn't it funny to think so? This, rather than any sexual performance, is the real performance of "Judy" and "Monique." "Judy" and "Monique" are discursive surrogates for an abeyant heterosexuality in the enterprise at hand—one might say. And one might only imagine further the aberrant performances—sexual and otherwise—that might result had Rodman named his hands "John" and "Roger" or, for that matter, "Rashad" and "Jamal."

What is made emphatically clear, in any case, is the tenuous cast of gender normally understood as obdurate and impermeable. All the more reason that Rodman's pronouncements on his relationship with Madonna are puzzling, a relationship openly admitted as one of the most intense and important romantic/sexual relationships of his life. If gender imperatives as they are symbolized by "Judy" and "Monique" are insubstantial then, strangely, these imperatives appear overwhelmingly substantial as they are rehearsed in "An Old-Fashioned Tale of Romance." Again, there seems to be no individual position here, so that rather than contained by the boundaries of "individualizing or psychologizing theories of subjectivity," the issue is really lodged in the diffuse and insinuating rationalizations of heterosexual domestication.[36]

More relevant than an essentialism of the individual is a series of transactions played across and over the figure of the individual. What is in evidence is the warring trajectories of a variety of appeals to social meaning, which vie with each other through the figure of the individual, and which do not necessarily find coherent resolution in any singular configuration or body. The inconsistency or incoherence in question is not so much Rodman's as it is indicative of perpetual productions of desire constantly inviting self-identifications in order to ensure corresponding and equally perpetual material/economic transactions.

One must not underestimate on this point the role of desire. Desire seeks pleasure(s) it can never fully attain, which is to say it is oddly "condemned to figure that *beyond*"—which is its sought-after object—"again and again within its own terms," and the perpetual loop of this movement is crucial to the profitability of the spectacles staged by the NBA and even more generally to grooming a population of consumers on which such profitability depends.[37] However, the processes of strict rationalization involved in these perpetual transformations of "individual" self-identifications into the rapid circulation of commodities seem also to require with some regularity gestures at abandoning the strict rationalism of this perpetual loop. The culture paradoxically seems to invite the population in the maw of constant consumption to imagine themselves in ways without and abrogating the straitened structures of desire and order to which they are overpoweringly confined. Rodman in his outrageousness is a paradigmatic figure of this abrogation and herein lies, it seems to me, so much of his appeal, even as he himself exhibits the resulting inconstancy and vacillation that may be more rightly a common feature of the cultural order than a sign of being "something else."

Although the production and harnessing of desire is marked in this way by extreme rationalism and irrationalism, they by no means cancel each other out. The rationalism is pronounced and lucrative: Throughout the contests staged by the NBA, the specular pleasure of professional play is translated, via regularly aired commercials, into anticipatory identification with some further moment of pleasure objectified in the form of a "readily" acquired product and image. As stated earlier, this circuit centered "around the theme of consumption" entails the extremely unlikely combination of blackness, masculinity, the market, and an acute moral imaginary.[38] Moreover, the circuit formed by this unlikely combination is most effective and most rationalized when particularly adulated players in the mix of NBA competition also occupy the narratives of exchange punctuating that play. In the most economical versions of NBA events, indispensable catalysts of this phantasmatic production of desire are select physically adept African-American "young guys" spectacularized within the acrobatics of the NBA as well as proliferating within the commercial narratives underwriting the broadcast. To identify with these figures in their technological displacement from basketball courts to vignettes of available consumption and new pleasures is to be bound up in an extremely economical set of manipulations. It is to be beckoned, on one level, to equate one's residence with one's imagination, for the NBA and other commercial interests count on the fact that when one sits down with the notion to watch NBA games, one also sits down with the notion to figure one's "place" through imagining what one might acquire in and for it. When one sits down with the notion to watch NBA games, one is situated in relation to the infinitely desirable marketplace through the translation of African-American "young guys" into crucial figures in the articulation of one's desires.

The trouble with this unlikely arrangement arises from the fact that the dynamics of racialization and the circuit of NBA spectatorship stand as antagonistically bipolar imperatives of desire, pleasure, and self-regard: "This schism is played out daily in the popular tabloid press. On the front page headlines black males become highly visible as a threat to white society, as muggers, rapists, terrorists and guerrillas: their bodies become the imago of a savage and unstoppable capacity for destruction and violence. But turn to the back pages, the sports pages, and the black man's body is heroized and lionized; any hint of antagonism is contained by the paternalistic infantilization of [black men] to the status of national mascots and adopted pets—they're OK because they're 'our boys.'"[39] The identifications and desires channeled through this precarious equipoise of racialized meanings might very easily—and in the most untoward ways—overwhelm the closed circuits in which they would be fixed. The employment of African-American young men in the production and exploitation of desire in late capitalism marks an enormous potential threat to "sanitary normativity," given that "the only viable models of black male sexuality trafficked in a mainstream economy are variations on outlaws and gladiators."[40] For, at its most proprietary, the specular network of relations sponsored by the NBA parallels in rationalization—not only in point of reception—the closed economy of heterosexual domestication. Rationalization is a key term in this context, because heterosexual domesticity seeks to make characteristically unruly and treacherous sexual impulses unquestionably rational insofar as it renders them *objective*, that is, insofar as it would place them in the vehemently acknowledged service of one incontrovertible goal: utter satisfaction and dissipation in procreation. The economy of sensual intimacy codified by heterosexual domesticity and the economy of vicarious investment sponsored by the NBA would ideally correspond to each other in the extremely rational efficiency and reserve of their independent circuits.

The irrational or wayward, in this scheme, amounts to any fantasy or practice confounding or circumventing these sparing systems of expenditure and return. Yet, strangely enough, this is precisely what happens whenever the correspondence between the two circuits proves too impeccable. To patently confuse libidinal urges of sexual desire with commercial urges of consumerism is to compromise the stated objectives of both sexuality and consumerism (though more patently of the first). Yet, to have this troublesome conflation refracted and exacerbated through proliferating figures of African-American "young guys" is, without a doubt, much more unsettling. (For African Americans are assumed to be agents of desire not easily nor fully subsumable within the customary equations of either the market or heterosexual domesticity.) Energies that should return to starkly economical circuits become lodged elsewhere, caught not in a fully mediated circuit of longing, but a more puzzling one in which first "blacks are looked down upon and despised as worthless, ugly and ultimately unhuman ... [then] in the blink of an eye, whites look up to and revere black bodies, lost in awe and envy as the black subject is idolized as the embodiment of ... [a momentary] ideal."[41] Indeed, Rodman writes of his own position in a popular imaginary: "When it comes to sex, I think I've heard it all. The wildest thing I get is from married couples. They'll come up to me in a bar or after a game, and the man will tell me he wants me to fuck his wife. He wants me to do her while he watches. It's her fantasy, and the man's too."[42]

What clearer statement could there be of what the NBA and U.S. cultures—racial, masculine, market, and moral—*must* not stand for? What more emphatic representation could there be of the potential specter of adulated African-American "young guys" being anomalously introduced into the residences and imaginations of a rapt U.S. populace? The infelicities of this proposition underscore the imbalance that, if propriety and its "most positive light" come only in one form, conversely impropriety *comes* in many. From the perspective of the "most positive light," the improprieties are prodigious: If race is, at bottom, a series of fundamental prohibitions on the discharge of sexual energies aimed at the transmission of valenced physical traits, it is severely ruptured. If masculinity is, at bottom, one of two requisite placeholders guaranteeing heterosexual symmetry, then it is severely ruptured as well. If the market depends foremost on simplifying and exploiting virtually all orders of the imagination, then it is exceptionally eluded. If the U.S. moral imaginary enshrines demure domestic wards above all, then it is defied to its core.

This is a moment that, one might suspect, Rodman would relish (whether or not he obliges). But he professes incredulity: "The first time I got this proposition was in a club in Dallas. I couldn't believe it. I was blown away. Since then, it's happened many times—a bunch of times in a rest room, for some reason. The husband will follow me in there and ask me to do it. They actually want me to do this."[43] Plainly, Rodman is not the only badboy to emerge in the aptly titled *Bad as I Wanna Be*. What should be the occasion for an unremarkable bodily function becomes an occasion, instead, for the airing of highly remarkable, surreptitious longings. The relief sought is not from routine physiological pressures but from the convergence of parallel, yet ideally separate, market-sponsored circuits of vicarious investment and sensuous intimacy. Apparently, to be as bad as one wants to be is to overreach and thwart constantly naturalized cultural orders and their rationalizations. It is to fail to domesticate or groom desire so that *pleasure* is willfully translated into and installed as the *pleasant*. One embraces, instead, what passes as the unseemly and unthinkable. The pressures at hand, so to speak, are much more complex than those of any physiological commonplace and much more difficult and hazardous to relieve, and Rodman's reported response in this situation points up those perils: "I look at the guy and say, 'Okay. You want to see me fuck your wife? I'd like to see the expression on your face if I ever *did* fuck your wife. How would you feel when your wife likes it? I think you'd be standing there saying, "Oh, shit." And then what if she comes up to me and says, "I want to do it again, without my husband knowing about it"?' "[44] Rodman unearths the powerful irrationality of the request. He acknowledges that actually granting it would be strangely incompatible with its structures of desire and the spirit in which it is made. His response plays on the fact that the proposition irreconcilably both disrupts and reinforces the premises of heterosexual domesticity. In terms of its mathematics as well as its explicit masturbatory voyeurism, the proposed encounter exceeds prescribed heterosexual coupling yet, at the same time, ultimately returns these illicit pleasures to a domestic symmetry only momentarily abrogated—and strengthened, supposedly, for its brief abrogation. The husband and wife seek an encounter that would momentarily nullify, or stand in for, their own sexual coupling but which, nevertheless, allows them subsequent enjoyment of that nullification as a rearticulated couple. The economy of their unseemly desires is not nearly as strict or sparing as prevailing cultural prescriptives would have it but still returns to the terms of enshrined heterosexual domesticity, and Rodman's quip plays precisely on the potential derailment of this errant circuit: Were the fantasies to be realized in this encounter too delightful, what might, in fact, be placed overwhelmingly in peril is the unproblematic rearticulation of the couple so anxious to exceed their own coupling. Unanticipated desires might arise which could not be contained within the terms of heterosexual domesticity. Desire might play itself out in no prescribed terms at all, no terms except those of its own treacherous and unruly drives. Rodman unearths the untenable position the men facing him in restrooms place themselves in vis-à-vis their own daring—their desires to be as bad as they want to be.

Significantly, however, such a contrary position is ironically the very position Rodman also occupies throughout *Bad as I Wanna Be*, as shown, for example, in his odd rhetorical resemblances to Diana Ross, or his rendition of his relationship with Madonna. Both Rodman and the husbands he faces down in restrooms share a muddled position within and without the cultural orders they appear to disregard, and the upshot of the resemblance is not an exposure of comparable stances of ironically similar individuals but, quite differently, an exposure of the usually unacknowledged irrationalities of prevailing cultural orders—cultural orders never fully able to contain all the energies they invoke.

This paradox is certainly all too evident in the realm of the NBA when city-wide celebrations of national championships turn raucous and violent despite all "reasonable" pleas to the contrary. The city of Chicago in anticipation of Rodman's 1996 championship win with the Bulls spent four million dollars in security measures and deployed over five hundred city policemen and state officers in efforts to preempt and contain what turned out to be a relatively mild spree of looting and vandalism yielding about one hundred arrests—timorous unrest compared to previous championship years. This crisis attests to the strength of the appeals that the NBA makes to its zealous consumers, as well as to the force those appeals exert on a populace otherwise posturing themselves within or seeming to accede to the most positive light of "sanitary normativity." It is a crisis on the part of a populace generally able to answer charges to contain themselves. The appropriate container, of course, is that of the "individual" and, in accordance with ideally rational economies of desire, one can only presume that more exemplary responses might be moderate and circumscribed gestures—a sanguine toast, a reckless grin, an outburst of absorbed applause—followed by a return, with equanimity, to matters of business, romance, child rearing or, say, any other number of commodified and televised pleasures consumable at leisure.

This is to say that, above all, a series of penetrating appeals and their trajectories through a population figured as consumers prove the most substantive and viable principles of the cultural order. Either as a concept or lived term, the "individual" is more functional than substantive within the idealized rationalisms of the prevailing social disposition—irrelevant, more than anything else, except perhaps as a point of uninvited crisis. Ideally and foremost, the individual is overdetermined by processes aimed at accruing commodified "surplus-value . . . which can only be made real (realised) through the sale of those commodities" in which it is lodged, since "a lengthy period of circulation reduces cash flows, reduces the turnover of capital, and thus reduces the annual surplus-value."[45] In short, Rodman and the men he teases in restrooms are fixed in situations in which desire, self-regard, and the "individual" correspond in no enduring way to the cultural systems sponsoring desire, self-regard, and the "individual." The notion of the individual remains, more than a vested principle, a fetish through which other fetishes are refracted. As the interactions in the restrooms reveal, individuals are no more than loci for productions of desire to be harnessed, irrespective of how desire might resolve itself, even if only as an aporia that, "in contrast to the claims of academic deconstruction ... is rarely experienced as a purely textual event ... [but] rather [as] the point where politics and the contestation of power are felt at their most intense."[46]

Rodman in his cross-dressing, his iconoclasm, his retorts to sexual propositions, his unruly cultural exhibitions, exposes a discordant system of interlocking fetishes. In his astute study, *The Codes of Advertising: Fetishism and the Political Economy of Meaning*, sociologist Sut Jhally works through the crucial role of advertising and the media in this system and, drawing ultimately on Marx and Freud, defines fetishism as "seeing the meaning of things as an inherent part of their physical existence when in fact that meaning is created by their integration into a *system* of meaning."[47] This definition proves useful in the context of Rodman's narrative because, more than any singularity of identity, *Bad as I Wanna Be* reveals a political economy of the individual. Insofar as he fashions his body as an inscrutable cipher, and insofar as he revels in his reckless adventures, Rodman exposes that one's *person* is coherent much less often than usually thought, and largely because meaning invested in one's *person* is neither one's own nor "individual." In ways sometimes analogous to surplus value, self-identification is produced and extracted within the flows of daunting social forces—race, gender, capital, morality, or any combination of these with other factors. Such an exposure challenges sedimented views of the individual as, on the contrary, upholding or moving through the flows of social forces. The exposure does not suggest, however, that actual individuals do not exist. Of this there is incontrovertible physical evidence. It only reveals that, as confirmed by the anomalous figure of Rodman, the meaning of individual personhood is "questionable." Starkly removing the individual from "the most positive light" of U.S. culture amounts to one critical way of questioning—even to the point of dispelling—the individual.

Nevertheless, the moments when Rodman faces down sexually titillated admirers in restrooms disclose more than the questionability of the "individual." These moments also go a long way toward answering the conundrum of how exactly African-American young men come to figure so crucially in some public arenas of post–civil rights U.S. culture. It would be remiss, that is, to overlook the glaring homosociality of the scene; indeed, much of the threat of Rodman's reply to his overardent admirers is that it returns the acute homosociality of their propositions to a preemptive heterosexuality: Were the perils of Rodman's reply to come true, what would come to an end is the titillating "intercourse" occurring between the men.

Numerous feminist scholars have theorized the role of male homosociality in structuring heterosexual paradigms and, among them, Laura Doyle writes: "the heterosexual relation for a man often emerges not as the end but as the means to a relationship with another man or men. Heterosexuality becomes secondary to the homosocial intercourse it makes possible."[48] In short, even those facets of cultural life one would least suspect remain subordinate to relations "strictly between men, attesting once more to the extraordinary difficulty men have—not in speaking *through* or *for* women to each other—but in *addressing* women."[49] Rodman's reply cuts discordantly to the center of this relationship because, by invoking a heterosexual encounter which would disrupt rather than reinforce the homosociality of the moment, the reply forecloses the homosocial stance that would couple Rodman with his admirer.

Homosocial regard is not by any means new, as recent feminist scholarship also makes clear, but the type of open regard described by Rodman, in fact, is. Indeed, rather than an overwhelming contestation of homosocial privilege itself, one substantial outcome of the cultural upheavals of the 1950s and 1960s is the nominal expansion of the circle of homosocial regard. Such an understanding of recent historical events does not dismiss important gains made by a variety of feminist movements associated with or renewed in the 1950s and 1960s, but remarks the daunting challenge facing them. U.S. culture—as it also does in terms of "whiteness," "heterosexuality," or "class"—continues fundamentally to imagine itself as a male domain, with both material and psychic resources accruing primarily on the male side of the gender divide. Thus, while in all likelihood to be more troublesome than intraracial homosociality, interracial homosociality is not extraordinary in the post–civil rights United States. In many ways, the signal turn of events of the 1950s and 1960s seems limited admission of nonwhite men into the most public circles of homosocial regard and, particularly, the most intense arena of homosocial appeal—professional sports. Sut Jhally's understanding of select gender-based imperatives of contemporary capitalism is useful for gauging the import of these changes. Jhally redacts the collective concerns of manufacturers, advertisers, and broadcasters in their appreciation of the fact that "the audience for sports includes a large proportion of adult males whom advertisers of high-price consumer articles (such as motor cars) are anxious to reach. To reach 1000 males advertisers of those products will be willing to pay more than to reach 1000 female viewers through prime-time advertising. . . . It is exactly this type of reasoning that has resulted in the huge expansion of televised sports in the last twenty years."[50] The appeal men have to and for each other cannot be underestimated as a factor in determining the dynamics of commercial and material cultures in the United States nor those rituals U.S. culture celebrates most conspicuously. African-American men, after the social upheavals defined as the civil rights movement, emerge as indispensable to U.S. economies of commerce and spectacle, insofar as they lend masculine prowess to certain public homosocial events. On closer consideration, then, Rodman's anecdote is not nearly as eccentric as it first seems: With all their homosocial suggestiveness, men's restrooms are patently appropriate, if not symbolic, sites for extreme admiration of him.

Still, restrooms are by no means the most widely practiced venues for celebrating Rodman in a culture and a market that, for more reasons than usual, should refuse him. John Edgar Wideman's shrill admiration of Rodman in the "Black in America" issue of *The New Yorker* (April 29–May 6, 1996) provides a more customary, if equally telling, example. In Wideman's brief "Playing Dennis Rodman," the homosocial appeal of Rodman is in no way understated. The article opens with astonishingly masculinist bravado:

> I knew the word *'tain't*. Old people used it, mainly; it was their way of contracting "it ain't" to one emphatic beat, a sound for saying "it is not" in African-American vernacular. . . . But I'd never heard it used to refer to female anatomy—not the front door or the back but a mysteriously alluring, unclassifiable, scary region between a woman's legs ("'Tain't pussy and 'tain't asshole, it's just the *'tain't*," to quote Walter Bentley) until a bunch of us were sitting on somebody's stoop listening to Big Walt, a.k.a. Porky, discuss with his cousin Donald some finer points of lovemaking.[51]

The resemblance between Wideman's recollections and the propositions recalled by Rodman requires little elaboration. In both instances, the homosocial site of heterosexual esteem is unmistakable. What does call for elaboration is the manner in which Wideman postures an absent Rodman within the scene on the porch and, on the other hand, the manner in which he postures the scene on the porch within the playing of Rodman.

Wideman's reader, as the very first order of business, is asked to consider the "mysteriously alluring, unclassifiable, scary" *'tain't* as somehow representative of Rodman's peculiarity. *'Tain't*, as it is defined here, is to be taken as a metaphor for Rodman himself: "Porky's crude connoisseur's riff on *'tain't* returns when I think about Dennis Rodman, the professional basketball player, and his gotta-have-it rebound jones."[52] This initial equation, however, is soon forgotten; Wideman contradicts it as quickly as he invokes it. One is not asked, in fact, to imagine Rodman in terms of the *'tain't* itself but, more fully, in terms of a masterful, heterosexual (and homosocialized) masculine gaze and tactility discovering, naming, and possessing female anatomy. Rodman is likened to a number of young men Wideman has seen on the playgrounds of Pittsburgh: "The best we could say about a guy like that was 'cockstrong': 'the brother's cockstrong.' Which meant all the above plus the insinuation that he wasn't getting much love action, so all the energy he should be using up in some sweeter place got dropped on you. 'Cockstrong' meant a guy was a load. And loaded."[53]

As it turns out, Rodman is not identified with female body parts at all but with what is emphatically presented as the more readable male sexual organs. He is not the *'tain't*, even though introduced as such, but the "irrepressible" male principle which would be its connoisseur. Curious. Again, it appears, Rodman is "something else"—an exceptionally exceptional anomaly. But, as is the case with Rodman's curious encounters in restrooms, the dynamics of the paradox exceed the terms of any individual figure. The irrationalities in question are more far flung. One witnesses, as with Rodman's other extreme admirers, Wideman dramatically failing to reconcile a "heteronormative vision" with an explicit homosocial appreciation of Rodman (and, in this case, other men on the playgrounds of Pittsburgh).[54] The incoherence of Wideman's divergent appeals might be masked by recourse to either configuration individually, but becomes plain when they are employed concomitantly. His laudatory gestures prove so irreconcilable that what in fact becomes enigmatic is the very obvious pleasure Wideman takes in seeing or thinking about Rodman playing.

However, what is clear is that whatever this pleasure may be it invites expression in explicitly sexual terms: The terms "cockstrong" and "cocksure" appear eight times in three paragraphs, with usually only a few words separating them. This virtual chant suggests, at the very least, that Wideman is delighted to take Rod/man's name very seriously. While similar fantasies might very well be possible in their cases, it is unimaginable that a similar chant could be taken up so effortlessly in nationally disseminated encomiums to, say, Grant Hill or Michael Jordan. One begins to understand that Rodman, as a result of his flagrant eccentricity, seems to enlist enthusiasms that lay bare the inherent and equally peculiar eccentricities of the circuits of market and imaginative forces shaping the U.S. population of cultural consumers. Yet, at all costs, even the cost of consistency, these forces would be defined by a "heteronormative vision," while a "heteronormative vision" is starkly inadequate to capturing Rodman and his flamboyance. Hence, the paradox is that Rodman's extraordinarily unlikely eccentricities remain the essence of his extreme appeal. Even Wideman acknowledges as much: "Cross-dressing, cross-naming himself (Denise), frequenting gay night clubs, going AWOL from his team, head-butting a referee, winning four rebounding titles in a row, painting his hair, dating Madonna, challenging the N.B.A. commissioner to suspend him, bad-mouthing the men in suits who pay his salary, Dennis Rodman, though not voted onto this season's All-Star team, verges on media superstardom."[55] The phenomenon of Rodman's national celebrity unearths eccentricities much greater and much more remarkable than his own. It highlights irrationalities endemic to the normative configurations of personhood and the normative ploys of self-identification most widely sponsored and routinely indulged in. Rodman's eccentricities call forth a kind of national attention and admiration which should be impossible, given the particular colonizations of desire idealized in the culture. The matters that place Rodman on the verge of "media superstardom" should exile him from public admiration altogether, because they result in self-promotion on Rodman's part betraying cherished visions of normalcy and, in particular, enshrined heterosexual domesticity. One might say, then, it is the culture Rodman stands athwart, more than Rodman himself, that is really—and grudgingly—"something else," a culture patently beside itself. For, although Rodman is taken as representative of energies uncontainable in starkly economical circuits of desire, he is celebrated precisely for this reason by a culture striving otherwise for containment within and to uphold starkly economical circuits of desire. These enormous inconsistencies, no doubt, account for the astonishing recklessness of Wideman's "Playing Dennis Rodman," especially its (daring?) opening gambit. And, like the larger culture itself, Wideman never fully fathoms his own recklessness.

Beyond the opening disquisition on the term *'tain't*, Wideman refers to women only two other times: once in parenthetical mention of the fact that "now . . . more women show up on outdoor courts," and once in acknowledgment of his "daughter playing in the regional finals of the N.C.A.A."[56] Both references seem to imply a social progressiveness characterized by greater inclusiveness and parity. Basketball is a field of endeavor and a point of concern, like many facets of post–civil rights U.S. culture, in which women (or choose any other group you wish) now receive more generous and overdue recognition. The primary tenor and logic of "Playing Dennis Rodman" overwhelming these references, however, only admits women in a profoundly different light than that of increasingly equal participants in an intricate and artful endeavor. Given the provocativeness of Wideman's introduction and subsequent, unmistakable equation of basketball with exhibitionist male heterosexuality, it would seem that the only way any woman (*even* a daughter) might enter this discourse is in terms of the distracting bodily topography of the *'tain't* and the attendant masculinism only barely able to contain itself in conceptualizing the *'tain't*. In a public statement openly styling itself on the order of male homosocial sites of heterosexual esteem, the appearance of a daughter is strikingly troublesome, for undifferentiated female flesh is the medium that Wideman imagines Rodman (and men like him) either exercising their ingenuity upon or in desperate need of exercising their ingenuity upon. Given the force of Wideman's introduction and his subsequent attention to which men are or are not "cocksure," the mention of any particular woman remains necessarily subordinate to an overarching characterization of women as undifferentiated flesh open, so to speak, to the execution of "the finer points of [ingenious male] lovemaking."

Stated differently, Wideman's mention of a daughter is strikingly out of place given the logic and tenor of his encomium, because the reference infers to him a paterfamiliar stance he can in no way sustain legitimately or credibly given both the specifics of the enthusiasms in question and usual understandings of paterfamilial postures. That is, although reference to a daughter signals on some level (in the midst of much homoerotic discourse) normative heterosexual congress, it also alludes to heterosexual domesticity greatly at odds with the enthusiasms unfolding. Heterosexual domesticity has more to do with prohibitions on sexual enthusiasms than homosocial esteem of "the finer points of lovemaking." Binding arrangements that would contain or domesticate male libidinal energy are not of the moment in "Playing Dennis Rodman" but, very differently, the mouth and hands and penis and scrotum as agents of pleasurable distraction and even disorder. In Wideman's reflections, the acute pleasures imagined in, through, and around sexual activity are broached—as in the instances in the restrooms—through the imagination of another man's sexual prowess, an act, whether in imagination or fact, exceeding the prescribed mathematics of heterosexual domesticity as well as its rationalization of libidinal energies (marked here by reference to a daughter). In short, Wideman goes the men in the restroom one better.

The arresting images of Rodman on the jacket of *Bad as I Wanna Be* provides a fittingly powerful rendition of these dynamics. On the dust jacket Rodman sits naked astride an imposing Harley-Davidson, his long muscled legs akimbo and contrasted against the black metal and chrome of the motorcycle, his torso lean and erect, his tattooed arms in open display, as is the left cheek of his butt, and as are five basketballs in close proximity, three on the ground next to the Harley, one pinned by a knee against the bike, the other in his crotch, a forearm resting casually across it. The lighting of the shot directs one's attention to this final detail. On the back cover, Rodman stands fully upright, his bare buttocks to the camera, the muscles of his butt and back prominently displayed, his legs stretched to their full length, as are his upreaching arms, a shading of other body parts barely visible through his open legs, six basketballs in proximity this time, four on the ground between or around his legs, two in the open palms of his hands. Thus, in addition to the invitation to see Rodman as having a powerful, brooding instrument between his legs which almost dwarfs the rest of him, the dust jacket poses the invitation to imagine, as do Wideman and innumerable others, that Rodman has balls. Big tan brown ones that are striped and so big and unwieldy they fit in your hand only one at a time. All of this at the same time Rodman must also be imagined as just one of the guys. All of this at the same time one is never invited to see in these images the incapabilities—glaringly evident—of keenly promoted systems of order making exacting colonizations of desire, pleasure, and self-regard.

By what startling set of imaginative feats readily practiced in the culture is Wideman able to see cross-dressing, cross-naming Dennis Rodman simply as one of the boys and simply to see one of the boys in Rodman's play? The mix of appeals, metaphors, and postures elicited by the elite mix of men on the basketball court, a mix the NBA struggles to put in "the most positive light," is so compelling that it seems overwhelming that its crises are generally overlooked, even in the unseemly antics of its most critical proponent. For these reasons, perhaps even more than it is about any individual, *Bad as I Wanna Be* seems more rightly about a compound crisis. Wideman and innumerable others are eager to imagine not just what the title, but also the dust jacket, of the book boldly proclaims. There exists an eager population of cultural consumers willing to undertake the highly profitable fantasy (both antagonistic to and in compliance with the cultural order) that Rodman has balls. Balls all the more intriguing and open to public consideration because they draw attention to themselves not only on the basketball court but at the site of sexual energy itself with its perilous crush of racial, gendered, domestic, and commercial prohibitions and imperatives. What a mix-up.

NOTES

Chapter 9, "Black Men in the Mix," was originally published in *Callaloo* 20, no. 1 (winter 1997): 106–26. Copyright 1997 Charles H. Rowell, and reprinted with permission of Johns Hopkins University Press.

    1. Kobena Mercer, *Welcome to the Jungle: New Positions in Black Cultural Studies* (New York: Routledge, 1994), 296.

    2. Julia Watson, "Toward an Anti-metaphysics of Autobiography," in *The Culture of Autobiography: Constructions of Self-Representation*, ed. Robert Folkenflik (Palo Alto, CA: Stanford University Press, 1993), 57.

    3. Candace Lang, "Autobiography in the Aftermath of Romanticism," *Diacritics* (1982): 5.

    4. Dennis Rodman with Tim Keown, *Bad as I Wanna Be* (New York: Delacorte Press, 1996), 122.

5. Rodman with Keown, *Bad as I Wanna Be*, 94.

6. Mercer, *Welcome to the Jungle*, 296; Judith Butler, "Desire," in *Critical Terms for Literary Study*, ed. Frank Lentricchia and Thomas McLaughlin (Chicago: University of Chicago Press, 1995), 374.

7. Butler, "Desire," 380.

8. Elizabeth Alexander, "'We're Gonna Deconstruct Your Life!': The Making and Un-making of the Black Bourgeois Patriarch in *Ricochet*," in *Representing Black Men*, ed. Marcellus Blount and George P. Cunningham (New York: Routledge, 1996), 167.

9. Rodman with Keown, *Bad as I Wanna Be*, 166, 184.

10. Rodman with Keown, *Bad as I Wanna Be*, 56.

11. Edward S. Herman, *Triumph of the Market: Essays on Economics, Politics and the Media* (Boston: South End, 1995), 3.

12. Rodman with Keown, *Bad as I Wanna Be*, 102.

13. Rodman with Keown, *Bad as I Wanna Be*, 102.

14. Rodman with Keown, *Bad as I Wanna Be*, 104.

15. Herman, *Triumph of the Market*, 4.

16. Rodman with Keown, *Bad as I Wanna Be*, 105.

17. Rodman with Keown, *Bad as I Wanna Be*, 13.

18. Robyn Wiegman, *American Anatomies: Theorizing Race and Gender* (Durham, NC: Duke University Press, 1995), 142.

19. Wiegman, *American Anatomies*.

20. See Kwame Anthony Appiah, *In My Father's House: Africa in the Philosophy of Culture* (New York: Oxford University Press, 1993), 34–37, for an elegant summation of this biological circumstance.

21. Naomi Zack, *Race and Mixed Race* (Philadelphia: Temple University Press, 1993), 27.

22. Abigail Solomon-Godeau, "Male Trouble," in *Constructing Masculinity*, ed. Maurice Berger, Brian Wallis, and Simon Watson (New York: Routledge, 1995), 74.

23. Rodman with Keown, *Bad as I Wanna Be*, 83.

24. Rodman with Keown, *Bad as I Wanna Be*, 83, 86.

25. Rodman with Keown, *Bad as I Wanna Be*, 13.

26. Rodman with Keown, *Bad as I Wanna Be*, 79.

27. Rodman with Keown, *Bad as I Wanna Be*, 178.

28. Diana Ross, *Secrets of a Sparrow* (New York: Villard, 1993).

29. Gayle Rubin, "Thinking Sex," in *The Gay and Lesbian Studies Reader*, ed. Henry Abelove, Michele Aina Barale, and David M. Halperin (New York: Routledge, 1993), 15. Rubin writes, "Variation is a fundamental property of all life, from the simplest biological organisms to the most complex human social formations. Yet [in the prevailing cultural order] sexuality is supposed to conform to a single standard. One of the most tenacious ideas about sex is that there is one best way to do it, and that everyone should do it that way," 15.

30. Rodman with Keown, *Bad as I Wanna Be*, 196–97.

31. Rodman with Keown, *Bad as I Wanna Be*, 200.

32. Rodman with Keown, *Bad as I Wanna Be*, 175.

33. Richard Delgado and Jean Stefancic, "Minority Men, Misery, and the Marketplace of Ideas," in *Constructing Masculinity*, ed. Maurice Berger, Brian Wallis, and Simon Watson (New York: Routledge, 1995), 211.

34. Delgado and Stefancic, "Minority Men, Misery, and the Marketplace of Ideas," 211.

35. Rodman with Keown, *Bad as I Wanna Be*, 157.

36. Mercer, *Welcome to the Jungle*, 296.

37. Butler, "Desire," 374, emphasis added.

38. Sut Jhally, *The Codes of Advertising: Fetishism and the Political Economy of Meaning in the Consumer Society* (New York: Routledge, 1990), 142.

39. Mercer, *Welcome to the Jungle*, 178–79.

40. Alexander, "'We're Gonna Deconstruct Your Life!,'" 160.

41. Mercer, *Welcome to the Jungle*, 201.

42. Rodman with Keown, *Bad as I Wanna Be*, 156.

43. Rodman with Keown, *Bad as I Wanna Be*, 156.

44. Rodman with Keown, *Bad as I Wanna Be*, 156, emphasis in original.

45. Jhally, *The Codes of Advertising*, 116.

46. Mercer, *Welcome to the Jungle*, 202.

47. Jhally, *The Codes of Advertising*, 29, emphasis in original.

48. Laura Doyle, *Bordering on the Body: The Racial Matrix of Modern Fiction and Culture* (New York: Oxford University Press, 1994), 82.

49. Leo Bersani, *Homos* (Cambridge, MA: Harvard University Press, 1995), 70, emphasis in original.

50. Jhally, *The Codes of Advertising*, 78–79.

51. John Edgar Wideman, "Playing Dennis Rodman," *New Yorker*, April 29–May 6, 1996, 94, emphasis in original.

52. Wideman, "Playing Dennis Rodman," 94.

53. Wideman, "Playing Dennis Rodman," 94.

54. Kendell Thomas, "Ain't Nothin' Like the Real Thing: Black Masculinity, Gay Sexuality, and the Jargon of Authenticity," in *Representing Black Men*, ed. Marcellus Blount and George P. Cunningham (New York: Routledge, 1996), 66.

55. Wideman, "Playing Dennis Rodman," 95.

56. Wideman, "Playing Dennis Rodman," 94, 95.

CH10

Dead Men Printed: Tupac Shakur, Biggie Smalls, and Hip-Hop Eulogy (1999)

The dead body is one thing; the dead black body another. For death is a site obdurately outside all desire and, opposingly, racial blackness a site so fully defined by and within desire it demands regulation, also by definition. In effect, the dead black body may be an ultimate figure of regulation, unruly desire and its risks fully mastered. Yet, as the unfolding history of the United States attests in particular, what is most interesting is that this form of death has a highly useful social valence, and the intrigue of how any form of social productivity might rest on such an inert figure is effectively suggested by Gilles Deleuze and Félix Guattari in their neo-Marxist usurpation of the interests of psychoanalysis. In *Anti-Oedipus: Capitalism and Schizophrenia*, Deleuze and Guattari aim to theorize the contingency, coincidence, and continuity of social and phantasmatic productions. They pursue individualizing and collective "flows" of desire passing through what they call "machinic" psychic and social structures that cohere concomitantly as both the subject and the collective of capitalism. These flows, they claim, yield every objective reality as an immediate attestation to psychic desire or, differently put, the phantasmatic appears to know no bounds in its extensiveness, and in its intensity the social appears to know no bounds. Subjectivity, or a subject-effect, falls out of these desirous flows only as a residuum of the psychic and material production fused almost seamlessly together. Deleuze and Guattari write: "The truth of the matter is that *social production is purely and simply desiring-production itself under determinate conditions*. We maintain that the social field is immediately invested by desire, that it is the historically determined product of desire, and that libido has no need of any transformation, in order to invade and invest the productive forces and the relations of production. *There is only desire and the social and nothing else.*"[1] The contention here is that to realize a highly consequential social production from dead black bodies proves to be, all at the same time, a substantial feat of phantasm and a profitable social transaction, as well as a thoroughly subjectivizing exercise.

To begin, one might grant that the individual subject is fundamentally a highly prized *point of articulation* in which one *also* views an (over)determined foreclosure of other possibilities of desire, phantasm, social production. Because the individual subject is always both desired and desiring, the problem for the interests of collectivity is rendering these two positions fully coincident. The propitious subject speaking through *Newsweek*, *Time*, the *New York Times*, the *Los Angeles Times*, the *Washington Post*, etc., may not advertise that "cruelty has nothing to do with some ill-defined or natural violence that might be commissioned to explain the history of mankind [or African Americans, or gangsta rap, for that matter]; cruelty is the movement of culture that is realized in bodies and inscribed on them, belaboring them. That is what cruelty means. This culture is not the movement of ideology: on the contrary, it forcibly injects production into desire, and conversely, it forcibly inserts desire into social production and reproduction. For even death, punishment, and torture are desired, and are instances of production."[2] One might ask, witnessing the eulogizing of Shakur and Smalls, what is it that is *always* being articulated? To what end or use is the "visible" subjective most readily and concertedly put in this crisis? Notions of tragedy and crisis remain crucial to mass mediated responses to the murders of Tupac Shakur and Biggie Smalls; however—rather than *whether or not* African Americans (and young black men in particular) are a site of cultural and social crisis—the paramount question involves precisely what kind of social subject is allowed to take public form in collective recognition and negotiation of the crisis. Formulating an answer begins with the recognition that, if the violence of gangsta rap—discursive or physical—is a tragedy, it always attests to (failed) individual fortunes.

Nelson George ends as follows his September 24, 1996, *Village Voice* commentary on the death of Tupac Shakur: "A gangsta can't out rhyme a bullet. And real gangsters rarely outlive them. Tupac Shakur—gifted black artist, reckless young man, and now the hip hop James Dean—always knew both of these things. Guess he just ran out of time to do anything about it. May God bless his divided soul."[3] The structure of George's parenthesis captures the drama and meaning of Shakur's tragedy: "gifted black artist, reckless young man, and now the hip hop James Dean." The unresolved conflict or division articulated through Shakur's life remains how his status as a "gifted black artist"—a status that, if properly negotiated, could have been translated into virtually unassailable market and civic rewards—is troubled, even negated, by his status as a violent, irreverent "reckless young man." However, any tragic *break* from the virtually invisible system and logic that might be called capitalism as culture and culture as capitalism is literally repaired by the third term of the parenthesis, the reference to James Dean. The reference pits the starkly different lives and "rebellions" of the (incommensurate?) Shakur and Dean unobtrusively as equivalent within a system in which a staggering variety of productions and consumptions remain fixed and relayed through individual identity and the unfailing axiomatic of the system, cash, the fundamental term of infinite substitutability, and market and civic rewards. Apparently, Shakur was given by interested onlookers, with generosity to a fault, time to execute a pending self-reclamation and self-reform, but he failed. In George's regret-ridden observations, the Judeo-Christian God comes to stand with sublime finality over the entire troublesome division, providing confirmation to the so vastly intuited capitalism as culture and culture as capitalism. One might recognize in the deeply regretful, and subjectivizing, sentiments of George the sly effects of a suturing in the too elegant system described by Deleuze and Guattari, the subject, subjectivity, the subject-effect, resting as the final stitch.

Writing in *Newsweek* in the week of March 24, 1997, John Leland presents another rendition of these matters in his article "Requiem for a Gangsta." Leland, within the first paragraph, writes of Smalls: "Life was good. He was pushing for a movie deal, a TV deal, a book deal; he wanted to become a household celebrity like the Fresh Prince."[4] Leland presents phantasmatic relations between *good* and goods as if they stand beyond all reasonable, or even unreasonable, doubt. The statements might be called—in the vocabulary of Deleuze and Guattari—"machinic," since they so productively gloss an enormous complexity of machines enabling movie production and consumption, television production and consumption, literary production and consumption, in addition to glossing the concept of household celebrity status, which fuses the enormous complexes not only to aggregate domiciles—themselves primary situations for further machines—but, moreover, to the individuated subject desiring the complexes in the first place through the manifest subject-effect, always already a residual of the highly particular chain forming desire, lack, risk, and substitution. The only mark of itself *available* to the manifest subject-effect proves, ironically, the set of relations and substitutions united already—so completely?—as fused phantasmatic and real points of articulation. If the murder of Biggie Smalls is a tragedy in any measure, it is a tragedy only insofar as his life/death is rendered available as a further point at which to fix an ideally infinite—hence, risky—chain of possibilities and substitutions.

A brief, but more extended, engagement with Deleuze and Guattari's project of tracking desire away from its psychoanalytic moorings is helpful for pursuing these observations more fully. In an important strand of *Anti-Oedipus: Capitalism and Schizophrenia*, Deleuze and Guattari align desire with production, rather than lack: "Producing is always something 'grafted onto' the product; and for that reason desiring-production is production of production, just as every machine is a machine connected to another machine."[5] This position allows them the theoretical vantage to insert desire immediately in a social fabric without the apparent digressions psychoanalysis would present as fundamental. They argue that "desire produces reality, or stated another way, desiring-production is one and the same thing as social production. It is not possible to attribute a special form of existence to desire, a mental or psychic reality that is presumably different from the material reality of social production. Desiring-machines are not fantasy machines or dream-machines, which supposedly can be distinguished from technical and social machines. Rather, fantasies are secondary expressions, deriving from the identical nature of the two sorts of machines in any given set of circumstances. Thus fantasy is never individual: it is *group fantasy*."[6] One might amend this final statement to read that no individual posture is ever entirely about fantasy and, equally, no fantasy is ever simply about an individual posture. Fantasy is never individual but always *at some* level group fantasy, for even as the fantasy may individuate the individual, the individualizing emerges through terms gaining their systematicity and—hence, articulated—through group affiliation (even in instances that this shared group affiliation takes repudiation as its primary form). Provisionally, one might reduce these issues to the formula that—again, in the words of Deleuze and Guattari—"the reality of the object, insofar as it is produced by desire, is thus a *psychic reality*."[7]

Some of these implications for understanding capitalist formations, as elaborated by Deleuze and Guattari, recall Baudrillard's theoretical drive to get beyond a Marxist conception of use value *cum* need. In proposing that desire "then becomes this abject fear of lacking something," Deleuze and Guattari repudiate understandings of desire *as* lack.[8] They write:

> Lack is a countereffect of desire; it is deposited, distributed, vacuolized within a real that is natural and social. Desire always remains in close touch with the conditions of objective existence; it embraces them and

follows them, shifts when they shift, and does not outlive them. For that reason it so often becomes the desire to die, whereas need is a measure of the withdrawal of a subject that has lost its desire at the same time that it loses the passive syntheses of these conditions. This is precisely the significance of need as a search in a void: hunting about, trying to capture or become a parasite of passive syntheses in whatever vague world they may happen to exist in.[9]

It is important to understand that Deleuze and Guattari theorize the withdrawal of the subject, not only as a sign of passivity but as, concomitantly, the sign of active participation in the collective system or organization through which need becomes *articulated and visible* in the first place. This state of affairs obtains even for what passes as the most basic of needs. For example, the human body does not *need* to eat, as demonstrated by the anorexic or bulimic body or, conversely, the human body may *need* not to eat. The anorexic or bulimic, of course, risks death and may die. However, in claiming that need does not mark a passive withdrawal into a precarious and discrete self where it originates as a given, Deleuze and Guattari present need as never really addressing the (inevitably expendable) individual but, rather, always inexorably, even if obliquely, the collective, systematicity, or productive phantasm mapping itself in/onto/through the individual. Put another way, need inexorably addresses the collective, systematicity, or productive phantasm in relation to which the individual must position herself or himself *in the first place* in order to take (or to refuse to take) any morsel into its mouth.

The condition of desire proves the position actively refusing any such passive withdrawal. Hence, desire, in its necessarily revolutionary nature, inexorably threatens established needs or order, patterns, of withdrawal: "Desire does not threaten a society because it is a desire to sleep with the mother, but because it is revolutionary. And that does not at all mean that desire is something other than sexuality, but that sexuality and love do not live in the bedroom of Oedipus, they dream instead of wide-open spaces, and cause strange flows to circulate that do not let themselves be stocked within an established order. Desire does not 'want' revolution, it is revolutionary in its own right, as though involuntarily, by wanting what it wants."[10]

Capitalism, Deleuze and Guattari argue, is the system that most deliberately attempts to master, install itself in, and exploit this condition, calling for repeated passive withdrawals of individuals into the needs of its collective fantasy, even as it concomitantly seeks perpetually new sites and terms of—hopefully always newly commodifiable—withdrawal. There is always a risk (more so than a lack) definitive of desire; one of which in the structural dimensions of capitalism and its risky installation within desire is that the next revolution of capitalism as culture and culture as capitalism yielding it to new terms and new sites may equally bring it to terms and sites calling for withdrawal into a dynamics of collective fantasy it cannot ultimately commodify and that, therefore, would mark its rupture, if not, in fact, its long-forecast dissolution.

If there is risk—for desire is always risky, because it is revolutionary, and capitalism transacts concertedly in desire—then, the risk is borne disproportionately in this instance at the site of young black bodies. The risk is not shared evenly by all of us enmeshed in the collective fantasy structured as/by capitalism. Desire is always alarming, because it does not *necessarily* attach itself to any *particular* thing: desire can be the desire for anything. Hence, "the prime function incumbent upon the socius has always been to codify the flows of desire, to inscribe them, to record them, to see to it that no flow exits that is not properly dammed up, channeled, regulated."[11] Capitalism looks to young black bodies as sites of open, unregulated flows of desire but, paradoxically, only in order productively and profitably to inscribe and channel these unregulated flows. On the other hand, these young people, who necessarily participate in the cash nexus capitalism phantasmatically and realistically promotes, proclaim for/through themselves that the terms of the transaction are highly problematic. The risk in every attempted (re)inscription or (re)channeling of the flows of desire is that the (re)inscription itself will present or intimate other options, other options that in another field of "desiring-production" would reform the socius and thus the apparent *limits* of desire itself. This risk produced at the site of young black people and their words and postures must be foreclosed because of the absolute risk of other options and change lurking in/beyond their bodies, an absolute risk capitalism as culture and culture as capitalism irresolvably wants and never wants to embrace.

It is useful to consider more public sentiments. Kevin Powell writes for *Rolling Stone*: "Like Kurt Cobain, before him, Shakur had become a living symbol of his generation's angst and rage, and for that he is now looked upon as a martyr. But his fame and the controversy and misunderstanding that surrounded his life have also rendered Shakur—Cobain, Marvin Gaye, James Dean, Jimi Hendrix, Jim Morrison and even Malcolm X—an enigma."[12] The mechanisms "rendering" Shakur a generational symbol, a martyr, controversial, misunderstood, and, ultimately, an interchangeable point on a chain linking dead, *troubled* celebrities—and the trouble rests acutely with them?—remain not only unimaginable but, moreover, unattainable: "an enigma." It is (suturing) subjectivity, however, that remains plain—even if supposedly an enigma.

Any angst and rage in question has to do with the dynamics of generational positioning—i.e., natural processes of youth and *growing up*—natural forces oddly able to assail and squander even the abilities of those individuals fortunate enough to hold in their grasps immense opportunities to translate their personal situations into properly unassailable market and civic rewards.

After the murder of Biggie Smalls apparently recalls or reopens the (inter)national trauma of Tupac Shakur's death, Farai Chideya, writing a brief "Viewpoint" column for *Time* (March 24, 1997), opines: "In the weeks to come as we try to make sense of the death of two of the youngest, richest, best-known black men in America, we'll probably succumb to a natural temptation to divide the 'good kids' from the 'hip-hop kids.'"[13] There are several matters to notice already. The ultimate (public) imperative, of course, is to make—or, in fact, remake—*sense*, a subjectivizing desire or drive fully determining Chideya's adjectives: The adjective "richest" invokes and frames the two men and the entire issue within that fundamental axiomatic of capitalism as culture and culture as capitalism—money—a principle ideally transforming all possible phantasms and material objects into an endless chain of substitutable equivalents; "best-known" frames the issue and the two men within the dynamics of public notoriety, dynamics guaranteeing that "fame itself can sell a product," that "connecting fame with a product enhances the value of both."[14] The terms on which Chideya accounts a public loss or lack reconstitute rudimentary grounds of capitalism as culture and culture as capitalism, to which there may be no outside, except apparently death itself.

Further, there is the impulse to reclaim "hip-hop kids" within the citation of the *good*. And, as it just so happens to turn out, within the citation of consumer goods. Chideya continues: "I'm not buying it. I grew up listening to hip-hop. In elementary school I tuned my radio to the techno-influenced chant *Planet Rock* and innocent party jams like *Rapper's Delight*. By high school and college, hip-hop was everything from the pop female braggadocio of Salt-n-Pepa to the black nationalism of Public Enemy. Today, in addition to music that ranges from alternative rock to techno, I listen to rough-edged rappers the Wu Tang Clan—and, yes, Biggie and Tupac as well."[15] Chideya draws out a long list of goods consumable as musical styles made equivalent, or mutually substitutable, or interchangeable, at the cash nexus. One glimpses in her observations the machinic world Deleuze and Guattari address: an overtly invoked radio, implicitly invoked CD players, and stereo systems, and cash registers, all in addition to the "satisfiable" desires so clearly connected to these machines, desires that might be characterized as more ineffable machines themselves producing the sense-making capacity of those material machines. The reference to the two slain rappers by their first names reiterates the compelling certainty of subjectivity, but never as an effect, a residual directly conceivable as a lack itself—needless to say, as a risk exercised through desire. The ultimate *need* raised in the commentary stands as follows: "That's why we, the hip-hop generation, bear the ultimate responsibility for shaping the art form we love. Hip-hop used to lift us above the struggles we faced; then it tried to inform us about the struggles we faced; now it's *become* one of the struggles we face."[16] Hip-hop, as a consumer good, and by a convulsive sleight of reason, becomes a struggle that supercedes the social and individual struggles hip-hop attempts to record in the first place.

In the same issue of *Time*, in a more extensive column, Christopher John Farley reports details of the events leading to the death of Biggie Smalls, also ultimately in order to put the situation in perspective. Essential elements of that perspective are redacted in a quotation Farley attributes to a "record-industry executive who knew [Smalls]." The executive asks: "Why must artists still pimp the idea that life is an ugly reality? It's time to give people dreams back. [Wallace] moved on, out of the drug dealing. The images he was conveying were still rooted in the ghetto. He wasn't showing his fans that there is another life."[17] Clearly, the idea that life can be an ugly reality for anyone is very threatening. For whom? In what circumstances? On the level of individuated fantasy and desire? On the level of the socius? Further still, the structure of these observations, moving as they do from "reality," to "dreams," to "images," and back to "life," reiterates and reinforces the great *consequence* of always contingent, contiguous, and coherent phantasm and reality. It is helpful to turn again to Deleuze and Guattari: "There is no such thing as the social production of reality on the one hand, and a desiring-production that is mere fantasy on the other. The only connections that could be established between these two productions would be secondary ones of introjection and projection, as though all social practices had their precise counterpart in introjected or internal mental practices, or as though mental practices were projected upon social systems, without either of the two sets of practices ever having any real or concrete effect upon the other."[18] The two theorists propose that the apparently real—or the collectively phantasmatic—is fantasy pure and simple. The collective fantasy underwritten through Farley and the unnamed recording-industry executive pronounce that no "ugly reality" can, in fact, be *real* because there is, of course, always "another [way of] life." What is not articulated and what is virulently resisted is the knowledge that the enabling violence of capitalism as culture and culture as capitalism forecloses the possibilities of "another life" for an enormous amount of people. What is resisted in this perspective, through the productive contiguousness of the phantasmatic and the actual, is any acknowledgment that "in all regions [of the United States], when black people in large numbers have become relatively assertive in their pursuit of a fair share of the good things in life [i.e., the psychic and material resources of an industrial capitalist order, now a postindustrial order], white people have proved themselves ready for violence."[19] As the effects of transnational capitalism make abundantly clear, these same observations also pertain and always have pertained to much more than the situation of the United States and African Americans. Farley and the executive, through violent, measured reason, resist fully imagining that those "fans" of gangsta rap "rooted in the ghetto" are acutely aware of "another [way of] life" and, what is more, are often fully cognizant of their violent, though "reasoned," disbarment from it.

Farley, in this vein, also invokes friends of the slain Biggie Smalls: "Friends say Wallace only rapped about violence to make enough money to leave it all behind. Says Lance Rivera, a close friend of Wallace's: 'He said he wanted to move his family down to Atlanta, build them a house there and write a book.'"[20] One witnesses machinic relations between the phantasmatic and the real played out, in this instance, through the paramount, but unobtrusive, phrase (and social act): "make enough money." Biggie Smalls not only lived as a crisis for capitalism as culture and culture as capitalism but comes to be a properly assimilable point of articulation for the formation, a point of *becoming* that to some extent marks the end of his status as a crisis, marking instead a (re)new(ed) status as a desiring-machine for capitalism as culture and culture as capitalism. In light of this particular transfiguration, Chideya's brilliant metaphorical flourish of "I'm not buying it" becomes all too resonant, a flourish situating both authors as/through a subject-effect *in the need* of not recognizing the figurality of that phrase (or individual position) as, in point of fact, all too literal. To recognize oneself as living so thoroughly in the figural (the arational? the phantasmatic?) is, at the very least, to burst violently the bounds of irony, to *become oneself* too problematic for coherence as generally understood, to *become oneself* too problematic in relation to the terrain of social violence, nonetheless, subjectivity.

Dealing with Too Much Attitude

But, this is to say, the occasions of the slayings of rappers Tupac Shakur and Biggie Smalls, in September 1996 and March 1997 respectively, present the U.S. media with the rare occasion to write of African Americans, particularly young black men, and African-American cultural production, particularly rap and gangsta rap, in one of the most effective poses for safeguarding its mystifications of black/white racial polarization. This pose is one of open censure laced freely but disingenuously with apparent concern, concern lamenting and anatomizing the problematic situation of young black men as one in which what these wayward citizens need "is to escape the idea that posing as a gangster is the only authentic role to play if you are black and 17."[21] The argument apparently runs that what these wayward citizens require to extricate themselves from their inevitably violent lives and circumstances is an epiphanic moment in which they acknowledge the distinction between an ill-chosen, unappealing self-performance and a more authentic self-performance deferred, often fatefully, by the other.

In conjunction with similar commentaries appearing in the *Los Angeles Times*, *Newsweek*, *Time*, etc., this curious argument presented by the *New York Times* in December 1996 forwards at least two assumptions. The first ascribes to young black men a seemingly inherent relation to violence, one aspect of which fixes them as legitimate objects of violence merely as a result of their "untoward" appearance. The second assumption takes for granted that a recoverable, fully sanctioned, and more authentic social subject is obscured by the public bravado of black masculinity as framed by hip-hop culture: this authentic, sanctioned social subject would be visible even in the form of menacing black male bodies, but only subsequent to the appropriate, collective epiphany on the part of the difficult purveyors of black masculinity. In and of themselves these assumptions are intriguing for understanding routine machinations of the dominant U.S. racial imagination, but they are especially intriguing in light of the fact that the commentary appears in the aftermath of a fatal shooting occurring over "the Thanksgiving weekend [1996] when five black teen-agers walked into a Brooklyn bodega and swaggered around the joint, playing the only role they knew. The store had never been robbed. But the proprietor was edgy—and armed."[22] The outcome of this cultural collision between swaggering on the one hand and entrepreneurial edginess on the other is the death of one of the five teenagers (fifteen years old) and the wounding of another (seventeen years old).

To begin, one must note that, in a culture that otherwise vociferously celebrates and idealizes—even to the point of infantilization—those persons it legally fixes in childhood, the commentary in the *New York Times* aims to condone the death and wounding of the teenagers. Even though in the end U.S. celebrations and idealizations of childhood too frequently have nothing to do with the actual terms of the lives of those persons legally marked as children, what is absolutely clear in this instance is that diagnostic confrontations with racial blackness, as a matter of course, obliterate even so cherished and instinctive a reflex of the U.S. social imagination. Ultimately pushing its readers to believe that the death and wounding of the two black teenagers are logical and justifiable outcomes of the encounter, the commentary is able to maneuver so patently and unapologetically in this direction in large part because of the sensational slaying of Shakur, approximately two months prior to the incident and, proleptically, the slaying of Smalls, yet some four months away. The murders of these music industry celebrities function culturally to provide the event in Brooklyn with its apparently reasonable inevitability through a set of alignments reifying swaggering black male bodies as somehow equivalent to weapons—weapons counterposed to the deadly handguns discharged by the edgy storekeeper and the unapprehended murderers of the two rap stars.

In her analysis of the acquittal of Rodney King's assailants in the first legal case to follow his brutal encounter with Los Angeles law enforcement, Judith Butler outlines this peculiar logical torque. In the essay "Engendered/Engendering: Schematic Racism and White Paranoia," Butler codifies as follows a circuit of white paranoia:

> They [the jurors] are perhaps King as well, but whitewashed: the blows he suffers are taken to be the blows they *would* suffer if the police were not protecting them from him. Thus, the physical danger in which King is recorded is transferred to them; they identify with that vulnerability, but construe it as their own, the vulnerability of whiteness, thus refiguring him as the threat. The danger that they believe themselves always to be in, by virtue of their whiteness (whiteness as an episteme operates despite the existence of two nonwhite jurors). This completes the circuit of paranoia: the projection of their aggression, and the subsequent regarding of that projection as an external threat.[23]

In these highly publicized incidents, violence "returns" to African-American male bodies, even though violence does not necessarily emanate from those persons in the first place, and it is this mystified circuit of what Butler terms white paranoia that, one might say, positions the several discrete incidents as equivalent for U.S. culture logic (the beating of King, the shootings in Brooklyn, the murders of Shakur and Smalls). In each incident threatening black male bodies stand as weapons met by the violence of other, more legitimate weapons. However, one recognizes further in the *New York Times* report the reduction of black male subculture and its social meaning to the violent deaths of the celebrity gangsta rappers. Whereas the violent attack on King is often made to seem a random or freak social event, the attacks on Shakur and Smalls are primarily made to seem a self-fulfilling apotheosis of the cultural production the two so lucratively sponsor. Restated, the untenable logic of the article seems to run as follows: if—unlike most young black men—one is astute enough to understand the social meaning of their subculture, one recognizes that subculture as foremost a dire warning to the young men creating and perpetuating it. Brent Staples, the author of the *New York Times* article, writes further: "Playing at gangsterism may be harmless for suburban white kids who roam the mall. But in places like Bedford-Stuyvesant, the same postures and clothing can get you killed."[24] Summarily put, it is a racial geography and the racial designation of the person beneath the clothing and informing the postures that accounts for any fatal difference: "More of the same," the article forewarns, "could lie in store for young black boys who play the gangster role too well."[25]

What is important to witness is not only the insidious rhetorical transfigurations of black male bodies into weapons, but the larger context or terms enabling the transfigurations. This context, very strictly circumscribing the meaning of *public* geographies, comprehends public geographies to be foremost "spaces that are privately owned and determined by the profit motive, making them bourgeois public spaces."[26] Insofar as the incident occurs in a public space, it is a proprietary public space wherein—in both its grandest as well as most minor executions—capitalism emerges as "the sole arbiter of enjoyment through [means of an ostensibly] free and ideologically uncontaminated flow of consumption."[27] The commentary centers cultural citizenship irrevocably in this arrangement and the very select set of negotiations attendant to it. In other words, one reason the actions of the edgy entrepreneur never call for or receive any pronounced scrutiny in the article is the fact that the violent response of the proprietor is elicited not only by recognition of black male bodies as "weaponry" but, as a corollary, in protection of orderly processes of exchanging commodities for cash and vice versa. Most starkly put, the swaggering poses of the black teenagers—sufficient provocation for violent retaliation—intervene between the edgy merchant and an idealized consumer. Importantly, it is not threatening demands for cash or goods intervening between the merchant and an idealized consumer. The property the merchant must protect is not the material property within the store but, rather, property coalescing in the form of an overcivil commerce and hyperbolic decency, with the phrase "Have a nice day!" indemnifying the ubiquitous pleasures of ceaseless transactions. From all indications, what is placed in most immediate danger are two presiding abstractions of idealized merchant and consumer—hardy, enduring abstractions, even though they remain hardly commensurate with the circumstances of New York City or, for that matter, virtually any location in the United States.

To say the least, the forged affability of these abstractions is glaringly incommensurate to the social circumstances of young black men as a demographic group. The social disposition of young black men by U.S. cultural forces cannot by *any stretch of the imagination* be captured by vapid notions of "nice days," a circumstance made statistically clear, for example, by Roderick J. Harrison and Claudette E. Bennett's report "Racial and Ethnic Diversity" in *The State of the Union: America in the 1990s, Volume Two: Social Trends*.[28] Young black men face a set of social circumstances in which odds have it that, on the "level playing field" of free-market society, they will achieve less educationally than their white male counterparts, will earn less financially, and are much more likely to be singled out as criminal perpetrators than their white male counterparts (especially in relation to drug use, even as statistics document higher drug use among their white male counterparts). It is statistically more likely that they and their families will live below the poverty line and, indeed, that their familial configurations will fail to conform to dominant prescriptions of what appropriately stands as a family—as if any such arbitrary configuration were foremost a sign of anything more than the prescription itself or the allowance to make the prescription. In short, their relation to what this culture takes as its primary indicators of "life chances" suggests that young black men (and African Americans, young and old, female and male) may not, in fact, have many "nice days" before them.

In "Racial and Ethnic Diversity," Harrison and Bennett disclose, for instance, that black men were approximately three times (1970), two and one half times (1980), and two and one quarter times (1990) less likely to earn a college degree than their white male counterparts—circumstances roughly identical to those of Native American and Hispanic men. In 1990 black men twenty-five years old and older earned, at best, approximately 87 percent of their white male counterparts' earnings regardless of the level of educational accreditation at which the comparison might be made. Drawing further on 1990 U.S. Bureau of the Census statistics, these researchers reveal that, as opposed to 75.2 percent of white men, 66.5 percent of black men sixteen years old and older officially participate in the labor force. For those with less than a high school degree the figure is 53.7 percent for black men as opposed to 69.2 percent for white men; for those with a high school degree the rate is 78.1 percent for blacks and 83.1 percent for whites; for those with a bachelor's degree 88.6 percent of black men participate in the workforce as opposed to 88.9 percent of white men.

If young black men learn to esteem normative domesticity (and U.S. culture propounds this dissembling "value" with the most unsubtle of pedagogies), then, on the contrary, their immediate environment alerts them to the likelihood that they will be able to insinuate themselves into such an arrangement with less apparent success than other young men (whether white or any other racial designation): In 1970, 1980, and 1990 respectively 67.7 percent, 57.1 percent, and 49.9 percent of black families correspond to the married-couple configuration, while that same configuration defines 88.0 percent, 86.5 percent, and 84.4 percent of white families in 1970, 1980, and 1990 respectively; female-headed households account for 27.4 percent, 37.2 percent, and 43.2 percent of black family configurations in 1970, 1980, and 1990, as opposed to 9.0 percent, 10.6 percent, and 11.8 percent in those same years for white families; male-headed households account for 4.8 percent, 5.7 percent, and 6.9 percent of black family configurations in those years, while the same type of household accounts for 3.0 percent, 2.9 percent, and 3.8 percent of white families.

The economic fortunes of these black and white families are divergent. The median family income for the black married couple in 1989 is $33,000 compared to $39,915 for the white married couple. For female-headed black families the figure is $13,500 in comparison to $21,023 for female-headed white families. For male-headed black families the figure is $21,000 and for male-headed white families $30,000. It is far from surprising that these domestic configurations in tandem with their median earning power yield racially skewed rates of poverty: 29.8 percent (1969), 26.4 percent (1979), and 23.9 percent (1989) of black families fall below the poverty line, and 8.6 percent (1969), 6.6 percent (1979), and 7.0 percent (1989) of white families.

Some features of this racial determination of economic fortunes are not always made visible by trends mapped across decades, an insight underscored by the historian Gerald Horne in "The Political Economy of the Black Urban Future: A History," in which he notes:

> According [to the September 14, 1993, *Wall Street Journal*], blacks were the only racial group to suffer a net job loss during the 1990–1991 economic downturn at companies reporting to the Equal Opportunity Commission. Whites, Hispanics, and Asians [Horne omits Native Americans] meanwhile gained thousands of jobs, according to an analysis of EEOC records. At Dial Corporation, for instance, blacks lost 43.6 percent of the jobs cut, even though they represented 26.3 percent of Dial's work force going into the recession. At BankAmerica Corporation and ITT Corporation, blacks lost jobs at more than twice the rate of their companies' overall work force reductions.[29]

Moreover, Horne reads recent economic crises and transformations in immediate relation to drastic changes in the social landscape for African Americans.

Drawing his evidence from the first statewide assessment of the status of black men by the California legislature, undertaken in 1993, Horne reports:

> The findings were startling. One-sixth of California's 625,000 Black men age sixteen and older are arrested each year, records that hamper job prospects. It was discovered that men of African descent are more likely than Euro-Americans or Latinos to be arrested on drug charges and later released for lack of evidence. Black men comprise forty percent of the felons entering state prisons and they are three times more likely than Euro-Americans to drop out of high school. And those with less than a high school education are twice as likely to be unemployed as Euro-Americans with the same education.[30]

Horne claims that

> most significant [to this state of affairs] is the erosion of semi-skilled jobs in which Blacks were employed disproportionately. This has set in motion a rapid slide in the income not only for black men ... but for Black families generally. The state's heavy dependence on military spending meant that, inevitably, down-sizing would occur once the Cold War subsided. In any case, African Americans historically have had difficulty in securing work in this important sector of the state's economy, and the entertainment industry, the other engine of the state's economy, has been similarly inhospitable to Blacks.[31]

These observations concerning structural economic changes and their interests in fully criminalizing a once industrially useful black labor force are echoed and extended in George Lipsitz's historical and social analyses in *The Possessive Investment in Whiteness: How White People Profit from Identity Politics*; Lipsitz proceeds at length to document his claim that the "neoracism of contemporary conservativism plays a vital role in building a countersubversive consensus because it disguises the social disintegration brought about by neoconservativism itself as the fault of 'inferior' social groups, and because it builds a sense of righteous indignation among its constituents that enables them to believe that the selfish and self-interested politics they pursue are actually part of a moral crusade."[32] Some aspects of Lipsitz's commentary on an escalating system of criminal (in)justice warrant quoting at some length:

> A 1990 study by the National Institute on Drug Abuse revealed that while only 15 percent of the thirteen million habitual drug users in the United States are black and 77 percent are white, African Americans are

four times more likely to be arrested on drug charges than whites in the nation as a whole, and seven to nine times more likely in Pennsylvania, Michigan, Illinois, Florida, Massachusetts, and New Jersey. A 1989 study by the Parents' Resource Institute for Drug Education discovered that African American high school students consistently showed lower levels of drug and alcohol use than their European counterparts, even in high schools populated by residents of low-income housing projects. Yet, while comprising about 12 percent of the U.S. population, blacks accounted for 10 percent of drug arrests in 1984, 40 percent in 1988, and 42 percent in 1990. In addition, white drug defendants receive considerably shorter average prison terms than African Americans convicted of comparable crimes. A U.S. Sentencing Commission study found in 1992 that half of the federal court districts that handled cases involving crack cocaine prosecuted minority defendants exclusively. A *Los Angeles Times* article in 1995 revealed that "black and Latino crack dealers are hammered with 10-year mandatory federal sentences while whites prosecuted in state court face a minimum of five years and often receive no more than a year in jail." Alexander Lichtenstein and Michael A. Kroll point out that sentences for African Americans in the federal prison system are 20 percent longer than those given to whites who commit the same crimes. They observe that if blacks received the same sentences as whites for these offences, the federal prison system would require three thousand fewer prison cells, enough to close completely six of the new five-hundred bed institutions.[33]

It is important to recognize, as a supplement to Lipsitz's observations, however, that contemporary cultural developments by no means stand as the singular episode in U.S. history of disingenuous "use of the law to redefine class and property relations and enhance labor discipline" by means of the callous disposition of African-American bodies.[34] For contemporary machinations reiterate earlier episodes, perhaps most notably the political motives of southern Redemption following the engineered collapse of the social experiment of Reconstruction, in which the "law attempted to accomplish what planters by themselves had failed to achieve: the complete separation of the freedmen from the means of production, the creation of a true agricultural proletariat."[35] In the late nineteenth century, "criminalization" of African Americans emerges as a powerful means of reapproaching, or approximating, in virtually everything but name, "a system of permanent, hereditary, racialized servitude reducing human persons to the status of property, legally defenseless against beatings, whippings, and rapes."[36] The United States has insistently displayed not only its willingness, but its profound intent, to expend the population into which young black persons are husbanded by racial designation.

All this is to say that one might easily suspect and, indeed, respect the fact that the teenagers in the Brooklyn bodega do not proffer postures of pleasant mutual regard mandated to circulate with the exchange of cash and goods. They appear in guises dismissive of precisely the most routine aspects of the social world enclosing them, a set of dismissive postures proliferated as well by Tupac Shakur, Biggie Smalls, and various other rappers. These postures do not signal satisfaction with or enjoyment of the cultural landscape through which the young men bearing them must move but signal, admittedly with dire repercussions, the opposite: "It is no surprise that rap is frequently viewed as the musical expression of delinquency. Intensifying the matter is rap's lyrical commitment to historicizing what the artists perceive as everyday reality. Due to their position as the socio-economically under privileged targets of repressive rhetoric and policies, their account of daily life is explosive and, for many, too much to take."[37] At stake, more than anything else, in the Brooklyn confrontation as well as larger cultural confrontations over rap and hip-hop culture are *protocols* of consumption, particularly when one recognizes that abrogation of these protocols does not by any means amount to foregoing or precluding normal flows of cash and goods.

The question of protocols may be precisely the social meaning of black male subculture and its gangsta rapper representatives. Indeed, open *solicitation*—in the Derridean sense of the word—of the protocols of individualist capitalist exchange might be precisely the social meaning of black male subculture prompting the murderous gunfire from the storekeeper, violence distorted, in turn, by the critical torsions of the *New York Times* article into a friendly but dire warning not so surreptitiously figuring young black men as weapons.[38] If the *New York Times* article presents no evidence that the teenagers precluded or interrupted operations of the cash nexus, then in very unintended ways its governing analogy between the five young men and gangsta rappers does—ironically—obtain. By no stretch of the imagination can gangsta rappers be imagined as, in fact, precluding or interrupting the cash nexus at the center of the material operations of the culture as well as at the center of its highest estimations of human intercourse. Gangsta rap, as the article itself acknowledges, is a highly lucrative enterprise—most especially for corporate USA. Shakur and Smalls, like the five teenagers, swagger, and for all the swaggering, none of the normal operations of the cash nexus are interrupted. Rather, as undertaken by Shakur and Smalls, these swaggers prime the exchange of cash for goods and goods for cash. Irrefutably, it is this circumstance, above any other—especially any aberration within the culture—that accounts for why the cultural productions of Shakur and Smalls loom large in the United States and internationally. Johnnie L. Roberts observes that in 1996 "rap generated more than $1 billion in receipts."[39]

Gangsta rap represents one of the most recent subcultural forms documenting how through "recognizing white culture's exotic interests in black music, dance, style, fashion, and linguistic innovation, consumer capitalism has played a pivotal role in the commodification of black culture in order to expand its middle-class white luxury consumer market."[40] Gangsta rap underwrites enormous flows of capital—through CD sales, concerts, merchandising, media coverage, etc.—however, it does so at the same time it attempts to critique the very culture and system of exchange in which it participates. Like the young men in the store, gangsta rappers, to say the least, do not take up postures of pleasant, mutual regard that can be easily circulated and recirculated along with the exchange of cash for goods and goods for cash. As already suggested, the circumstances in which African Americans find and conceive of themselves are usually circumstances at which the conditions of pleasant mutual regard do not always easily obtain.[41]

All of this is to underscore that a crucial part (if not the crucial part) of every economic transaction is a phantasmatic (self-?)insertion into a *territorialized*—to borrow a term from Deleuze and Guattari—real social field, a phantasmatic act never easily or truly recuperable at all times from everyone, nonetheless from those most socially disenfranchised by "the consequences of deindustrialization and economic restructuring . . . and their institutions, and the social and moral bankruptcy of a market economy that promotes materialism, greed, and selfishness, that makes every effort to assure the freedom and mobility of capital while relegating human beings to ever more limited life chances and opportunities."[42] Even as it fulfills the imperatives of the cash nexus, gangsta rap and the subculture it represents expose and stress structures of desire that, in the opinion of some (such as the *New York Times*), are best left idealized, best left codified by such an evacuated phrase as "Have a nice day!"

Insofar as perpetual colonizations of desire always remain at stake in normative primings of the cash nexus, open recognition of these processes and violences mapped in/through psychic and social territories *must be intuited (blown?) away by any means necessary*. For the very mapping of these violences in/through both psychic and social territories is the act producing or yielding the always already constituted fields in the first place. The constitutive (in)stability of these fields rests on a performative occlusion, forgetting, oversight—a performance no less performative because it is (almost) never recognized as such. Every nebulous "Have a nice day!" remains, this is to say, an utmost productive guarantee of collective, though individualist, exchanges forwarding capitalism as culture and culture as capitalism.

The media occasions to eulogize Tupac Shakur and Biggie Smalls make it particularly clear how an onerous amount of this risky business is borne by young African Americans and the culture they produce, as well as the relations both young African Americans and their culture bear to commodification. The idealized merchant and consumer, functioning to hypostasize a collective meaning of cash nexus and, in this way, haunting individual declarations of "Have a nice day!," prove the real property imperiled by the African-American teenagers fired on, or by gangsta rap. The standard of these idealizations is the real property that the "sense" of the *New York Times* article struggles to recover. But sense is never *there*. It must be fashioned collectively. The strict parameters of sensibility drawn by capitalism as culture and culture as capitalism force sensibility within structures always seeking out new things in the interests of translating them into the terms of the very systematicity they have eluded so far. The peculiar calculus of capitalism as culture and culture as capitalism would render money, goods, the self, affective kinship and other relations, the materialities of bodily maintenance, general tidiness, and ultimately everything as equivalent insofar as they can be rendered susceptible to the perpetual circularity of exchange at the cash nexus, the endless substitutability of money as an axiomatic.

If the idealized merchant and consumer redacted in "Have a nice day!"—the evacuated phrase, which stands for a hyperbolic civility, which stands in turn for a nebulous sociality, standing in turn for an even more nebulous matrix of needs and desires, standing in turn for those matrices rendering the individual—prove to be abrogated by the swaggering postures of young black men at the cash nexus, then, more patently than usual, capitalism as culture and culture as capitalism have not yet fully secured their redaction at this new(?) site wherein they aim to play out, in their likenesses, the self-collapsing substitution of the real and the phantasmatic constituting individual and collective life. To restate the point, what is refracted starkly through the figures as well as the materiality of young African-American bodies is the violent collective and individual phantasm of capitalist social formation as it "engineers (*machine*) and mobilizes flows that are effectively decoded, but does so by substituting for the [decoded] codes a quantifying axiomatic (*une axiomatique comptable*) that is even more oppressive. With the result, capitalism—in conformity with the movement by which it counteracts its own tendency—is continually drawing near the wall, while at the same time pushing the wall further away."[43]

Literally and figuratively, the bodies of Shakur and Smalls and the young black men who resemble them have this capitalistic and psychic limit forcibly inscribed upon them. They represent one very patent point at which the capitalist socius must account for (if not fully see) its own violences working to (re)produce the *limit* of the socius as a *relative limit* rather than an absolute limit. Insofar as these young black men do not, through their words and postures, possess or circulate idealizations of merchant and consumer, which fix a nebulous collective chain of real/phantasmatic substitutions they are already caught in, they challenge the cash nexus through a peculiar kind of theft, a phantasmatic theft, sensed as real, for which they risk dire retribution, even incarceration or death.

This is to say, the *reactive* subject-effect of the capitalist socius cannot be one collectively producing the remark: "The thing is, once this gangsta image is out there, you've got the people, who love it, the politicians, who use it, and the police, who hate it. They didn't have any love for [Tupac Shakur] when he was a homeless kid, and they certainly didn't show any love for him when he grew into a defiant young man."[44] Not only the bounds of reason, but of decency, are troubled by this perspective, since it rests athwart the collective phantasm defining reason and decency: "Have a nice day!" The violence of this perspective, as a point of articulation, represents an always individual machinic residual, always and ideally to be (re)claimed for the collective:

> The real is the end product, the result of passive syntheses of desire.... Desire does not lack anything; it does not lack its object. It is, rather, the *subject* that is missing in desire, or desire that lacks a fixed subject; there is no fixed subject unless there is repression. Desire and its object are one and the same thing: the machine, as a machine of a machine. Desire is a machine, and the object of desire is another machine connected to it. Hence the product is something removed or deducted from the process of producing: between the act of producing and the product, something becomes detached, thus giving the vagabond, nomad subject a residuum.[45]

One is pressed to subjectivity in/through passivity—a passive withdrawal through desire into the needs of the collective—so that the subject is never the center of desire, but always its residual, and those who make such statements as Frank Alexander, this is to say—who grew up on Chicago's South Side in the Robert Taylor projects, a dangerous place "that fueled rebellion" and who was Tupac Shakur's assigned bodyguard the night leading to Shakur's death—deprive the culture of a certain, highly valuable form of property: Never simply rendered as an idealized merchant and consumer and a phantasmatic sociality insinuating through them, this property is subjectivity itself as well as the efficient economies of reclamation without which subjectivity never stands.[46] The violence of Alexander's perspective and its subject(s) are intelligible as assaults, assaults forcing one to intuit *without* one's own subjectivity (a relative limit?) and *without* the socius (an absolute limit?). This point of articulation registers a different (or Other) desire, leaving behind a different and always threatening residual. To emphasize the point, the property most ultimately placed in jeopardy is subjectivity itself and its efficient economies of reclamation, a crisis holding various possible outcomes: edginess, gunfire, death (the absolute limit?). Also: regret, anguished reason, censure laced freely and openly with apparent concern.

Dealing with the Visible Subject

Directly stated, what Alexander addresses is the way Tupac Shakur, Biggie Smalls, and gangsta rappers are collectively seen. What does, or can, one see in them? One sight that *Newsweek*, *Time*, the *New York Times*, the *Los Angeles Times*, the *Washington Post*, and other media outlets certainly never sponsor in these figures is the vision of how racial blackness collectively proves most specific to the regime of capitalism as culture and culture as capitalism as a foreclosed moment of absolute *cum* relative challenge. The general concept of race as well as its formalization in racial blackness situates personality, subjectivity, individuation in the phantasmatic collective through a particular, pacifying set of needs, one of which is the enabling subjectivizing need to perform a break with the socius that, nonetheless, impels one back into it. One might posit— far beyond any convulsions of the late twentieth-century entertainment industry—one particularly spectacular instance of this continual, individual and collective, convulsive challenge to be the mid-nineteenth-century abolition of racial slavery in the United States. The historians John Ashworth, David Brion Davis, and Thomas L. Haskell undertake drawing out significant dynamics of this U.S. convulsion in their essays collected in *The Antislavery Debate: Capitalism and Abolitionism as a Problem in Historical Interpretation*, while Eric Foner, another celebrated historian, states in *Nothing but Freedom: Emancipation and Its Legacy*: "Among the revolutionary processes that transformed the nineteenth-century world, none was so dramatic in its human consequences or far-reaching in its social implications as the abolition of chattel slavery."[47] Brief reference to this earlier crisis and its seemingly staggering reversal of fortunes aids in clarifying what appears to be at stake in the mediated gaze turned to Shakur, Smalls, and gangsta rap.

For illustrative purposes in what follows, the visual regime of abolished racial enslavement is represented by the scopic implied by defining Hegel's master/slave dialectic and the "secured" entry of African Americans into market society by the scopic dynamic simplified by the evacuated "Have a nice day!" and uniting idealized merchant and consumer and, through them, a market collective. In the first instance, the scopic is entangled in a production of consciousness through a tarrying with the negative. Autonomous consciousness produces itself through mastery of an Other, who seeks the same self-production, yet is unwilling to engage fully the risk of the desire for recognition, unwilling to engage fully the very satisfaction of its own life yielded through the very risk of its own life. Autonomous consciousness—the Master—arrives at itself through a violent will or force, and slavish consciousness—the Slave—only through a secondary recognition premised on the greater recognition already wrested from it by the Master. Nonetheless, the anguished violence of the engagement is even more pronounced because, insofar as the Slave carries the will of the Master into the world, this very transportation ironically figures the profound dependence, rather than independence, of the Master, the very form of recognition the Master would refute in the first place. The two competing subjects constituted through the mutual gaze, which yields anything but equivalent positions, are caught in a dialectic never able to refuse or disengage from the originary violence bringing them together in the first place.

On the other hand, subjects constituted through the implied mutual regard of merchant and consumer sharing "Have a nice day!" seem to stand outside any violent controversion. There is nothing to see but the vision of mutual regard itself; mutual regard rendered as/through "Have a nice day!" yields subjects equivalent in their sociality. It neither marks nor yields incommensurability, dominance and subordination, or forms of violence fixing inequality in place but, rather, essential similarity, compatibility, and substitutability—like (in fact, because of) the cash—joining together the subjects in their open difference, or individuation, in the first place. There is, in other words, nothing to witness but uncanny self-reflexivity, identity that is reassuring.

However, in the United States, the difference *between* these two forms of historical regard is violent: the U.S. Civil War. One sees in the disjunction between the two scopics, taken as historical configurations, a violent difference that oddly can never be acknowledged *in/as* the productive and profitable, phantasmatic or real, terms—the uncanny self-reflexivity—of the second. One recognizes, oddly, capitalism vanquishing its earlier need for racial blackness (as unfree), an earlier specification of race, in a gesture that "decodes" already channeled "flows" of desire (and needs) in order to (re)channel and market them productively and profitably. One witnesses an exceptionally grand instance of capitalism in perpetual war with itself. Through the ubiquitous "Have a nice day!"—in which everyone is *equally* produced—capitalism as culture and culture as capitalism productively reinscribes its own rupture (its violent precedents) as the rupture of that rupture (hypercivil decency). Capitalism reinscribes, as itself, its definitive self-difference (endless substitutability) as a *relation* of suturing individual identity. The entire exchange, it seems, merely boils down to the assurance that there is another social animal—as decent as you!

On the contrary, Susan Strange, in *The Retreat of the State: The Diffusion of Power in the World Economy*, by providing a telling rendition of the collective results of these exchanges, clarifies what is as assuredly one patent absurdity of this form of individuation. The results, Strange writes, are: "in the Anglo-American financial systems ... a marked rise in the rewards to managers, both in terms of salaries, of severance payments—golden handshakes or parachutes—and of stock options, to say nothing of the perquisites of office in first-class air travel, expense accounts for restaurant bills and luxury hotel accommodations and not least the regiment of chauffeurs, gardeners, masseurs, social secretaries, even doctors, dentists and lawyers—who *in olden times* would have made up the retinue of a landed aristocracy."[48]

Strange's analogy aligning a powerful, corporate elite with an apparently superceded (possibly feudal? possibly despotic?) aristocracy announces a peculiar social *difference* in relation to which suturing individual *identity* is nonetheless yielded by subjectivizing hypercivility powerfully (con)fusing the phantasmatic as the real. Strange reveals an immense silence at the center of the immense violence of capitalism as culture and culture as capitalism that ruptured the master/slave scopic of ascendant capitalism with the ostensibly more equalizing scopic of *free*-market capitalism. What is finally most assured in and by the momentary civil exchanges are various forms of privileged nonsociality premised on massive, unequal accumulation of wealth. What seems most guaranteed as an outcome of the innumerable exchanges is not commensurability, substitutability, identity at all, but those differentiating forms of power already collectively known. Power—"simply the ability of a person or group of persons so to affect outcomes that their preferences take precedence over the preferences of others"—yields forms of nonsociality by definition.[49] One sees, unaccountably, through the identity properly produced at the cash nexus the nonsociality premised on massive, unequal accumulation of wealth somehow yielding the *difference* understood to *individuate* so acutely.

The moment of exchange is not at all one of mutual regard. Rather, to imagine such a profound situation of nonsociality *as sociality* requires an enormous feat: the feat seems to be the denial of one's own relative—relating?—difference in an inscription of galvanizing—absolute?—difference elsewhere, the inscription of a horizon making one's own relative position of difference disappear, just as the absolute, visible difference of the physical horizon reaffirms the impossibility of seeing the relative position at which one is at that moment standing. One thing certainly happens: one imagines collectively. The sharing of "Have a nice day!" priming the exchange of cash and goods both risks and wards off temporary social death within a systematicity effectively producing such desired *exchanges* as real in what may be, in fact, the paramount moment of individual aggregate fantasy. The gesture (con)fuses the mobile and infinitely *exchangeable* terms of the gesture with what effectively passes as the most real: a personality yielded unaccountably from nonsociality *cum* sociality. There is at the center of the exercise a phantasmatic foreclosure, limit, or suture; these *socializing* phrases in standard contextualizations of/at the cash nexus assuredly allow one to glimpse Deleuze and Guattari's convictions about the contingency, fusion, and coherence of phantasmatic and material productivity, as well as about the residual of those productions, the subject-effect. The socializing gesture—"Have a nice day!"—in its formulaic repetitiveness, discloses, despite itself, the first horizon of utter difference, the utter difference from one's collective self *first* marked as mutual regard; it discloses needful "humanizing" desire as a formalizing of nonsociality—relative difference—always already impelling one into sociality through *individuating terms*, terms marking—though not finally (not as a subject)—the utter difference from one's collective self *first* marked as mutual regard. Always, one must somehow respond to galvanizing (utter) difference.

A diametrically opposed instance at which to marvel at the centrifugal contradictions, absurdities, and potential violences of the *socializing* performances yielded at the cash nexus is proposed by the anthropologist Bill Maurer in what he describes as the "post-human" conditions of post-Fordist transnational economic strategies. Maurer, towards the conclusion of "Complex Subjects: Offshore Finance, Complexity Theory, and the Dispersion of the Modern," relates how transnational economic strategies have managed to bring about what he terms "the end of time-space," which are fundamental vectors the individual "human" subject can never overcome within a proper suturing *identity*, or any sense of reality a proper suturing identity collectively affords.[50] One body that might do so is the dead body, or the body Deleuze and Guattari theorize as a body-without-organs. In any case, to quote Maurer at length:

> The world offshore financial centers provide a series of stepping-stones for investments and business operations to continue, without interruption, around the clock. An investor in New York wishing to establish a fund with a Tokyo bank could request that a series of transactions be carried out in tax havens, each generating nontaxable revenue as it makes its way toward the next business day in Tokyo. The overlapping business hours of the global ring of tax havens permit investors to continue 24 hours a day. A multinational company in its various guises can conduct business continuously. And since such a company creates itself by domiciling in various havens and onshore centers around the world, it has already worked into its design a mechanism for solving the (non)problem of time.... There are no temporal constraints to economic activity because they are already solved by the very structure of the multinational corporation.
>
> Nor are there spatial constraints. We cannot conceive of our prototypic multination as limited or even bounded by space, since it can be everywhere. The Banco Ambrosiano is a fine example of how international financial networks put a multinational into a space that, once scrutinized, dissolves into no-place. The "Free and Independent Republic of Minerva"—a haven supposedly consisting of a few reefs 250 miles from Tonga in the Pacific, but "really" only a node in an international computer network—pushes the point further: its present existence in computer networks demonstrates that space as such is not even necessary to the business of offshore finance.[51]

What Maurer convincingly illustrates is how power has been able to disengage itself more and more from any seductive fiction of the subject, even and especially as any productive and profitable subject does not do so, or perhaps more rightly cannot do so. Maurer underscores the profitable and materially productive work of a very select "post-human" phantasm.

The point being made for this analysis of hip-hop eulogy is that, if "the 'subject' of complexity theory—and of offshore finance—is posthuman," then, in certainly more ways than one, the same might be said of the mediated figures of Shakur and Smalls, although the question appears to remain one of subjects.[52] If the post-Fordist strategies of (re)globalizing capital reveal a dispersal into "networks of power with no originary point ... and nonoriginary unfoldings," then the same can be said of the exchanges produced over the bodies of Shakur and Smalls. The point, accordingly, is to query what exactly is pressed into service through open exchanges over these two African-American bodies.

Pursuing the query suggests the urgency of meaningfully rethinking the situation of the subject, not as an always available "originality," but as an always overwhelming "(non)originality." Pursuing the query seems to suggest that, despite the always apparently urgent question of individual or collective racial blackness (or, say, gender or sexuality, for that matter), it is an uncanny moment of irrecuperable, irresolvable impetus toward the startling socius that may be the "actual" moment standing as primary or originary difference, the horizon of utter difference making one's own relative position of difference invisible, a horizon of utter difference from oneself marked *first*, but not finally, not as a subject, as mutual regard. One must concede that this *first* moment precipitates a leap of faith, or blindness, that constitutes in turn an *attitude* in the socius as the instance of self-production. And, as it happens, the socius (for centuries now) that one irresolvably confronts remains the phantasm of capitalism as culture and culture as capitalism in which collective subjectivizing moments and their productivities are never, in point of fact, grounded, only tightly economic, because fused to the principle of endless substitutability itself—money. What this leap of faith or blindness yields within capitalism as culture and culture as capitalism is, above all, always detachable, and mobile, and always—in this way—(re)animating, a moment of high risk that, as it yields dividends, effectively yields *signs* of person-ality as one of them.

This is to say that the original fetish—the primary instance of irrecuperable disavowal and substitution—may be the threateningly undifferentiated (*deterritorialized*) world. The primary scene, because of its terrific undifferentiation, its utterly bald originality *cum* utter difference, must be always foreclosed and redeployed to obtain signs of person-ality. In the (closed?) infinitude of capitalism as culture and culture as capitalism, it is replayed productively in the uncanny self-fashioning of material exchanges.

The claim is that the primal scene of collective self-identification never is inscribed simply at the node of heterosexist risk—therefore Deleuze and Guattari's rallying cry of "Anti-Oedipus"; it never is inscribed simply at the node of gender differentiation on which that particularly risky social scene is premised, as many theorists would propose; it never is inscribed simply, for that matter, at the node of race. Beyond them, very differently, the primary scene seems to be the flight that first seeks to relieve an untenable situation of *absolute* difference, of baldly original trauma codifiable as phantasm? hysteria? uncanny? paranoia? psychosis? the mirror stage? the body-without-organs? death? The unnameable but productive fetishist moment in question is one necessarily manufacturing the less daunting terms of relative difference, less daunting terms through which absolute difference might be more *assuredly* scripted, one of these being subjectivity itself. Further, then, this *socializing* moment refracted through an endless(?) chain of material equivalents may just be endlessly productively (re)nameable: tragedy, reason, decency, reflexive civility, growing up, open censure laced freely and disingenuously with apparent concern.

An *unaccountable* confrontation with primary difference constitutes the original threatening break with the socius, which at the same time always calls for the suturing of that break, and which at the same time always mistakenly (re)produces relative difference—race? gender? sexuality? class? etc.—as *apparently* recuperable, though ever-receding, primary difference. If not absurd, this situation is at the least contradictory, complex, subtle. One would be hard pressed, for instance, to explain how the verities and fixities of race, gender, sexuality, class, religion, etc., are ideally elided, in this violently fractured social landscape, at any social moment marking the exchangeability of cash and goods. What this *ideally social* moment offers under the guise of so much more is the boundless possibilities of money—as an unanchored principle—comprehending the possibilities of life. Like this later scene, the primary scene is one in which desire—a temporary social death of the subject-effect which nonetheless carries it back to the socius—responds to galvanizing needs: one of which is the (re)figuring through an individual attitude of the utter difference first tallied as the socius itself. Very risky business, and African-American bodies, among others, bear an onerous amount of this risk.

The crux of hip-hop eulogy is that—even or especially as they swagger with contempt for a culture authorizing their widespread disregard—young African Americans do not *necessarily* interrupt or contravene normative dynamics of the cash nexus, but do abrogate the most idealized postures, pleasures, and sensibilities of those transactions. Young African Americans, as one locus of lucrative media sponsorship, always subtend an enormous number of the exchanges of capitalism as culture and culture as capitalism and, even outside such media sponsorship, of course, engage in them. What their gesturing bodies signal, even when fully aligned with a supposedly collective cash nexus, is patent disrespect for the cultural circumstances and cultural meaning of capitalism as culture and culture as capitalism, the cash nexus. Young African Africans and their postures, in more ways than merely marked by hip-hop, revile and reject the collective phantasm of human relations by which the cash nexus is falsely and officially advertised. It is a rejection of this interpellative or constitutive ground, one might say, that is met with exorbitant and untenable violence—frequently incarceration, or gunfire, or both—nevertheless, dissembling discursive violence.

For the *New York Times* and other media outlets, the social tragedy to be gleaned from the shooting in Brooklyn, if there really is any, is that the five teenagers apparently mimicked "the only role they knew," a dangerous and potentially deadly role in which they are schooled by the wayward superstars of gangsta rap.[53] In its distortion of this *racialized* posture and its cultural rejections (taken up with less consequence by white suburban youth), hip-hop eulogy attempts to preserve forms of cultural property very much more difficult to locate or fix than the material property on the shelves of any Brooklyn bodega or, equally, within the gargantuan portfolios of any tentacled transnational corporation.

Even though it may not seem immediately so, childhood is also at the crux of the matter. In exemplary fashion, Kenneth Carroll writes for the *Washington Post* that the analyses proliferating after the shooting of Shakur from "commentators, reporters and critics on the left and right . . . lacked the style or economy of [his] 14-year-old son, who *sadly* proclaimed Tupac 'stupid.'"[54] In Carroll's eyes the development and maturity of his son is registered in the *attitude* positioning the fourteen-year-old boy to the socius, an attitude not only aligning him with the socius, but doing so with an economical starkness that seemingly conflates, or confuses, stylization with the real. The no-nonsense style in which the fourteen-year-old renders what he understands and *feels*, and prompting Carroll to hyperbolic appreciation, seemingly postpones (forecloses?) for the moment all *individual* questions of desire or need—propitiously—through an exchange deferring succinctly to what both subjects already collectively understand as real. To some people, the mind and imagination of the fourteen-year-old boy seem prescient, incisive, and laudable.

Courtland Milloy, similarly eulogizing in the *Washington Post*, also introduces the figure of youth into the matter: "I learned that Tupac Shakur had been shot when my 18-year-old daughter, Takiesa, walked into the kitchen one morning last week and declared with mock urgency, 'I've got to go out to Las Vegas to be with my man.'"[55] The mocking at the center of this exchange, it seems to me, inordinately produces the currency of the exchange, as did the stern sadness in the last. The eighteen-year-old's mocking *attitude* performs a complicity with the renegade Shakur that, however, only knows itself ironically. Even more, the form of knowledge in question is the most intimate and consequential imaginable, since sexuality—in what is styled as its essence—is never in any way at all about style but always about what is perhaps most real: the fully passionate circuit in which it persists rightly to achieve utter satisfaction and dissipation as nucleated procreation. All things being equal, the matter ultimately (re)forming any child's body *into* the figure of a mature body (and attitude) is inflaming, proprietary carnal knowledge. Thus, with even more consummate skill than the insights of the fourteen-year-old, the eighteen-year-old's mocking exchange over Shakur's wounded body—in a commentary (absurdly? convincingly?) aspiring to make anguished sense of those wounds—again postpones (or forecloses) individual questions of desire or need through an exchange deferring unmistakably to what is already collectively understood as real: the fully passionate circuit in which sexuality persists rightly to achieve utter satisfaction and dissipation as nucleated procreation. This second exchange marks a performance of greater skill, of greater risk, because it openly engages what is conceivably the most daring of all possible terms, any sexual attitude. To most people, what is risked in the latter exchange is certainly greater than anything risked in the first. If one is doubtful, imagine the exchanges reversed.

Childhood then, as one might suspect, is also a desiring-machine, and apparently one of the most consequential, which is to say, childhood is not so much about children but "truly" what can be inscribed and ascribed at the site of children. Insofar as Deleuze and Guattari alert us that every objective reality is a psychic reality, one might conceive, for a moment, of the objective (space-time) reality of *bodies growing up* in relation to the clock against which the drama plays itself out. Of the objective/psychic reality of the clock, Deleuze and Guattari write, "the same machine can be both technical and social, but only when viewed from different perspectives: for example, the clock as a technical machine for measuring uniform time, and as a social machine for reproducing canonic hours and for assuring order in the city."[56] In the duplicity of the instrument one might recognize a seamlessness with which the phantasmatic and the real are conjoined as a collective one enters through individualizing postures, poses repeatedly transacted, if not variously extracted through an endless chain of "nice days." One can also imagine childhood standing collectively as the extended moment when the seamlessness of all exchanges *might* appear most seamless, suturing most beguiling, because also entirely threatening (as well as threatened).

Yet the suturing of childhood, a temporary condition, is always threatened by its looming end, an end assuredly arriving in the most patently recognized figure of uncoded desire: any sexual attitude. If so much of a collective risk resides here, no wonder figures of childhood persist as significant to the dynamic of eulogizing Shakur and Smalls: Childhood must be protected, especially as much of that protection must be from its too wayward (African-American?) self: five black teenagers swaggering in a Brooklyn bodega as the swaggering is measured by an edgy entrepreneur with a gun. It is no wonder, then, that the force of gangsta rap can be rendered by Mikal Gilmore in *Rolling Stone* in unmistakably masculinist and sexual terms, public terms of individuation assuredly threatening to childhood itself: "I have never heard anything remotely like Tupac Shakur's breathless performance on this track in all my years of listening to pop music. It contains a truly remarkable amount of rage and aggression—enough to make anything in punk seem *flaccid* by comparison."[57] To extrapolate the sexual innuendo, if punk is flaccid, gangsta rap is startlingly erect—in public. Intriguingly, the question of style or delivery returns to, of all things, perhaps the most remarkable question of the real: any sexual attitude, the ultimate conflation or confusion of stylization with the real. Supposing Gilmore's observations on points of style remain salient—in an article beginning oddly enough with a comparison of Tupac Shakur to Kurt Cobain, even as it simultaneously laments that black urban realities remain ones "mainstream culture and media are loath to understand or respect"—then the whole matter never really seems to turn on anything real at all, except perhaps the "productive" exchanges themselves afforded by the occasions of the deaths of Shakur and Smalls.[58]

What, in fact, are difficult purveyors of black masculinity doing at the cash nexus, especially when, in the sleight of infinite substitutability, one can collectively imagine oneself and, indeed, unprotected children there as well? It is important to note that, unlike Carroll or Milloy, Gilmore is not openly concerned with children; however, it is equally important to recognize in his remarks the ever-present imputation of a risk to young African-American male bodies and their productions (an erection in this case). This curious set of alignments and misalignments, now a highly significant strand of capitalism as culture and culture as capitalism, teeter very regularly on violating all propitious thought or, perhaps more importantly, teeter on violating young African-American persons. Whatever type of exchange is possible at the cash nexus, it is not what was imagined by the five teenagers in Brooklyn or, equally, Tupac Shakur or Biggie Smalls. What the cash nexus does not violate, even as it occasions gunfire, is a long-sedimented residuum or ideal of desiring and productive flows: subjectivity taking the form of a socializing effect of capital. Beyond money and goods, whatever materializes at the cash nexus is both individual and collective: the subject-effect, or suturing, always rendering the individual and collective an overly elegant (closed) system in the first place and, therefore, always already problematic. There persists, needless to say, much attitude at the cash nexus. Apparently somehow, the five teenagers in the Brooklyn bodega, Tupac Shakur, and Biggie Smalls brought the wrong attitudes to bargain with.

NOTES

Chapter 10, "Dead Men Printed," was originally published in *Callaloo* 22, no. 2 (spring 1999): 306–32. Copyright 1999 Charles H. Rowell, and reprinted with permission of Johns Hopkins University Press.

Acknowledgments: I thank Thelma Foote, John Carlos Rowe, and Brian Carr for their always helpful engagements with this essay. Also, I gratefully acknowledge the research assistance of Rasaan Boykin at the University of Virginia and Kyle Julien at the University of California, Irvine.

1. Gilles Deleuze and Félix Guattari, *Anti-Oedipus: Capitalism and Schizophrenia* (Minneapolis: University of Minnesota Press, 1983), 29, emphasis in original.
2. Deleuze and Guattari, *Anti-Oedipus*, 145.
3. Nelson George, "Master of His Own Fate," *Village Voice* 42, no. 1 (1996): 29.
4. John Leland, "Requiem for a Gangsta," *Newsweek* 129, no. 12 (March 24, 1997): 74.
5. Deleuze and Guattari, *Anti-Oedipus*, 6.
6. Deleuze and Guattari, *Anti-Oedipus*, 30.
7. Deleuze and Guattari, *Anti-Oedipus*, 25, emphasis in original.
8. Deleuze and Guattari, *Anti-Oedipus*, 27.
9. Deleuze and Guattari, *Anti-Oedipus*, 27.
10. Deleuze and Guattari, *Anti-Oedipus*, 116.
11. Deleuze and Guattari, *Anti-Oedipus*, 33.
12. Kevin Powell, "Tupac Shakur: Bury Me Like a G.," *Rolling Stone* 746 (1996): 44.
13. Farai Chideya, "All Eyez on Us: It's Time for the Hip-Hop Generation to Get Real," *Time* 149, no. 12 (1997): 47.
14. George Lipsitz, *The Possessive Investment in Whiteness: How White People Profit from Identity Politics* (Philadelphia: Temple University Press, 1998), 107–8.
15. Chideya, "All Eyez on Us," 47, emphasis in original.
16. Chideya, "All Eyez on Us," emphasis in the original.
17. Christopher John Farley, "Rhyme or Reason," *Time* 149, no. 12 (1997): 47.
18. Deleuze and Guattari, *Anti-Oedipus*, 28.
19. Joel Williamson, *A Rage for Order: Black-White Relations in the American South since Emancipation* (New York: Oxford University Press, 1986), 285.
20. Farley, "Rhyme or Reason," 47.
21. Brent Staples, "Dying to Be Black," *New York Times*, December 9, 1996, A16.
22. Staples, "Dying to Be Black," 16.
23. Judith Butler, "Engendered/Engendering: Schematic Racism and White Paranoia," in *Reading Rodney King: Reading Urban Uprising*, ed. Robert Gooding-Williams (New York: Routledge, 1993), 19, emphasis in original.
24. Staples, "Dying to Be Black," A16.
25. Staples, "Dying to Be Black," A16.
26. Stephen Nathan Haymes, *Race, Culture, and the City: A Pedagogy for Black Urban Struggle* (Albany: State University of New York Press, 1995), 19.
27. May Joseph, "Soul, Transnationalism, and Imaginings of Revolution: Tanzanian Ujamaa and the Politics of Enjoyment," in *Soul: Black Power, Politics, and Pleasure*, ed. Monique Guillory and Richard C. Green (New York: New York University Press, 1998), 126.

28. Roderick J. Harrison and Claudette E. Bennett, "Racial and Ethnic Diversity," in *The State of the Union: America in the 1990s*, vol. 2: *Social Trends*, ed. Reynolds Farley (New York: Russell Sage, 1995).

29. Gerald Horne, "The Political Economy of the Black Urban Future: A History," in *Globalization and Survival in the Black Diaspora: The New Urban Challenge*, ed. Charles Green (New York: State University of New York Press, 1997), 260–61.

30. Horne, "The Political Economy of the Black Urban Future," 253.

31. Horne, "The Political Economy of the Black Urban Future," 253.

32. Lipsitz, *The Possessive Investment in Whiteness*, 16.

33. Lipsitz, *The Possessive Investment in Whiteness*, 10–11.

34. Eric Foner, *Nothing but Freedom: Emancipation and Its Legacy* (Baton Rouge: Louisiana State University Press, 1983), 60.

35. Foner, *Nothing but Freedom*, 61.

36. George Lipsitz, *The Possessive Investment in Whiteness*, 224.

37. Raquel Z. Rivera, "Rap in Puerto Rico," in *Globalization and Survival in the Black Diaspora: The New Urban Challenge*, ed. Charles Green (New York: State University of New York Press, 1997), 109.

38. See Alan Bass, "Translator's Introduction," in *Writing and Difference*, by Jacques Derrida (Chicago: University of Chicago Press, 1978). Bass explains: "The counterviolence of *solicitation*, which derives from the Latin *sollicitare*, meaning to shake the totality (from *sollus*, 'all' and *ciere*, 'to move or shake'). Every totality, [Derrida] shows, can be *totally shaken*, that is, can be shown to be founded on that which it excludes, that which would be in *excess* for a reductive analysis of any kind. (The English *solicit* should be read in this etymological sense wherever it appears)" (xvi, emphasis in original).

39. Johnnie L. Roberts, "Music, Money, Murder," *Newsweek* 129, no. 12 (1997): 74.

40. Haymes, *Race, Culture, and the City*, 49.

41. This condition holds true not only in the present moment, but, indeed, in terms of prospects for the future as well, a future Gerald Horne warily understands as follows: "For now, with the Cold War ended, yet another pervasive transformation is sweeping through the economy of the United States, which is likely to change radically the role and status of Black workers. With the dissolution of the Soviet Union and the collapse of the socialist camp in Eastern Europe, not only has a new pool of labor been opened that will compete directly with the U.S. working class but further, this has been a material and psychological boost to capital generally with no immediate benefit to African American workers particularly" ("The Political Economy of the Black Urban Future," 256).

42. Lipsitz, *The Possessive Investment in Whiteness*, 82.

43. Deleuze and Guattari, *Anti-Oedipus*, 176.

44. Frank Alexander with Heidi Siegmund Cuda, *Got Your Back: The Life of a Bodyguard in the Hardcore World of Gangsta Rap* (New York: St. Martin's, 1998), 199.

45. Deleuze and Guattari, *Anti-Oedipus*, 26, emphasis in original.

46. Alexander with Cuda, *Got Your Back*, 5.

47. Thomas Bender, ed., *The Antislavery Debate: Capitalism and Abolitionism as a Problem in Historical Interpretation* (Berkeley: University of California Press, 1992); Foner, *Nothing but Freedom*, 1.

48. Susan Strange, *The Retreat of the State: The Diffusion of Power in the World Economy* (Cambridge: Cambridge University Press, 1996), 64, emphasis added.

49. Strange, *The Retreat of the State*, 17.

50. Bill Maurer, "Complex Subjects: Offshore Finance, Complexity Theory, and the Dispersion of the Modern," *Socialist Review* 25, nos. 3–4 (1995): 136. Maurer uses the term "post-Fordism" to mean "from large-scale, industrial production using skilled labor and geared toward mass consumption to more flexible production strategies using unskilled or deskilled labor and geared toward niche markets. With its emphasis on just-in-time production and niche marketing, post-Fordist production strategies rely heavily on the kinds of computer technologies that make possible the rapid transfer and management of capital" (119–20).

51. Maurer, "Complex Subjects," 136–37.

52. Maurer, "Complex Subjects," 125.

53. Staples, "Dying to Be Black," A16.

54. Kenneth Carroll, "Tupac's Squandered Gift," *Washington Post*, September 22, 1996, C1, C5, emphasis added.

55. Courtland Milloy, "At a Loss over Shakur's Two Faces," *Washington Post*, September 15, 1996, B1.

56. Deleuze and Guattari, *Anti-Oedipus*, 141.

57. Mikal Gilmore, "Why Tupac Should Be Heard before He's Buried," *Rolling Stone* 746 (1996): 51, emphasis added.

58. Gilmore, "Why Tupac Should Be Heard," 49.

IV. CALCULATIONS OF RACE AND REASON
Theorizing the Psychic and the Social

Introduction

ROBYN WIEGMAN

It may seem strange to introduce the final section of this collection by pointing toward Lindon Barrett's citations, given the scope no less than the gravity of the questions his scholarship sets out to answer about the implicit racialization of reason in the modernity of the West. But it is precisely in the constitution of his archive that we witness a signature feature of Barrett's work: his commitment to a historically rich critical practice that follows the past in order to trace its power to stalk and haunt the world of our present. This past is neither uniform nor unitary, which is why the essays in "Calculations of Race and Reason" can collectively study the impact of the Enlightenment's heralded man of reason—and the manners and sentiments that rose to prominence with him—while addressing vastly different cultural materials, from literature, political economy, history, and philosophy to the divergent itineraries of post-structuralist theory. To be sure, readers of this volume will already be familiar with the remarkable breadth of Barrett's intellectual preoccupations and with his ability to travel across three centuries of the Enlightenment's world-making without abandoning his characteristic intimacy with texts and their weighted details. They will have come to know his ability to reorganize our understanding of the essentializing hermeneutics of race and the clarity with which he can render legible the racial aesthetics of the genres and technologies of everyday life. Most crucially, they—let me say *we* here—will have been buoyed by the signing voice of a critic whose craft is dedicated to unearthing the violence of the transit between words and worlds in ways that render incomprehensible the current proposition that literary critics must choose between suspicious reading and a hermeneutics of repair. Without suspicion, Barrett's archive would lose its power to cite racial reason in those places where it has otherwise remained illegible or obscured; without repair, the archive would mock the psychic value it affords as a resource for the critical insurgency his work enacts and models for our own.

Suspicion and repair then, or what we might better call, in a gesture toward this section's subtitle, critique and the aspiration toward social and psychic reparation that incites it. The affective intuitions mobilized by these seemingly divergent forms of literary reading are palpably present in the essays collected in this book, underscoring Barrett's attachment to and stunning revision of the most influential critical turns that differentiated his generation from those that came before: identity studies, cultural studies, and post-structuralist theory. The most formative turn is, of course, identity studies, which politicized the humanities by retrieving as subjects of knowledge the suspect figures of modernity—black, female, native, queer—from their denigration as mute objects of the scholarly (read colonial, masculinist, and Eurocentric) gaze. For Barrett, this retrieval is threatened from all sides by the very model of sovereignty it reinforces as it repairs the violence, both social and psychic, of the suspect subject's historical abjection. For Barrett's generation, cultural studies likewise revised scholarly assumptions about the political organization of subject worlds and social life but its critical agency resonated most strongly—as it still does—in its thoroughgoing critique of the priority given to elite cultural forms, defetishizing the literary monotheism of New Criticism by training attention on the popular, quotidian, and ephemeral. Barrett's work bears witness to the lasting impact of this critical turn, even as he insists, with Toni Morrison and other critics of the African American literary tradition, on the province of the literary as an indispensable site for reading and resisting the multiple dimensions of race making in the New World. In addition to these influences, Barrett's incisive approach to the racialized character of authorship, language, meaning, and representation is in debt to the intoxicating rise of post-structuralism and the theoretical space it provided for casting suspicion on some of the most coveted tenets of Western humanism, including the equation of the sovereign self with enlightenment and freedom. All of Barrett's writing affirms these critical turns as important transformations of the poverty of the known while specifying what must be confronted in order to sustain—at times reinvigorate—their analytic and political capacities against the deadening force of institutionalized legitimacy. In this double move, the essays in "Calculations of Race and Reason," as elsewhere in this collection, are not only performative instances of

Barrett's ability to register and rework the epistemological conditions of the present, but also articles of faith, quite literally, in the possibility of criticism as the venue and vehicle for dismantling the calculating mind as the supreme figure and fiction of white racial essence.

If we were to give the first essay in this section its own theoretical designation, we might say that "Presence of Mind" ups the ante of suspicious modes of reading by using a deconstructive sensibility to rearrange the startlingly stunted discussion of race in the literary criticism centered on Edgar Allan Poe, that canonical figure whose signature work, *The Narrative of Arthur Gordon Pym*, did not even register as a racial discourse until Morrison used it as primary evidence in *Playing in the Dark: Whiteness and the Literary Imagination*, her groundbreaking 1992 study of the Africanist presence in American literature and culture.[1] Morrison's argument influenced Barrett's thinking throughout the 1990s, serving as a major reference point in *Blackness and Value: Seeing Double*, which grapples with the relationship between literacy, literature, and value in ways that established his reputation as a highly theoretical interpreter of both African American writing and national discourses of race.[2] His 2001 essay sustains this engagement by turning to a different Poe text, "The Murders in the Rue Morgue," arguing that it "stand[s] as a monument to Reason itself" in ways that demonstrate how profoundly reason has served as "the figure of *race*" not simply in Poe's oeuvre, but more broadly and more decisively "in the West."[3] In doing so, "Presence of Mind" pairs the literary criticism on Poe that followed Morrison's radical revision with a rereading of the detective tale in order to insist that there is much work left to do to understand the historical and textual complexities of the claim that scholars must continue to pursue: that "racial taxonomies form a set of social knowledges virtually impossible to elude." In using the protocols of detection to read Poe's signature work of detective fiction, Barrett analyzes the binding force of race to reason at the scene of Western humanism's most enduring crime.

In "Family Values / Critical Values," published here for the first time, Barrett interrupts a long-standing debate in African American literary studies concerning the racial politics of writing by women in the last decade of the nineteenth century. Often collated around the figures of Frances Harper and Pauline Hopkins, the debate largely centers on whether or not sentimental fictional forms can be said to instantiate a radical African American political vision. While one side of the debate says *no*, describing the genre in suspect terms as white bourgeois mimicry, and the other side says *yes*, highlighting its hopeful subversive potential, Barrett fastens his attention on the critical suppositions that these two sides share. Both, he argues, conflate and analogize family and race, and in this they collectively ignore the historical weight of the domestic and its effects on the rationalized management of sexuality in the modern West. In thus failing to consider the values already at stake in the domain of domestic life, the critical archive that constitutes this signature debate forfeits the opportunity, in Barrett's words, "to uncover *in the construct of the family* the fraudulent nature of *race* as a representational category."[4] Turning to the works of Audre Lorde and Leo Bersani, Barrett's argument unfolds in distinctly queer theoretical terms, with the libidinal defined simultaneously as corporeal and affective, making sexuality excessive to every attempt to anchor family and race in a seemingly natural biogenetic origin. Here, Barrett reads sexuality within the framework of what has been called the "antisocial thesis," but rather than citing it as antithetical to thinking race, he marshals it to lay claim to the idea that sexuality's resistance to socialization is crucial for discerning reproduction as ground zero of the global dispersal of Eurocentric race thinking. In the end, Barrett urges critics to return to the archive of African American women's writing in the 1890s to grapple with the way that sexuality, citizen sovereignty, and the nuclear family were complexly interwoven in post-Emancipation struggles, at times enforcing the very logics of race through which white supremacy reinvigorated itself. It is through such attention to what Barrett calls, referencing Lorde, "the chaos of our strongest feelings" that "Family Values / Critical Values" limns the relationship between the social and the psychic to offer a fuller picture of how the history of race and sexuality can be told.

While the first two essays of this section consider the imbrications of race and reason by turning in quite different ways to the nineteenth century and its literatures, the volume's closing piece demonstrates Barrett's growing interest in the philosophical, economic, and political conjunctures through which Europe's modernity was forged in the centuries before the United States took national form. "Mercantilism, U.S. Federalism, and the Market within Reason" was first published in an anthology devoted to excavating the historical bonds between property and personhood, and was the only preview in print of the monograph *Racial Blackness and the Discontinuity of Western Modernity* that Barrett was completing at the time of his death.[5] It revises Michel Foucault's account of the emergence of modern biopower and its specification of the "species" in an argument that traces the enormity of the fact, along with its stunning denial, that the annulment of the captive African's personhood is the foundation on which the political economy and philosophical character of Western modernity depends.[6] No longer working solely within the object orientations of literary criticism and cultural studies, the essay demonstrates Barrett's ability to inhabit Marxian and psychoanalytic theoretical traditions while pressing each to their limits. His elegant extension of the conceptual yield of fetishism as the term Marx and Freud most shared is arrayed through a compellingly diverse archive that taunts those who might resist his central contention that "African-derived populations, conscripted under the rubric of racial blackness, become the decisive point of nullification in the geopolitical, economic and phantasmatic confluence ... of the modern market ... and modern subjectivity" ("Mercantilism, U.S. Federalism"). In this, his argument deepens the contours of his long-standing consideration of blackness and value in order to calculate, against market logics, the *longue durée* in which race and reason have colluded simultaneously to entrench and obscure the ontological violence that attends the West's vast material accumulation. As readers will surely detect, the force of the essay lies not only in the sheer brilliance of its rhetorical maneuvers but in the affective atmosphere it generates as Barrett locates in the documents of national founding the disavowed history of racialized dispossession.

While the essays gathered in "Calculations of Race and Reason" might rightly be said to end this volume, they should not be taken as constituting anything as final as Barrett's last words. On the contrary, what we learn from reading both these essays and those in the volume as a whole is that what appears to be past is not over and what has left the scene of the present is not dead. These are metaphoric interpretations, to be sure, and while they can be used to mystify the violence of the history they refer to, their import to Barrett's way of thinking is decidedly the obverse. The uncanny effect of reading *Conditions of the Present: Selected Essays* lies here: in the elegance of Barrett's critical voice as it continues to do battle with modernity's ghosts.

NOTES

1. Toni Morrison, *Playing in the Dark: Whiteness and the Literary Imagination* (New York: Vintage, 1992).

2. Lindon Barrett, *Blackness and Value: Seeing Double* (New York: Cambridge University Press, 1999).

3. Lindon Barrett, "Presence of Mind: Detection and Racialization in 'The Murders in the Rue Morgue,'" chapter 11, this volume.

4. Lindon Barrett, "Family Values / Critical Values: 'The Chaos of Our Strongest Feelings' and African American Women's Writing of the 1890s," chapter 12, this volume.

5. Lindon Barrett, *Racial Blackness and the Discontinuity of Western Modernity*, ed. Justin A. Joyce, Dwight A. McBride, and John Carlos Rowe (Champaign: University of Illinois Press, 2014).

6. Lindon Barrett, "Mercantilism, U.S. Federalism, and the Market within Reason: The 'People' and the Conceptual Impossibility of Racial Blackness," chapter 13, this volume.

CH11

Presence of Mind: Detection and Racialization in
"The Murders in the Rue Morgue" (2001)

The misadventures that constitute Edgar Allan Poe's *Narrative of Arthur Gordon Pym* end with, what seems to Poe's mind, the most horrible and unthinkable of misadventures, encountering a "body of savages . . . [who] appeared to be the most wicked hypocritical, vindictive, bloodthirsty, and altogether fiendish race of men upon the face of the globe."[1] In landscapes, in seascapes, as well as in human anatomies, the closing details of the narrative contrast images of blackness and whiteness, marking out a world of irreconcilable divisions fixed ultimately as the clash of peoples and civilizations. These closing images and sentiments affirm that issues of race, as much as or more than any other issue, are integral to the narrative. In *Playing in the Dark*, Toni Morrison discusses these closing images in elaborating a figurative "darkness from which our early literature seemed unable to extricate itself, suggest[ing] the complex and contradictory [racial] situation in which American writers found themselves."[2] Morrison believes that no early U.S. writer is more important to this situation than Poe, a comment that is rare in a critical conversation around Poe that seems, at best, circumspect concerning race and, at worst, disingenuous.

Although Morrison highlights some of the most patent racial features of Poe's work in making this point, some of the premises of *Playing in the Dark* suggest that patent acknowledgments of race may not be the most compelling element of customary treatments of race in U.S. culture. At the outset Morrison posits that mechanisms of denial, indirection, and erasure rule U.S. racial thought—denial, indirection, and erasure not at all intended to challenge racial meanings themselves but devoted to maintaining them as unobtrusively as possible. Morrison understands that patent reflection on race (or an "Africanist presence," in her terms) is by no means the singular or even paramount sign of the influence of race or racialized thought in U.S. culture and literature and, thus, she disregards prevalent knowledge, which holds "that traditional, canonical American literature [and culture] is free of, uninformed, and unshaped by the four-hundred-year-old presence of, first, Africans and then African-Americans in the United States. It assumes that this presence—which shaped the body politic, the Constitution, and the entire history of the culture—has had no significant place or consequence in the origin and development of that culture's literature. Moreover, such knowledge assumes that the characteristics of our national literature [and culture] emanate from a particular 'Americanness' that is separate from and unaccountable to this presence."[3]

One of the integral components of U.S. racial thought, in other words, is the *unreasonable* effort to mask or overlook the systemic racial differentiation and subordination cultivated in the United States. In what manner are issues of race integral not only to openly Gothic and brooding elements of Poe's canon but also to narratives seemingly far afield of open considerations of race? The response to this question presented here assumes that racialization may be a more telling or provocative component of Poe's "Murders in the Rue Morgue" than *The Narrative of Arthur Gordon Pym* precisely because of its seeming irrelevance or invisibility.

The first of Poe's famed trilogy of detective stories, "The Murders in the Rue Morgue" aims, as does the entire trilogy, to document and stand as a monument to Reason itself—at its most sophisticated. The story presents its protagonist's extraordinary powers of apprehension, and the terms on which Reason itself is posed prove instrumental to uncovering issues of race and racialization. For "race and the various exclusions it license[s] became naturalized in the Eurocentered vision of itself and its self-defined others, in its sense of *Reason and rational direction*."[4] Modern Eurocentric Reason and rational direction provide effective, elaborate justifications for political, economic, social, and psychic systems of racial order guaranteeing that racially "distributive management of bodies ... [results in] the massive generation and redeployment of surplus value."[5]

The issues of racialization integral to "The Murders in the Rue Morgue" are signaled by three details crucial to its denouement confirming extreme powers of Reason in Dupin, its protagonist: first, the seemingly irresolvable controversy concerning the language of the murderer; second, the invocation of the French naturalist Georges Cuvier; and, third, references to distant and exotic

Borneo. These details yield the identity of the murderer (the deceptively humanlike ape), as well as underwrite incontestable proof of Dupin's ingenious and exemplary mind. The duality or duplicity of this outcome is key, because two figures are paramount by the end of the narrative, one merely mimicking and, therefore, mistaken as human, the other figuring the zenith of human potential. The capacity for thought marks the distance between these figures as nadir and zenith, and insofar as these pairings resolve the mystery of detection in the narrative, they also redact entrenched figurations of the racial animus of "blackness" and "whiteness."

That reason, formidably so, becomes the figure of *race* in the West is a peculiarity evident in both learned and popular traditions. Recently, for example, Ronald Judy, in *(Dis)Forming the American Canon*, confronts Kant over his offhanded equation of racial blackness with stupidity in *Observations on the Feeling of the Beautiful and the Sublime*—Kant being only one leading figure of the venerated Western intellectual tradition in which the equation is so routine that it never warrants careful exposition or expostulation.[6] What and who stand beyond the pale of Reason in the West is for some so plain that the question never seems openly to bear reasoning itself. Similar traditions exist popularly and less formally. In the antebellum United States, both North and South, open dismissals of blackness in this particular vein are all too easy to document. Writing in 1858, in the decade after Poe's death, Ralph Butterfield, MD, for instance, puts the matter starkly when he states the following in *American Cotton Planter and Soil of the South*: "Everybody knows that negroes are deficient in reason, judgment and forecast—that they are improvident, and thoughtless of the future, and contented and happy in the enjoyment of the mere animal pleasures of the present moment. If negroes can have plenty to eat and to wear, if they can freely indulge their amorous animal propensities, and then if to these are added a liberal allowance of whiskey and tobacco, they are indeed supremely blessed, and they sigh for no higher or brighter state of existence."[7]

The belief in an inverse relation between racial blackness and Reason is emphatic. In terms of the cultural logic of the United States, to speak of Reason is already to a very significant degree to make a racially exclusive move. The valence of the gesture is especially intriguing in the era of the escalating debate concerning the U.S. meaning of racial blackness taking place in Poe's lifetime.

It bears repeating that the circumspection around questions of race in the work of Poe is disingenuous, because the very contours of the culture in which Poe finds himself and the terms of subjection open to him are defined by highly consequential notions of race and racial blackness, influences virtually impossible to escape, and from which escape would be marked, no doubt, by unequivocal announcements of repudiation on Poe's part—of which there are none. In the same way that, without explicit evidence to prove otherwise, one must assume that Poe is a *native* speaker of English given the culture he lived in, one must assume that, given the culture he lived in, Poe necessarily refracts notions of racial hierarchy in which racial whiteness is privileged extraordinarily over racial blackness. It cannot be surprising that Poe imagines and refracts the culture in which he is steeped. In the words of social historian David Roediger, the imagined and legislated "pleasures of whiteness ... [effectively] function as a 'wage,'" or apparent boon, in the United States, for even the most dispossessed of those certified racially white nonetheless pursue opportunities to become acknowledged cultural figures.[8] Restated, the contention is that the exemplary presence and life of the mind central to "The Murders in the Rue Morgue" iterate and reflect the oppositions of racial blackness and whiteness established *as Reason* by the cultural logic of the United States and the West. If racial opposition is absent, so is Reason.

One might say that the focus in "The Murders in the Rue Morgue" on the measured, urbane, and exclusive display of Reason functions as an analogue of the images of "impenetrable whiteness" Morrison examines in *The Narrative of Arthur Gordon Pym*: "These images of impenetrable whiteness need contextualizing to explain their extraordinary power, pattern, and consistency. Because they appear almost always in conjunction with representations of black or Africanist people who are dead, impotent, or under complete control, these images of blinding whiteness seem to function as both antidote for and meditation on the shadow that is companion to this whiteness—a dark and abiding presence that moves the hearts and texts of American literature with fear and longing."[9]

According to Morrison, meditations or representations of whiteness are conjoined to their antithesis at the very point of their articulation. This claim constitutes one of the many restatements in *Playing in the Dark* that race insinuates itself into the fabric of the U.S. literary imaginary in the most circumspect of ways.

The approach of historian Alexander Saxton in exploring the racial attitudes of the young John Quincy Adams is very much to the point here. In explaining how his analysis will proceed in *The Rise and Fall of the White Republic: Class Politics and Mass Culture in Nineteenth-Century America*, Saxton writes: "The first of the sections that follow reconstructs the ideas and attitudes about race available to John Quincy Adams in the milieu of his youth, and presumably accessible to other young men of his class and generation."[10] Saxton re-creates what must have been the racial universe of the youthful Adams by assessing the racial circumstances and attitudes of Adams's family and acquaintances as well as those fostered and disseminated in the public domain. Saxton infers, in the absence of any direct statements on the part of Adams here or later contradicting this social and cultural inheritance, that he shares these views defining his age and culture. Indeed, evidence from subsequent years demonstrates "Adams modifying and adjusting those [racial] ideas and attitudes to suit the strategic needs, as he perceived them, of the class coalition that was moving him forward as a leader."[11] The same principles are pertinent to issues of race insinuated in "The Murders in the Rue Morgue." What evidence exists in the narrative, one must ask, that confirms or belies the racial attitudes of the culture in which Poe lived?

It would be mistaken, however, to suggest that the critical conversation on Poe completely circumvents open discussion of matters of race. Dana Nelson, in *The Word in Black and White*, recounts the long-standing controversy concerning whether Poe held pro- or antislavery sentiments. Spanning decades, these exchanges debate whether Poe is, in fact, the author of an unsigned proslavery book review published in April 1836 in the *Southern Literary Messenger*, a journal for which he served as editor at that time. In detailing this intellectual history, Nelson carefully states her wish to avoid narrow concerns about intentionality and Poe; she wishes, rather, to consider "the racist dimension of Poe's work ... [and] the cultural work performed *now* by masking that aspect of his work."[12] She proposes the issue of settling the authorship of the single book review as less than relevant because it makes little sense to imagine that issues of race in Poe's literary work should rest foremost on the question of the authorship of a tangential document. She claims it much more productive to see that complexities of race reside in Poe's texts themselves and in the cultural systems those texts both reflect and participate in. In brief, the question of Poe's personal dispositions may be interesting but is not in fact crucial. What is crucial for a sound investigation of the racial exigencies of his canon is gauging his relation to a U.S. national imaginary continually playing in the dark, in Morrison's apt phrase.

John Carlos Rowe, in "Poe, Antebellum Slavery, and Modern Criticism," puts the matter well when he points out that one cannot reasonably overlook the fact that "Poe's prose and poetry is, of course, full of abused, murdered, dismembered women, of native peoples represented as the embodiment of primitive evil, of visionary aristocrats, of royalty 'saved' by poetic manipulation, of the hateful 'masses.'"[13] Poe's work is so steeped in the material intrigues of cultural power and political control that it makes little sense to imagine that the significance of its racial issues turns on determining the authorship of an isolated declaration of political sentiment. Rowe, even more so than Nelson, reminds readers that the incidents and relations set out in Poe's works ineluctably engage the "materiality of history" and culture—as one must suspect of all literature.[14] Even as the tales (and perhaps especially the detective fiction) work to present the "argument that language, the essence of reason, is the basis of all reality and thus the only proper 'property,'" they profess as strenuously, though more surreptitiously, that "as the 'enlightened ruler' of language, the essence of reason, its rational governor, the poet works to recontain that savagery the mob—the black, the lunatic—within poetic form."[15] Rowe presumes along with Nelson that the question rests, rather than simply with declared or documentable political allegiances, in imaginative configurations found in the literature itself.

However, Rowe, like Morrison and Nelson, looks foremost to *The Narrative of Arthur Gordon Pym* to make the case for the significance of race and racialization in Poe's work. Allegorizing aspects of the narrative in terms of dynamics of the antebellum South, Rowe writes, for instance: "Like Nat Turner, the Black Cook [in *Pym*] strikes his victims on the head, testifying to the symbolic danger to reason posed by the emergence of the irrational savagery so many Southern whites imagined would accompany slave rebellion or even legal emancipation."[16] Rowe suggests the great importance of the conflation of blackness and irrationality to both the allegorized terms of Poe's imagination and the historical terms of the moment in which Poe lives. The threat of racial blackness takes the form of a threat to rational conduct and to social organization, and, although Rowe questions the role of reason in the detective narratives, he never openly proposes that the same dynamics of reason so evident in *Pym* might also be crucial to the detective narratives in which the display of reason is paramount.

David Van Leer, in "Detecting Truth: The World of the Dupin Tales," makes the opposite gesture. While Van Leer does query the exemplary display of Reason in Poe's detective fiction, he never imagines or poses any conjunction between matters of Reason and matters of racialization. His ultimate concern is the peculiarity that in the fictive world of these tales the reasoning presented is finally specious because it posits "no difference between seeming and being."[17] Like Rowe, Van Leer implies that it is the question of representation—who holds the authority to represent, as well as representational strategies themselves—that is at stake. Both Van Leer and Rowe understand reason as tied to processes of the construction and elaboration of what is forged as visible and comprehensible, rather than to any primary access to "truth." Van Leer presents extended suspicions concerning the "bravada demonstration of Dupin's ability to predict his friends' thoughts" that opens "The Murders in the Rue Morgue."[18] While this demonstration would stand ideally as a preface to more astounding displays of Dupin's genius to follow, displays of genius that will solve the mystery of the unfathomable murders, Van Leer dismantles the display as follows:

> Such an analytic tour de force is . . . not truly ingenious. Yet it does suggest how Dupin's method deduces its conclusions from generalized concepts rather than inducing them from observed reality. The outside world barely intrudes on Dupin's analysis: The narrator murmurs a word, looks up to heaven, smiles, and stops stooping. Not arising from an exact observation of details, Dupin's reasoning depends on the logical inevitability of any thought process. The narrator "could not say" a word "without being brought" to think of another word. Once thinking that second word he "could not avoid" looking upward or fail to associate the constellation he sees with yet another word. "From certain pungencies" (which Dupin forbears to enumerate) the narrator necessarily relates this Latin word to its use in a hostile review of the actor. Thought, by this account, is merely a passive review of the actor. Though Dupin claims to have "correctly followed" his friend's thoughts, he actually anticipates them. There is nothing in the passage that counts as evidence. Most of the narrator's actions—his skyward glance, smile, and posture—corroborate what Dupin has already concluded to be the necessary train of his thoughts.[19]

In sum, Van Leer closely analyzes what Poe represents as Reason; he considers what features pass for Reason (with its access to truth) in Poe's fictive world.

The narrative would ostensibly have it otherwise, but one recognizes at last not simply individual genius at its center but also a system of racial stratification in the prodigious display of mindfulness. Whereas Van Leer probes the suspect Reason of Poe's tales, and Nelson and Rowe emphasize the relevance of race to Poe's work, the interest here is to uncover the ineluctable complication of Reason and race.

The disinterested capacity for human genius recorded in "The Murders in the Rue Morgue" is occasioned by a violent central crime that is a disturbing and puzzling antithesis to any world of perceptual order and mental acuity. If night and simulated darkness stand as the preferred element for the narrator and his friend Dupin in indulging their "souls in dreams—reading, writing, or conversing," then as it turns out, this preferred environment for their radical immersion in the life of the mind proves equally the cloak for bizarre and disconcerting events.[20] The darkness of night, insofar as it is the preferred element for the life of the mind in the narrative, seems concomitantly the very seat of the unreasonable, for what makes the murders of Madame L'Espanaye and her daughter so bizarre and disconcerting is not simply their extreme, macabre violence but the fact that they seem to defy all logical or reasonable explanation. Dupin's self-appointed charge to isolate, penetrate, vanquish what, as it turns out, is only *apparently* unreasonable reasserts the supremacy of the life of the mind. Only to those with powers of reasoning unequal to Dupin's do the murders ultimately seem unreasonable and to underscore the point, the tale ends with Dupin musing over the lesser powers of the prefect of police, whom he overshadows with his spectacular solution to the murders: "I am satisfied with having defeated him in his own castle. Nevertheless, that he failed in the solution of this mystery, is by no means that matter for wonder which he supposes it; for, in truth our friend the Prefect is somewhat too cunning to be profound. In his wisdom is no *stamen*. It is all head and no body, like the pictures of the goddess Laverna,—or, at best, all head and shoulders, like a codfish."[21]

Predictably, Dupin's intervention into the macabre, baffling events begins with his digesting all available information. However, although there are abundant clues at the scene of the crime, as well as an abundance of reports from witnesses who were within earshot of the crime, all this information seems to point only to its own oddity or to prove contradictory. One of the most salient pieces of evidence investigators have to work with, the series of voices overheard by witnesses during the fatal altercation, amounts to only irreconcilable reports. Two voices other than the women's are heard, and, while there is a fairly stable consensus among witnesses that one of the two voices heard during the altercation was that of a Frenchman, there is absolutely no agreement on the language of the very unusual second voice also heard in the apartments. The singular point of corroboration by the witnesses is that it was a "shrill voice [which] was that of a foreigner."[22] The confusion is remarkable: a gendarme on the scene believes the peculiar voice was Spanish; a neighbor thinks the voice Italian; a restaurateur, native to Amsterdam, believes it belonged to a Frenchman; an English tailor believes the voice to be German; an undertaker, native to Spain, deposes the voice was English; an Italian confectioner believes the voice was Russian. Each witness names a language he does not speak or understand, so that their collective testimony registers, in essence, only the absolute alienness of what was heard.

What is truly alien, of course, according to the terrain the depositions mark out is all that lies outside the geography of the leading European powers. Each of the witnesses names a European language with which they are unfamiliar as the language of the unidentifiable voice. Deftly, Dupin fathoms that the mistake each witness makes is to draw the scope of their reckoning much too narrowly. To each witness the "foreign" is that which is unfamiliar within the parameters of Europe, while, opposingly, an important measure of Dupin's brilliance rests on the fact that he fully recognizes that what is most strange, peculiar, and unfamiliar lies, with certainty, without rather than within European geographies. All but Dupin overlook the fact that attempts to identify the second voice may be so baffling precisely because those paradigms against which it is measured are themselves overly familiar, rather than aberrant or extraordinary. Dupin remarks: "Each spoke of [the voice] as that *of a foreigner*. Each is sure that it was not the voice of one of his own countrymen. Each likens it—not to the voice of an individual of any nation with whose language he is conversant—but the converse.... Now, how strangely unusual must that voice have really been about which such testimony as this *could* have been elicited!—in whose *tones*, even, denizens of the five great divisions of Europe could recognise nothing familiar!"[23]

The matter in question must be profoundly outré to exceed "the five great divisions of Europe." All that is truly reasonable or reckonable must be legible within the terms set out by at least one of these five great divisions, Dupin's logic seems to run.

Hence, what will turn out to be the triumphant logic articulates a vast world map, one with a patent center and with all lying beyond this center unmistakably suggestive of the bizarre or virtually unthinkable. The racialized imperative of this logic is not as bald, however, as it at first seems, for the culprit, of course, turns out to be not an otherwise racialized (i.e., non-European) person but a frenzied orangutan. Indeed, Dupin quickly dismisses the possibility of any "Asiatic" or "African" being the culprit: "You will say that it might have been the voice of an Asiatic—of an African. Neither Asiatics nor Africans abound in Paris; but, *without denying the inference*, I will now merely call your attention to three points."[24] He does not so much remove suspicion—and ultimately culpability—from "Asiatics" or "Africans" as move it through racially distinct peoples. He proclaims that one is perfectly right in imagining that the unrecognizably strange voice might be that of an Asiatic or an African. The inclinations are correct but the odds are against it, he reasons, and even as he undermines this line of speculation, he nonetheless equates the bizarre and unfathomable with these "exotic" cultures and peoples. Dupin, in other words, is never quite willing to dispel or dismiss the insight even as he proceeds to point out evidence that will lead him not to "Asiatics" or "Africans" but to the actual culprit.

Suggestively, Dupin's preeminent reasoning finally reveals the bizarre and fatal intrusion into the apparently orderly world of modern urban life to be a threat from without in the form of a volatile, foreign agent unfit by nature for unrestrained civil intercourse. Such reasoning is precisely at the center of the escalating debate concerning the meaning of racial blackness in the antebellum United States. The trajectory of Dupin's triumphant exposition in significant measure resembles widespread notions in U.S. culture of African Americans as a lurking "pathogen"—to use a telling term employed by historian Clarence Walker.[25] Walker writes: "In the eyes of these statesmen [Thomas Jefferson, John C. Calhoun, William Lowndes Yancey, and Alexander Stephens] and the people they represented, Negroes were primitive, comical outsiders who were governed more by appetite than reason. . . . To most nineteenth-century white Americans the Negroes' racial difference and inferiority were not mere abstractions. Race was a physical fact."[26] By marshaling evidence to represent popular nineteenth-century U.S. sentiment in his essay "How Many Niggers Did Karl Marx Know? Or, a Peculiarity of the Americans," Walker mounts a challenge to U.S. historiography of slavery and race relations invested primarily in analyses of class to the negligence of the fact that "to most nineteenth-century white Americans . . . racial difference and inferiority were not mere abstractions."[27] As both learned and popular sentiment make plain, to live with Africans and African descendants in one's midst is to live in extreme proximity to the dangers of a foreign and primitive presence understood, as Walker argues, as no less than pathogenic. Moreover, in the West, in both the learned and the popular mind, the wild primitive state of the orangutan remains an important analogue for the natural condition of Africans and their descendants:

> If Negroes were likened to beasts, there was in Africa a beast which was likened to men. It was a strange and eventually tragic happenstance that Africa was the habitat of the animal which in appearance most resembles man. The animal called "orangoutang" by contemporaries (actually the chimpanzee) was native to those parts of western Africa where the early slave trade was heavily concentrated. Though Englishmen were acquainted (for the most part vicariously) with monkeys and baboons, they were unfamiliar with tail-less apes who walked about like men. Accordingly, it happened that Englishmen were introduced to the anthropoid apes and to Negroes at the same time and in the same place. The startling human appearance and movements of the "ape"—a generic term though often used as a synonym for the "orangoutang"—aroused some curious speculations.[28]

What Dupin seems to insinuate with his equivocation is a subtle though inviolable connection between whatever lies beyond the wards of Europe and its five great divisions and what, in solving the murder mystery, is eventually revealed as the bestial. It is important to note, however, that this coimplication of the non-European and the bestial remains suggestive above all at this point in the narrative, for as yet there is no reasonable or reasoned figure in which and by which such a coimplication is confirmed. Ultimately, of course, this figure will be Dupin in his exposition of the guilty orangutan, its temperament, mimicry of human behavior, and origins.

Dupin's subsequent references to naturalist Georges Cuvier in elaborating his solution to the murders invokes these curious speculations much more directly. Both in terms of intellectual notoriety and in assuming the coimplication of the bestial and the non-European, Cuvier stands in the narrative as the figure of reason who precedes and in many ways validates the triumphant figure of Dupin. A leading European naturalist of the early nineteenth century, Georges Cuvier was also "regarded by contemporaries as the arch placeman, the greatest manipulator of patronage in science and in some branches of the administration, notably those of education and the Conseil d'Etat, of his day."[29] A leading scientific and public figure, Cuvier, "through studying the various structural means by which animals carried out the major processes of life, . . . believed he could establish rational criteria for a 'natural system' of classification."[30] This certainly extended, furthermore, into considerations of the ostensible varieties of humankind, and one of Cuvier's most famous associations, that with southern African native Sarjte Bartmann (also known as the "Hottentot Venus"), underscores this point, as well as his position as both scientist and public figure: as part of the lucrative nineteenth-century vogue for "the exhibition of unusual humans . . . in both upper-class salons and in the street-side stalls," twenty-year-old Sarjte Bartmann was brought from southern Africa to Europe and displayed to eager audiences in both London and France from 1810 until her death in 1815.[31] Drawing intense interest and large crowds for her embodiment of "steatopygia, or protruding buttocks, . . . which captured the eye of early European travelers [to Africa]," Bartmann proved as fascinating in death as in life.[32] The young woman's autopsy "was written up by Henri de Blainville in 1816 and then, in its most famous version, by Cuvier in 1817," a version "reprinted at least twice during the next decade."[33] Emphasizing "any point of superficial similarity [of Bartmann] with an ape or monkey," Cuvier's report reveals sensibilities and intentions plainly in line with enduring but specious speculations proposing the subhumanity, or inferior developmental or evolutionary state, of Africans and their descendants.[34] Bartmann's dissected genitalia remain in the back reaches of the Musée de l'Homme in France, a trophy testifying to unabashed nineteenth-century efforts to "define the great scale of human progress, from chimp to Caucasian."[35]

This is to say that, if one can point to a figure in "The Murders in the Rue Morgue" for whom Africans and their descendants undoubtedly hold "a grim fascination, not as a missing link in a later evolutionary sense, but as . . . creature[s] who straddled that dreaded boundary between human and animal" and for whom this assumption underwrites an exhibition of intellectual prowess, it is certainly Georges Cuvier—who, as it turns out, is key to Dupin's comprehension of the baffling events in the apartments of Madame L'Espanaye.[36] In sum, one man of preeminent learning and perception executes his skills of apprehension by taking his cue from another. The figure of Cuvier represents a form of genius reiterated in Dupin and his deductions, since, as Dupin himself openly acknowledges, his recognition of the solution to the mystery of the murders turns on Cuvier. Having solved the mystery for himself, Dupin asks the narrator to read a passage from Cuvier's work that "was a minute anatomical and generally descriptive account of the large fulvous Ourang-Outang of the East Indian Islands. The gigantic stature, the prodigious strength and activity, the wild ferocity, and the imitative propensities of these mammalia are sufficiently well known to all. I understood the full horrors of the murder at once."[37]

The full horrors have to do with the bestial nature of the threat now understood by the narrator to be in their midst—a bestial nature that Cuvier in his career does not confine to wild animals, a presumption Dupin, in referencing Cuvier, reiterates at least implicitly. In all its suggestiveness, the pivotal reference to Cuvier does more than echo and reinforce the schemes of racialization implicit in Dupin's earlier equivocal comments concerning the language of the assailant. Allusions to the figure of Cuvier signal in substantial ways that schemes of racialization dismissive of "Asiatics" or "Africans" are themselves unquestionable signs of Reason. These particular signs are instrumental to Cuvier's notoriety, so that part of what constitutes the public knowledge on which Dupin draws is a racially stratified notion of intellect itself.

Summarily or directly stated, Dupin and Poe share Cuvier: in the fictive nineteenth-century world of Dupin, Cuvier is a notable international figure, as he also is in the nineteenth-century United States of Poe. Stated differently still, insofar as Poe labors for verisimilitude, he fixes instrumental elements of that verisimilitude on an internationally known celebrity who posits Africans to be "the most degraded of human races, whose form approaches that of the beast and whose intelligence is nowhere great enough to arrive at regular government."[38] These ideas, of course, are central to U.S. national identity and policy—official and unofficial: "In the United States of the mid-nineteenth century, racial prejudice was all but universal. Belief in black inferiority formed a central tenet of the southern defense of slavery, and in the North too, many

PRESENCE OF MIND   289

who were undecided on the merits of the peculiar institution, and even those who disapproved of it, believed that the Negro was *by nature* destined to occupy a subordinate position in society."[39] In the absence of contravening references and in conjunction with other collaborating details, the pivotal reference to Cuvier succinctly suggests that the racial assumptions of the narrative remain strictly in line with the social and cultural inheritance informing quotidian U.S. notions of race.

Emphatically, the contention here is not that "The Murders in the Rue Morgue" is about U.S. slavery or in any way *directly* about the position of Africans and African descendants in U.S. society. The point is that the "materiality of history," to borrow the phrase of John Carlos Rowe, directly impinges on the narrative by characterizing its exposition and celebration of extraordinary reason in widespread (international) racist formulations proposing subordinate evolutionary, social, and intellectual positions to nonwhite peoples. Mental apprehension of the offending orangutan in many ways supplants the need for open declarations about race, or might in itself signal such a declaration. No dark-skinned person or persons need be singled out as guilty, and the reference to Cuvier subtly and with calculated verisimilitude substantiates this knowledge.

Still, beyond the key position of Georges Cuvier in the intellectual drama, the disclosure of the origins of the offending orangutan in Borneo is a further important element in the narrative's understated meditation on race. The "third largest island in the world after Greenland and New Guinea," Borneo is "one of numerous islands in the humid tropics of Asia which are scattered around the southern and eastern rim of the South China sea."[40] Encircled by the South China Sea, the Java Sea, and the Celebes Sea, Borneo rests southeast of Malaysia and directly east of Sumatra. While the island fell mainly within the sphere of Dutch imperial power in the seventeenth century, the nineteenth century ushered in the island's primary period of colonization, which took place under the British rather than the Dutch; accordingly, the exotic location, landscape, and peoples of Borneo proved a catalyst for ardent Western imaginations in the nineteenth century, which "saw Borneo natives as living in a state of nature, closely in tune with their natural environment. In some cases, the European imagination merged humans and animals."[41] The orangutan, as it happens, was conceived to be the primary figure of such a merger. For instance, "Englishman Capt. Daniel Beeckman following his visit to southern Borneo was the first to portray the forest ape, the *orang utan* (Pongo pymaeus) as a creature of fable," and Norwegian Carl Bock ventured to Borneo "in search of the 'missing link': living creatures with combined human and animal characteristics."[42]

As a result of falling increasingly under the sway of Western imperialism, Borneo in the nineteenth century serves as a point on the globe that marks for the West a hotbed of primitivism, exotic adventure, and encounters with startling, dangerous beasts. It is an enticing locale for both popular fiction and travelogues, such as *The Expedition to Borneo of H.M.S. Dido for the Suppression of Piracy: With Extracts from the Journal of James Brooke, Esq. of Sarawack (Now Agent for the British Government in Borneo)* published by Harper and Brothers in 1846 and written by Captain the Hon. Henry Keppel, R.N. In sum, "crossed by the equator a little below its center, so that about two thirds of its area lie in the northern and one third lies in the southern hemisphere," Borneo furnishes an ample and remarkable arena for reveries of racial superiority, as the African interior similarly would once it became fully accessible to European explorers in the latter half of the nineteenth century (as Thomas Pakenham closely documents in his extensive study *The Scramble for Africa*).[43] Both in the Western popular imagination and in "The Murders in the Rue Morgue," the enormous compass of Borneo—several times larger than England and "from the sea-coast to the summits of the highest mountains ... covered with a dense forest"—represents the antithesis of the Western metropole and serves as a compelling site for aggrandizing fantasies.[44]

The importance Borneo holds in Dupin's solution documents Poe's familiarity with the popular meanings of distant geographies associated with "Asiatics" and "Africans." Further, it ideally fixes as the occasion for the murders the force of alien brutality eluding civilized restraint. Differently, the reason there seems to be *no* explanation for the murders is because there is no *reasonable* explanation. The murders are so alien not only in physical circumstances but also in possible motive that they *make no sense*. The force behind them is the chance and irrational brutality of a primitive agent. And the incontrovertible sign that this alien force stands *without* reason is the neglected economic windfall of the fatal encounter. For, although it was fairly well known that Madame L'Espanaye and her daughter "lived an exceedingly retired life [and] were reputed to have money," and although three days before the murders Madame L'Espanaye "took out in person the sum of 4000 francs, ... which was paid in gold, and a clerk sent home with the money," the money was not stolen during the fatal altercation.[45] All of Paris is left puzzling over the incident and musing: "why did [the perpetrator] abandon four thousand francs in gold to encumber himself with a bundle of linen? The gold was abandoned. Nearly the whole sum mentioned by Monsieur Mignaud, the banker, was discovered, in bags, upon the floor."[46] In one instance, one might "imagine the perpetrator to be so vacillating an idiot as to have abandoned his gold and his motive together."[47]

The perpetrator, however, is beyond idiocy and *foreign* to the principles of economic exchange and accumulation understood profoundly as the hallmark of civilized and rational social being.

Even the wayward sailor, a member of the abundant lower classes, who is indirectly responsible for the murders through illicit ownership of the orangutan, is patently guided by principles of economic self-interest. In his unfolding mastery of the convoluted circumstances, Dupin places a false newspaper report of the capture of the beast, certain the sailor will appear to claim the animal because he "will reason thus:—'I am innocent; I am poor; my Ourang-Outang is of great value—to one in my circumstances a fortune of itself—why should I lose it through idle apprehensions of danger?' "[48] He attributes economic motives to the sailor's ill-fated stewardship of the beast in the first place. That is, the desperate and unwise actions of the lower orders are eminently comprehensible (even if misguided), whereas the unfettered "intractable ferocity" of the inhabitants of foreign wards well beyond the geography of Europe is governed by no such recognizable principles of reason. Dupin's genius rests on providing an account of the unquestionable and unimaginable other—which is, as gingerly outlined as it may be, sketched in nineteenth-century codes of racialization. The prodigious intellectual powers of Dupin, then, reach beyond the limits of reason itself to provide most unexpectedly a logical account of circumstances seeming to defy all logic.

Dupin's duel here is with principles of unreason that are articulated through subtle markers of race. As much as the offending orangutan represents a principle of unreason, it also connotes in nineteenth-century cultural parlance signifiers of race: linguistic, anatomical, physiognomic, geographic. Oblique invocations of non-European racialization as a principle of violent unreason are at the center of Dupin's ruminations, and it is imperative to note that this is not an aberration. The larger principle at work here is one of exclusion and exclusiveness, one establishing the singular claims of racial "whiteness" to sites of value and acclamation by evacuating racial otherness from the conceptual field in question. This is the principle the fictive world of Dupin closely shares with the antebellum world of Poe. Eric Foner's redaction of the charged political concepts increasingly dominating the U.S. cultural conversation in the decades prior to the Civil War underscores this commonality, for "in a nation in which slavery was a recent memory in the North and an overwhelming presence in the South; whose westward expansion (the guarantee of equal opportunity) required the removal of Indians and the conquest of lands held by Mexicans, it was inevitable that the language of politics . . . would come to be defined in racial terms."[49] Just as racial others are discharged from the condition and exposition of reason in "The Murders in the Rue Morgue," nonwhites are excluded, in fact, from ironically universalist rhetoric in the antebellum United States: "Despite its universalist vocabulary, the [triumphant republican] idea of free labor had little bearing on the actual conditions of nonwhites in nineteenth-century America."[50] It is not open declarations of racial sentiments on the part of Poe that are so telling but, rather, the continuity between his work and widespread racial and racist constructions.

In the essay "Amorous Bondage: Poe, Ladies, and Slaves," Joan Dayan makes a similar proposal in a relatively broad survey of Poe's work. She interrogates the way in which, "without mentioning blacks, Poe applies the accepted argument on the 'nature' of negroes and the 'spirit' of women—both feeling, not thinking things—to the white men usually excluded from such categorizations."[51] She believes that "for Poe the cultivation of romance and the facts of slavery are inextricably linked" and that his "gothic is crucial to our understanding of the entangled metaphysics of romance and servitude."[52] Dayan sets out to interpret the obliquely evident racial imperatives of Poe's imaginative world and proceeds by often reading Poe's work allegorically or by referring to aspects of his personal history—for instance, his "relationships with the leading proslavery advocates in Virginia" or the fact that his "guardians, the Allans, had at least three servants (all slaves, but at least one of these was owned by someone else and bonded to Mr. Allan)."[53]

Equally, one might disclose powerful correspondences between Poe's imaginative vision and the cultural vision of his society, as well as the terms that conjoin them. How is it possible, in a culture in which an antipathy between racial blackness and whiteness stands as a rudimentary principle, for one to understand oneself as a racial subject, a U.S. social subject, or a literary subject outside of the psychic as well as the legislated denigration of racial blackness? Racial taxonomies form a set of social knowledges virtually impossible to elude or not to imbibe which codify and advertise African Americans as confined by nature to bodily existences having little or nothing to do with the life of the mind and its representation. In the absence of evidence that Poe stood far outside these cultural assumptions, it would be absolutely misguided not to conceive *as a matter of course* that such attitudes inform his delineations of great mindfulness, reason, and ingenuity—and, indeed, his entire canon. The burden of proof, it seems, rests with the opposing position. Literacy, for instance, is a primary issue through which the dynamics of racial blackness are emphatically played out in the cultural moment of the antebellum United States. Cultural fiats surrounding literacy point out that the body within the ideologies of the dominant U.S. community holds the ultimate terms of identity for

African Americans.[54] As the dominant community would have it, the identity of African Americans is bound up primarily, if not exclusively, with the terms of the body, a signal identification, since in European philosophizing the body is restricted to being the object of thought and never its subject. Literacy provides manifest testimony of the mind's ability to extend itself beyond the constricted limits and conditions of the body, so that to enter into literacy is to gain important skills for extending oneself beyond the condition and geography of the body. In other words, because literacy provides the most manifest formalization of the life of the mind, it is indispensable to this elaborate cultural construct.

Granting this perspective even tentatively in the case of "The Murders in the Rue Morgue," one begins to "see that the cool analytical rigor of Dupin's solutions, their masterly appropriation of the forms of scientific induction, might also serve to mask an underlying web of prejudices, received opinions, and unfounded ideological presumptions, lending them at second-hand, as it were, respectability and seemingly impeccable intellectual credentials."[55] More generally, the conviction that Poe operated within, rather than substantially without, the terms of the antebellum culture in which he lived is to a significant degree shared by Dayan: "When we note varying denigrations of blacks in Poe's early works, it becomes even more unsettling that issues of race, like those of gender, have not figured significantly in Poe criticism."[56] A gulf between Poe and normative U.S. racial ideology is an unlikely proposition, one in which, given its unlikeliness, the burden of proof rests with those subscribing to it.

Nonetheless, if Reason is conflated subtly with whiteness in "The Murders in the Rue Morgue," how might one account for the final disposition of its central characters, all of whom are white, but only one of whom, Dupin, stands confirmed fully by the logic of the narrative? John Bryant, in "Poe's Ape of UnReason: Humor, Ritual, and Culture," addresses this issue indirectly in an analysis that argues for Poe's "comic development."[57] According to Bryant, the dynamic from which Poe wrings his humor is one in which "the irrational (a human function intimately conjoined with sexuality) allows for a tentative spiritual connection to Beauty and Ideality, but that same irrationality, when manifested artistically in the grotesque of the imp of the perverse, debases, or even denies regenerative human faculties."[58] In reconstructing this humor, Bryant also acknowledges the speciousness of Dupin's triumphant reasoning: "Dupin knows the murderer is just an ape but has us rehearse the case so that we will conclude falsely that the perpetrator is a madman and hence that, by association, Dupin too is mad. But he fingers the Ape before we can draw such conclusions, thereby demolishing any implications of his actual irrationality."[59]

The joke seems to be that there are two apes in the narrative—Dupin in his performance of an "ape of UnReason" being the second. The pun confirms the long-standing principle that if racial opposition is absent, so, too, is Reason, since the competing figurative and literal uses of "ape" only reiterate the diacritical relations (nadir and zenith) drawing together in the tale language, Cuvier, and Borneo.

Insofar as whiteness is vulnerable to bizarre intrusions into its apparently orderly world in the form of volatile, foreign agents (or impulses) unfit by nature for unrestrained civil intercourse, Dupin plays with—thereby signaling his mastery of—the threat. This singular mastery places Dupin in the most authoritative and advantageous position in the narrative. He sees the inexplicable horror beyond the scope or reach of the prefect, the horror that his friend, the narrator, recognizes only through proximity to Dupin, and which consumes two innocent white female victims. Dupin understands Reason, the analogue of whiteness, in ways that none of the other racially white characters do but, significantly, in ways that almost blur the distinction on which the terms of Reason—by racial fiat—rest. Dupin, in his closer mental proximity to the profoundly foreign intrusion, maintains, to his advantage, the full terms of his racial whiteness. In this paradox, the narrative returns its readers to peculiarities well articulated by Toni Morrison: "What does positing one's writerly self, in the wholly racialized society that is the United States, as unraced and all others as raced entail? . . . How do embedded assumptions of racial (not racist) language work in the literary enterprise that hopes and sometimes claims to be 'humanistic'?"[60] In effect, there is more than one alarming puzzle offered by Poe's narrative of individual brilliance, since Dupin's triumph documents that the truly white person always looks necessarily and intently beyond Europe and whiteness.

NOTES

Chapter 11, "Presence of Mind," was originally published in *Romancing the Shadow: Poe and Race*, ed. J. Gerald Kennedy and Liliane Weissberg (Oxford: Oxford University Press, 2001), 157–76. Republished with permission of Oxford University Press; permission conveyed through Copyright Clearance Center, Inc.

I gratefully acknowledge the many suggestions of the editors, as well as an unknown reader for Oxford University Press, concerning this chapter.

1. Edgar Allan Poe, *Collected Works of Edgar Allan Poe: Tales and Sketches, 1831–1842*, ed. Thomas Ollive Mabbott (Cambridge, MA: Belknap, 1978), 1:201.

2. Toni Morrison, *Playing in the Dark: Whiteness and the Literary Imagination* (Cambridge, MA: Harvard University Press, 1992), 33.

3. Morrison, *Playing in the Dark*, 4–5.

4. David Theo Goldberg, *Racist Culture: Philosophy and the Politics of Meaning* (Cambridge: Blackwell, 1993), 10, emphasis added.

5. Goldberg, *Racist Culture*, 53.

6. Ronald Judy, *(Dis)Forming the American Canon* (Minneapolis: University of Minnesota Press, 1993).

7. Ralph Butterfield, *American Cotton Planter and Soil of the South* 2 (1858): 293–94, in *Advice among Masters: The Ideal in Slave Management in the Old South*, ed. James O. Breeden (Westport, CT: Greenwood, 1980), 212.

8. David R. Roediger, *The Wages of Whiteness: Race and the Making of the American Working Class* (London: Verso, 1999), 13.

9. Morrison, *Playing in the Dark*, 33.

10. Alexander Saxton, *The Rise and Fall of the White Republic: Class Politics and Mass Culture in Nineteenth-Century America* (London: Verso, 2003), 25.

11. Saxton, *The Rise and Fall of the White Republic*, 25.

12. Dana D. Nelson, *The Word in Black and White: Reading "Race" in American Literature, 1638–1867* (New York: Oxford University Press, 1994), 92, emphasis in original.

13. John Carlos Rowe, "Poe, Antebellum Slavery, and Modern Criticism," in *Poe's Pym: Critical Explorations*, ed. Richard Kopley (Durham, NC: Duke University Press, 1992), 136.

14. Rowe, "Poe, Antebellum Slavery, and Modern Criticism," 126.

15. Rowe, "Poe, Antebellum Slavery, and Modern Criticism," 127.

16. Rowe, "Poe, Antebellum Slavery, and Modern Criticism," 128.

17. David Van Leer, "Detecting Truth: The World of the Dupin Tales," in *New Essays on Poe's Major Tales*, ed. Kenneth Silverman (New York: Cambridge University Press, 1993), 68.

18. Van Leer, "Detecting Truth," 68.

19. Van Leer, "Detecting Truth," 70–71.

20. Edgar Allan Poe, "The Murders in the Rue Morgue," in *Selected Poetry and Prose of Edgar Allan Poe*, ed. T. O. Mabbott (New York: Rinehart, 1951), 533.

21. Poe, "The Murders in the Rue Morgue," 568, emphasis in original.

22. Poe, "The Murders in the Rue Morgue," 540.

23. Poe, "The Murders in the Rue Morgue," 549, emphasis in original.

24. Poe, "The Murders in the Rue Morgue," 550, emphasis added.

25. Clarence Walker, *De-romanticizing Black History: Critical Essays and Reappraisals* (Knoxville: University of Tennessee Press, 1991), 10.

26. Walker, *De-romanticizing Black History*, 5.

27. Walker, *De-romanticizing Black History*, 8.

28. Winthrop D. Jordan, *The White Man's Burden: Historical Origins of Racism in the United States* (New York: Oxford University Press, 1974), 15.

29. Dorinda Outram, *Georges Cuvier: Vocation, Science, and Authority in Post-revolutionary France* (Manchester: Manchester University Press, 1984), 5.

30. Toby A. Appel, *The Cuvier-Geoffroy Debate: French Biology in the Decades before Darwin* (New York: Oxford University Press, 1987), 4.

31. Stephen Jay Gould, "The Hottentot Venus: A Sensation from Piccadilly to Paris, She Drew Crowds from All Classes, Including Scientists," *Natural History* 91, no. 10 (1982): 20.

32. Sander Gilman, "Black Bodies, White Bodies: Toward an Iconography of Female Sexuality in Late Nineteenth-Century Art, Medicine, and Literature," in *"Race," Writing, and Difference*, ed. Henry Louis Gates Jr. (Chicago: University of Chicago Press, 1986), 232.

33. Gilman, "Black Bodies, White Bodies," 232.

34. Gould, "The Hottentot Venus," 22. Gould adds parenthetically: "I hardly need to mention that since people vary so much, each group must be closer than others to some feature of some other primate, without implying anything about genealogy or aptitude" (22).

35. Gould, "The Hottentot Venus," 20.

36. Gould, "The Hottentot Venus," 22.

37. Poe, "The Murders in the Rue Morgue," 559.

38. Georges Cuvier, *Recherches sur les ossemens fossiles de quadrupèdes, où l'on rétablit les caractères de plusieurs espèces d'animaux que les révolutions du globe paroissent avoir détruites*, 4 vols. (1812), 105.

39. Eric Foner, *Politics and Ideology in the Age of the Civil War* (New York: Oxford University Press, 1980), 77, emphasis added.

40. Victor T. King, *The Peoples of Borneo* (Oxford: Blackwell, 1993), 7.

41. King, *The Peoples of Borneo*, 10.

42. King, *The Peoples of Borneo*, 10–11, emphasis in original; 13.

43. Charles Hose and William McDougall, *The Pagan Tribes of Borneo* (New York: Barnes and Noble, 1966), 1; Thomas Pakenham, *The Scramble for Africa: White Man's Conquest of the Dark Continent from 1876 to 1912* (New York: Avon, 1992).

44. Hose and McDougall, *The Pagan Tribes of Borneo*, 5–6.

45. Poe, "The Murders in the Rue Morgue," 539, 541.

46. Poe, "The Murders in the Rue Morgue," 256.

47. Poe, "The Murders in the Rue Morgue."

48. Poe, "The Murders in the Rue Morgue," 561.

49. Eric Foner, *Free Soil, Free Labor, Free Men: The Ideology of the Republican Party before the Civil War* (New York: Oxford University Press, 1995), xxvii.

50. Foner, *Free Soil*, xxvii.

51. Joan Dayan, "Amorous Bondage: Poe, Ladies, and Slaves," *American Literature* 66 (1994): 239–73, reprinted in *Subjects and Citizens: Nation, Race, and Gender from Oroonoko to Anita Hill*, ed. Michael Moon and Cathy N. Davidson (Durham, NC: Duke University Press, 1995), 223–65, and in *The American Face of Edgar Allan Poe*, ed. Shawn Rosenheim and Stephen Rachman, 119–209 (Baltimore: Johns Hopkins University Press, 1995), 189.

52. Dayan, "Amorous Bondage," 110, 111.

53. Dayan, "Amorous Bondage," 134.

54. See, for example, Janet Duitsman Cornelius, *"When I Can Read My Title Clear": Literacy, Slavery, and Religion in the Antebellum South* (Columbia: University of South Carolina Press, 1991). Also my article "African-American Slave Narratives: Literacy, the Body, Authority" (chapter 4, this volume).

55. Louisa Nygaard, "Winning the Game: Inductive Reasoning in Poe's 'Murders in the Rue Morgue,'" *Studies in Romanticism* 33 (1994): 253.

56. Dayan, "Amorous Bondage," 256.

57. John Bryant, "Poe's Ape of UnReason: Humor, Ritual, and Culture," *Nineteenth-Century Literature* 51 (1996): 52.

58. Bryant, "Poe's Ape of UnReason," 29.

59. Bryant, "Poe's Ape of UnReason," 33.

60. Morrison, *Playing in the Dark*, xii.

CH12

Family Values / Critical Values: "The Chaos of Our Strongest Feelings" and African American Women's Writing of the 1890s

The erotic is the measure between the beginnings of our sense of self and the chaos of our strongest feelings.—AUDRE LORDE, "Uses of the Erotic: The Erotic as Power"

In her essay "The Occult of True Black Womanhood: Critical Demeanor and Black Feminist Studies," Ann duCille considers the manner in which the fortunes of black feminist literary studies have greatly increased in the recent academy.[1] DuCille is concerned foremost with the issue of who has come to "profit" most by the dramatic emergence of the field and aims to expose the racial politics insinuated with its increasing visibility. Just as duCille queries troubling features of what might be called the institutional management of the field, one might query leading approaches and paradigms elaborated in the critical terrain tagged as black women's writing of the 1890s, which has come to be recognized as one of the most significant and productive moments in African American women's writing in the United States. The point elaborated here is that what has come to stand as the foremost debate in the field, contesting whether or not this body of work measures up as radical racial discourse (particularly in comparison to the fictional writings of African American men), mistakes important features of the cultural situation under examination. These positions, in addition to sharing anachronistic premises, share an exorbitant conflating and analogizing of family and race, even as in many ways the constructs remain conceptually (and socially) opposed.

The paramount concern of the debate is the extent to which African American women's writing of the 1890s employs "the vehicle of the sentimental novel, producing heroines who celebrate domesticity, marriage, and motherhood, and who reflect a dominant white model of womanhood."[2] Critics dismissing this writing argue "variously that the sentimental novel is bad art, white art, bourgeois art—or all three—and that it is, moreover, incompatible with political protest fiction."[3] Critics undertaking the recuperation of these works, crediting the writers with innovative use of constricting narrative forms, investigate the "use [of] sentimental forms as a means of cultural intervention."[4] However, both positions mistake the intraracial dynamics of African American communities in the 1890s—the extent to which the fictional concerns of Frances Harper, Pauline Hopkins, and their contemporaries appear unique in terms of radical racial discourses and practices as well as the tradition of the African American novel at the close of the nineteenth century—and both misconstrue that family and race, despite their unflagging imprecisions, negotiate differently a paradox of self-recognition and yield different public logics.

Race draws an absolutely broad circle of abstracted acquaintance secured by the recognition of physical markers, whereas family draws a relatively close circle of supposedly actual acquaintance secured by the recognition of physical markers *as well as issues always involving more particular* discriminations. Respectively, race and family take physical embodiment as either the sole arbiter or one of several aspects of a powerful social purpose: Family would announce *more than nominal* access to those with potentially unlimited physical resemblances to one; conversely, race announces *nominal* access to those with what amounts to severely limited physical resemblances to one. Even though family and race codify dramatic social affiliations in the service of managing different types of bodies, their incommensurability is underscored by the issue of physical embodiment, obdurately tied to the logic of race and holding a somewhat inverted aspect in the logic of family. The terms of physical embodiment would be coextensive with the term of race, but not with family.

Nonetheless, despite their pronounced differences, the two do hold common interests, since their abstracted matters are also finally corporeal ones. The logics of family and race, in "guaranteeing" community, interrogate what is always potentially, if not always in fact, "irresponsible" individual practices and moments. As distinct net systems of (dis)affective management, family and race establish profoundly instrumental relations to sexual engagement, in effect, making "responsible" the always potentially irresponsible attractions of sexual arousal and its various outcomes.

The competing positions in the debate establish gender as the signal issue, critical positions best represented, respectively, by the work of Houston Baker (*Workings of the Spirit*) and Claudia Tate (*Domestic Allegories of Political Desire*). Even as the latter stance remains the more prevalent, as well as seems the more tenable, the interest here is not in resolving the dispute but, very differently, in examining some of the critical shortcomings proceeding from this misstep. In the critical debate subtended foremost by gender, one recognizes that, despite varying postures to the contrary, unexamined reiterations of normative domestic agendas are never fully in dispute, so that cultural capital steadfastly accrues, even if in never fully accounted ways, to the disciplinary construct of the family, which in significant measure secures the abjected cultural position of racial blackness, even as the most routine terms of African American advocacy in the 1890s attempt to resignify the construct.

Despite the terms of the debate, one finds that there is no less urgency or insistence on matters of family in writing by African American women or men in the 1890s, although narrative and representational emphases vary according to gender. Further, the irrefutable feature of the debate remains an unquestioned respect for the signifying powers of bourgeois domesticity, respect considerable enough to obscure the certainty that the dynamics of the bourgeois family do not summarily offer (even analytical) "liberation" to either gender, regardless of race—nonetheless, a mass African American population against which the normative bourgeois family is defined historically. What is ultimately diminished is the role of the domestic space as a mystified cathexis of civic and commercial management or regulation—not in spite of but precisely because of its affective character. The debate finally overlooks the family as a site of forced and virtually ubiquitous cultural value, value the African American racial elite of the 1890s forthrightly embraces, in order to make (extra)ordinary claims on it. What is obscured is that

> the nineteenth-century bourgeois family is one of the primary social forces that constructed subjectivity, especially as Americans confronted the social transformations brought about by industrialization and urbanization.... Because the family appears at once to be based on a natural relation among its members and yet depends crucially upon the production of its members, both in its domestic space and in the larger economy, the family serves a crucial function in naturalizing individuals' relations to ideology. Because the family's means of production seems so self-evidently *natural* and *biological*, the family is an especially attractive medium for

disguising ideological messages and thus contributing to the naturalization of new social relations.[5]

All the more puzzling, then, that the established debate comprehends focus on the family as principally a point of dismissal or praise, failing to credit, as fully as the matters under investigation call for, that negotiating the imperatives of the nuclear family amounts to negotiating the most traversed and insistent complex of modern Western and U.S. cultures. In the cultural doxa of the United States, the family, whatever else it may involve, signifies for virtually all those championing and deploying it an intense normalized cum respectable orientation and installation in the social, and its relays of financial, civic, psychic, and legal rewards.

The debate misses this point, never adequately acknowledging that African American writers and race leaders of the 1890s do not simply imagine themselves portraying and championing a vast African American collective but, as evident in one instance in the work of African American women writers, undertake their historically contingent version of championing racial blackness by idealizing a set of conditions that do not define the circumstances of the majority of African Americans. Race men and women able to signify themselves at the close of the nineteenth century in the exemplary terms eliciting "class-related sympathy and respect" from white advocates possess a measure of racial authenticity the majority of African Americans in the 1890s, residing outside those protocols, does not.[6] At the close of the nineteenth century, the fully representational African American demonstrates or embodies the potential of the majority of African Americans, a majority standing contradistinct. African American racial discourses of the 1890s reference a set of conditions that might be taken as representative of the majority of African Americans for whom they advocate only insofar as it provides an example for that majority to emulate or, at the very least, admire—the nuclear family and the cultural capital accruing to it being an integral part of the example. Unacknowledged in the debate, then, are the strikingly different sets of representational dynamics functioning around race in the era of Francis Harper and Pauline Hopkins, dynamics diametrical to those presiding at present in U.S. culture.

For the rhetorical and cultural force of a mass black population proves the unmistakable feature of African American racial representation only in the latter half of the twentieth century. Patent forms of mass representational power are unmistakably granted to, or grasped by, an African American population at large only well into the twentieth century, and reckoning the historical difference is significant. One might, for the sake of illustration, mark the two distinct historical configurations by the date 1954, the year *Brown v. Board of Education* ushered in a racial protest movement unmistakably dependent for its efficacy on the sheer numbers of African Americans in the United States. Only subsequent to this point in U.S. history does the rhetorical and cultural force of a mass black population prove in no way peripheral to national racial debates or gains in political, civil, and economic opportunities and cultural representation. There are, of course, precedents for effective mass mobilization in African American struggles in the United States before 1954, particularly in political intrigues of the 1930s, as the historian Nancy J. Weiss demonstrates in her important 1983 study *Farewell to the Party of Lincoln*.[7] Nevertheless, the civil rights movement of the 1950s and 1960s marks the codification of the representational power of a mass African American population. Very much on the contrary to the dynamics of the 1890s, present standards of racial authenticity and fidelity are set by a mass African American population, with middle- and upper-class African Americans risking being racially dismissed for their cultural differences and proving their racial authenticity routinely in terms set by or in reference to the differently situated cultural majority.

Hazel Carby, one of the earliest literary critics openly reconsidering African American women's writing of the 1890s, acknowledges this complex historical situation in *Reconstructing Womanhood: The Emergence of the Afro-American Woman Novelist*: "The relation of the black intellectual elite to the majority of blacks changed drastically as a result of the migration north of Southern blacks. Before World War I, the overwhelming majority of blacks were in the South, at a vast physical and metaphorical distance from those intellectuals who represented the interests of the race. After the war, black intellectuals had to confront the black masses on the streets of their cities and responded in a variety of ways."[8] Differently stated, no racial group is a monolith, and the black leadership at the turn of the century proceeds to great lengths to remind both their white advocates and adversaries of this fact, a point that cannot be overstated. In the 1890s, with national and cultural circumstances radically different from those of the latter half of the twentieth century, the masses of African Americans and their linguistic and cultural preferences are resoundingly disqualified as either the exemplum for racial representation or as the measure of racial authenticity. What African American cultural elites and their white advocates share and "were eager to foster, if only through verbal encouragement, [was] *individual* Black mobility, for it not only gave credibility to their own social ideals, but suggested that the race problem could be reduced to a matter of individuals."[9]

Similarly, and more recently, Carla Peterson observes in *"Doers of the Word": African-American Women Speakers and Writers in the North (1830–1880)*:

> One important consequence of Reconstruction for the black community was a deepening of class and gender divisions that had already made themselves felt before the Civil War. Indeed, the postbellum period witnessed the slow emergence of a new class structure and sensibility that separated the mass of common laborers from a growing black professional and business class. This class was not always able to comprehend the labor issues facing black workers and felt at times that the political and social interests of the two groups no longer necessarily coincided. Moreover, within this nascent bourgeoisie black women found themselves increasingly pressured toward privatization in the domestic sphere, and their presence in the ongoing public work of racial uplift often unwelcome.[10]

The late nineteenth century is a period in which the most influential discourses championing racial blackness are invested in overtly acknowledging and grooming "authenticating" differences within the African American population, differences constituted in large part through the cultural capital of the nuclear family.

Several historians have also outlined these matters. The historian Kevin Gaines in his important study *Uplifting the Race* also describes what might be called the intraracial differential of turn-of-the-century African American advocacy. Gaines documents "black bourgeois and nationalist ideologies that equated race progress with male dominance and Victorian ideals of sexual difference in both political and domestic life."[11] He documents strategies of racial leadership in which "black elites seize upon the status of the family and moral and cultural distinctions (with their inevitable radical overtones) between themselves and the black masses to affirm the class differences among African Americans that racist whites were loath to acknowledge."[12] This style of leadership, Gaines argues, was taken to the point at which "elite blacks' use of uplift ideology to forge a sense of personal worth and dignity in an anti-black society pointed to intraracial division along class lines virtually as an end in itself, as a sign of race progress."[13] Gaines's project demonstrates that attentions given the bourgeois entanglements of family cannot be considered exclusively, or even primarily, as if those entanglements merely configure a boundary demarcating separate gendered imaginaries, rather than an important means for "the articulation of a positive racial identity for African Americans [or, in other words,] a divisive struggle whose contradictions often went unnoticed in favor of the unifying, uplifting rhetoric of self-help and solidarity."[14] An important challenge for race men and women in the 1890s and "racial uplift ideology ... [is a] quest for the authentic, or 'positive' black middle-class subject," a challenge not so nearly obtaining in the most prevalent protocols of African American racial representation in the latter twentieth century.[15]

In his 1981 article, "A Politics of Limited Options: Northern Black Politics and the Problems of Change and Continuity in Race Relations Historiography," the historian David A. Gerber describes the scope of African American political advancement in the 1890s, as well as the integral role of class in fixing its limitations. Gerber states that, groomed by the exigencies of the political mechanisms of their day, African American leaders "were less interested in race solidarity, institutionalized self-help, and other group-oriented values and goals ... than in equality before the law and the gradual integration of talented, worthy individual Blacks into the bourgeois, capitalist, American mainstream."[16] From their positions of advocacy, "the racial duties of ambitious, striving Blacks who attained upward mobility in this climate lay not so much in establishing concrete bonds of solidarity with the masses of Blacks as in playing the role of 'representative men'—role models of moral excellence and practical achievement who would inspire young Blacks to go forth and do likewise."[17] By enumerating dimensions of the local-machine operation around which Republican and Democratic party politics were organized, as well as the parameters within which black political agents were allowed to operate in these organizations, Gerber clarifies the necessity of categorically dismissing assumptions that public representations of African American populations, interests, and culture were (or even could be) singular and undifferentiated. In the cultural climate of the late nineteenth century, "social mobility was not a *consequence* of but a *prerequisite* for Black patronage, which to begin with was concentrated among the educated and affluent."[18]

The question of who could and should "speak for the race" is a radically different one from who, in point of fact, constitutes the African American population in the 1890s, just as the question of what could and should be spoken in the name of the race is vastly different from the variety of expressive and cultural forms African Americans in point of fact embrace. Gerber's anatomization of the organized political culture of the period bears quoting at length:

> To encourage the systemization of Black politics to facilitate segregated campaigns and large voter turn-outs among Blacks, and to preserve acceptable, though not necessarily static, racial boundaries, white party leaders often chose a few dependable, higher status Black liaison agents, who were accountable to the party, not to the masses of Black voters.

Often these agents were, like Cincinnati's William Parham, Chicago's John Jones, Cleveland's John P. Green, or Detroit's Robert Pelham, businessmen, professionals, artisans, or domestic servants who, in the days before the development of a race consumer market in the northern ghettos, based their livelihoods entirely on white economic patronage. This economic dependence combined with social exclusivity and bourgeois life styles, expectations, and aspirations to make them the natural allies of the whites they served, but limited their ability to create an independent power base among their own people.[19]

With these remarks in mind, it bears repeating that the established debate proceeds mistakenly as though the work of African American women writers of the 1890s simply aspires, successfully or unsuccessfully, to untroubled racial representation.

Neither easily nor neatly translated across the barrier of 1954 are cultural circumstances in which "black elites [in general, not just African American women writers] tried to gain recognition of *their* humanity by ranking themselves at the top of an evolutionary hierarchy within the race based upon bourgeois morality."[20] Even though alterations in African American cultural life make the "uplift" challenge of a century ago appear suspect, these discrepancies must be closely accounted in theorizing textual productions of the era.

Further still, beyond its points of anachronism, the established debate does not acknowledge the oppositions distinguishing the logics of family and race. The chimerical figure of untroubled racial representation insinuated in the debate rests on an enduring collusion of the constructs of family and race and, because these oppositions are, in fact, stark (and therefore the misstep pronounced) they bear clarifying at some length. As already suggested, the logic of the family, as a biological relation, marks and claims a significantly circumscribed gene pool, whereas the logic of race does not. Ideally, the managerial, or interpellative, work of family depends on relays of affective, intimate knowledges, while this is precisely the type of work, by definition, race would foreclose across the different bodies it maps. Coveting a very different, very broad perspective opposed to the logic of family, race is, rather, "*a concept which signifies and symbolizes social conflicts and interests by referring to different types of* human bodies."[21] The logic of the nuclear family is also premised on the certainty of different types of human bodies—male and female, immature and mature—however, with the intent to produce unity across the differences it highlights.

The logic of race, on the contrary, would signify and substantiate conflict across difference. Family wants to yield affective bonds premised foremost on expectations of in-group dissimilarity, and race wants to yield disaffective conflicts premised foremost on expectations of in-group similarity. The stability of both are also contradistinct, since the nuclear family approaches dissolution or dispersal when its different types of human bodies prove too similar, whereas race never remotely seems to risk dissolution regardless of the mutable conditions of the different types of bodies it regulates. Even as they would seem to collude as a point of identity, family and race are points of reference against which to measure individual and group identity in deeply opposed ways.

Particularly as metaphors credited on biological terms, family and race remain starkly incommensurate. Genetic variation within racial groups is often larger than variation between racial groups, a circumstance elegantly rehearsed, for example, in scientific and post-structuralist terms by Anthony Appiah in his study *In My Father's House: Africa in the Philosophy of Culture*.[22] Because the nuclear family proves a superintendent—but provisional—articulation of a gene pool, it is fundamentally incongruent with race, a supposed articulation of a gene pool so vast it cannot hold up under scrutiny as a genetically based reality. Put differently, the phenotypical—rather than genotypical—traits signifying race correspond to genetic information incidental to the biological well-being of human organisms, particularly in comparison to genetic information regulating metabolism or hormonal cycles, for instance, or protecting one from or predisposing one to certain diseases. Race, in short, is not a genetically encoded or physical proposition significant to the human organism. Race fails to be meaningful as a biological premise, and only succeeds at being a meaningful social premise under the most contrived and violent of conditions. Family and race, as concepts or principles, never easily have coincided—only by remarkable fiat—and one of the chief efficacies of the collusion of family and race stands as the masking of the fiat. Following again the insights of John Carlos Rowe in *At Emerson's Tomb: The Politics of Classic American Literature*, racialization in the history of the United States "reminds us that such formal division only arbitrarily divides a community in which family relations are already fundamentally miscegenated. This may well be why Linda [Brent]'s choice of Sands as father of her children is so significant, not only for its practical consequences but also for the visibility it gives to the otherwise hidden, yet tacitly acknowledged, interracial relations of the antebellum South."[23] For a variety of reasons the conceptual trouble of race can be mapped against the conceptual trouble of family, but never in ways finally suggesting a basic commensurability or congruence.

If race and family are taken to conflate at a point of supposed, fixed identity, thus passing off what is, in effect, a point of forced communication as a point of correspondence, then the obfuscatory work of both, particularly in collusion, is phenomenal. What is obscured is that, rather than representing genotypical or phenotypical uniformity, social or class status, family relations, innate intelligence or criminality, group affinity, cultural singularity, or whatever traits one might wish to place upon it, race merely represents in the most attenuated, diffuse, and mystified of forms—to borrow insights from the economic historian Immanuel Wallerstein—"sizeable groups of people to whom [are] reserved certain occupational/economic roles in relation to other such groups living in geographic proximity."[24] Race marks as well sizeable groups for certain psychological, moral, and recreational roles or, at least, characterizations, and what African American racial advocacy of the 1890s fully recognizes and counts on are characterizations placing the majority of African Americans askance of the privileged site of the nuclear family. The established debate in large part forecloses these issues.

Championing the novels of Frances Harper and her contemporaries, Claudia Tate positions her project in *Domestic Allegories of Political Desire* as a fundamentally historical one, aimed at drawing aside contemporary perspectives on "the novels' first readership" in order "to discern the efficacy of the domestic genre for expressing the social desire and despair, the personal and political dreams and frustrations of late-nineteenth-century black people."[25] Tate understands "that marriage is a viable medium for developing the self, the Other, and the community" and, to this end, sets out to prove that the discursive strategies of these writers constitute an "interior political matrix permit[ting] the prosperous marriage story to move forward to its consummation, while implicitly constructing an external, fictive world in which marriage as the sign of private prosperity is also the sign of civil justice."[26] Tate clarifies that she writes in respect of a "middle-class eroticism" and "black middle-class values," invoking at one point the fictional, adult Huxtables of NBC's long-running 1980s *The Cosby Show*.[27] Yet the project never clarifies the ways in which a "middle-class eroticism" and "black middle-class values" are tied necessarily to collective racial liberation in the 1890s or at present.

Tate does not interrogate marriage as an arbitrary mechanism with functions beyond its appearance as a normative human situation. Instead, the domestic spaces of bourgeois marriage are posed as untroubled registers of collective African American racial interest. Tate writes: "Marriage in these novels serves the interest of racial uplift by constructing it as an aggregate of happy, enterprising conjugal units. For this society, 'the household, not the individual, is the unit of the State.' By contrast, modern desire seems motivated by isolated self-interest rather than governed by group interests, social institutions, or attendant conduct codes."[28] Tate never questions as, for instance, Saidiya Hartman does in *Scenes of Subjection: Terror, Slavery, and Self-Making in Nineteenth-Century America*, ideological machinations grooming such a viewpoint in the late nineteenth century. Hartman traces the surreptitious bonds of obligation forged through public discourses of proper conduct, morality, and the gratifying responsibilities of work fostered for a freed African American population in order to supplant (in a prime Foucauldian sense) the overt coercions of legal enslavement. When approaching the construct of the family, Hartman is concerned with "the reach of the law and, in particular, the acquiescence of the law to sentiment, affinity, and natural distinctions."[29] This line of thought highlights much of the trouble with the premise that the social project of marriage simply "express[es] the social desire and despair, the personal and political dreams and frustrations of late-nineteenth-century black people."[30] Indeed, insofar as desire remains in question, one might ask: to what extent does marriage and its "middle-class eroticism" and "black middle-class values" effect evacuations or colonizations of desire rather than coincide with those vicissitudes?

Baker's position on the other side of the debate seems more curious. His project is more diffuse. *Workings of the Spirit* is less systematic than *Domestic Allegories of Political Desire*; Baker's elaborations are as generally influenced by historical, generic, or disciplinary paradigms as Tate's are closely circumscribed by them. Baker situates *Workings of the Spirit* as the third installment of a trilogy, the first two parts of which "develop an autobiographical sounding of Afro-American expressive culture predicated on ... 'spirit work.'"[31] *Workings of the Spirit* extends this investigation to the specifics of African American women's expressive culture and proceeds by considering the extent to which African American women's expressive culture adequately demonstrates "allegiance or obligation to the field of Afro-American particulars."[32] It is on this score that African American women's writing of the 1890s proves of interest to Baker since, in contrast to the fictional, autobiographical, and anthropological writings of Zora Neale Hurston, or the drama of Ntozake Shange, for example, writing of the 1890s fails in these obligations. Baker establishes the poles of betrayal and fidelity in class or, more particularly, antibourgeois terms, also rendered in geographic terms. He states that "a nineteenth-century black woman's vernacular southern culture in the heroism of its economic survival, and then in the resonances of its quilts, gardens, conjuration, supper-getting-ready songs, churched melodies, woven baskets of Charleston wharves, and culinary magnificence, is a *great absence* in the texts of the escaped northern daughters *as authors*."[33] Referring in particular to Pauline Hopkins's *Contending Forces*, Baker proposes: "The suppression of southern horror and the transmutation of patriarchal seduction into a new, classical species of intelligent colored life are, finally, in the service of the cultivation of *an approving white public opinion*."[34] Baker dismisses the type of writing represented by Hopkins as "a propaganda topos for a progressive historical reading of African American life in America."[35]

The dismissal is odd, however, because, as in Tate's work, the family remains a poorly examined but pronounced proposition. More particularly, the dismissal is odd because it is inconsistent with the use of domestic constructs as figures of racial discourse in earlier portions of the trilogy. The initial installment, *Modernism and the Harlem Renaissance*, concludes in part as follows: "My tale, then, to say again what I have said, is of a complex field of sounding strategies in Afro-America that are part of a family. The family's history always—no matter how it is revised, purified, distorted, or emended—begins in an economics of slavery."[36] Baker highlights these observations with a composite of four photographs, featuring his father and father-in-law, wife and son, as well as grandparents and brothers. In other words, the initial terms of the trilogy posit the U.S. national collective of African Americans as a "family," a proposition underscored—and as certainly undermined—by discursive and graphic references to any particular family. Baker's project, like Tate's, provides no sense that domestic constructs remain desperately embroiled in the paradox of race, rather than distantly or symmetrically reflecting the paradox. No principle emerges to confirm domestic constructs as the necessary complement of racial arrangements—affective or disaffective. On the other hand, Angela Davis in *Blues Legacies and Black Feminism*, also referencing turn-of-the-century U.S. culture, outlines the immense social powers articulated meticulously through the raveling imbrications of family, race, gender, and sexuality. Davis, when she considers the sentiments of early mass-mediated music, understands the family, rather than a template for race, as a site of highly focused and particularly misogynist management coimplicated with race: "The expression of socially unfulfilled dreams in the language and imagery of sexual love is, of course, not peculiar to the African-American experience.... In the context of the consolidation of industrial capitalism, the sphere of personal love and domestic life in mainstream American culture came to be increasingly idealized as the arena in which happiness was sought. This held a special significance for women, since love and domesticity were supposed to constitute the outermost limits of their lives. Full membership in the public community was the exclusive domain of men."[37] This line of thought highlights much of the trouble with Baker's implicit premise that domestic images and concepts might patently bolster one type of racial discourse or project and not another, particularly those marked by differing attentions to gender. In brief, in impulses to racial annunciation, what claim to domestic arrangements does either gender necessarily bear?

As these competing positions of the debate imply, the signal issue is libidinal, but the issue is foreclosed in large part by the missteps of the debate that hypostatize only two positions for racially black bodies in the historical movement from enslavement to emancipation. African American bodies are figured "as either possessed property or as an object of [the most conventional] romantic possession."[38] This very neat resolution to ultimately libidinal questions is secured in large part by the collusion uniting family and race, the extreme analogy confusing the far from complete correspondence of the two as libidinal complexes. The philosopher Naomi Zack writes: "Individuals who are designated black have the ability, through the mechanism of their heterosexuality, to destroy the white identity of families, and because race of kin determines race of individuals, to destroy the white identity of the relatives of their descendants. Thus the asymmetrical kinship system of racial inheritance in the United States... defines black people as intrinsically threatening and dangerous to white families" and (less urgently) vice versa.[39] Most ascertainably tracked through family, race is like the family, guaranteed through the colonization of libidinal desires and the management of sexual congress. That is, race is insinuated in the notion of the family in as ineluctably physical a manner as possible—or, more carefully put, in the most pointedly physical manner inviting returns to its exorbitant physicality ad infinitum.

In short, even though the difficulties of characterizing them as analogous are readily apparent, the logics of family and race do hold crucial investments in common and, for many, it is their shared libidinal interests that effectively conflate the two. The logics of family and race idealize sexual congress from which *jouissance* is rationalized and economized strictly (or even potentially to a point of nullification). Both foreclose open-ended desire in order to supervise closely regulated or reserved systems of sexual expenditure—systems operating as fundamentally distinct technologies of self-identification; yet the problems of these subjectivizing technologies as well as their potentially violent cross-purposes inhere in the fact that no necessary relation exists between orgasm, procreation, or any civic configuration that would propose ineluctable alignments. Rather than sexual engagement, orgasm, and procreation holding inflexible relations to one another, the necessity of any such relations resides always in the demands of subjectivizing protocols aiming to align the finally unarbitrated but signal matters on which the nuclear family and race so strictly depend.

What must be kept in mind is that to grant unquestioned credence to either family or race in this way amounts to abiding perhaps too easily by hegemonic provisos, as well as failing to interrogate fully some of the most subtle measures of force on which those provisos rely. In these provisos, the terms of family and race are so linked, so intertwined, that failure to interrogate fully one equals in many ways failure to interrogate fully the other. There can be nothing intrinsically to disqualify any group from a position of cultural protest by engaging so fundamental a construct as the family and, also, there can be nothing intrinsically to celebrate in any group employing the construct of the family as a platform for social protest, nuanced or unnuanced. (The second position is—to the point of distraction—a deeply entrenched posture in U.S. culture.) Like race, the family is a calculus, a site of subjection, and never a discrete social artifact to be either engaged or foreclosed. The family, like race, is a forced site of cultural value. As dysfunctional, bankrupt, or unreliable as any number of actual families within Western modernity might be, the institution, like racialization, nonetheless guarantees vital elements of social and civic order.

Significantly, however, the self-shattering enticement of sexual engagement, with its risks and rewards of jouissance, draws one into indulgences that are never fully civic. Civic protocols resting on the libidinal conscript it for ends always at some point frustrated, distressed, by the illogically circular demands ad infinitum of the practices in question. The extremity of this quandary is reflected in the routinely acknowledged complexities of the Freudian family romance with its inevitable generation of traumas and neuroses. Indicated by the arduous path of "normal" development, the fraught management of sexual energies within the family yields, to follow Freud, a spectacular array of problems more so than any neat solution or resolution to the crisis of management. What is more, the fretful set of negotiations undertaken through the paradigm of the family the competing paradigm of race frets even further, because the transmissions of phenotypical traits on which the viability of race depends can only be effected through the mechanism of heterosexual procreative sex (or its technological correlates), which, coincidently, is the paramount formulation the nuclear family acclaims by superintending. Simply stated, as the logics of family and race struggle to codify continually what they represent as natural, it is important to acknowledge that the struggle contradicts any reported claims of the inevitability or soundness of their protocols.

It is imperative to recognize that, while the nuclear family stands as the routinely accepted site for the proper management of all libidinal quandaries, the recognition, materiality, and certainty of race depends on attempts to guarantee the transmission and stability, from generation to generation, of a set of dangerously unstable phenotypical traits: the darkness or lightness of skins, the textures of hair, the shapes of eyes, noses, cheekbones, buttocks, and so on. Family and race forge separate but occasionally isomorphic prohibitions on the discharge of sexual energy. Insofar as the family attempts to represent fully ordered and disciplined libidinal energies, it attempts a representational gesture, just as does race (and in concert with race) that, in fact, it never can wholly or successfully match to lived or psychic experience.

The insights of the philosopher Naomi Zack highlight the powerful tensions and misalignments of the project family and race set for themselves, since historically in the United States, the ascertainable intrusion of African American phenotypes onto the body of a white family member severs that member from the family on the terms of radical dissimilarity, which are, nevertheless, exactly the terms the configuration of the family acclaims to manage so rightly and successfully. Moreover, the severance of the reracialized person from the former family is so pronounced that it is not only traceable materially but temporally as well, as if the infiltration were accountable not only in physical terms but in the even more distressing recklessness of the libidinal. The crisis is managed as if the exposed structures of desire require an extended quarantine to safeguard further the hegemonic racial whiteness placed emphatically and momentarily in peril. The reconstitution of the identity of the descendants of the many reckless white individuals susceptible to these structures of desire effects one version of quarantine. Easily, the libidinal can respect too fully, rather than forego, the logically circular, or nonrational, demands of sexual engagement, which reportedly are so well mastered by sedimented protocols.

This point is evident especially within the exceptional legal and extralegal licenses held by those persons inhabiting the most fully sovereign white male relations to family and race in the history of the United States. The logical, legal, and, compoundingly, libidinal confusion produce historical circumstances in which "through successive generations, a visible, albeit culturally inauthentic, 'whiteness' was reproduced from 'black' female bodies."[40] The extensive trouble accruing to the broad licenses of these individuals substantiates, this is to say, the unruliness of libidinal impulses (especially when claimed to be strictly managed). These circumstances witness the transfiguration of the nonrational into the irrational. They witness that the unarbitrated relations of sexual engagement, orgasm, and procreation, in fact, routinely disrupt the material and rational bases of both family and race. Nonetheless, even as they cannot adequately manage the rationalizing, affective, or speculative exigencies pressed upon them, family and race stand as social mechanisms of the very highest priority—as a consequence of the orderliness, even propriety, they appear to represent despite all indications to the contrary.

Competing transgressions yield similar exposures. "Free African Americans," writes the historian Martha Hodes in her study *White Women, Black Men: Illicit Sex in the Nineteenth-Century South*, "were troublesome to white Southerners throughout the antebellum era, but the children of white women and black men carried in their identity the added burden of displaying defiance not only of race and status but also of the rules of patriarchy: whether with direct intention or not, white women had defied white men, and black men had defied white men."[41] One immediately understands from Hode's observations how family and race resoundingly articulate social power. To be sure, one understands further that these overly simple terms of extraordinary authority—extralegal and, especially, legal—insinuated in these circumstances are allegedly to be never so crudely or obdurately settled within the ken of the rational, the justifiable, the democratic. Hode's observations underscore the extraordinarily deep irrationalities masked in both erudite and common doxas of the European Enlightenment, or Age of Reason, and its gargantuan, international experiment named the United States.

Summarily stated, in ways that a simple gender binarism does not allow one to recognize, the circumstances under which race holds sway as a violent premise regiments, in a prime Foucauldian sense, the most seductive of forces. In order to designate, efficiently, "sizeable groups of people to . . . certain occupational/economic roles in relation to other such groups living in geographic proximity," sexual expenditure and its desires must be reimagined, if not recuperated, through very particular channels. The logics of family and race, in their normalizing of desire, produce public knowledges that are never as secure as they seem, for their attempts often fail conspicuously. Arising from the nonrational knowledge and the appeals of orgasm, potential crisis threatens every sexual arousal. Sexual congress and the never necessarily consequent domestic/racial relations it ideally would underpin are marshaled to resolve a recurring libidinal crisis never managing to expend itself fully as a sparing system of psychic and cultural negotiation. The logics of family and race propose, or attempt to make desirable, the capacities for a strict orderliness in what is an impulse that more or less gainsays all meticulous ordering of the self.

Leo Bersani's interrogations of Freudian theories of sexuality in *The Freudian Body* are provocative in considering this point: since the self-shattering experience of sexual engagement is repeatedly sought out by the very self ineluctably shattered by the engagement, sexuality rests askance all forms of socialization, even so fundamental, rudimentary, and enabling a proposition as the individual, much less the more abstracted notions of family or race. In Bersani's view, "Freud subverts views of pleasure as inherently social by suggesting that even the most sublimated forms of pleasure are ontologically grounded in a *jouissance* at once solipsistic and masochistic, a *jouissance* which isolates the human subject in a socially and epistemologically 'useless,' but infinitely seductive, repetition."[42] All indications are that sexual engagement and orgasm in their seductiveness, bearing "the traces of a prelinguistic shattering of the human subject," distress the most persistent structures: psychic, linguistic, aesthetic or, as fully, familial, or racial.[43] Sexual pleasure and orgasm recurringly present themselves as incompatible with the very proposition of the individual—to say nothing of the considerably more abstracted paradigms and protocols that would subject and array the propitious individual. Sexuality, in its pleasurable and unruly recklessness, distresses and may necessarily abrogate, even if only momentarily, all formalities to which it would be bound. Nonetheless, "sexuality is an optimum sphere for social regulation, because it constitutes a point of intersection between the individual and the social body which thereby also provides a [potential] site for the resolidification of individual and social investments, with the currency of pleasure as lubricant."[44]

It is not surprising that race persists pointedly and invidiously in a culture in which (like many others) virtually everyone seems intent on desiring to be or desiring a parent. In this calculus, one discovers significant responsibility in duties posed almost entirely in affective terms. This particular characterization of the libidinal makes exorbitant, in a Foucauldian sense, the realm of responsibility and work and (as quarantines imply, for example) "reduces work to a travesty of necessities, a duty by which we earn bread or oblivion for ourselves and those we love."[45] The shared aim of family and race is to organize strictly, to rationalize, what the cultural critic and commentator Audre Lorde nonetheless describes in the essay "The Uses of the Erotic" as "our deepest and nonrational knowledge."[46] In the frustrated rationality of this scheme, the erotic, because always an excess of duty, remains an always haunting formulation. Over against these very tightly organized and ever-receding logics, Lorde's acclamation of the erotic as "the measure between the beginnings of our sense of self and the chaos of our strongest feelings" revises notions of responsibility so that it is not nearly so propitious. Lorde suggests that, unlike confrontations with race and family, sexual arousal amounts to confronting compelling matters one never fully understands in any entirely rationalized sense.

And, ultimately, the corporeal basis of this nonrationality cannot be overlooked, for as the cultural critic Elaine Scarry's concept of "analogical verification (or substantiation)" reminds one, the acuteness of corporeal sensation is always an important ideological concern. Analogical verification (or substantiation) is most evident, in Scarry's view, at "particular moments when there is within a society a crisis of belief... [so that] the sheer material factualness of the human body will be borrowed to lend that cultural construct the aura of 'realness' and 'certainty'"; in the case of torture, for example, "the physical pain [of the victim] is so incontestably real that it seems to confer its quality of 'incontestable reality' on the power that has brought it into being."[47] Pain, as anatomized by Scarry, is a form of compelling, involuntary withdrawal from the social landscape, "a state that has at its center the single, overwhelming discrepancy between an increasingly palpable body and an increasingly substanceless world."[48] Sexual arousal and orgasm, although in different ways, approximate such an individual withdrawal and state and, what is more, are socially questionable in ways not applicable to the condition of pain. Because they impose an "overwhelming [and exploitable] discrepancy" between the palpabilities of the body and its firm symbolic obligations, the libidinal is a virtually matchless cultural resource to be claimed. The libidinal is particularly to be claimed in the less-than-tidy U.S. circumstances in which "race, sex, and gender have been inextricably linked first through a system of slavery that placed white men in control of the productive labor of black men and the productive and reproductive labor of both black and white women, and then nationally through an economic and political system and a cultural ideology that established a fundamental racist and sexist hierarchy of privilege and oppression."[49] Regardless of how similar or different the engagements, if one might lose oneself in the physical impress of pain, one might lose oneself in the physical impress of sexual arousal and orgasm. Family and race, regardless of their pronounced differences, both would guarantee community by interrogating what is always potentially, if not always in fact, irresponsible individual practices and moments. Family and race, to their own consternation, depend decidedly on the disorderly interests of sexual arousal and orgasm.

Insofar as questions of the bourgeois nuclear family prove central to the work of African American women writers of the 1890s, gender divisions far from define the dynamic under examination. Given the characterization of the 1890s set out by the debate, it is not clear how one considers the equally salient (though differently situated) presence of sentimental devices, tragic mulattas and mulattoes, and bourgeois codes of morality operating in the work of African American male writers of this time—Charles Chesnutt and Sutton Griggs perhaps providing the most significant examples. Moreover, there is in the fiction of an African American racial and literary vanguard of the 1890s a set of anxieties unmistakably isomorphic with many of the anxieties of, say, William Dean Howells's *The Rise of Silas Lapham*. Whether authored by men or women, what African American fiction of this period shares across gender (and racial) lines is an overt investment in the ordered nuclear family as well as the cultural capital accruing to that investment.

What Audre Lorde's insights suggest in terms of these questions, and with a decidedly different anachronistic aspect, might be restated as follows: The family and its structures do not strictly exhaust the possibilities of affective arrangements, racial, gendered, sexual, economic, or any set of arrangements one might imagine or pursue; as clearly, race and its structures do not consume the possibilities of affective arrangements, familial arrangements, gendered, sexual, or economic arrangements. These knowledges arrive recklessly, to quote Scarry again, by drawing a "single, overwhelming discrepancy between an increasingly palpable body and an increasingly substanceless [social/civic] world."[50] The finally corporeal interests of family and race diminish otherwise firm protocols and otherwise firm purposes, because in the form of the less public knowledges Lorde alludes to, they confirm that "the erotic is not a question only of what we do; it is a question of how acutely and fully we can feel in the doing."[51]

These dynamics yield a type of chaos that, as one can imagine, remains readily apparent in African American women's intellectual culture of the 1890s. However, the established debate engages this chaos only in deference to "a host of discursive inductions through which the African American body historically became signifiable within the bounds of a decidedly bourgeois humanism governed by the bodily integrity of sexual difference."[52] Neither pole of the established debate aims to uncover in the construct of the family the fraudulent nature of race as a representational category, and the danger to the field amounts to misconstruing the circumstances in which African American sexuality is "one of the most tangible domains in which emancipation was acted upon and through which its meanings were expressed. Sovereignty in sexual matters marked an important divide between life during slavery and life after emancipation."[53] Moreover, if race and family amount to sometimes competing, sometimes conflated sets of prohibitions on the discharge of sexual energy, then by what means, given the specific historical watershed of the 1890s, do these prohibitions fuse purposefully with the strict protocols of capitalist consumption? What relations do these sets of prohibitions on the discharge of sexual energy bear to a national culture fully engaged in forging in the 1890s the social and psychic relations of incipient consumer capitalism, a sociocultural order in which African American participation becomes accordingly a keynote of racial advocacy? There are a host of questions indicating that, in all likelihood, it may be rewarding not to order the chaos of African American women's writing of the 1890s precipitously.

NOTES

1. Ann duCille, "The Occult of True Black Womanhood: Critical Demeanor and Black Feminist Studies," *Signs* 19, no. 3 (1994): 591.

2. Kate McCullough, *Regions of Identity: The Construction of America in Women's Fiction, 1885–1914* (Stanford, CA: Stanford University Press, 1999), 23.

3. McCullough, *Regions of Identity*, 23.

4. McCullough, *Regions of Identity*, 24.

5. John C. Rowe, *At Emerson's Tomb: The Politics of Classic American Literature* (New York: Columbia University Press, 1997), 67.

6. David A. Gerber, "A Politics of Limited Options: Northern Black Politics and the Problem of Change and Continuity in Race Relations Historiography," *Journal of Social History* 14, no. 2 (winter 1980): 241.

7. Nancy J. Weiss, *Farewell to the Party of Lincoln: Black Politics in the Age of FDR* (Princeton, NJ: Princeton University Press, 1983).

8. Hazel V. Carby, *Reconstructing Womanhood: The Emergence of the Afro-American Woman Novelist* (New York: Oxford University Press, 1987), 166.

9. Gerber, "A Politics of Limited Options," 241, emphasis in original.

10. Carla L. Peterson, *"Doers of the Word": African-American Women Speakers and Writers in the North (1830–1880)* (New Brunswick, NJ: Rutgers University Press, 1998), 198.

11. Kevin K. Gaines, *Uplifting the Race: Black Leadership, Politics, and Culture in the Twentieth Century* (Chapel Hill: University of North Carolina Press, 1996), xviii.

12. Gaines, *Uplifting the Race*, 11.

13. Gaines, *Uplifting the Race*, 21.

14. Gaines, *Uplifting the Race*, 4.

15. Gaines, *Uplifting the Race*, xvii.

16. Gerber, "A Politics of Limited Options," 241.

17. Gerber, "A Politics of Limited Options," 241.

18. Gerber, "A Politics of Limited Options," 241, emphasis in original.

19. Gerber, "A Politics of Limited Options," 239.

20. Gaines, *Uplifting the Race*, 75, emphasis in original.

21. Michael Omi and Howard Winant, *Racial Formation in the United States: From the 1960s to the 1990s* (New York: Routledge, 1994), 55, emphasis in original.

22. Kwame Anthony Appiah, *In My Father's House: Africa in the Philosophy of Culture* (New York: Oxford University Press, 1993), 34–37.

23. Rowe, *At Emerson's Tomb*, 142.

24. Immanuel M. Wallerstein, *Historical Capitalism: With Capitalist Civilization* (London: Verso, 1995), 76.

25. Claudia Tate, *Domestic Allegories of Political Desire: The Black Heroine's Text at the Turn of the Century* (New York: Oxford University Press, 1996), 19.

26. Tate, *Domestic Allegories of Political Desire*, 77, 9.

27. Tate, *Domestic Allegories of Political Desire*, 106.

28. Tate, *Domestic Allegories of Political Desire*, 77.

29. Saidiya V. Hartman, *Scenes of Subjection: Terror, Slavery, and Self-Making in Nineteenth-Century America* (New York: Oxford University Press, 1997), 175.

30. Tate, *Domestic Allegories of Political Desire*, 19.

31. Houston A. Baker, *Workings of the Spirit: The Poetics of Afro-American Women's Writing* (Chicago: University of Chicago Press, 1991), 2.

32. Baker, *Workings of the Spirit*, 64.

33. Baker, *Workings of the Spirit*, 30.

34. Baker, *Workings of the Spirit*, 26.

35. Baker, *Workings of the Spirit*, 26.

36. Houston A. Baker, *Modernism and the Harlem Renaissance* (Chicago: University of Chicago Press, 1987), 104–5.

37. Angela Y. Davis, *Blues Legacies and Black Feminism: Gertrude "Ma" Rainey, Bessie Smith, and Billie Holiday* (New York: Pantheon, 1998), 9–10.

38. Brian Carr, "At the Thresholds of the 'Human': Race, Psychoanalysis, and the Replication of Imperial Memory," *Cultural Critique* 39 (spring 1998): 136.

39. Naomi Zack, *Race and Mixed Race* (Philadelphia: Temple University Press, 1993), 27.

40. Elaine K. Ginsberg, *Passing and the Fictions of Identity* (Durham, NC: Duke University Press, 1996), 5.

41. Martha Hodes, *White Women, Black Men: Illicit Sex in the Nineteenth-Century South* (New Haven, CT: Yale University Press, 1999), 120.

42. Leo Bersani, *The Freudian Body: Psychoanalysis and Art* (New York: Columbia University Press, 1986), 90.

43. Bersani, *The Freudian Body*, 107.

44. Linda Singer, *Erotic Welfare: Sexual Theory and Politics in the Age of Epidemic* (New York: Routledge, 1993), 76.

45. Audre Lorde, "Uses of the Erotic: The Erotic as Power" (Tucson, AZ: Kore, 2000), 55.

46. Lorde, "Uses of the Erotic," 53.

47. Elaine Scarry, *The Body in Pain: The Making and Unmaking of the World* (New York: Oxford University Press, 1985), 14, 27.

48. Scarry, *The Body in Pain*, 30.

49. Ginsberg, *Passing and the Fictions of Identity*, 5.

50. Scarry, *The Body in Pain*, 30.

51. Lorde, "Uses of the Erotic," 54.

52. Carr, "At the Thresholds of the 'Human,'" 136.

53. Davis, *Blues Legacies and Black Feminism*, 4.

CH13

Mercantilism, U.S. Federalism, and the Market within Reason:
The "People" and the Conceptual Impossibility of Racial Blackness
(2006)

> About 1730 in Bristol it was estimated that on a fortunate voyage the profit on a cargo of about 270 slaves reached £7,000 or £8,000, exclusive of the returns from ivory. In the same year the net return from an "indifferent" cargo which arrived in poor condition was £5,000. Profits of 100 percent were not uncommon in Liverpool, and one voyage netted a clear profit of at least 300 percent. —ERIC WILLIAMS, *Capitalism and Slavery*

> The dirty, get-on-down music the women sang and the men played and both danced to, close and shameless or apart and wild.... Just hearing it was like violating the law.
> —TONI MORRISON, *Jazz*

In the still-debated *Capitalism and Slavery* (1944), the historian Eric Williams details the economic purchase secured by the circumscription of the lives of African-derived persons never forthrightly admitted in modern certainties of human being. As summarized by the historian Colin A. Palmer, *Capitalism and Slavery* aims to show "how the commercial capitalism of the eighteenth century was built upon slavery and monopoly, while the industrial capitalism of the nineteenth century destroyed slavery and monopoly."[1] The following attempt to synthesize some of the key modalities of Western modernity and its forms of personhood—phantasmatic, geopolitical, economic, and racial—accepts this premise that the enslavement of African-derived persons is fundamental to the economic and political development of the modern West. The synthesis interrogates what seems the conceptual impossibility of the human being, as well as the loss of the sub-Saharan populations bound to the commercial traffic of the mercantilist era and also bound, in one instance at the conclusion of the mercantilist era, to the Atlantic federation of the former British North American colonies newly vying for the economic values generated in the Atlantic arena. The perplexity is that at stake originally, as the "modern," is the animation of a conceptual *form*—the commodity—as the principle of economic (and general) rationality, in the face of the already fully animate individual and collective *forms*—in human proportions—of racial blackness. Beginning in the fifteenth century, the modern episode exceeds the bounds of economics simply, and discloses the conceptual license overlapping the modern Western market and modern Western reason by means of the material disposition of African-derived populations.

The perplexity, then, is that the *impossibility* of racial blackness seeming to lie within the limits of the economic fundament of the modern West as well as within the limits of modern psychic rudiments belies the signal importance of the emergent circumstances of the concept of racial blackness: the rise of the Atlantic system of trade on which the articulation of the modern depends. African-derived populations, conscripted under the rubric of racial blackness, become the decisive point of nullification in the geopolitical, economic, and phantasmatic confluence that ultimately betrays the large coextensiveness of the modern market, the ideally infinite arena of ideally infinite exchange, and modern subjectivity, the animating turns of the imagination yielding functional self-coherence, "our inaccessibility to ourselves," in the phrase of the Lacanian psychoanalytical critic Joan Copjec.[2] For following the Portuguese descent down the long swath of the West African coast, which accelerates after 1434, racial blackness forms the enabling point of "disintegration" for the paradigms of Western modernity and, in this way, seems an eccentricity of the modern, even as the violent formation of the African diasporic communities of the Americas discloses the conceptual *impossibility* to be, on the contrary, that the Atlantic coast of Africa describes the point of possibility for modern "civic animation," or in the words of the postcolonial historian Dipesh Chakrabarty, "the bureaucratic construction of citizenship, modern state, and bourgeois privacy that classical political philosophy has produced."[3]

Because the transforming metropolises along the Atlantic coastlines of Europe and the "New World" forge their exemplary modern profiles by means of the immense surplus values that depend on the depletion and the disordering of the political jurisdictions along the Senegambian, Guinea, and west-central African coastline and the stark regimes of enforced labor in the Americas, the paramount peculiarity of mercantile capitalism seems the selective criteria by which *almost no* "human suffering was too high to pay for the monetary gain from trade in slaves and from the extension of capitalist production into the New World."[4] The conceptual obfuscation, or upshot, is that the economic boon secured and resecured by Europe and some of its outposts at each node of the Atlantic system of trade—the boon radically augmenting European diets, shipping, and markets—massively introduces sub-Saharan Africans and their descendants into the European "New World" or, differently put, into the newest mechanisms of European viability and, as forcefully, into individual and collective European imaginations. The economist G. R. Steele explains that "mercantilism originated during the transition from the feudal economy to merchant capitalism and international commerce, in the sixteenth and seventeenth centuries. A strong central authority was considered essential to the expansion of markets and it was a mercantilist imperative that the power of the state should be enhanced by an accumulation of national wealth."[5] In deference to the conceit of modern nationality, mercantilist policies eschew free trade, promoting instead the cultivation, transportation, and processing of the goods circulating in the new Atlantic trade within national (albeit newly geographically distant) jurisdictions. The European annexation of the Americas inaugurating mercantilist policies and the enormous economic significance of the Caribbean basin cannot be overemphasized in the modernizing progress of Europe and its permutations.

The commercial exchanges bolstered by modern national configurations and agencies bind the subject to the market economically and otherwise by means of the values of "the socially necessary labor time" accruing to the modern centers of European commercial supervision and their outposts. The national articulation of the former British seaboard colonies strikingly exemplifies this imaginative, geopolitical, economic, and racial complex. The fundamental proposition (or feint) of the modern, the certain proposition that "human being" configures the market and conversely the market configures "human being," openly informs the constitutive federal postures of the fledgling union of North American territories, insofar as the rhetorical appeal to "the people" of the incipient national formation apparently glosses the aggregate populations of the former colonies, yet still more forthrightly comprehends the Atlantic circuit of goods premising modern forms of exchange. The importance of the seaboard geography of the former colonies, if not the newly national rhetoric, betrays the subvention of the national identity and its visible sign, "the people," in the ideally infinite arena of ideally infinite exchange constituted and secured through the inconceivability of the fully animate African-derived populations providing "the socially necessary labor time" of the intercontinental trade derived from the Americas. The foreclosure of the certain "human being" of the African-derived populations in the Atlantic theatre discloses that modern nationalisms hold fundamentally supranational coordinates never admitted readily. Stated more particularly, insofar as in "the eighteenth century two features of the market economy fascinated contemporaries: the reliance upon individual initiative and the absence of authoritarian direction," this primary misrecognition of the operations of the market negates the human significance of the African and African-derived populations conscripted into the Atlantic theatre.[6] The tumultuous significance of African-derived persons in the Atlantic arena is occluded by the figure of "an invisible flow of goods and payments girdling the globe and crisscrossing the English countryside," radically reforming across the Western hemisphere civic and subjective protocols—modernity—as marked emphatically by the independence of the former British seaboard colonies.[7]

Because psychoanalytic paradigms do not fundamentally rely on the trajectories of history, as Joan Copjec argues in *Read My Desire*, these interrogations of the modern are not broached primarily in psychoanalytic terms. The overwhelming problem for psychoanalytical paradigms is that, because the emergent subject of "European" modernity is forged during the earliest phases of capital accumulation, mercantile capitalism, the perplexity is at once historical and paradigmatic. Nonetheless, the coincident development of the modern market and modern subjectivity remains an important issue for Marxist paradigms, in which the concept of commodity fetishism designates the coincidence. The economists Jack Amariglio and Antonio Callari, in their consideration of the concept of commodity fetishism, provide a succinct rendition of the Marxist codification of subjectivity. "Marx," they write, "has had a theory of the subject, the theory of commodity fetishism. To the extent that it attempts to conjoin the analysis of commodity production and circulation with a discussion of 'ideology,' commodity fetishism does discuss the peculiar subjectivity typical of capitalist social formations."[8] In particular, they point out that the Marxist understanding of "socially necessary labor time" as the essential value masked in commodity fetishism clarifies the subjectivizing force of the modern market, which is to say, the imperatives "naturalizing" the difference between the social conditions of the labor yielding the commodity and the failure of the commodity to resemble those conditions in the exchange. In this way, "the act of exchange is not simply the site of an economic process but also one of the key locations within capitalism where a symbolic order is particularly constituted and learned."[9] The concept of commodity fetishism describes the phantasmatic torque of rational exchanges so as to abrogate the "unnecessary gulf [that] has come to exist between two important areas of theoretical work in contemporary Marxism, with the theory of value (the economics, if you will) on one side and the nature and role of subjectivity (an antieconomism) on the other."[10] The ideally infinite arena of ideally infinite exchange of the modern abstracted market forms the most efficient nexus of material and conceptual exchange. In the historical trajectory, the cultural trajectory, and the trajectories of subjection, commodity fetishism depends on and stands for the fantastic *impossibility* by means of which not only the possible seems coherent but, more importantly, the *force* of the actual seems coherent. This nexus is racial in character insofar as the phantasmatic, geopolitical, and economic coincidence yields the declensions of humanity and subhumanity, the attendant disclosure being that "the history of European people on both sides of the Atlantic indicates that responsiveness to the market economy cannot be taken for granted, for it reflects values and ideas even more than material conditions."[11] This is to say that the emergent subject of European modernity—the relay of the perplexity of commodity fetishism—and the intrigue of mercantilist agendas form coimplicated registers of the social, economic, and cultural reorganizations of Europe and its extensions following the fifteenth century.

By 1830, as one outgrowth of the competition over the economic values trafficked through the Atlantic theatre, the number of novel military and administrative jurisdictions, modern nation-states, emergent in the "New World" includes: Haiti (1803), Argentina (1816), Chile (1818), Venezuela (1820), Mexico (1821), Great Colombia (1822), Bolivia (1825), Paraguay (1826), and Uruguay (1828).[12] The resulting macropolitical effect—the nation—and the micropolitical effect—the ineffability of "the people" as the collective representation of individual subjects—reveal that "the act of exchange is not simply the site of an economic process but also one of the key locations within capitalism where a symbolic order is particularly constituted and learned."[13] As with the feint of commodity fetishism, there is an enabling slippage, the wholly viable misperception that configures the matter of nationality as simply the cohesion or coherence of an "imagined community," in the well-known phrase of Benedict Anderson. In this way, in the exemplary Federalist intrigues of the United States, the articulation of "the people," the effective concept yielding the sign of *national* visibility, conflates the fiscal management of commodity exchange within the strict protocols of modern rationalized accumulation with the legibility of human being. Beyond the macropolitical reorganizations, the affective principle, the feint, is the semblance of discrete viability (whether national or individual), as nonetheless sustained through the reified, ideally infinite arena of ideally infinite exchange.

The Conceptual Impossibility

The geopolitical, historical, and social palimpsest is intricate. The annexation of the Americas and the policies governing the opportunities to raise and traffic enormous quantities of goods in the new Atlantic economies transforms the premodern axes of long-distance trade: the significance of the sea lanes of the Baltic trade, the Mediterranean Sea, the Indian Ocean, and the intercontinental arena of the silk roads. The newly promoted European desires for sugar and other tropical products formalize in the seventeenth and eighteenth centuries the enormous trade circuit termed the triangular trade, fusing the formerly disparate economies of the Americas, Western Europe, and the West African coast from Senegambia, Sierra Leone, the Windward and Gold coasts, and the Bight of Benin, to Benguela beyond the Bight of Biafra—jurisdictions inhabited by Akans, Angolans, Ashante, Bambara, Igbo, Kongolese, Kru, Mandingas, Mende, Oyo, Vais, Yoruba, and others, who are hard-pressed by the demands of European modernity. In the triangular circuit of the new Atlantic economies, European manufactured objects are disposed on the African coast in trade for slaves, who are shipped across the Atlantic as the requisite labor force for the massive production of the cash crops that in the final segment of the circuit are traded under the nationally protectionist policies of the European metropolises to serve the rearticulated desires of mass populations.

The historian David Eltis directly considers the compound economic and imaginative impress disposing of sub-Saharan Africans and their descendants in European modernity. Rehearsing in particular the unpursued but potentially far greater economic promise of European enslavement in the Americas, he queries "which groups are considered eligible for enslavement" in the mercantilist era and its aftermath, proposing that the "crux of the matter is shipping costs, which comprised by far the greater part of the price of any form of imported bonded labor in the Americas."[14] The scope of this argument, rather than being bound by national jurisdictions, is international, in order to demonstrate "that economic motivation should be assigned a subsidiary role in the rise and fall of the exclusively African-based bondage that Europeans carried across the Atlantic."[15] The shorter voyage from Europe to the Americas, the less closely packed ships of these routes, the lower mortality and morbidity rates in North Atlantic as opposed to South Atlantic transportation, and the accessibility to European convict labor given that major European population centers abut navigable waterways, David Eltis argues, all attest to the far from complete role of economics in the arrangement of mercantilist labor forces. Rather, he states that "the most cursory examination of relative costs suggests that European slaves should have been preferred to either European indentured labor or African slaves."[16]

The confluence of imagination, economics, and race is plain: "The most that can be said by way of comparison is that the spread of African slavery in the Americas coincided with the spread of forced labor in punishment systems within Europe (transportation in the English case). But no one was in any doubt about the distinctions between the two."[17] The ultimate point is that the "absence of European slaves, like the dog that did not bark, is perhaps the clue to understanding the slave trade and the system it supported."[18] The more than simply economic question foregrounds the *imagination* of the European subject as well as attendant political and material forces, the quandary being "that the peoples with the most advanced capitalist culture, the Dutch and the English, were also the Europeans least likely to subject their own citizens to enforced labor," circumstances disclosing that "the celebration of British liberties—more specifically, liberties for Englishmen—depended on African slavery."[19] Drawing a circumference around the entire Atlantic circuit, David Eltis's argument extrapolates in important ways the thesis of the historian Edmund Morgan's *American Slavery, American Freedom*, broadening it so as to encompass the psychic and political subjectivity of modernizing Europe generally. In sum, the thesis of Edmund Morgan's classic examination of colonial Virginia is "not . . . that a belief in republican ideology had to rest on slavery, but only that in Virginia (and probably in other southern colonies) it did."[20]

David Eltis's more general rendition of the principle bears noting. If, in the episode of mercantile capitalism, the "early modern Europeans shifted property rights in labor toward the individual and away from the community," then, as clearly, these reorganizations shift property rights in labor (as well as in epistemological and cultural systems) across continental divisions: toward Europe and the Americas and away from the west coast of Africa.[21] The Atlantic accessibility of the African continent provides the means for dismantling the long-standing systems of property rights, of commercial trade, legal and penal systems, and intercultural contact of the self-governing jurisdictions arrayed along the broad continental swath in which "few—perhaps no—West African peoples appear to have been living on the very margin of subsistence during the eighteenth century . . . [for] research almost always seems to disclose some surplus output and some interregional trade even in the most isolated areas."[22] In short, the modern transfer of rights toward the European(ized) individual and away from the community has patent inverse effects on the eastern and western arcs of the Atlantic rim. Summarily stated, the fact that the modern "individual" and its revolutionary civic and political protocols *did not precede* the transfer of rights from the community to the individual, or from the eastern to the western arcs of the Atlantic, reveals plainly the powerful turns of the imagination that accrue along the eastern rim of the Atlantic in the modernizing centers of Europe and its outposts—fully in tandem with the vast economic values in question.

The modernity of *individual* psychic positions is forged from the very same enterprise as the modernity of mercantilist agendas as well as their revised, dramatic, and exorbitant nationalisms. For these reasons, the conceit of racial blackness, which indiscriminately catalogues dark-skinned Africans and their descendants, can be understood as a powerful analogue of the complex of commodity fetishism, insofar as the extended quarantining of this key population largely and effectively promotes key turns of the imagination that *naturalize* the gulf between the social conditions of the labor yielding the commodity for exchange and the failure of the commodity to resemble those conditions in the exchange—in other words, the powerful dissemblance by which it is not as plain as it might be that rational economic transactions dispossess some of the parties attendant to the exchange. In the most routine protocols of the Atlantic economies, the difference of phenotypes hyperbolically redacts the diacritical positions on either side of the commodity form, positions opposed as *production* and *consumption*. The difference of phenotypes in these turns of mind *naturalizes* and imbricates the subjective and economic feints of commodity fetishism, that "producers" and "consumers" contend equally within the interests of modern market relations. These turns of the imagination are also racialized in key and stark ways for the modern West, because of its radical dispositions of populations according to continental origin. The radical dispositions dichotomized Europe and Africa, consumption and production, supervision and subordination, and reason and unreason as indices of race given the unprecedented proximities of populations: "Although data on the immigration of free persons to the Americas are much less precise, it seems probable that enslaved African immigrants to the New World outnumbered Europeans by about four or five to one during the eighteenth century."[23]

That is, as opposed to the occurrences in Europe and the Americas, the personal securities of the populations of the various polities along the coast of West Africa "evaporated to facilitate a trade that was a constant threat to their existence."[24] For instance, Senegambia, the northernmost coastal region disrupted in the vast triangulation of the Atlantic economies, includes the polities of the Bijangos, Mande, and Mandingas, among others, and, although it is the region that supplies the smallest number of enslaved conscripts to the expansion of capital accumulation, it nonetheless registers fully the effects of the international violence. Beyond the widespread warfare that does not arise necessarily from—but necessarily inflames—regional political animosities, a variety of legal and extralegal threats reorganizes and frustrates quotidian life across Senegambia: various systems of land tenure based on land stewardship by the nobility (Papels) or reciprocal labor (Balantas) are compromised; penal systems are recalculated in order to broaden and expedite the possibilities of seizure for enslavement; the means of exploiting personal and class rivalries expand enormously; and the enticements to lawlessness, such as kidnapping, alter both personal and organized political calculations. Most importantly, drawing the region into even greater entanglements with the European and "New World" ideally infinite arena of ideally infinite exchange, the enveloping threat to travel and unfamiliar intercourse weakens the internal commercial relations of the Senegambia. The disruption of the political economies along the lower Guinea and west-central coasts, territories of the Angolans, Kongolese, Oyo, Yoruba, and others, is even more acute, providing "ample proof that the economic pull of the American market could force a fundamental change within Africa."[25] Paul Lovejoy notes the volume, rapidity, and high consequence of the overwhelming transfer of the African labor forces to the western rim of the Atlantic:

> The largest exporting region in the early seventeenth century was west central Africa, which continued sending thousands of slaves a year to the Americas, thus consolidating a pattern that had begun a century earlier. Senegambia and Benin maintained their relatively modest share of the trade as well, each providing about a thousand slaves a year. Slaves came from elsewhere too. The really dramatic expansion of the Atlantic trade began after 1650, and from then slave exports affected ever larger parts of Africa, not just the Kongo region. In the last fifty years of the seventeenth century, more slaves were sold to Europeans on the Atlantic coast than in the previous two hundred years combined. This phenomenal growth was a response to the spread of plantation slavery in the Americas. From the 1640s through the 1660s, sugar spread from Brazil to the lesser Antilles—Barbados, Martinique, Guadeloupe, St. Kitts, Antigua—and these new colonies acquired tens of thousands of slaves. The figure of the third quarter of the seventeenth century was double the previous twenty-five-year period, averaging 17,700 per year, while in the last quarter, almost 30,000 slaves were exported annually. By now sugar plantations were being established on Jamaica and Saint Domingue, which rapidly became the two largest producers of sugar. As a result, the dramatic

surge in slave exports continued into the eighteenth century, reaching figures in the order of 61,000 slaves per year for the whole century.[26]

It is important to understand that the violence of the Atlantic conscription is neither random nor absolute. Lovejoy notes the closely deliberative aspects of the undermining of the political jurisdictions of the coast: "The introduction of new crops from the Americas increased food production and thereby helped to maintain population levels despite the export of slaves. Advances in commercial institutions, including credit facilities, currency, bulking, and regularized transportation, assisted in the movement of slaves."[27] In short, while the intrusive transatlantic contact "implies disorder in the social framework wherever the external trade was important, the effective organization of slave supply required that political violence be contained within boundaries that would permit the sale of slaves abroad."[28]

The fact that "the export of about 11.3 million slaves from 1500 to 1800, including the astronomical increase between 1650 and 1800 in the Atlantic sector, could not have occurred without the transformation of the African political economy" is corroborated by the economists Henry Gemery and Jan Hogendorn, who construct a hypothetical West African economy as it might have existed outside of the slave trade in order to make a comparison to the actual economic outcomes of the episode.[29] They measure the net economic loss to the region based on figuring five factors: (1) the levels of subsistence production under both economies, (2) the average surplus production per person above subsistence requirements, (3) the longer working life of those transported to and enslaved in the Americas, (4) mortality during slave acquisition and delivery prior to the transatlantic transportation, and (5) the greater economic contributions of the younger, more productive, and more highly conscripted groups of the labor force. They write: "As noted, any one of these independent factors 1–5 would in itself convert the net impact of the slave trade into an economic loss for West Africa. The implication is overwhelming that when these factors are taken in combination, the economic costs of the trade exceeded its gains on an overall basis. Let us reemphasize that this conclusion is reached without any reference to the massive intangible costs of the trade."[30]

Dramatically, there are inverse effects on the other side of the Atlantic. The historian Ronald Bailey describes the importance of the Caribbean, its commodity routes, and African-derived labor forces to both the colonial development and industrialization of New England—never mind, say, South Carolina, the state with the most direct ties historically and economically to the Caribbean basin. Ronald Bailey summarizes the rehearsal as follows:

I have argued in this article, as others have done, that New England's maritime trade and shipping laid the foundation for, raised the infrastructure of, and funded early industrial development. This was particularly the case for the cotton textile industry between 1815 and 1860. Maritime trade and shipping depended largely on the slave trade and on the slave-based Atlantic economic system of the seventeenth, eighteenth, and nineteenth centuries. The early industries, such as ship building and rum distilling, were directly tied to the slave trade and to maritime activities in general. These helped pave the way for the establishment of the cotton textile industry, which, together with the production of the cotton textile machinery, became the leading sector of U.S. industrialization in the nineteenth century.[31]

The final observation is that "the contribution of the slave trade and New World slavery to the entire process is hard to exaggerate."[32] The historian Robin Blackburn writes:

> The birth of the North American republic had a large impact on the plantation-related trade of the rest of the Americas. United States exports to the French, Spanish, Portuguese, and Dutch colonies reached nearly £1 million annually in 1790–92, representing 24 percent of the total. . . . The tonnage of US shipping registered as engaged in overseas commerce totaled 346,000 tons, twice that of the tonnage of British shipping involved in the Atlantic trade, in 1770; by 1801 the tonnage of US commercial shipping more than doubled to 718,400. Merchants from New York, Boston and Philadelphia traded with all parts of the Caribbean and Americas in sugar, cotton, coffee, cacao, and indigo, much of which was then re-exported to Europe. They offered powerful economic as well as ideological encouragement to creole aspiration to American independence. The total export trade of the United States grew fivefold in the period 1790 to 1807, swelled by its role as entrepôt for the plantation produce of the Americas, to reach over $60 million (over £10 million).[33]

Still, the full measure of the trajectory of mercantile capitalism and its modernizing transfers of economic values and peoples in the transatlantic circuit rests in the subtleties and protocols of mercantilist capitalism that understand human congress (and progress) as inseparable from the exchanges (and feints) of the unwieldy abstracted market. Differently put, the full trajectory of the modern West is clarified in the revolutionary certainty that functional human being—individual and especially collective—is inseparable from the ideally infinite arena of ideally infinite exchange, an arena that even the broadest modern legislative, military, and rhetorical resources fail to articulate coherently as often as not. The complex is a matter of subjectivity, the full reach of which—paradoxically—is never the discrete subject but, rather, turns on the (ideally collective) imagination by which discrete subjection reforms and adheres to the coveted processes and values of transatlantic (and global) commodity circulation, a rarefied intersubjective template questionable only under the most pressed of circumstances.

The beguiling and basic national proposal—the proposal of an ineffable, "psychological bond that joins a people and differentiates it, in the subconscious convictions of its members, from all other people in a most vital way"—credits the nation as a centrifugal, if not fully cohesive entity.[34] In 1882, Ernest Renan writes famously, a "nation is a soul, a spiritual principle" the outcome of a "great aggregation of men, [which] with healthy spirit and warmth of heart, creates a moral conscience which is called a nation."[35] In the subjectivizing premise of the modern nation-state, the assumption of basic or fundamental cohesiveness, there is, then, the foreclosure of the recognition of the more openly destructive imperatives and force of national formations. For example, the historian Alfred Cobban writes: "As an agency of destruction the theory of nationalism proved one of the most potent that even modern society has known. Empires or states that were not homogeneous in culture and language were undermined from within, or assaulted from without."[36] Similarly, the sociologist Anthony Richmond observes that "the internal cohesion and social integration of the nation-state depended upon an elimination of previous local, tribal or provincial attachments and the inculcation of loyalty to the larger territorial unit dominated by the secular state."[37] The case seems, however, that the profound reverberations of national formations (and reformations) in the mercantilist era do not apply foremost or finally to the Western communities redrawn within (and as) the national territories but, as fully, to the instrumental bearers of the "socially necessary labor time" who are never calculable strictly, given the transatlantic protocols of mercantile capitalism, by any national designations.

The violence in question, unlike the apparent cohesion it subtends, never merely is equivalent to or circumscribed by the national formation. The insufficiencies and obfuscations of the rubrics of nationalism for effectively scoring this violence is plain, because "simply put, people from one continent forced those from a second continent to produce a narrow range of consumer goods in a third—having first found the third's native population inadequate to their purpose."[38] Instead of innate sets of psychological bonds or easily calculated moral gestures, the phenomenon of nationalism details the necessity of the *micropolitical* redescription, in addition to the *macropolitical* reformulation, of social power. These redescriptions of power—according to the political economist Susan Strange, "the ability of a person or group of persons ... to affect [the] outcomes that their preferences take precedence over the preferences of others"—fix the always vulnerable margins between the conceptual and the inconceivable, between the proximity to and the attenuation of the violence yielding the apparent cohesion in question.[39]

The Civic Premise

The historian John Brewer, in *The Sinews of Power*, summarizes mercantilism, rather than being a coherent set of policies, as an "era in which the relationship between state power and international trade was seen as a problem of exceptional importance, one which was normally formulated as a debate between the interventionist obligations of rulers rather than a matter of free trade."[40] The emphatically modern historical break of the British mainland colonies from their national origins is evident in these imperatives of mercantilism, its matters of state jurisdiction, international trade, and sovereign intervention. The British Sugar Act of 1764, which imposes tariffs on the seaboard colonies that result in the enormous, economically crucial smuggling between the colonies and the Caribbean basin, followed in 1773 by the Stamp Act, which lowers the tariffs in order to make British intervention in the smuggling more viable, remain important points of escalation in the transatlantic tensions that result in the successful independence of the seaboard colonies, as well as the scrupulous, developing alignment of economic and social life as the paramount premise of modern national agency. Mercantilist principles, exacerbating economic jealousies, chafe at long-standing concepts of national agency. The point Brewer demonstrates is that in the seventeenth- and eighteenth-century histories of England, by shaping the international flow of goods and wealth by the means of intercontinental markets, mercantilism articulates and reinforces modern forms of nationality as bureaucratic, administrative entities. The inaugurating episodes of mercantilism, which is defined in opposition to free trade, witness measures such as the British Navigation Acts and the French *exclusif*, measures aiming to ensure that the tropical products cocoa, coffee, indigo, rum, sugar, and tobacco (as well as gold and silver) extracted from New World outposts by means of African-derived labor are shipped exclusively on the vessels of their respective metropolitan centers and then refined and marketed in those metropolitan territories by national agents and industries. At the conclusion of the era, the fledgling United States, as the sign of its emphatic modernity, both redescribes national territories and presents new conceptual forms. The historian Andrew Cayton observes: "Indeed, many saw the efforts of nationally oriented men to attach people to the new republic as essentially radical innovations designed to undermine traditional social relationships. Not only were Federalists elevating imperial authority above local authority. By privileging abstract impersonal principles above particular personal ties, they were redefining the nature of social and political relationships."[41]

Given its recalculation of social and political relationships, the specification of "the people" devised in the crisis of the independence of the seaboard colonies provides a historical correlate to the theoretical conceptualizations of the large coextensiveness of the market and the forces of subjectivity. The articulation of national independence dramatically clarifies the enormous material boon, as well as the subjectivizing turns of the imagination secured by means of the Atlantic economies, a historical progress describing the coimplicated investments of the macropolitical and the micropolitical.

At once, the force in question is *macropolitical*, which is to say broadly historical and supranational, enforcing the economic circuits imbricating the West African, "New World," and European polities within the adamant antinomies of race following the sixteenth century. In the era that follows, "in less than one hundred years the world's economic situation had altered completely.... Negro slaves, who were of only nominal value in 1500, had become indispensable to the maintenance and development of this new plantation economy."[42] Concomitantly, the force in question is *micropolitical*, which is to say insinuates and enforces, the interpellation of a "model of economic life that borrowed its order from ... the newly conceptualized nature of predictable regularity. As this economy absorbed more and more of the attention of men and women it supplied a new identity for them. By the end of the eighteenth century the individual with wide-ranging needs and abstract rights appeared to challenge the citizen with concrete obligations and prescribed privileges."[43]

For these reasons, it is important to acknowledge that in the British mainland colonies "African slaves, if taken together ... [are] the largest single group of non-English-speaking migrants to enter the North American colonies in the pre-Revolutionary era."[44] The historical progress reveals that, rather than being foremost the vector of human coherence, the modernity of the national formations, especially in the Americas, provides foremost the novel, beguiling means by which individual and communal detachments are created, channeled, and exploited, in the transcontinental arrangements yielding unprecedented demographics and proximities. The matter is not economic simply but rather involves as specifically the turns of the imagination that demand the impossibility—violently secured—of racial blackness being a feature of readily recognized human being.

This is to say that the profound conceptual problems yet pronounced political efficacy of the figure of "the people" are unmistakable in the finally supranational intrigue of the independence of the seaboard colonies and subsequent American Federalist era. The Federalist era ranges from the 1780s, fomenting the debate over supplanting the Articles of Confederation with a new constitution, to the election of Thomas Jefferson to the presidency in 1800. Still, this is to say further that, in the matter of nation building, the aporetic force in question is not simply the military drama of the Revolutionary War but the effects of the African-derived "socially necessary labor time" on which the modern Atlantic market and its various national articulations (and rearticulations) depend. The material and conceptual effects of the African-derived "socially necessary labor time" redoubles the incongruity of the local, federal, and individual renditions of "the people" that mark the political urgencies of the Federalist era. The developing historiography of the Federalist era draws out the perplexity of the figure of "the people" forming the national register of the independent British mainland colonies. The historian Robert Shalhope outlines the work of Bernard Bailyn, Gordon Wood, and J. G. A. Pocock, and their formation of the historiographical "republican synthesis," or the related set of convictions that, insofar as early U.S. history "revealed a continual struggle between the spheres of liberty and power, the American Revolutionaries quickly formed a consensus in which the concept of republicanism epitomized the new social and political world they believed they had created."[45] Shalhope positions principally the scholarship of Joyce Appleby against the contentions of the "republican synthesis," so as to describe a "major weakness of earlier analyses of republicanism, . . . namely, a focus on political and constitutional issues to the detriment of economic analysis."[46] What is clear from the discrepant perspectives, he contends, is that the "American Revolution created a single political nation but certainly did not fashion a cohesive national community."[47] Appleby, in her own consideration of the historiographical tensions, forthrightly rejects the earlier "insistence that the classical republican paradigm controlled how eighteenth-century men reacted to change," claiming the historical record demonstrates, instead, that the colonial elite "living with sensibilities formed in an agrarian society and struggling to interpret change with an ideology pivoting on the preeminent importance of stasis could only be disconcerted by the intrusive vigor of the [effects of the] market."[48] To this end, the historian T. H. Breen outlines pointedly the shortcomings, or the explanatory limits, of the historiographical investments of the "republican synthesis":

Intellectual historians encounter a different, though equally thorny set of problems. They transform the American Revolution into a mental event. From this perspective, it does not matter much whether the ideas that the colonists espoused are classic liberal concepts of rights and property, radical country notions of power and virtue or evangelical Calvinist beliefs about sin and covenants. Whatever the dominant ideology may have been, we find that a bundle of political abstractions has persuaded colonists living in scattered regions of America of the righteousness of their cause, driving them during the 1760s and 1770s to take ever more radical positions until eventually they were forced by the logic of their original assumptions to break with Great Britain. Unfortunately, intellectual historians provide no clear link between the everyday world of the men and women who actually became patriots and the ideas that they articulated. We are thus hard-pressed to comprehend how in 1774 wealthy Chesapeake planters and poor Boston artisans—to cite two obvious examples—could possibly have come to share a political mentality. We do not know how these ideas were transmitted through colonial society from class to class, from community to community.[49]

In short, as much as the "republican synthesis" advances ideal propositions of historical and narrative continuity, it cannot account for the way in which radically distinct geographical populations as well as social classes arrived at the collective apprehension of a national "people," revolutionary acts of imagination yielding the "mobilization of strangers in a revolutionary cause [that] eroded the stubborn localism of an earlier period."[50] This episode that produces finally the federal compact, more than a political theoretical inheritance, turns on novel economic and conceptual priorities.

Brief considerations of the roles of the three authors of the composite *Federalist*, which famously appeals in the 1780s for the new national compact, begin to illustrate the point. The three exemplary figures are Alexander Hamilton, who is the successful architect of the federal economic policy within the first administrations; John Jay, who is a New York lawyer and, like Alexander Hamilton, one of the representatives from New York at the constitutional convention who in *The Federalist* pinions nativist appeals for the new national agency; and James Madison, who is the instrumental figure of the 1787 constitutional convention. The architectural economic strategies of Alexander Hamilton underscore the immediate conceptual force that the relays of commodity exchange hold for the national endeavor. The nativist appeals of John Jay betray the occlusions of the international complex equally necessary to the endeavor. The role of James Madison highlights the representational quandary—yet nonetheless political efficacy—of the rhetorical figure of the people. The imbrications of their positions are fundamental to and productive of the enterprise they conceive and debate.

Alexander Hamilton—"the colossal genius of the new system," notwithstanding James Madison's more preeminent role in the details of constitution making—recognizes keenly the neomercantilist dilemma of the incipient national union:

> Believing economic independence was inseparable from political freedom, Hamilton was alarmed by American dependence on British imports. He opposed commercial coercion, fearing that the young nation would be devastated by such a contest. His less confrontational design envisioned ridding the United States of British economic domination by developing American manufacturing. He concluded that American technological backwardness stood in the way of American manufactures and urged the federal government to launch an aggressive campaign to acquire England's protected industrial secrets.[51]

In the policies sponsored by Alexander Hamilton, the "intrusive vigor of the market" is undisguised: the pursuit of public credit for the federal agency, the establishment of the national bank, the championing of domestic taxation in support of public credit, the redrawing of economic relations with Britain while at the same time supporting rival domestic manufacturing by flouting British patent laws, the championing of a well-funded national military in the service of international force, and the elimination of the federal land grant program for fear of losing to the skilled immigrant workers of the more open South and West—in effect, the twinning of the fortunes of the new republic with the interests and influence of financiers, bankers, merchants, manufacturers, and land speculators. Jeffersonian opposition to these inaugural federal policies is intense, as is the resolve of the governing Federalists under the presidency of John Adams in the few years before the 1800 presidential election of Thomas Jefferson. The observations of Doran Ben-Atar and Barbara Oberg concerning the tense political atmosphere of the early national union are apt: "Twice in a period of two years [the Federalist] maneuvers brought the nation to the brink of disunion and civil war. Their attempt during the Quasi-War with France to muzzle the opposition with the Alien and Seditions Acts in 1798 moved Jefferson, in the Kentucky Resolutions, to advocate nullification. Two years later, in response to the Federalists' Burr maneuver, Republican leaders in Virginia and

Pennsylvania considered raising an army and marching on the nation's capital to place Jefferson at the helm."[52]

It is important to note that a significant part of the Jeffersonian opposition to the programs of Alexander Hamilton and the initial Federalist administrations draws on the popular opposition to the expansion of the national military in support of international influence, the policy dependent on formalizing domestic taxation as the perpetual supplement to the revenues collectible from customs and tariffs. The local populations, "as their representatives in Congress made clear, and some of them also made clear out of doors were not prepared to pay taxes to support a powerful military and aggressive posture in foreign affairs."[53] The policies and impress of the first federal administrations compromise plainly the simple figurativeness of the people, particularly as "in principle, central government was antithetical to liberty, which most Americans associated with local self-rule."[54]

The question of the independent powers of the federal agency subordinates to the international coordination of economic values the individual subjections and subjects on which it depends for its representative basis. The historian James Ferguson places the question of the powers of the federal agency in the international context that determines it more completely. He outlines that before the complications of the initial intrigues of the independent seaboard states, "an analogous political-economic process affected British development."[55] The Bank of England, in order to underwrite more ample business credit as well as provide more efficient means of general exchange, is established in 1694, establishing as well as the British innovation of the funded debt, the innovation that provides the national government access to immense funds with the exceedingly generous license that "no pledge was given ever to repay the principal."[56] The effect—also considered by Brewer—is that "the ability to borrow, limited only by having to pay interest, was the crucial factor in Britain's victories in eighteenth-century wars."[57] In Britain and subsequently the independent seaboard states, the alternatives to the expanding system of commercial credit are repudiated. In England, the scheme to employ land banks, which base credit in real property, is forestalled, and in the North American states, the greater powers of federal taxation finally override the policies of "currency finance," in which governments raise capital by issuing their own paper money or certificates redeemable at a later date and, since guaranteed by the government agency, exchangeable as currency. These policies, undertaken separately by the newly independent states, would allow them to assume the federal debt accumulated in the Revolutionary War and thus curtail the powers of the new federal agency. The retention of the national debt at the federal level, the crucial measure of the viability of the new federal agency and effectively bestowing much wider federal authority, allays the quandary paramount to the Federalist vision: the concern that "Union was a league of states rather than a national system because Congress lacked the power of taxation."[58] The quizzical specification of the people that is the rhetorical hallmark of the struggle remains deeply troubled—ultimately overwhelmed as a viable appeal—since "in the closing years of the Revolution, the Nationalists under the aegis of such leaders as Robert Morris, Gouverneur Morris, and Alexander Hamilton started a secondary revolution directed against the political-economic establishment of the American states."[59] The federal agency garners its sovereignty by diminishing the former, wider prerogatives of the more local state agencies.

These indeterminacies of the federated or national people, to follow the perspective of Appleby, betray ultimately that "no concepts existed for analyzing a trading system that had not only moved beyond the confines of political boundaries but had created wealth essential to the conduct of politics. There was no classical language for understanding a commercial system that was public, progressive, and orderly. However appealing civic humanism was to English gentlemen involved in public issues, it did not help persons who sought to understand the private transactions that were determining the shape and direction of the Anglo-American economy."[60]

Further still, beyond the discrepancy of the local and federal imperatives, the new proposition of individual national identity discloses the subjectivizing—rather than merely the individual—puzzle brought into being by the exigencies of the Atlantic economies. The New York jurist John Jay, one of the negotiators of the 1783 Treaty of Paris arranging independence from Britain, and the first chief justice of the U.S. Supreme Court, as well as governor of New York, advocates the principle of nativism in support of the new national identity. He presses for the prerequisite of presidential native birth, and in *Federalist* #2 misstates hyperbolically the cultural unity and common sensibilities of the internationally disparate population of the independent mainland states: "This country and this people seem to have been made for each other, and it appears as if it were the design of Providence that an inheritance so proper and convenient for a band of brethren, united to each other by the strongest ties, should never be split into a number of unsocial, jealous, and alien sovereignties."[61] The hyperbole is undisguised since, in fact, John Jay is familiar intimately with "the already ethnically and religiously cosmopolitan New York City and was himself three-eighths French and five-eighths Dutch, without any English ancestry."[62] In other words, John Jay, as does Alexander Hamilton, understands the scrupulous set of international dynamics and equipoise on which the experiment of the new nationality depends. This comprehension is evidenced as much in his characterization of the radically diverse and changing human landscape of the independent states as "one united people" as it is in his role in negotiating the 1794 Jay Treaty, which brings further economic and political rapprochements with Britain, thereby imperiling U.S. relations with Britain's chief European rival, France.[63] The translation of the *unprecedented* ethnic and racial coordinations of the mainland states into "a people descended from the same ancestors, speaking the same language, professing the same religion, attached to the same principles of government, very similar in their manner and customs" patently reimagines the diverse immigration to the mainland territories and their dynamic social atmosphere.[64] Bernard Bailyn describes the late eighteenth-century immigration to the North American mainland, revealing the extremities of John Jay's entreaties to the singularity of the new individual national identity:

> The migration to America in the fifteen years between the end of the Seven Years War and the Revolution was remarkable by the standards of the time. Between the end of warfare in the mainland colonies and the disruption of empire in 1775, over 55,000 Protestant and Irish emigrated to America, over 40,000 Scots, and over 30,000 Englishmen—a total of approximately 125,000 from the British Isles—in addition to at least 12,000 from the German states and Switzerland who entered the port of Philadelphia, and 84,500 enslaved Africans imported to the southern colonies. This grand total of about 221,500 arrivals in the fifteen-year period (a conservative figure, yet almost 10 percent of the entire estimated population of mainland America in 1775) meant an average *annual* influx of approximately 15,000 people, which was close to the total estimated population of Boston during these years; and, except for the slaves, the great majority of these tens of thousands of newcomers crowded initially into a few small port towns, almost all of them south of New England.[65]

In short, as do its local and federal assignments, the new subjective assignment of nationality remains as conceptually fraught as it is effective.

Particularly because the Virginia lawyer James Madison registers and calculates keenly the representational antagonisms of the concept of the people, he holds a highly exemplary role in these political and subjectivizing revolutions. James Madison's insights into the delicacy of reimagining the federal compact in the 1780s, as "state rivalries blocked formation of a common front against British trade policies," are galvanizing for the new national viability.[66] The historian Jack Rakove observes: "Far more than was the case at the state level of politics, where the task of correcting the errors incorporated in the first constitutions seemed open-ended, reform of the confederation could proceed only through the pursuit of a carefully delineated agenda. So at least it seemed to James Madison, the most thoughtful and eventually the most influential of these reformers, and to the relatively small circle of like-minded men who shared his interest in national political problems."[67]

In the unraveling intrigue, James Madison is the leading proponent of the U.S. Constitution, serving as the "chief spokesman at the Federal Convention for a radically new plan of government... subsequently champion[ing] the Constitution as 'Publius' in *The Federalist* and as a delegate to the Virginia ratifying convention... [and further bringing] the process of constitution-making to a successful close by guiding through the First Congress the amendments that became the Bill of Rights."[68]

Charles Hobson remarks on James Madison's motives for, fluctuating opinions of, and compromises accepted in the specific form of government taken by the United States. The two most severe blows to James Madison's political vision at the 1787 convention are the rejection of the proposals "for proportional representation in both houses of the legislature and... to give the national legislature a 'negative,' or veto, over the laws of the states."[69] James Madison is intent to diminish the local influences represented by the states in deference to the more completely abstracted generality of national influence. For—as registered by the insistent fears of the larger states, like Massachusetts, Pennsylvania, and Virginia by the smaller states, like Delaware, New Jersey, and Rhode Island—forms of interstate conflict and commercial rivalry precipitate in large part the move to the new federated combination, fears James Madison rehearses throughout *Notes of Debates in the Federal Convention of 1787*.[70] The perspective of the smaller states is argued most strenuously by William Patterson of New Jersey, which is an agricultural state fated to supplement, through the excises and tariffs transacted at its busy ports, the welfare of its commercial neighbors New York and Pennsylvania. The federal agency authorized in the way James Madison champions would meet more effectively these and other matters of interstate rivalry. In sum, the federal agency would be one with authority accruing not only over the several states but, by virtue of their national singularity, also, at best, over the newly reordered competition over the transatlantic flow of property and currency, as well as the rest of the vast North American continent. The envisioned interstate organization and comity aspires to this end above all. As recorded by James Madison in *Notes of Debates in the Federal Convention of 1787*, John Dickinson, the successful lawyer and one of the representatives of Delaware, who achieves much of his social standing by marrying into "one of the first and wealthiest commercial families" of Philadelphia, states the jurisdictional quandary plainly: "We must either submit the states to the danger of being injured by the power of the Nat'l Gov't or the latter to that of being injured by the states."[71] The concept of the national "people" is pinioned, rather than clarified or highlighted, in the metonymic tensions that trouble the "nation" and the "state" as coherent markers of identity, not to mention the reportedly disinterested organization of social and political power.[72] The proposal of the veto power that would discipline fully the local legislative determinations of the aggregate national populace redacts powerfully, this is to say, the conceptual peculiarity of the notion of the people.

It is important to grant that, as disclosed by the conclusion of *Notes of Debates in the Federal Convention of 1787*, the unanimous approval of the new constitutional document is foremost symbolic and carefully orchestrated—particularly by Benjamin Franklin, Alexander Hamilton, and James Madison. If the magnitude of the U.S. federal powers is not as great as he first imagines, James Madison recognizes nonetheless in the compromised document that is the product of the 1787 convention the adequate means to the bolder federation of the states. Hobson describes the trajectory of James Madison's changes of perspective as follows: "On the very eve of his debut in *The Federalist*, Madison was highly dissatisfied with, not to say, contemptuous of, the proposed government. The October 1787 letter [to Thomas Jefferson] was a strong dose of nationalism that contrasted sharply with 'Publius's' celebration of the Constitution and indeed with all of Madison's subsequent writings. After this full and candid critique he ceased his advocacy of the negative on state laws and never again spoke ill of the Constitution."[73]

The dilemma of the proposed veto—in which the notion of the "people" is vexed between the antagonisms of their state and federated renditions—provides an important measure of James Madison's alterations, or alternately circumscriptions, of mind. That is, the federal veto might attenuate the influence of the larger states yet—as readily as it might exercise it—can do so in no final way. For, with or without the federal veto, given the strength of proportional representation obtaining in the first legislative chamber (then attenuated in the Senate), the scheme retains the always potentially greater influence of the larger states—whether applied alternately as states or as elements of the larger conglomerate. It is unlikely that the representatives of large states would endorse policies directly injurious to the interests of their states, or veto (or sanction efforts to veto) policies directly bolstering the interests of their states. In tandem, particularly, James Madison's defeated proposals of proportional representation in the Senate and the federal veto strengthens the position of the large states. Large states that more fully would constitute the legislative agency would also have a greater power to protect their interests by means clearly distinct from their local political renditions. In all the permutations of authority, the influence of the state of Virginia, the largest Revolutionary state—and the state that James Madison represents—remains well disposed and, as much as the federal veto he champions obfuscates the looming influence of the large states, it exacerbates in doing so the vexations of the concept of the people.

The entreaties of James Madison in support of the new federal compromise are instructive. In *Federalist #35*, beginning by outlining the dangers to government represented by the disparate interests of "the people," James Madison by its conclusion redefines "the people" so as to conflate the concept virtually with the principles and effects of the market, the ideally infinite arena of ideally infinite exchange. James Madison's focus is taxation: "There can be no doubt that in order to a judicious exercise of the power of taxation, it is necessary that the person in whose hands it is should be acquainted with the general genius, habits, and modes of thinking of the people at large and with the resources of the country. And this is all that can be reasonably meant by a knowledge of the interest and feelings of the people. In any other sense the proposition has either no meaning, or an absurd one."[74]

Evidenced by the juxtaposition of "the general genius, habits, and modes of thinking of the people at large" and "the resources of the country," "the people," as a national formula for self-imagination, reveals that the appearance of cohesion is merely the beguiling or subjectivizing effect of the new relays of accumulation generated in the modernizing episode of mercantilism. Any notion that otherwise holds "the people" and the market as essentially distinguishable, James Madison emphasizes, risks absurdity. James Madison in the *Federalist*, as he does before the first congress, exposes "the people" as the device of elite colonial subjects forging their advantage and modernity in the revolutionary national expression.

Even as he is an important figure in the Jeffersonian opposition to the administration authorized by the new federal document, James Madison, having served in the Virginia state assembly from 1784 to 1787, arrives at the 1787 constitutional convention with the fear that "in republics the majority made the laws but too often these laws, rather than reflecting the public good or general interest of the whole society, ratified the self-interests of a dominant faction in that society—whether debtors, creditors, planters, merchants, manufacturers, members of a certain religious sect, inhabitants of a particular region, or some other political, economic, or cultural group. Whenever the opportunity presented itself, there was nothing to restrain a majority faction from seizing control of the government and imposing its designs on the minority."[75]

James Madison's motives for, fluctuating opinions of, and compromises accepted in the specific form of government taken by the United States turn always on the absolute representative impossibility of the figure of the people, even as it certifies and ideally humanizes the relays of wealth and power that in the late eighteenth century remain, as yet, radically or relatively unassumed (depending on perspective).

The unprecedented political opportunities and calculations on the North American seaboard and its environs ensure, as Lance Banning writes, that "the era of the American Revolution was a period of political paranoia. Social and political events were seldom conceived to have causes apart from conscious purpose, and the purposes of any group organized to have an impact on government were automatically thought of as malignant."[76] Banning further argues that the intense climate of the Revolutionary era yields the precipitous stature of the new, compromised constitutional document. In the aftermath of its framing, the constitutional document that James Madison worries over is seized as an exceptional resource in the political rivalries it licenses to unfold. "Paradoxically, then, it was the appearance of a deeply felt opposition to the policies of our first administration, which assured the quick acceptance of the Constitution that had been committed to its care. More than the government itself, the opposition had to have an unchallengeable constitution on which to rely."[77] The new constitutional document is arrayed against the policies, in large part, of Alexander Hamilton, who represents New York at the 1787 convention and, as the first secretary of the treasury (resigning in 1795), is the triumphant strategist of the fledgling national economic policy.

> During the first year of the new government, while Jefferson made his way back from France, Madison acted as congressional leader of the forces who meant to assure a strong and independent executive power. He parted with the administration only on the questions of discrimination and national assumption of the debt, policies Virginians considered sectionally unjust. On these issues, however, both Madison and Jefferson were willing to compromise for the sake of federal union. The two Virginians did not move firmly into a more general opposition until they were confronted with Alexander Hamilton's proposal of a national bank. Then, already troubled by what seemed to them a growing sectional bias in the laws, they saw in the broad construction of federal powers which Hamilton advanced in support of the bank a powerful blow at

the barriers against an indefinite expansion of federal authority and, with it, the enhancement of the dangerous power of a northern majority.[78]

Hobson codifies the opposition as follows:

> Despite its extended sphere, the government proved more susceptible to faction than [James Madison] had foreseen in 1787. The threat of oppression, moreover, came not from a *majority* faction (whose dangers his previous warnings had dwelled on almost exclusively) but from a highly organized and influential "moneyed interest" that had somehow seized the reins of power and was adroitly maintaining its control through "corruption." To combat the Hamiltonian system of funded debts, banks, and encouragements for manufactures, Madison adopted a strategy of opposition that necessarily forced him to retreat from his high nationalism of 1787 (even to the point of flirting with the doctrine of "state interposition" in 1799).[79]

The exemplarity of James Madison, Alexander Hamilton, and John Jay is not to fix the feints of the rhetorical and nationalizing "people" as original to any personality, but to underscore that as the sign of its emphatic modernity the fledgling United States redescribes national territories and presents new conceptual paradigms, attending always to the immense transatlantic economic values generating the series of macropolitical confrontations for well over a century, as in the First and Second Anglo-Dutch Wars (1652–54, 1664–67), the Nine Years War (1689–98), the War of Spanish Succession (1702–13), the War of Austrian Succession (1740–48), the Seven Years War (1756–63), and the American Revolution (1776–83). The forthright glosses of the "people," as does the macropolitical context eliciting the concept, give modern forms of commercial exchange the priority shaping the renewed coordination of the former mainland colonies.

The "People"

Literary critic David Kazanjian acknowledges the queried role of taxation in the political vision in which commodity exchange remains the unassailable end of the new national formation of the British mainland colonies and, moreover, its self-representations. He states:

> On July 4, 1789, four months into its first session, the U.S. congress celebrated thirteen years of formal U.S. independence by passing its first tariff

bill. The bill placed duties of 5–15 percent on approximately thirty different goods, ranging from nails to carriages, with the highest rates reserved for "articles of luxury." When Madison proposed this "endeavor" with the first non-procedural words uttered in the new congress, he represented the tariff as a means of restoring the lost unity of the nation.... For Madison, "The deficiency in our Treasury" threatens the "union" with disintegration into the implicitly plural and antagonist realm of the Representatives' "constituents." In response, he calls the Representatives' "first attention" and "united exertions" to a national economic policy. However, Madison suggests that this tariff will do more than fill the treasury, it is precisely a *national* policy because it promises to transform these potentially plural and antagonistic "constituents" into unified subjects abstracted from their particularities and antagonisms and represented as formally equivalent units of a national population—units he elsewhere calls "citizens" who will engage in lively economic exchange.[80]

The imaginative torque and the relays of order confirmed in the settlement of federal taxation for the seaboard enterprise pivots on racial blackness as the impossible point of consideration for the viability of national identity. Because "as merchant capital flooded the Atlantic theatre after the sixteenth century, European mercantilist measures emerged almost immediately to regulate that flood, to give it social and political shape," "the people," the revolutionary form of social organization promulgated by the union of the former seaboard colonies, the newest and most preeminent of these social and political shapes, discloses the intercontinental circuit of commodity exchange and its articulation of the vastly abstracted "market," which are more conceivable than the vast numbers—particularly the racialized numbers of—its increasing compass of the conscripts conflated with the market.[81]

As the Federalist era demonstrates, the United States is, above all, a concept, with its conceivability, effectively the matter of the turns of the imagination, resting finally on the programs of force that, as the fundamental characteristic of European modernity, fails the report of force. This conceptual turn is fundamental, as documented by the historian Howard Ohline, who outlines the constitutive role of the African-derived "socially necessary labor time" yielding—beyond the material artifacts of the Atlantic economies—the inaugural compromises and coalitions of the revised experiment in the seaboard nationality. Ohline examines the role of interest-group politics, "the tendency of individual congressmen to pursue the priorities of his constituents while shaping the policy of the nation as a whole," in order to argue that, "afraid of alienating possible southern support for assumption of state debts, no northerner consistently supported the first abolitionist attempt to transform Revolutionary antislavery ideals into the explicit policy of the national government."[82] The political compromise in question arises when petitions to define congressional powers over slavery and Alexander Hamilton's recommendations concerning public credit are considered by the national representatives on the same agenda in 1790. The principle that "humanity unconnected with material interest was not within the limits of republican legislative actions"—which is used to refute the abolitionist entreaties of the Quakers, who have no immediate connections to slave property—is evident as well in the regional alliances producing the policies that both foreclose the assumption of the national debt by the states and federal abolitionist measures.[83] "The reason that historians have failed to understand that northerners, too, were engaged in special-interest politics in 1790 is that they have looked at the issue entirely in terms of slavery versus antislavery."[84] Northern representatives and their commercial interests, understanding that "in a country in which the operative fiscal systems were those of thirteen local and diverse entities, a federal debt was anomaly," understand further that "loss of the debt portended disaster to the Nationalist movement. Without a debt there would be little reason to ask for the [federal] taxing power, since . . . paying the debt was about the only thing that Congress would need much money for."[85] Ohline summarizes the national compromise and coalition of the distinct interest groups: "As republicanism helps one to understand why Americans accepted slavery in a society dedicated to freedom, special-interest politics helps one to understand why congressmen who claimed to be antislavery accepted slavery as they constructed a modern political system bound together by economic self-interest. The belief of northern congressmen that the national government should foster economic stability and growth created a functional relationship between slavery and economic measures."[86]

The open fiat on which the new guarantor of national viability, federal taxation, depends designates racial blackness as the conceptual and political, if not *human*, point betraying the premises and dilemmas of modern political community. The civic proposition of self-coherence granting national identity as its most hyperbolic form proceeds from the conscription of sub-Saharan Africans and their descendants into the severest routines of the Atlantic commercial cycles, as well as the severest routines of individual and administrative European imaginations. The disposition of racial blackness constitutes the impossible point of human conception in the enterprise—foreclosed as the unnamed violence of human visibility.

The priority given modern forms of economic exchange in the specification of "the people" reiterates that both actually and figuratively, "the people," historically and paradigmatically, depend on the massive production and movement of the cash crops cocoa, coffee, indigo, rum, sugar, and tobacco, which elicit the international competition waged over the economic values of the Caribbean basin—competition sponsoring and orienting modern national formations. In not merely the historical but also the paradigmatic move, the reasoning in question forcefully determines racial blackness to be the ideal, adamant recognition of African-derived peoples as if exploitable, indispensable, fully accounted quantities. At stake originally, as the "modern," is the phantasmatic animation of the conceptual form (the commodity) in the face of the already fully animate individual and collective material forms (in human proportions) of racial blackness. Given the reasoning feint of commodity fetishism and the ideally infinite arena of ideally infinite exchange, other forms of historical and cultural presence remain so too, although not the expansive limits of the market.

NOTES

Chapter 13, "Mercantilism, U.S. Federalism, and the Market within Reason," was previously published in *Accelerating Possession: Global Futures of Property and Personhood*, ed. Bill Maurer and Gabriele Schwab, 99–131, Critical Theory Institute Books. Copyright 2006 Columbia University Press, and reprinted with permission of Columbia University Press.

This paper was completed in part under a fellowship from the University of California Humanities Research Institute. I gratefully acknowledge the conveners of the seminar, Kathleen McHugh and Chon Noriega.

1. Colin A. Palmer, introduction to *Capitalism and Slavery*, by Eric Williams (Chapel Hill: University of North Carolina Press, 1944), xii.

2. Joan Copjec, *Read My Desire: Lacan against the Historicists* (Cambridge, MA: MIT Press, 1994), ix.

3. Dipesh Chakrabarty, "Provincializing Europe: Postcoloniality and the Critique of History," *Cultural Studies* 6, no. 3 (1992): 351. On Portuguese exploration, see Hugh Thomas, *The Slave Trade: The Story of the Atlantic Slave Trade, 1440–1870* (New York: Simon and Schuster, 1997).

4. Walter Rodney, *A History of the Upper Guinea Coast, 1545–1800* (Oxford: Clarendon, 1970), 121.

5. G. R. Steele, "The Money Economy: Mercantilism, Classical Economics, and Keynes' General Theory," *American Journal of Economics and Sociology* 57, no. 4 (1998): 486.

6. Joyce Appleby, *Capitalism and a New Social Order* (New York: New York University Press, 1984), 22.

7. Appleby, *Capitalism and a New Social Order*, 30.

8. Jack Amaragilio and Antonio Callari, "Marxian Value Theory and the Problem of the Subject: The Role of Commodity Fetishism," in *Fetishism as Cultural Discourse*, ed. Emily Apter and William Pietz (Ithaca, NY: Cornell University Press, 1993), 188.

9. Amaragilio and Callari, "Marxian Value Theory," 215.

10. Amaragilio and Callari, "Marxian Value Theory," 186.

11. Amaragilio and Callari, "Marxian Value Theory," 47.

12. Fernando Lopez-Alves, *State Formation and Democracy in Latin America: 1810–1900* (Durham, NC: Duke University Press, 2000).

13. Lopez-Alves, *State Formation and Democracy*, 215.

14. David Eltis, "Europeans and the Rise and Fall of African Slavery in the Americas: An Interpretation," *American Historical Review*, December 1993, 1400, 1405.

15. Eltis, "Europeans and the Rise and Fall," 1401.

16. Eltis, "Europeans and the Rise and Fall," 1404.

17. Eltis, "Europeans and the Rise and Fall," 1411.

18. Eltis, "Europeans and the Rise and Fall," 1422.

19. Eltis, "Europeans and the Rise and Fall," 1423. The torque and quandary are reckonable, to follow the arguments of the historian William Pierson, as a type of aesthetic transaction in which "certain black and white designs can be made to contain two vastly different pictures, the observed pattern depending upon which color our mind perceives at a particular moment to be dominant. . . . What would happen if we shifted our normal perspective so as to make our nation's black legacy, a primary point of reference? Just as in the visual image, the patterns of American history would instantly seem to reverse themselves. Such a process would not change the history, but it would offer a flash of Afrocentric insight—how changed the world could be if only we thought differently about things, at least for a moment." William D. Pierson, *Black Legacy: America's Hidden Heritage* (Amherst: University of Massachusetts Press, 1993), ix.

20. Edmund S. Morgan, *American Slavery, American Freedom: The Ordeal of Colonial Virginia* (New York: Norton, 1975), 381.

21. Eltis, "Europeans and the Rise and Fall," 1423.

22. Henry A. Gemery and Jan S. Hogendorn, "The Economic Costs of West African Participation in the Atlantic Slave Trade: A Preliminary Sampling for the Eighteenth Century," in *The Uncommon Market: Essays in the Economic History of the Atlantic Slave Trade*, ed. Henry A. Gemery and Jan S. Hogendorn (New York: Academic Press, 1983), 153.

23. Robin Blackburn, *The Making of New World Slavery: From the Baroque to the Modern 1492–1800* (London: Verso, 1997), 384.

24. Rodney, *A History of the Upper Guinea Coast*, 259.

25. Paul E. Lovejoy, *Transformations in Slavery: A History of Slavery in Africa* (Cambridge: Cambridge University Press, 1979), 57.

26. Lovejoy, *Transformations in Slavery*, 46.

27. Lovejoy, *Transformations in Slavery*, 68.

28. Lovejoy, *Transformations in Slavery*, 66.

29. Lovejoy, *Transformations in Slavery*, 66.

30. Gemery and Hogendorn, "The Economic Costs of West African Participation," 161.

31. Ronald Bailey, "The Slave(ry) Trade and the Development of Capitalism in the United States," *Social Science History* 14, no. 3 (1990): 402.

32. Bailey, "The Slave(ry) Trade," 403.

33. Blackburn, *The Making of New World Slavery*, 483.

34. Walker Connor, "A Nation Is a Nation, Is a State, Is an Ethnic Group, Is a...," *Ethnic and Racial Studies* 1, no. 4 (1978): 379–88.

35. Ernest Renan, "Qu'est qu'une nation?," in *Nationalism*, ed. John Hutchinson and Anthony D. Smith, trans. Ida Mae Snyder (Oxford: Oxford University Press, 1994), 26, 29.

36. Alfred Cobban, *The Nation State and National Self-Determination* (New York: Crowell, 1969), 249.

37. Anthony Richmond, *Global Apartheid, Refugees, Racism, and the New World Order* (Oxford: Oxford University Press, 1994), 291.

38. Eltis, "Europeans and the Rise and Fall," 1399.

39. Susan Strange, *The Retreat of the State: The Diffusion of Power in the World Economy* (Cambridge: Cambridge University Press, 1996), 17.

40. John Brewer, *The Sinews of Power: War, Money, and the English State, 1688–1783* (Cambridge, MA: Harvard University Press, 1988), 169.

41. Andrew R. L. Cayton, "'Radicals in the Western World': The Federalist Conquest of the Trans-Appalachian North America," in *Federalists Reconsidered*, ed. Doron Ben-Atar and Barbara B. Oberg (Charlottesville: University of Virginia Press, 1998), 78.

42. Harry A. Gailey, *History of Africa*, vol. 1: *From Earliest Times to 1800* (Malabar, FL: Krieger, 1970), 119.

43. Joyce Appleby, "Republicanism in Old and New Contexts," *William and Mary Quarterly* 43 (1986): 32.

44. Peter H. Wood, *Black Majority: Negroes in Colonial South Carolina from 1670 through the Stono Rebellion* (New York: Norton, 1974), xiii.

45. Robert E. Shalhope, "Republicanism and Early American Historiography," *William and Mary Quarterly* 39 (1982): 334.

46. Shalhope, "Republicanism and Early American Historiography," 345.

47. Shalhope, "Republicanism and Early American Historiography," 354.

48. Appleby, "Republicanism in Old and New Contexts," 31.

49. T. H. Breen, "'Baubles of Britain': The American and Consumer Revolutions of the Eighteenth Century," *Past and Present* 119 (1988): 75.

50. Breen, "'Baubles of Britain,'" 74.

51. Charles Beard, *An Economic Interpretation of the Constitution of the United States* (1913; reprint, New York: Free Press, 1986), 100; Doran Ben-Atar, "Alexander Hamilton's Alternative: Technological Piracy and the Report on Manufactures," in *Federalists Reconsidered*, ed. Doran Ben-Atar and Barbara B. Oberg (Charlottesville: University of Virginia Press, 1998), 59–60.

52. Doran Ben-Atar and Barbara B. Oberg, "Introduction: The Paradoxical Legacy of the Federalists," in *Federalists Reconsidered*, ed. Doran Ben-Atar and Barbara B. Oberg (Charlottesville: University of Virginia Press, 1998), 2.

53. Herbert E. Sloan, "Hamilton's Second Thoughts," in *Federalists Reconsidered*, ed. Doran Ben-Atar and Barbara B. Oberg (Charlottesville: University of Virginia Press, 1998), 67.

54. James E. Ferguson, "The Nationalists of 1781–1783 and the Economic Interpretation of the Constitution," *Journal of American History* 56 (1969): 242.

55. James E. Ferguson, "Political Economy, Public Liberty, and the Formation of the Constitution," *William and Mary Quarterly* 40 (1983): 389.

56. Ferguson, "Political Economy, Public Liberty," 390.

57. Ferguson, "Political Economy, Public Liberty," 391; Brewer, *The Sinews of Power*.

58. Ferguson, "The Nationalists of 1781–1783," 244.

59. Ferguson, "Political Economy, Public Liberty," 411.

60. Appleby, "Republicanism in Old and New Contexts," 31.

61. Alexander Hamilton, John Jay, and James Madison, *The Federalist Papers*, ed. Clinton Rossiter (1787–88; reprint, New York: Penguin, 1961), 38.

62. Rogers M. Smith, "Constructing American National Identity," in *Federalists Reconsidered*, ed. Doran Ben-Atar and Barbara B. Oberg (Charlottesville: University of Virginia Press, 1998), 23.

63. Hamilton, Jay, and Madison, *The Federalist Papers*, 38.

64. Hamilton, Jay, and Madison, *The Federalist Papers*, 38.

65. Bernard Bailyn, *The Peopling of British North America: An Introduction* (New York: Vintage, 1988), 9.

66. Jonathan Dull, *A Diplomatic History of the American Revolution* (New Haven, CT: Yale University Press, 1985), 157.

67. Jack Rakove, "From One Agenda to Another: The Condition of American Federalism, 1783–1787," in *The American Revolution: Its Character and Limits*, ed. Jack P. Greene (New York: New York University Press, 1987), 82.

68. Charles Hobson, "The Negative on State Laws: James Madison and the Crisis of Republican Government," *William and Mary Quarterly* 36 (1979): 215.

69. Hobson, "The Negative on State Laws," 216.

70. James Madison, *Notes of Debates in the Federal Convention of 1787* (1787; reprint, New York: Norton, 1987).

71. Beard, *An Economic Interpretation of the Constitution*, 87, 91.

72. Hobson, "The Negative on State Laws," 215.

73. Hobson, "The Negative on State Laws," 233.

74. Hamilton, Jay, and Madison, *The Federalist Papers*, 217.

75. Hobson, "The Negative on State Laws," 222.

76. Lance Banning, "Republican Ideology and the Triumph of the Constitution, 1789–1793," *William and Mary Quarterly* 21 (1974): 171.

77. Banning, "Republican Ideology," 187.

78. Banning, "Republican Ideology," 180.

79. Hobson, "The Negative on State Laws," 234–35.

80. David Kazanjian, "Race, Nation, Equality: Olaudah Equiano's *Interesting Life* as a Genealogy of U.S. Mercantilism," in *Post-national American Studies*, ed. John Carlos Rowe (Berkeley: University of California Press, 2000), 130.

81. Kazanjian, "Race, Nation, Equality," 131.

82. Howard A. Ohline, "Slavery, Economics, and Congressional Politics, 1790," *Journal of Southern History* 46 (1980): 335–36, 336.
83. Ohline, "Slavery, Economics, and Congressional Politics," 342.
84. Ohline, "Slavery, Economics, and Congressional Politics," 357.
85. Ferguson, "The Nationalists of 1781–1783," 245–46.
86. Ohline, "Slavery, Economics, and Congressional Politics," 359.

AFTERWORD. Remembering Lindon Barrett
ELIZABETH ALEXANDER

I met Lindon in September 1986 in the front hallway of Bennett Hall at the corner of 34th and Walnut Streets in Philadelphia at the University of Pennsylvania. He was walking down the grand stairwell under the looming portrait of Shakespeare, the portrait we would one night completely cover with pictures of James Baldwin, Zora Neale Hurston, Ann Petry, W. E. B. Du Bois, and other black literary lights. It was the age, you will remember, of much canonical revision. Lindon and I both entered the PhD program in English that year with master's degrees, each having written creative MA theses. Mine, at Boston University, was a collection of short stories, and Lindon's, at the University of Colorado, was prose some beautiful where between fiction and criticism, which he showed me one day in its hard black binding. The thesis was titled "Diane," the family name for one of his great idols who inspired the collection and much else in Lindon's life, Diana Ross.

Lindon had friends already when I first met him that day. But he looked up from his friends, saw me, and walked away from the first group: love at first sight. And black love at first sight, for Lindon, coming from Winnipeg, Canada (the 'Peg, as he called it) and then Denver, who had never studied black literature (as we then called it, still black for just a minute) before, had never studied in a community of black people, which is to say, with any black people other than himself. His excitement upon spotting me had everything to do with that unprecedented possibility. And from that moment on we were brother and sister.

We studied that whole year together with four others for our oral exams, which at Penn was called the fifty-book exam. It did not then represent a revised canon, and for Lindon and me it felt like much was at stake in mastering the master's tools. Lindon was certainly, certainly the most diligent, focused, and plainly brilliant in our group. His mind worked faster and better, had snapping turtle jaws that held on to all that went in, and processed what he read into spun gold. We completed our exams in the spring and were emancipated Negroes, ready to become scholars of black literature.

We grew a community at Penn: Kim Hall and Roland Williams were there when Lindon and I arrived, and David Anderson and Karen Chandler came in with us. The next year came Jennifer Brody, then Nicole King and Amy Robinson and Michele Frank, and Gale Ellison: black graduate students in the same place studying black literature in the late 1980s: a potent and unprecedented convergence we still can't take for granted. John Roberts and Sandra Pouchet Paquet taught us and supported our work under circumstances that sometimes seemed impossible, and Herman Beavers and Manthia Diawara, when they arrived as faculty, were also a part of the moment. I call all these names to remember, to say that it was real, to mark the space in which we were learning together at a moment where everything seemed possible for black literary study. There were few enough of us in the profession that we could know or hope to know everyone whose work was important to us, and that our cohort could develop together. Lindon knew absolutely nothing about black literature when I first met him—not one word, not a syllable. No one was more excited to be in the presence of smart black people (past and present, dead and alive) than Lindon Barrett. No one could have loved us more. Having grown up in a West Indian home in the middle of the tundra (I would listen wide-eyed to Lindon's stories of Vaseline smeared on the face before you could even think of going to school, exhaust that froze coming out of the car's pipes), perhaps you appreciate a black community more than if you grew up in the Negro metropolises of the United States.

Here are some things about Lindon that were true then: he was a vegetarian who fasted one day a week, every week. His mother sent him Guyanese herbs and roots from Canada that we would brew, hold our noses, and drink. He was an innocent then, except that there was always something hyperdeveloped about his brain. Next to him I felt a little smutty, a bit like a fast big sister, though also like a nerdy, annoying little sister who needed her big brother to drive her to the store. That was the yin-yang of it.

I called Lindon when faced with a mouse in my kitchen, and he stayed on the phone with me as I swept it out the door. I called Lindon in the middle of the night when the Guyanese potion started to do its work. Those first years in Philadelphia he gave heart and soul without a moment's hesitation to all he did: his work, his friendships, his new niece Ashley. Lindon loved to drive and loved to drive the long distances that had become the norm in his Canadian childhood. So he would always choose the farther movie theater or grocery store and off we'd go.

Black pop music—and I mean POP, not soul or funk—was his great love. He loved the crystalline voices, loved Jody Watley and Janet Jackson and his cherished Diane. We went to see Luther Vandross in concert and screamed the whole way through. And in black literary study, he exhibited the same degree of fandom and passion for our field's superstars. We idolized Hortense Spillers to an embarrassing extent, every single tiny thing about her, every word she wrote, every utterance she made, every extraordinary outfit we ever saw her in. We talked about Barbara Johnson's brilliance in the same breath that we described the way we'd watched her eat chocolate at a conference. We revered our West Indian Papa, Arnold Rampersad, and followed him around like puppies at MLA. This is to mark for you a moment in the profession when you knew who all the black people were and when we could admit, and did admit, that these people were our idols. Lindon was a fan in the same way that he was a fan of the music, and he was unabashed and generous in his admiration.

Next to Lindon I felt like Lisa Fischer, Luther's tall and gorgeous backup singer. For he made me feel that fabulous. I remember the exact moments when he told me something I had written was, in his opinion, brilliant, and how much that compliment meant to me coming from him, and how much it meant for words in the wilderness to be RECEIVED.

And we were embodied. Our brains lived in our bodies; our bodies loved to move, and it was all part of the same thing. Lindon danced liked he used his mind. That boy could DANCE. He danced with utter commitment. His dancing, like his mind, was brilliant, tireless, precise, dazzling, relentless, beautiful, and nasty. He danced like he saw his mother dance; he used to describe his mother—an elegant and extremely composed woman—hitching up her skirt and dancing all the way across the floor, screaming. In dance was catharsis (Lindon used to SWEAT when he danced) and in dance was communion. He was a demanding dance partner. If you were hanging back against the wall he'd come and grind all up on you until you entered the fray. You had to participate fully in his presence, in the same way that his mind left no small detail unattended.

We were a devoted, hard-working, and loving community of black scholars aspiring to contribute to a newly flourishing field. We worked as well and as hard as I have ever seen. Within our community, one of our elders wronged us profoundly, and that wronging scooped a chunk out of Lindon's soul that was never right again. I am sure of that. To see that innocent heart broken was a terrible thing.

Lindon finished quickly despite many obstacles and took a job at UC Irvine. He brought a group of us together in April 1993 at Irvine for a conference called "Contested Boundaries in African-American Textual Analysis." We were all assistant professors: Saidiya Hartman, Phil Harper, Jennifer Brody, Thelma Foote, Tricia Rose, Arthur Little, Kim Hall. I think it fair to say we all individually came to critical voice in some way at that conference, knowing that we had to bring our very best game to this group, and that even if far flung we were once again operating in community. That was where I first presented an essay called "Can You Be Black and Look at This? Reading the Rodney King Video." To our minds that conference marked us as a mission-driven generation.

Life changed for him in California. He grew away from many of his friends in ways we still struggle to understand. But his accomplishments are known and indelible: his extraordinary book, *Blackness and Value: Seeing Double*; his building of African American studies at Irvine; his nurturing of graduate students who have gone on to do wonderful work at other institutions.

No one I've ever known before or since reminds me of Lindon, not even a little bit.

NOTE

This essay was first delivered at the American Studies Association Conference, October 18, 2008, Albuquerque, New Mexico.

Contributors

ELIZABETH ALEXANDER is currently the Director of Creativity and Free Expression at the Ford Foundation in New York City. She received a BA from Yale University, an MA from Boston University, and a PhD in English from the University of Pennsylvania. Her collections of poetry include *Crave Radiance: New and Selected Poems 1990–2010* (2010); *American Sublime* (2005), which was a finalist for the Pulitzer Prize; *Antebellum Dream Book* (2001); *Body of Life* (1996); and *The Venus Hottentot* (1990). Her memoir, *The Light of the World* (2015), was a finalist for the Pulitzer Prize. Alexander's critical work appears in her essay collection, *The Black Interior* (2004). She also edited *The Essential Gwendolyn Brooks* (2005) and *Love's Instruments: Poems by Melvin Dixon* (1995). Her poems, short stories, and critical writing have been widely published in such journals and periodicals as the *Paris Review*, *American Poetry Review*, the *Kenyon Review*, the *Southern Review*, *Prairie Schooner*, *Callaloo*, the *Village Voice*, the *Women's Review of Books*, and the *Washington Post*, and her work has been widely anthologized. In 2009, she recited "Praise Song for the Day," a poem she composed and read at President Barack Obama's first Presidential Inauguration. She served as the first director of the Poetry Center at Smith College, was a member of the founding editorial collective for the feminist journal *Meridians*, and has served as a faculty member for Cave Canem Poetry Workshops. In 2015, Alexander was elected a Chancellor of the Academy of American Poets. She has been a fellow at the Radcliffe Institute for Advanced Study at Harvard University, and at the Whitney Humanities Center at Yale University. She previously served as the Thomas E. Donnelley Professor of African American Studies and inaugural Frederick Iseman Professor of Poetry at Yale University, and the Wun Tsun Tam Mellon Professor in the Humanities at Columbia University.

JENNIFER DEVERE BRODY serves as the Director of Stanford's Center for Comparative Studies in Race and Ethnicity. She chaired the Department of Theater and Performance Studies at Stanford University from 2012 to 2015. She holds degrees from Vassar College and the University of Pennsylvania and has taught at several universities, including UC Riverside, Duke University, and Northwestern, where she held the Board of Visitors Research and Teaching Professorship. Her books, *Impossible Purities* (Duke University Press, 1998) and *Punctuation: Art, Politics, and Play* (Duke University Press, 2008), discuss relations among sexuality, gender, racialization, visual studies, and performance. She served as the President of the Women and Theatre Program and on the board of *Women and Performance*, and she co-edits *GLQ*. Her work in queer and race studies has been supported by the Ford and Mellon Foundations as well as by the Monette Horowitz Trust for Research Against Homophobia. She has published essays in journals including *Screen, Callaloo, Genders, Theater Journal*, and *Signs*. Currently, she is working on republishing James Baldwin's illustrated book *Little Man, Little Man* and completing a new monograph about the intersections of sculpture and performance.

DAPHNE A. BROOKS, Yale Professor of African American Studies and Theater Studies, is the author of two books: *Jeff Buckley's Grace* (2005) and *Bodies in Dissent: Spectacular Performances of Race and Freedom, 1850–1910* (Duke University Press, 2006), which won the Errol Hill Award for Outstanding Scholarship on African American Performance from American Society for Theatre Research. Brooks is currently working on a new book entitled *Subterranean Blues: Black Women Sound Modernity*. She has authored numerous articles on race, gender, performance, and popular music culture in *Amerikastudien/American Studies, The Oxford Handbook of the African American Slave Narrative, Callaloo*, and *Meridians*. Brooks is also the author of the liner notes for *The Complete Tammi Terrell* (2010) and *Take a Look: Aretha Franklin Complete on Columbia* (2011). She is the editor of *The Great Escapes: The Narratives of William Wells Brown, Henry Box Brown, and William Craft* (2007) and the *Performing Arts* volume of the Black Experience in the Western Hemisphere series (2006).

LINH U. HUA earned her doctorate in English from UC Irvine under the direction of Lindon Barrett, with emphases in feminist and critical theory. Her first publication on black feminist sentimentality was awarded the Joe Wiexlmann prize in 2009 by *African American Review*. She has since written critically on affect and intimacy in teaching and coalition for the *Feminist Wire*, and has a chapter forthcoming in the volume *Teaching and Emotion*. She is a Rhetorical Arts Fellow in English at Loyola Marymount University, where she has taught in African American studies, Asian American studies, and women's studies. She is currently working on a manuscript entitled *To Love and Die: Scaling Affect, Narrative Discrepancy, and Intersectional Theory*.

JANET NEARY is an Associate Professor of English at Hunter College, City University of New York. She earned her doctorate in English from UC Irvine, with emphases in feminist and critical theory. Her book *Fugitive Testimony: On the Visual Logic of Slave Narratives* (2017) traces the long arc of the African American slave narrative from its origins to its expression in contemporary visual art in work by artists such as Kara Walker and Glenn Ligon. Recent essays have appeared in *J19, ESQ, African American Literature*, and *MELUS*. Her current research focuses on African American literature of Western migration in the wake of the California Gold Rush and the passage of the Fugitive Slave Law.

MARLON B. ROSS, Professor of English at the University of Virginia, is the author of *Contours of Masculine Desire: Romanticism and the Rise of Women's Poetry* (1989) and *Manning the Race: Reforming Black Men in the Jim Crow Era* (2004). His essays and articles on queer theory, masculinities studies, African American literature, and British romanticism have appeared in collections such as *Black Queer Studies: A Critical Anthology*, *Claiming the Stones/Naming the Bones: Cultural Property and the Negotiation of National and Ethnic Identity*, *Masculinity Studies and Feminist Theories: New Directions*, and *Modernism, Inc.: Essays on American Modernity*. He is completing a study entitled *Sissy Insurgencies: Racial Enactments of Un/fit Manliness across Twentieth-Century America*.

ROBYN WIEGMAN is Professor of Literature and Women's Studies at Duke University, where she teaches courses in feminist and queer theory, U.S. studies, and critical race studies. She has published *Object Lessons* (Duke University Press, 2012) and *American Anatomies: Theorizing Race and Gender* (Duke University Press, 1995) and edited numerous anthologies that focus on the institutional and political formation of identity knowledges, including *The Futures of American Studies* (Duke University Press, 2002), *Women's Studies on Its Own* (Duke University Press, 2002), and *Feminism Beside Itself* (1995). Her current work includes *Arguments Worth Having*, which locates points of critical tension and dissension in contemporary encounters between feminist and queer theory, and *Racial Sensations*, a study that considers the affective politics of race thinking. She is the former Director of Women's Studies at both Duke and UC Irvine, and former Co-director of the Dartmouth Institute for the Futures of American Studies.

Index

Abdur-Rahman, Aliyyah I., 17
Abel, Elizabeth, 186–87
Abrams, M. H., 101
abuse, as theme in African American literary studies, 41–44
Activist Sentiments (Foreman), 88
Adams, Henry, 69–70
Adams, John Quincy, 281–82
advertising industry, cultural history of, 6, 196–98
Africa, economic impact of slavery in, 327–44
African American feminism: Barrett's discussion of, 88–90, 171–89, 275–77; research initiatives in, 175–76; slave narratives and, 49–50, 53–56; women writers of the 1890s and, 299–317
African American literary studies: canonical theory and, 39–40; critical theory and, 1–3, 33–34; dualism of knowledge in, 34–35; evolution of, 15–19; institutional status of, 5; limits of neutrality in, 35–36; marginal and preferred in, 37–38; politics in university and, 25–30; racial influences in, 274–77; Rowe's contributions to, 61–82; slave narratives in, 31–33; textual analysis in, xii–xiii; women writers in, 6, 8–10, 299–317
"African-American Slave Narratives: Literacy, the Body, Authority" (Barrett), 16, 87–90, 92–114
African American Theatrical Body, The (Colbert), 90
"Afro-American Criticism and Western Consciousness: The Politics of Knowing" (Cornwell-Giles), 43

Afro-American Literature: The Reconstruction of Instruction, 94
Afro-pessimism, 14–15, 21n18
Aijaz, Ahmed, 11
alethic, Rowe's use of, 70
Alexander, Elizabeth, xii, 18, 353–56
Alexander, Frank, 256–57
Althusser, Louis, 12
Amalgamation Waltz, The (Nyong'o), 90
Amariglio, Jack, 323
American Adam (Lewis), 67, 76
American Anatomies: Theorizing Race and Gender (Wiegman), 181
American Cotton Planter and Soil of the South (Butterfield), 280
American Freedmen's Inquiry Commission, 98
American Literary History, 87–90
American Literature, 87–90
American Novel and Its Tradition, The (Chase), 67
American Renaissance, 80
American Renaissance: Art and Expression in the Age of Emerson and Whitman (Mathiessen), 39, 66, 80
American Romanticism and the Marketplace (Gilmore), 80
American Slavery, American Freedom (Morgan), 326
"Amorous Bondage: Poe, Ladies, and Slaves" (Dayan), 293–94
analogical verification, Scarry's concept of, 101–2, 315–16
Anderson, Benedict, 324
Anderson, David, 354

Andrews, William, 43, 94
antebellum culture, literacy and the body in, 96–98, 104–5
Anti-Oedipus: Capitalism and Schizophrenia (Deleuze & Guattari), 237–40, 262–63
Antislavery Debate: Capitalism and Abolitionism as a Problem in Historical Interpretation, The (Ashworth, Davis & Haskell), 257–58
antisocial thesis, 276–77
Anzaldúa, Gloria, 171
"Apology for Poetry, An" (Sidney), 39
Appiah, Kwame Anthony, 105, 307
Appleby, Joyce, 334, 338
Aristotle, 39
Articles of Confederation, 334
Ashworth, John, 257
At Emerson's Tomb: The Politics of Classic American Literature (Rowe), 66, 71–73, 307–8
authenticity: of black body, in slave narratives, 119–36; and experience, 25–30, 48–59
autobiography by African Americans: Barrett's analysis of, 89; critical theory and, 39–44; Rodman's *Bad as I Wanna Be*, 213–34; self-knowledge and law in, 139–58; slave narratives as, 31, 90–92, 115n4

Babylon Girls (Brown), 90
Bad as I Wanna Be (Rodman), 6, 213–34
Bailey, Ronald, 329–30
Bailyn, Bernard, 334
Baker, Houston, 301, 309–10
Baldwin, James, 51–52, 67–68, 77, 82
Bambara, Toni Cade, xii, 6, 17, 171–89
Banta, Martha, 196, 205
Barnhart, Bruce, 15
Barrett, Lindon: death of, 3, 10; legacy of, xi–xiii, 16–19, 29–30, 353–56; on politics of African American literary studies, 25–30. *See also specific essay titles*
Barthes, Roland, 79, 214
"Bartleby the Scrivener" (Melville), 70
Bartmann, Sartje, 288
Bates, Edward, 154–58
Baudrillard, Jean, 240–41

Beavers, Herman, 354
Behind the Scenes; or, Thirty Years a Slave, and Four Years in the White House (Keckley), 52, 54–56, 122–23
Ben-Atar, Doran, 336
Bennett, Claudette E., 249
Bercovitch, Sacvan, 76
Berry, Polly, 139
Bersani, Leo, 196, 205, 276, 314–15
Best, Stephen, 17, 21n25, 88
Bhabha, Homi, 43
Bibb, Henry, 98, 106–7
Big Sea, The (Hughes), 8, 193–209; public and private in, 202–7; sexuality and violence in, 198–202
binarism, African American literature and, 36–37
Black Autobiography in America, 140
black body: capitalism and, 17, 241–42; centrality of female body in slave narratives, 89–90; death and, 237–66; evolution from slavery to emancipation of, 311–17; gender and, 107–14; as inferior status symbol, 102; as intensive and extensive, 106–7; Jefferson's perspective on, 121; knowledge and, 110–14; language and, 104–5; literacy and, 95–114; "obdurate materiality" of, 5; pain and abuse of, in African American literary studies, 41–44; in Rodman's *Bad as I Wanna Be*, 230–34; self-authorization and, 108–9; in slave narratives, 12, 88–89, 92–114, 119–36; white body in relation to, 122–30. *See also* mulatto bodies, culture of; white body, in slave narratives
Blackburn, Robin, 330
black intellectuals, evolution in U.S. of, 303–6
Black Marxism: The Making of the Black Radical Tradition (Robinson), 21n25
black masculinity: in Bambara's "The Hammer Man," 183–89; Barrett's discussion of, 5–6, 17; deaths of Shakur and Smalls and, 265–66; Rodman's cross-dressing and, 212–34
"Black Men in the Mix: Badboys, Heroes, Sequins, and Dennis Rodman" (Barrett), 8, 212–34
blackness: African American women writers' championing of, 302–17; Barrett's

analysis of, 14–15, 17, 21n25; capitalism and, 320–21, 327–47; limiting nature of, 50–51; media images of, 246–57; pathogenicity of, 286–95; pedagogy of, 25–30; sanitary normativity and, 217; slave narratives as experience of, 48–59; stupidity linked to, 280; as visible subject, 257–66
"Blackness and Nothingness (Mysticism in the Flesh)" (Moten), 1, 14, 21n29
Blackness and Value: Seeing Double (Barrett), xi–xiii, 4, 12, 89, 275–77, 356
Black Skin, White Masks (Fanon), 15
black sociality, Barrett's discussion of, 14–15
Blassingame, John, 93
Blithedale Romance (Hawthorne), 70
Blues Legacies and Black Feminism (Davis), 310
Bodies and Machines (Seltzer), 196
Bodies in Dissent (Brooks), 90
Bodies That Matter (Butler), 126
Body in Pain, The (Scarry), 41, 101–2, 104–5
Borneo, racialized images of, 290–95
Brantlinger, Peter, 115n7
Breen, T. H., 334–35
Brewer, John, 332, 337
British Navigation Acts, 332
British Sugar Act, 332
Brody, Jennifer DeVere, xi–xiii, 354, 356
Brooks, Daphne A., 5, 87–90
Brown, Gillian, 205–6
Brown, Jayna, 17, 90
Browne, Simone, 17
Brown v. Board of Education, 303
Bryant, John, 294–95
Butler, Judith, 10, 126; African American feminism and, 175, 178–79; on black masculinity, 214; on ethnicity and race, 188; on Rodney King, 247
Butterfield, Ralph, 280
Butterfield, Stephen, 140

"Calculations of Race and Reason" (Barrett), 273–77
Callari, Antonio, 323
canonical texts: African American literary studies in relation to, 32–44; Barrett's discussion of, 28; Rowe's discussion of, 69–79
canonical theory, 39–44
Canons and Contexts (Lauter), 81

"Can You Be Black and Look at This? Reading the Rodney King Video" (Alexander), 356
Capital (Marx), 39
capitalism: black bodies and, 10–12; Deleuze and Guattari on, 241–42; identity and, 259–60; nationalism and, 4; race and, 6; Rowe's critique of, 80–81; slavery and, 14–15, 257–59, 320–47
Capitalism and Slavery (Williams), 320–21
Carby, Hazel, 88–89, 160n26, 187, 303
Carpenter, Faedra, 90
Carroll, Kenneth, 264, 266
Cayton, Andrew, 333
Chakrabarty, Dipesh, 61, 321
Chandler, Karen, 354
Changing Our Own Words (Wall), 39
Chase, Richard, 67, 80
"chattel principle," 53
Chay, Deborah, 56–57
Chesnutt, Charles, 316
Chideya, Farai, 243–45
Child, Lydia Maria, 110
childhood, insights of, 264–66
Chopin, Kate, 71–72
Christian, Barbara, 26, 187
City of Quartz (Davis), 13
class: African American feminism and, 171–72; African American middle class, 304–6; Rodman's challenge on basis of, 216–34
classroom, politics of race and blackness in, 25–30
Cobban, Alfred, 331
Codes of Advertising: Fetishism and the Political Economy of Meaning, The (Jhally), 228–29
coercion, as efficiency or progress, 4
Colbert, Soyica, 17, 90
colonialism: capitalism and, 320–47; geopolitics of, 61–62; internal colonization in U.S. and, 77–78; statutory law and, 150–53; subaltern theory and, 43–44
Coloring Whiteness (Carpenter), 90
commercial credit, Federalism and expansion of, 337–47
commodity fetishism, 323–24, 327–44; politics and, 344–47
complex political technology, in Delaney's *From the Darkness Cometh Light*, 140

"Complex Subjects: Offshore Finance, Complexity Theory, and the Dispersion of the Modern" (Maurer), 260–61
consumption, commodity fetishism and, 327–47
Contending Forces (Hopkins), 309–10
Copjec, Joan, 321, 323
Cornelius, Janet Duitsman, 96, 116n16
Cornwell-Giles, JoAnne, 43
Cosby Show, The, 308
courtroom, in African American autobiography, 151–58, 161n57
Craft, Ellen, 90, 107–8, 112–14, 119, 125–36
Craft, William, 5, 88–90, 107–8, 112–14, 119–36
Crenshaw, Kimberlé, 175
criminalization of African Americans, 252–57
critical theory: African American literary studies and, 1–3, 26–30, 32–44; Barrett's contributions to, 12–15; definitions of, 45n3; depersonalization of knowledge and, 34; fiction in 1890s by African American women writers and, 300–317; institutional status of, 5; libidinal in, 10–12
Critique of Judgment (Kant), 39
cross-dressing: black masculinity and, 212–14, 219–34; in popular culture, 212
cruelty, desire and, 237–38
cultural criticism, Rowe's contributions to, 61–82
Cultural Critique, 64
Cultural Literacy (Hirsch), 33
cultural literacy, race and, 16, 33–34
cultural studies: advertising industry and, 196–98; African American feminism and, 172; African American literature in, 3, 25–30, 33–44; Barrett's contributions to, 274–77; definition of, 115n7, 115n9; identity in, 174–75, 181–89; race in, 278–79; Rowe's discussion of, 77–79
Cuvier, Georges, 278, 288–90

Davis, Angela, 310
Davis, David Brion, 257
Davis, Mike, 13
Dayan, Joan, 293–94
"Dead Men Printed: Tupac Shakur, Biggie Smalls, and Hip-Hop Eulogy" (Barrett), 9–12, 237–366

Dean, James, 238–39
death: in African American autobiography, 142–45; black body and, 237–66
de Blainville, Henri, 288
"Deconstructing America: Recent Approaches to Nineteenth-Century Literature and Culture" (Rowe), 63, 65–66
deconstructionism: in Barrett's work, 13–14, 28; of Derrida, 124; in Rowe's scholarship, 63–66, 68–79; sign in, 78–79, 124–25; subjectivity in autobiography and, 214
Delaney, Lucy, 4–5, 88–89, 110–11, 139–58
De Laurentis, Teresa, 159n3
Deleuze, Gilles, 7, 237–43, 254–57, 260–63, 265–66
depersonalized knowledge, lack of experience and, 33–34
Derrida, Jacques, 12, 42, 88, 120, 268n38; deconstructionism of, 70, 124; on Rousseau, 129–30; signs and bodies for, 126
desire: advertising and, 196–98; Barrett's analysis of, 4, 7–9, 19; death and, 240–66; family and race and, 308–9; in Hughes's *The Big Sea*, 198–202; in Rodman's *Bad as I Wanna Be*, 214, 218–34; social productivity and, 237–38
"Detecting Truth: The World of the Dupin Tales" (Van Leer), 283–84
detection, racialization and, 278–95
Devereux, Georges, 171
Diawara, Manthia, 354
Dickinson, John, 340–41
difference: Barrett's analysis of, 26–27; confrontation with, 263–66; identity and, 182–83; multiplicity and plurality and, 12–15; in slave narratives, 56
(Dis)Forming the American Canon (Judy), 280
Dissemination (Derrida), 70
dissociation: in African American feminism, 172–76; in Bambara's "The Hammer Man," 177–79; race and ethnicity and, 179–89
Django Unchained (film), 90
"Doers of the Word": African-American Women Speakers and Writers in the North (1830–1880) (Peterson), 304
Domestic Allegories of Political Desire (Tate), 301, 308–9

Domestic Individualism: Imagining Self in Nineteenth-Century America (Brown), 205–6
Douglas, Mary, 39
Douglass, Frederick: autobiography by, 107–10, 141; Barrett's discussion of, 41–42, 49–51, 71–72; on slavery, 88, 98, 134
Doyle, Laura, 229
Dubliners (Joyce), xii
duCille, Ann, 26, 299
Dufty, William, 42

economic conditions: capitalism and slavery and, 325–47; racial patterns in, 250–57
Edelman, Lee, 175, 201
education, for black men, 249–50
Ellison, Gale, 354
Eltis, David, 325–27, 348n19
emancipation, in slave narratives, 54–55
Emerson, Ralph, 71–72
empiricism, Locke's contributions to, 62–63
"Engendered/Engendering: Schematic Racism and White Paranoia" (Butler), 247
Enlightenment: black literary studies and, 88–89, 92–114, 273–77; family and race and, 314; mind/body dualism in, 121–22
ethnicity: dissociation and, 177–89; family and, 173–74, 179–80; feminism and, 171–73, 187–89; in Hughes's *The Big Sea*, 203–7; identity and, 173, 190n4
"Ethnicity" (Sollers), 171
Ethnic Studies programs, decline of, 76
eulogy, hip-hop as, 4, 10–12, 237–66
exchange, identity and, 260
Expedition to Borneo of H.M.S. Dido for the Suppression of Piracy: With Extracts from the Journal of James Brooke, Esq. of Sarawack (Now Agent for the British Government in Borneo), The, 291
experience: cultural literacy and absence of, 34–35; depersonalized knowledge and lack of, 33–34; facts versus, 37–38; in slave narratives, authenticity and, 25–30, 48–59
"Experiences of Slave Narratives: Reading against Authenticity, The" (Barrett), 2, 14, 48–59

Fables of Abundance (Lears), 196–98
family: in African American autobiography, 142–48; ethnicity and, 173–74, 179–80; race and, 6, 173–74, 179–80, 249–57, 300–317; sanitary normativity and, 217
"Family Values / Critical Values: 'The Chaos of Our Strongest Feelings' and African American Women's Writing of the 1890s" (Barrett), 8–10, 15, 275–77, 299–317
Fanon, Frantz, 15
fantasy, desire and, 240–66
Farewell to the Party of Lincoln (Weiss), 303
Farley, Christopher John, 244–45
Father Comes Home from the Wars, Parts I and II (Parks), 90
Faulkner, William, 71
federal agency, slavery and growth of, 337–47
federalism, mercantilism and, 4, 13–15
Federalist era, slavery in, 334–47
Federalist papers, 335–47
Feidelson, Charles, 67
femininity, in Hughes's *The Big Sea*, 193–95, 205–9
feminists of color. See African American feminism
feminist theory: African American feminism and, 186–89; class and, 171–72; male homosociality and, 229. See also African American feminism
Ferguson, James, 337
fetishism, Barrett's discussion of, 277
fiction: in African American autobiography, 142–47, 151–58; by African American women writers, 299–317
Fiedler, Leslie, 67, 80
"Figures of Colonial Resistance" (Sharpe), 44
film studies, Barrett's legacy and, 90
Finkelman, Paul, 151–52
Fischer, Lisa, 355
Foner, Eric, 257–58, 292–93
Foote, Thelma, 356
Foreman, P. Gabrielle, 17, 88
formalism, in U.S. literary scholarship, 66
Foster, Frances Smith, 53–54, 93–94, 120, 146
Foucault, Michel, 39, 78–79, 196; biopower concept, 276–77
Frank, Michele, 354
Franklin, Benjamin, 341
Freud, Sigmund, 277, 314–15
Freudian Body, The (Bersani), 314–15
From behind the Veil (Stepto), 95, 120

From the Darkness Cometh the Light (Delaney), 5, 110–11, 139–58
Fugitive Blacksmith, The (Pennington), 52
Fugitive's Properties, The (Best), 88
future-oriented temporality, Barrett's discussion of, 15

Gaines, Kevin, 304–5
gangsta rap, political economy of, 252–57
Gardley, Marcus, 90
Gates, Henry Louis, 94
Gates, Theaster, 90
"Gaze of Langston Hughes: Subjectivity, Homoeroticism, and the Feminine in *The Big Sea*, The" (Barrett), 6–9, 193–209
Gemery, Henry, 329
gender: advertising industry and, 197–98; African American autobiography and, 140–41, 159n3; African American feminism and, 172–74, 181–89; black body and, 107–14; fiction in 1890s by African American women writers and, 300–317; in Hughes's *The Big Sea*, 193–209; identity and, 175, 187–89; race and, 6, 9; in Rodman's *Bad as I Wanna Be*, 213–14, 219–22
genetics, race and, 307
Genovese, Eugene, 152
George, Nelson, 238–39
Gerber, David A., 305–6
Gilmore, Michael, 80
Gilmore, Mikal, 265–66
Glausser, Wayne, 62–63
Goldsby, Jacqueline, 17, 88
Gold Standard and the Logic of Naturalism, The (Michaels), 196
Gorilla, My Love (Bambara), xii, 176
Gould, Stephen Jay, 297n34
Graff, Gerald, 45n5, 81
Griffin, Farah, 17, 89
Griggs, Sutton, 316
Grimes, William, 98, 110–12
Guattari, Félix, 7, 237–43, 254–57, 260–63, 265–66
Gusdorf, Georges, 141, 214

Hall, Kim, xii, 58, 175–76, 354, 356
Hamilton, Alexander, 335–47

"Hammer Man, The" (Bambara), 6, 17, 172–77, 183–89
"Hand-Writing: Legibility and the White Body" (Barrett), 5, 12, 89–90, 119–36
Harper, Frances, 9, 275–77, 300, 302, 308
Harper, Phillip Brian, 175, 188, 356
Harrison, Roderick J., 249
Hartman, Saidiya V., 17, 88, 309, 356
Haskell, Thomas L., 257
Hawthorne, Nathaniel, 70
Hegel, G. F. W., 10, 40–41, 46n15, 258
Heidegger, Martin, 70
Henderson, Mae G., 43
Henry Adams and Henry James: The Emergence of a Modern Consciousness (Rowe), 66, 68–70
heroism: fiction in 1890s by African American women writers and, 300–317; Rodman's image and, 213–34
heteronormativity: in African American feminism, 172–73, 187–89; in Hughes's *The Big Sea*, 194–95, 203–7; Rodman's challenge to, 214–34
Hill, Grant, 231
hip-hop, as eulogy, 4, 10–12, 237–66
Hirsch, E. D., 31, 33, 37
Hispanic men, 249
historical materialism, in Barrett's work, 12, 28
history, postcolonial discussion of, 61, 320–47
"History of Mary Prince, a West Indian Slave, The," 42, 107, 112–14, 122–23
Hobbes, Thomas, 61–62
Hobson, Charles, 340–44
Hodes, Martha, 314
Hogendorn, Jan, 329
Holiday, Billie, 42
Holland, Sharon, 17
homoeroticism, in Hughes's *The Big Sea*, 193–95, 199–209
homosexuality: in African American feminism, 172–73, 187–89; masculinity and, 198–202; Rodman's references to, 220
homosociality: in Hughes's *The Big Sea*, 193–95; in Rodman's *Bad as I Wanna Be*, 228–29
hooks, bell, 33, 187
Hopkins, Pauline, 9, 275–77, 300, 302, 309–10
Horne, Gerald, 250, 268n41

Hottentot Venus. *See* Bartmann, Sartje
House That Will Not Stand, The (Gardley), 90
Howells, William Dean, 316
"How Many Niggers Did Karl Marx Know? Or, a Peculiarity of the Americans" (Walker), 287–88
Hua, Linh U., 5, 25–30
Hughes, Langston: Barrett's discussion of, 4, 8–9, 20n11, 193–209; homoeroticism in work of, 193–95, 198–202; personal efficiency and primal scene in work of, 196–202; public and private in work of, 202–9
Hull, Gloria T., 187
Hume, David, 39
Hurston, Zora Neale, 187, 309
Husserl, Edmund, 42
Hutchinson, Thomas, 152–54

"Identities and Identity Studies: Reading Toni Cade Bambara's 'The Hammer Man'" (Barrett), 2–3, 8, 171–89
identity: in African American feminism, 171–72; Barrett's analysis of, 26–27, 171–89, 274–77; black body as marker of, 102–3; literacy and, 96–114; race and ethnicity and, 173–89
ideology: African American autobiography and, 140–43; in Rowe's criticism, 68–79
Ideology and Classic American Literature (Bercovitch & Jehlen), 76
imagination, economics and race and, 325–47
Imperfect Union: Slavery, Federalism, and Comity, An (Finkelman), 152
Incidents in the Life of a Slave Girl (Jacobs), 108–10, 120, 141, 143, 149, 161n49
income, race and, 250–57
individualism: femininity and, 205–6; in Rodman's *Bad as I Wanna Be*, 212–13, 218–34
In My Father's House: Africa in the Philosophy of Culture (Appiah), 105, 307
institutional theory: African American literary studies and, 39, 41–44; race, gender, and ethnicity and, 181–89; in U.S. literary scholarship, 66
"Institutions, Classrooms, Failures: African American Literature and Critical Theory in the Same Small Spaces" (Barrett), 1–3, 14, 20n13, 26–28, 31–44

intertextuality, Rowe's discussion of, 64
In the Break (Moten), 88
In the Wake: On Blackness and Being (Sharpe), 14
"'I Was Born': Slave Narratives, Their Status as Autobiography and as Literature" (Olney), 95

Jackson, Janet, 355
Jacobs, Harriet, 71–72, 88, 161n49; slave narrative by, 106, 108–10, 120, 134, 141, 143, 149
Jacobs-Jenkins, Branden, 90
James, Henry, 69–71, 73–75
James, Winston, 3–4
Jay, John, 335–47
Jefferson, Thomas, 40–41, 121, 334
Jehlen, Myra, 76
Jhally, Sut, 228–29
Johnson, Barbara, 355
Jordan, June, 187
Jordan, Michael, 17, 231
jouissance: ethnicity/race and, 188–89; family and race and, 311
Joyce, James, xii
Judy, Ronald, 280
justice, conceptual and desire for, 29

Kant, Immanuel, 39, 280
Kasson, Joy S., 128–29
Kazanjian, David, 344–45
Keckley, Elizabeth, 49, 52, 54–56, 58–59, 122–23
Keown, Tim, 213
Keppel, Henry, 291
Kidwell, Jennifer, 90
King, Nicole, xii, 354
King, Rodney, 247
Kolodny, Annette, 81
Krasner, James, xii
Kristeva, Julia, 124

labor: by black men, 249–50; mercantilism and ideologies of, 321–47; slavery and, 14–15, 257–59, 320–47
Lacan, Jacques, 120
Laclau, Ernesto, 76
Lady Sings the Blues (Holiday & Dufty), 42
Lang, Candace, 141–42, 214

language: black body and, 104–5; in Delaney's autobiography, 149–50
Language, Counter-memory, and Practice (Foucault), 39
Lauter, Paul, 81
law: in African American autobiography, 139–58; Barrett's discussion of, 8, 11–12; slavery and, 156–58
Lay of the Land (Kolodny), 81
Lears, T. J. Jackson, 195–98
Le Conte, Joseph, 40
Leland, John, 239–40
Leviathan (Hobbes), 61
Lévi-Strauss, Claude, 205
Lewis, R. W. B., 67, 76, 80
libidinal economy: Barrett's discussion of, 9–12, 15; family and race and, 311–17; in Hughes's *The Big Sea*, 198–202, 205–7; Rodman's autobiography and, 214–34
Life of William Grimes, the Runaway Slave (Grimes), 110–12
Lincoln, Abraham, 40–41, 142
linguistics: Barrett on race and, 12–15; in Rowe's criticism, 68–79
Lippit, Akira, 82
Lipsitz, George, 251–52
literacy: in African American literary studies, 43–44; Barrett's essays on, 5; in Delaney's autobiography, 149–50; politics and poetics of, 88–90, 120–21; race and cultural literacy, 33–34; in slave narratives, 12, 27–28, 31, 92–114, 116n16, 126–36, 149–50
Literary Culture and U.S. Imperialism: From the Revolution to World War II (Rowe), 63, 67, 77–82
literature: African American literary studies and role of, 32–44; institutional status of, 5
Little, Arthur, 356
Locke, John, 62–63
Lorde, Audre, 7, 187, 276, 299, 315, 317
Los Angeles Police Department (LAPD), xiii
Los Angeles Times, 246
Love and Death in the American Novel (Fiedler), 67
Lovejoy, Paul, 328–29
lynch laws, Wells's indictment of, 12

Macherey, Pierre, 42
Machine in the Garden, The (Marx), 67, 76
macropolitics, slavery and, 333–47
Madison, James, 335–47
Madonna, 215, 220–22, 226–27
"Mama's Baby, Papa's Maybe" (Spillers), 39, 43
market forces, in Rodman's autobiography, 214, 222–34
marriage, race and, 308–9
Marx, Karl, 39, 277; James compared with, 73–75
Marx, Leo, 67, 76, 80
Marxism, commodity fetishism and, 323–24
Marxism and Deconstruction (Ryan), 124
Marxist scholarship, mercantilism and, 76
masculinity: homoeroticism and, 198–202; of professional athletes, 212; Rodman's autobiography and, 214–34; in slave narratives, 49–50, 107–14
Masks of Conquest (Viswanathan), 43–44
masochism, sexuality and, 201–2
master/slave dialectic (Hegel), 10, 258
Matthiessen, F. O., 39, 66, 80–81
Maurer, Bill, 260–61, 269n50
McAllister, Marvin, 90
McDowell, Deborah E., 49–50, 187
McKay, Nellie, 187
McLean, John (Supreme Court Justice), 157–58
media: rap music in, 246–57; visible subject in, 246–57
Melville, Herman, 70–71
mercantilism: civic premise in, 332–47; Marxist scholarship on, 76; nationalism and, 4, 6, 13–15; slavery and, 320–47
"Mercantilism, U.S. Federalism, and the Market within Reason" (Barrett), 13–15, 276–77, 320–47
Mercer, Kobena, 213
Metahistory (White), 70, 79
Michaels, Walter Benn, 160n45, 196, 205
micropolitics, slavery and, 333–47
Miller, Christopher, 43
Miller, Perry, 81
Milloy, Courtland, 264–66
mind/body dualism: black bodies and, 121–22; in slave narratives, 92–94, 106–14, 129–30

"Modern Art and the Invention of Postmodern Capital" (Rowe), 80
Modernism and the Harlem Renaissance (Baker), 310
modernity: American culture and, 63–65, 88–89; Barrett's critique of, 14–15; in Rowe's criticism, 69–82; slavery and, 323
Moore, William E., 151
moral imaginary, Rodman's autobiography and, 214
Morgan, Edmund, 326
Morrison, Toni, 28, 42, 187, 274, 278–79, 281–82, 320
Moten, Fred, 1, 14, 17–18, 21n29, 82, 88–89
mulatto bodies, culture of, 105–6
Muñoz, José Esteban, 17
"Murders in the Rue Morgue, The" (Poe), 275–77, 279–95

Narrative of Arthur Gordon Pym, The (Poe), 70, 275–83
"Narrative of the Female Body: *The Greek Slave*" (Kasson), 128–29
Narrative of the Life and Adventures of Henry Bibb (Bibb), 107
Narrative of the Life of Frederick Douglass (Douglass), 50, 108–10, 141, 149–50
Narrows, The (Petry), 42
National Basketball Association (NBA): commodification of young African American men in, 6; political economy of, 214–15, 222–34
nationalism: mercantilism and, 4, 13–15; race and, 6
nation-states, colonialism and emergence of, 324
Native Americans, 249
nativism, slavery and, 335–47
Neary, Janet, 1–19
"Negro, The" (Wilson), 121
Nelson, Dana, 282
neodualism, literacy and the body and, 97–98
neoliberalism, Barrett's fight against, 18
Neti, Leila, 19
New Criticism, 40
Newsweek (magazine), 239–40
New Yorker (magazine), 230–31
New York Times, coverage of Shakur and Smalls murders in, 246–57, 264–66

Northrup, Solomon, 88, 107, 134
Notes of a Native Son (Baldwin), 67–68
Notes of Debates in the Federal Convention of 1787 (Madison), 340–41
Notes on the State of Virginia (Jefferson), 121
Nothing but Freedom: Emancipation and Its Legacy (Foner), 257–58
Nyong'o, Tavia, 17, 90

Oberg, Barbara, 336
Observations on the Feeling of the Beautiful and the Sublime (Kant), 280
"Occult of True Black Womanhood: Critical Demeanor and Black Feminist Studies, The" (duCille), 26, 299
Octoroon, An (Jacobs-Jenkins), 90
Of Grammatology (Derrida), 70
"Of the Standard of Taste" (Hume), 39
Ohline, Howard, 345
Olney, James, 95, 120, 141, 214
one-drop rule, 190n8
Orientalism (Said), 39
Origins of Literary Studies in America: A Documentary Anthology, The (Graff & Warner), 81
Other, African American autobiography and knowledge of, 142–43
Other Henry James, The (Rowe), 63–64, 73–75

pain: in African American literary studies, 41–44; black body and, 106–14
Pakenham, Thomas, 291
Palmer, Colin A., 320
Paquet, Sandra Pouchet, 354
Parks, Suzan Lori, 90
"passing": family membership and, 173–74; in slave narratives, 125
Pateman, Carole, 195–96, 200, 202, 205
Patterson, Orlando, 15
Patterson, William, 340
pedagogy: Barrett's discussion of, 25–30; in Rowe's criticism, 68–79; sentimental literature as, 101
Pennington, James W. C., 49, 52, 58–59, 134
performance studies, black body in, 90
personal efficiency, Lears's concept of, 195–96, 208–9
Peterson, Carla, 304

INDEX 369

Petry, Ann, 42
Philosophy and the Mirror of Nature (Rorty), 97
physicality, in slave narratives, 50–51
Pierson, William, 348n19
"Playing Dennis Rodman" (Wideman), 230–34
Playing in the Dark: Whiteness and the Literary Imagination (Morrison), 28, 275–79, 281
plurality, multiplicity and difference and, 12–15
Pocock, J. G. A., 334
Poe, Edgar Allan, 6, 11–12, 20n11, 70–71, 120, 275–95; circumspection of race in works of, 279–95
"Poe, Antebellum Slavery, and Modern Criticism" (Rowe), 282–83
"Poe's Ape of UnReason: Humor, Ritual, and Culture" (Bryant), 294–95
Poetics (Aristotle), 39
"Political Economy of the Black Urban Future: A History, The" (Horne), 250–51
politics: in Delaney's *From the Darkness Cometh Light*, 140; race and, 251–57, 304–6; Rowe on culture and, 71–73, 76–79; slavery and, 332–47
"Politics of Limited Options: Northern Black Politics and the Problems of Change and Continuity in Race Relations Historiography, A" (Gerber), 305
pornography, homoeroticism and, 200
Possessive Investment in Whiteness: How White People Profit from Identity Politics, The (Lipsitz), 251–53
post–civil rights culture, Rodman's place in, 213–34
postcolonialism: slavery and, 321; subaltern theory and, 43–44
post-Fordism, 259–61, 269n50
postmodernism, Rowe and, 81–82
"Post-Nationalism, Globalism, and the New American Studies" (Rowe), 76–77
Post-Nationalist Studies, Rowe's introduction to, 75–76
post-structuralism: in Barrett's work, 12–15; in Rowe's criticism, 69–71, 76–79
Powell, Kevin, 242–43

power: Barrett's exploration of, 2–3; identity and, 259–60; language as index of, 16–17; literacy and, 92–114, 130–36; whiteness and, 67–68
Powers, Hiram, 128–29
"Preface to Blackness: Text and Pretext" (Gates), 94
"Presence of Mind: Detection and Racialization in 'The Murders in the Rue Morgue'" (Barrett), 11–12, 20n11, 275–95
Prince, Mary, 42, 88, 107, 112–14, 122–23
privacy, in Hughes's *The Big Sea*, 202–7
production: commodity fetishism and, 327–47; desire and, 237–40
proportional representation, 341–42
Provincializing Europe (Chakrabarty), 61
public and private, in Hughes's *The Big Sea*, 202–7
public geographies, black male bodies and, 248
Pudd'nhead Wilson (Twain), 70
Purity and Danger (Douglas), 39
Purloined Letter, The (Poe), 120

Queen Latifah, xiii
queer theory, 276–77

race: advertising industry and, 196–98; African American feminism and, 171–73, 187–89; Baldwin's discussion of, 67; Barrett's analysis of, 4, 6–9, 15; critical theory and, 33–34; detection and, 274, 278–95; dissociation and, 177–89; economic conditions and, 249–57; experience and, 35–36; family and, 173–74, 179–80, 300–317; in Hughes's *The Big Sea*, 203–7; identity and, 173, 190n4; institutional status of, 5; literacy and, 97–114; pedagogy of, 25–30; in Poe's writing, 279–95; production of difference and, 12–15; reason and rationality in context of, 279–81, 284–86, 291–95; Rodman's challenge on basis of, 216–34; sexuality and, 6, 195–209; slave narratives and cultural formation of, 48–59; of teachers of African American literature, 45n4; violence and, 4–5, 10–12, 28–30
"Race and Gender in the Shaping of the American Literary Canon: A Case Study from the Twenties" (Lauter), 81

"Race for Theory, The" (Christian), 26
"Racial and Ethnic Diversity" (Harrison & Bennett), 249
Racial Blackness and the Discontinuity of Western Modernity (Barrett), 3–4, 276–77
Rakove, Jack, 340
Rampersad, Arnold, 193, 355
rape, in Hughes's *The Big Sea*, 195, 198–200
rap music, media images of, 245–57
rationality: agency and, 99–100; black body in opposition to, 122–30; race and, 279–81, 284–86, 291–95
reading: Barrett's discussion of, 28–29; slave narratives and act of, 98–99
Read My Desire (Copjec), 323
reason: black body in opposition to, 122–30; race and, 279–81, 284–86, 291–95
Reconstructing Womanhood: The Emergence of the Afro-American Woman Novelist (Carby), 303
"Redoubling American Studies" (Barrett), 28
Renan, Ernest, 331
representation: in African American women writers' fiction, 302–17; NBA political economy and, 214–15; in slave narratives, 58–59, 106–14
"republican synthesis," formation of, 334–35
"Requiem for a Gangsta" (Leland), 239–40
Retreat of the State: The Diffusion of Power in the World Economy, The (Strange), 259–60
Richmond, Anthony, 331
Rise and Fall of the White Republic: Class Politics and Mass Culture in Nineteenth-Century America, The (Saxton), 281–82
Rise of Silas Lapham, The (Howells), 316
Rivera, Lance, 245
Roberts, John, 354
Robinson, Amy, 125, 354
Robinson, Cedric, 21n25, 76
Robinson, Max, 188
Rodman, Dennis, 4, 6, 8, 212–34
Roediger, David, 281
role models, Rodman's challenge to, 215–34
Rolling Stone (magazine), 242–43, 265–66
Rorty, Richard, 97
Rose, Tricia, 356
Ross, Catherine Sheldrick, 99–100
Ross, Diana, xii, 219–20, 226–27, 353, 355

Ross, Marlon B., 5–6, 10, 165–69
Rousseau, Jean-Jacques, 129
Rowe, John Carlos, 3–5, 13, 28, 307–8; cultural criticism and work of, 61–82; on Poe, 282–83, 290
Rubin, Gayle, 205, 220, 235n25
Running a Thousand Miles for Freedom; or, The Escape of William and Ellen Craft from Slavery (Craft), 5, 90, 107–8, 112–14, 119; black and white bodies in, 119–36
RuPaul, 212
Ryan, Michael, 124

Sacred Fount, The (James), 70
Said, Edward, 39
Sánchez-Eppler, Karen, 100–101, 132
sanitary normativity, Barrett's concept of, 217
Saussure, Ferdinand de, 12, 56, 69–71, 124
Saxton, Alexander, 281–82
Scarry, Elaine, 7–8, 41–42, 101–2, 104–5, 315–16
"scene of writing": in African American autobiography, 139–58; in slave narratives, 120
Scenes of Subjection: Terror, Slavery, and Self-Making in Nineteenth-Century America (Hartman), 88, 309
Scott, Joan W., 182–83, 190n6
Scramble for Africa, The (Pakenham), 291
Secrets of a Sparrow (Ross), 219–20
self-authorization, black body and, 108–9
Self-Discovery and Authority in Afro-American Narrative (Smith), 43, 120
self-evidence of race, slave narratives and context of, 49–59
self-knowledge, in African American autobiography, 139–58
"Self-Knowledge, Law, and African American Autobiography: Lucy A. Delaney's *From the Darkness Cometh the Light*" (Barrett), 8, 12, 89
self-production, in Hughes's *The Big Sea*, 194–95
Seltzer, Mark, 196–97, 205
Sensibility (Todd), 101
sentimental novel: African American women writers and, 9–10; body images in, 100–101
Sexton, Jared, 13–14, 21n18
Sexual Contract, The (Pateman), 200

sexuality: advertising industry and, 197–98; in African American feminism, 171–74; Barrett's discussion of, 6–9, 19, 20n11, 276–77; black female body and, 107–14; family and race and, 311–17; in Hughes's *The Big Sea*, 194–209; identity and, 175, 181–89; public and private and, 202–7; race and, 6, 195–209
Shakur, Tupac, 10–12, 237–66; media coverage of death of, 246–57
Shalhope, Robert, 334
Shange, Ntozake, 309
shared discourse, in slave narratives, 53
Sharpe, Christina, 14, 17
Sharpe, Jenny, 44
Sheppard, Scott R., 90
Sidney, Sir Philip, 39
sign: black bodies as, 125–30; deconstructionism and, 78–79, 124–25; of difference, 25–26; modernity and, 79–82; in Rowe's work, 13, 28, 61–65, 69–72, 78–79
Sinews of Power, The (Brewer), 332
"singing self" theories, 89
Slave Narrative: Its Place in American History, The (Starling), 115n4
slave narratives: in African American literary studies, 16–19; Barrett's essays on, 4–5, 11–12, 16, 87–90; cultural studies and role of, 93–94, 115n7, 115n9; experience and authenticity in, 25–30, 48–59; form and content analysis of, 89; representation of bodies in, 12, 88–89, 92–114; student alienation from, 27, 31–33; white body in, 112–14, 119–36
slavery: abolition of, 257–58; absence of laws establishing, 156–58; Afro-pessimism scholarship and, 14–15; capitalism and, 14–15, 257–59, 320–47; civic premise underlying, 332–47; cultural production and, 88
Slavery and Social Death (Patterson), 15
slave songs, 50, 52
Slave Testimony (Blassingame), 93
"Sly Civility" (Bhabha), 43
Smalls, Biggie, 10–12, 237–66
Smith, Barbara, 56, 187
Smith, Beverly, 171–72
Smith, James L., 88, 102–4
Smith, Valerie, 43, 88–89, 95, 120, 187

social practices, slave narratives and, 48–59
social theory, libidinal in, 10–12
solicitation, in rapper culture, 253–54
Sollers, Werner, 171
Song of Solomon (Morrison), 42
Southern Literary Magazine, 282
"Speaking in Tongues: Dialogics, Dialectics, and the Black Woman Writer's Literary Tradition" (Henderson), 43
"Speaking of Failure: Undergraduate Education and the Intersection of African-American Literature and Cultural Theory" (Barrett), 26–30
Spectacular Secret, A (Goldsby), 88
speech-act theory, 43
Speech and Phenomena and Other Essays on Husserl's Theory of Signs (Derrida), 42, 70
Spillers, Hortense, 39, 43, 88–89, 133, 175, 355
spiritual-material existence, in slave narratives, 98–114
Spivak, Gayatri, 45n3
Stallybrass, Peter, 42
Stamp Act, 332
Staples, Brent, 248
Starling, Marion Wilson, 115n3
State of the Union: America in the 1990s, Volume Two: Social Trends, The, 249
statutory law, African American autobiography and, 150–53
Steele, G. R., 322
Stepto, Robert, 16, 95, 120
Stowe, Harriet Beecher, 110
Strange, Susan, 259–60
"Stranger in the Village" (Baldwin), 51–52
Street, The (Petry), 42
structuralism, in Rowe's criticism, 69–71
students, experience versus facts for, 33–35, 37–38
stupidity, blackness linked to, 280
subaltern theory, African American literary studies and, 39, 41, 43–44
subjectivity (subject-effect): autobiography and, 214; Barrett's analysis of, 6–7, 237–38; blackness and, 12–15; desire and, 238–66; in Hughes's *The Big Sea*, 193–209; identity and, 185–89; Rodman's sexuality and, 215–34; slavery and, 333–47; visible subject and, 257–66

Subtlety, A (Walker), 90
Symbolism and American Literature (Feidelson), 67
syncretism, in African American feminism, 172–76

Tanner, Laura, xii, 120
Tate, Claudia, 301, 308–9
taxation, slavery and, 342–47
Taylored Lives (Banta), 196
"Technology of Gender, The" (De Laurentis), 159n3
territoriality, race and, 254–57
textuality: in African American autobiography, 154–58; in African American literary studies, 1–3, 32–44; politics of race and blackness and, 25–30; Rowe's discussion of, 66–67; in slave narratives, 48–59, 95–114, 126–30
theater studies, Barrett's legacy and, 90
Theoretical Dimensions of Henry James, The (Rowe), 66
"Theories of Africans: The Question of Literary Anthropology" (Miller), 43
theory. *See* critical theory; cultural studies
Theory of Literary Production (Macherey), 42
Things of Darkness (Hall), 58, 175–76
This Bridge Called My Back, 171–72
Thomas, Hank Willis, 17
Thomas, Kendall, 173, 175
Thoreau, Henry, 70
"Three Approaches to Locke and the Slave Trade" (Glausser), 62–63
Through the Custom-House: Nineteenth-Century American Fiction and Modern Theory (Rowe), 63–64, 66, 70–72, 79–82
Time (magazine), 243–45
Todd, Janet, 101
"'To Live Outside the Law You Must Be Honest': The Authority of the Margin in Contemporary Theory" (Rowe), 64–65
torture: desire and, 237–38; Scarry's discussion of, 41–42, 101–2; in slave narratives, 106–14
To Speculate Darkly: Theaster Gates and Dave the Potter (Gates), 90
To Tell a Free Story (Andrews), 43
Transcendentalists, The (Miller), 81
transnational economies: posthuman conditions in, 259–61; slavery and, 327–47

Treaty of Paris (1783), 338
Tropics of Discourse, The (White), 79
Twain, Mark, 70–71
12 Years a Slave (film), 90
Twelve Years a Slave (Northrup), 107
Two Treatises of Government (Locke), 62

UC Irvine, Barrett's career at, 12–15, 18, 21n16
UC Riverside, Barrett's career at, 18, 21n16
Underground Railroad Game (Kidwell & Sheppard), 90
United States, historical views of, 61–62
"U.N.I.T.Y." (Queen Latifah song), xiii
University of Pennsylvania: American Civilization program, 76; Barrett's career at, xi–xiii, 18, 353–56
Uplifting the Race (Gaines), 304–5
U.S. Civil War, 258–59
U.S. Constitution, slavery and evolution of, 340–47
"Uses of the Erotic, The" (Lorde), 315
U.S. exceptionalism: in Rodman's *Bad as I Wanna Be*, 219–34; Rowe's analysis of, 76

value, African American literature and hierarchy of, 38–39
Vandross, Luther, 355
Van Leer, David, 283–84
Village Voice, 238–39
violation, sexuality and, 198–202
violence: in Bambara's "The Hammer Man," 177–79; Barrett's discussion of racial violence, 4–5, 10–12, 28–30; black body and, 92–94, 106–14; Douglass's depictions of, 107–9; in slave narratives, 50–52; slavery and, 14–15, 327–47; young black men and, 248–57
Viswanathan, Gauri, 43–44

Walker, Clarence, 286
Walker, Kara, 90, 187
Wall, Cheryl A., 39, 175
Wallace, Michele, 187
Wallerstein, Immanuel, 76, 308
Walton, Jean, 175
war, Scarry's discussion of, 41–42, 101–2
Warner, Michael, 81
Washington, Mary Helen, 187

Washington Post, 264
Watley, Jody, 355
Week on the Concord and Merrimack Rivers, A, 70
Weheliye, Alexander, 17, 89
Weiss, Nancy J., 303
Wells, Ida B., 12
"What Is Criticism?" (Barthes), 79
"When I Can Read My Title Clear": Literacy, Slavery, and Religion in the Antebellum South (Cornelius), 96–97
"When the Revolution Comes" (Last Poets), 20n10
White, Allon, 42
White, Hayden, 70, 79
white body, in slave narratives, 112–14, 119–36
white feminism, African American feminism and, 186–87
whiteness: Morrison's examination of, 281; in Poe's fiction, 294–95; political economy of, 251–53; in slave narratives, 50–53, 90, 112–14
white paranoia, black bodies in death and, 247–48
White Women, Black Men: Illicit Sex in the Nineteenth-Century South (Hodes), 314

Whiting Up (McAllister), 90
Whitman, Walt, 71
Wideman, John Edgar, 230–34
Wiegman, Robyn, 6–7, 175, 181, 273–77
Wilderson, Franklin, III, 13–15
Wilkerson, Margaret, 187
Wilkinson, Mrs. Joseph, 98
Williams, Eric, 320–21
Williams, Linda, 200
Williams, Roland, xii, 354
Wilson, John S., 121
Witnessing Slavery (Foster), 93–94
women: in African American literary studies, 29; African American writing of 1890s by, 6, 8–10, 299–317; libidinal economy and, 205; in slave narratives, 49–50, 53–54, 107–14. *See also* African American feminism
Wood, Gordon, 334
Word in Black and White, The (Nelson), 282
Workings of the Spirit (Baker), 301, 309–10
writing: in African American autobiography, 148–49, 158; slave narratives and act of, 98–99, 126–36
Writing and Difference (Derrida), 70

Zack, Naomi, 7, 173–74, 179, 311–13

Credits

Chapter 1, "Institutions, Classrooms, Failures," was previously published in *Teaching Contemporary Theory to Undergraduates*, ed. Dianne F. Sadoff and William E. Cain, 218–32 (New York: Modern Language Association of America, 1994). Reprinted by permission of the Modern Language Association of America.

Chapter 2, "The Experiences of Slave Narratives," was previously published in *Approaches to Teaching* Narrative of the Life of Frederick Douglass, ed. James C. Hall, 31–41 (New York: Modern Language Association of America, 1999). Reprinted by permission of the Modern Language Association of America.

Chapter 4, "African-American Slave Narratives," was originally published in "Imagining a National Culture," special issue, *American Literary History* 7, no. 3 (autumn 1995): 415–42. Reprinted by permission of Oxford University Press.

Chapter 5, "Hand-Writing: Legibility and the White Body in *Running a Thousand Miles for Freedom*," was originally published in *American Literature* 69, no. 2 (June 1997): 315–36. © 1997.

Chapter 6, "Self-Knowledge, Law, and African American Autobiography," was originally published in *The Culture of Autobiography, Constructions of Self-Representation*, ed. Robert Folkenflik, copyright 1993 by the Board of Trustees of the Leland Stanford Jr. University. All rights reserved. Reprinted by permission of the publisher, Stanford University Press, sup.org.

Chapter 7, "Identities and Identity Studies," was originally published in *Cultural Critique* 39 (spring 1998): 5–29, and is reprinted with permission of the University of Minnesota Press.

Chapter 8, "The Gaze of Langston Hughes," was originally published in *Yale Journal of Criticism* 12, no. 2 (1999): 383–97. Copyright 2000 Yale University and The Johns Hopkins University Press, and reprinted with permission of Johns Hopkins University Press.

Chapter 9, "Black Men in the Mix," was originally published in *Callaloo* 20, no. 1 (winter 1997): 106–26. Copyright 1997 Charles H. Rowell, and reprinted with permission of Johns Hopkins University Press.

Chapter 10, "Dead Men Printed," was originally published in *Callaloo* 22, no. 2 (spring 1999): 306–32. Copyright 1999 Charles H. Rowell, and reprinted with permission of Johns Hopkins University Press.

Chapter 11, "Presence of Mind," was originally published in *Romancing the Shadow: Poe and Race*, ed. J. Gerald Kennedy and Liliane Weissberg, 157–76 (Oxford: Oxford University Press, 2001). Republished with permission of Oxford University Press; permission conveyed through Copyright Clearance Center, Inc.

Chapter 13, "Mercantilism, U.S. Federalism, and the Market within Reason," was previously published in *Accelerating Possession: Global Futures of Property and Personhood*, ed. Bill Maurer and Gabriele Schwab, 99–131, Critical Theory Institute Books. Copyright 2006 Columbia University Press, and reprinted with permission of Columbia University Press.

www.ingramcontent.com/pod-product-compliance
Lightning Source LLC
Chambersburg PA
CBHW061342300426
44116CB00011B/1954